MW00880018

Intersecting Traditions

by

Yvonne Aarden

Intersecting Traditions

Copyright 2022, Yvonne Aarden

ISBN: 9798422494088

All rights reserved. No reprint rights granted without the written permission of the author.

Reasonable excerpts or quotes used for review, educational, or other fair use purposes are permitted and encouraged.

Table of Contents

Where I'm From
by Yvonne Aarden

I am a girl from the White Earth Indian Reservation,
growing up with no electricity or running water
a heating with wood childhood.
From a village lacking modern conveniences
but overflowing with neighborly concern and love.

I am from dirt roads, biking on tree-rooted trails,
a jump-roper, hop-scotcher, marbles and jacks enthusiast,
swimmer, skater, slider,
playing outdoors until dark with village kids.

I am from pine, birch, maple, oak, pin cherry and chokecherry trees,
whose sap, berries, bark and wood gave us sustenance.
I am from gardens growing vegetables for year-round food,
and a family who lived frugally.

I am from venison, wild rice, kolaches and rohlikes,
from Ojibwe, French and Czech ancestry.
I'm from a Catholic go-to-church every Sunday family,
A pillars-of-the church family putting prayer into action.

I'm from the LaVoy and Rumreich branch
Post-Office in my home mother,
Jack-of-all trades father.

I'm from "Children are to be seen and not heard,"
Respect your elders, Hand-me-down clothes,
Basket and pie socials, bingo and movie nights,
Sunday baseball games, and village festivals.

I am from an extended family in Naytahwaush
encircling me with their love.
I am today because of who I was yesterday,
and where I came from.

Memory is the seamstress
that threads our lives together.
Virginia Wolf

This book is a gift to my family of past, present, and future. Life itself is a gift and all that happens during one's lifetime shapes whom we become. My life has been a rollercoaster of chapters, each chapter carving a possibility for the next.

At age eighty-one, I realize I am living the last chapter, and I wanted to record the experiences I have been so fortunate to have had in my earthly life.

My memories are within this book as best I could remember them. They are memories and traditions that have threaded my life together and made me who I am today.

May each of you who read this know how precious your thread is. Let us continue to make memories together with the threads remaining.

Yvonne Aarden

January, 2022

This book is dedicated to my parents—
Philomene LaVoy Rumreich and Alois Rumreich
who gave me life, love, and the courage to step into
the unknown, all the while offering their
unfailing guidance and support.

Mom and Dad working in the post office.

Chapter One

Tracing My Roots

From the roots of our ancestors we grow. With each generation
we learn to reach higher and bend more. Knowing we are all
connected yet each person, like a branch, individual and yet
part of the whole. One life force flows through us and unites us,
and yet, though one branch may break, we go on.

Through the cold of winter, the rebirth of spring, the heat of
summer and the changes of fall, we adapt and continue. Our
leaves constantly changing, our bark bearing the marks of our
story we stand strong against time and wind. We reach towards
the sky and grow from the strength of our roots and the warmth
of the sun. Our family goes on, reaches on, together.

Kevin Hall

Knowing my ancestry is key to understanding who I am! Therefore, I feel it is vital to begin the story of my life with the story of my ancestors.

The LaVoi Genealogy

The LaVoie family traces its roots back to France on my mother's side. When the family migrated to Canada in the 1600s, they were primarily farmers along the Lawrence River in Quebec, Canada. My great grandfather (Lawrence) was born in 1828 when all the available land was too limited to earn a living. Combined with drought and social conditions, many young men decided to look elsewhere to seek their fortune.

Lawrence decided to join the young gold seekers during the gold rush years and boarded a ship to Panama, crossing the isthmus.

He then had to find a boat that could carry him to California. After many unsuccessful hardships, Lawrence returned to farming in Quebec. In 1865 he married Philomen Beaugrand-Champagne and started a family the following year.

My great-grandfather's son, Alphonse LaVoie, was born on March 1, 1878, in St. Germane, Quebec. He was the seventh of eleven children and soon became known as Dick, not Alphonse. His parents migrated to Balico, Connecticut, where they lived for several years after his birth. At some unknown time, after living in the United States, the family dropped the last letter of their name, and the spelling became LaVoi.

In the fall of 1883, my great-grandfather heard about homesteading possibilities in the Midwest. He journeyed with his two oldest sons to Fosston, Minnesota, and began farming in Hanesville Township. That first year, they built a house, and later the rest of the family joined them. Each child had responsibilities. Dick's chores on the farm were to feed the horses, clean the barn, and haul water. As far as schooling, Dick only went to the third grade. He could read reasonably well, but could only write his name and little else.

Since he was a strong and sturdy young man, my Grandfather Dick had many jobs in his lifetime. In his early twenties, he was a teamster and hauled logs in northern Minnesota in the Bagley-Bemidji area. When he moved to Mahnomen County in his middle twenties, he met Flora Roy at a barn dance. At that time, she was a matron at the boarding house in Beaulieu.

My grandmother Flora's parents, Peter Roy and Philomen Chouinard, had mixed French and Chippewa parentage and lived in southern Minnesota near Little Falls. They raised fourteen children, with my grandmother being the thirteenth child. Peter Roy, my great-grandfather, was given the Indian name of Be-yun-ees when he was born. He became the first Native American to be elected as a legislator in Minnesota and served two terms from 1860-64. His name appears on many of the treaties with the Ojibway between 1840 and 1870. He was a man of large frame and generous impulses, liberal and open-handed, even to his financial disadvantage. Despite his excellent health, he dropped from his chair on June 21, 1881, dying instantly at fifty-three when serving as the town clerk.

(See Appendix A for his description of his early life discovered in his belongings after his death.)

Grandma LaVoi.

On March 19, 1867, during a treaty signing in Washington, DC., Ojibwe Indian chiefs met with President Andrew Johnson at the White House to negotiate the treaty that created the White Earth Indian Reservation. Originally the reservation covered 1,300 square miles (796,000 acres), with the western part being fertile prairie land and the eastern part rich timberland with beds of white clay under the black soil.

The Indian Allotment Act (Dawes Act) of 1887 broke up Indian reservations by allotting land to individual households recorded in tribal rolls. The Nelson Act of 1889 was a corollary law that enabled the land to be divided and sold to non-Natives. Land "suitable for agricultural and grazing purposes" was allotted in tracts of 160 acres to all heads of families, 80 acres to all single persons over eighteen and orphan children under eighteen, and 40 acres to all other

Grandpa LaVoi with his horses and dog.

children. Much of the land was improperly sold or seized by outside interests.

Since my grandmother's family was Ojibwe, they received a parcel of land in the township of Rosedale on the White Earth Reservation (Gaa-waabaabiganikaa), named because of the white clay that was abundant. After my grandparents married on November 15, 1905, they settled on her allotted land, where my grandfather earned a living by farming, a skill he had learned from his father. Their first child, Napoleon (Nip), was born in 1907, followed by Philomene (Phil) in 1909, Lawrence (Sid) in 1910, and Vincent (Howard) in 1912.

In 1914, Flora, my grandmother, became sickly with tuberculosis. People believed that the humid climate near a lake could cure the disease. Hoping this to be true, my grandparents purchased land in Naytahwaush (an Ojibwe word meaning "smooth sailing"), located near North Twin Lake on the White Earth Reservation. They built their two-story home with a huge screened porch where my grandmother slept in the cool outside air in an attempt to be cured of her illness.

As they settled into their new home in Naytahwaush, Dick decided to farm his twenty-plus acres of land on which he raised cows, pigs, and chickens—and he always had a dog or two. He also set up a livery business. In addition to that, Grandpa Dick hauled wood to Mahnomen. On his return trip, he brought freight back to the village. During the 1920s, my grandfather carried mail from Naytahwaush to Beaulieu with his horses. Because he loved being around people, he enjoyed meeting different people on his mail route. It also allowed him time to visit with his friends in Beaulieu.

Because the family members were devout Catholics with great faith in St. Anne, Grandpa Dick decided to find a way to have my grandmother transported to the shrine of Sainte-Anne de-Beaupre in Quebec. They believed that one could obtain miracles through St. Anne's intercession. The story goes that Louis Guimond helped build the shrine, even though he suffered from rheumatism. After placing three stones upon the shrine's foundation, St. Anne cured him of all his ailments. Testimonies of other healed people followed this, and the shrine soon grew popular. My grandmother made the pilgrimage journey in 1917, hoping for a cure.

Sadly, the trip did not result in a miraculous cure. My grandmother knew she was leaving four young children and a husband who would need help when she was gone. On her deathbed, she asked her sister, Mary Jane, who was not married at the time, to take care of her family after she died. Aunt Mary Jane promised she would do that for her sister.

In 1918, when my mother was nine, her mother died of tuberculosis at age forty. Since my mother was the only girl in the family, Grandpa decided to send her to an Indian boarding school in White Earth, Minnesota. The Benedictine nuns from St. Cloud, Minnesota, ran the school for Indian children where girls and boys attended the boarding school.

The story was that her father felt she could get a better education taught by the nuns. Though it was less than twenty miles from her home, my mother returned home only twice during the school year, Christmas and Easter, and then during the summers. Horse and buggy were the primary transportation, which prevented easy and frequent visits.

As requested by my grandmother, Aunt Mary Jane Roy came to live in Grandpa's home to take care of the young family left behind. At that time, Aunt Mary Jane was in love with a successful businessman, John Morrison. He wanted to marry her, but she she would have to move where he lived because his business was in a distant part of Minnesota. Since she had promised my grandmother to take care of her family, Aunt Mary Jane sacrificed the love of her life to fulfill her dying sister's wish.

Aunt Mary Jane did not want people to gossip about an unmarried woman living with a widowed man. It just wasn't proper in those days. John Terway, another suitor, lived in a nearby village and wanted to marry her. He loved her, and she consented to marry him despite her love for a different man named John. After she married John Terway, they lived with Mom's family until Mom was thirteen.

When Mom came home from boarding school during the summers, Aunt Mary Jane taught her how to cook, do laundry, and clean the house. One weekend, when Aunt Mary Jane went somewhere, Mom had to cook for the family. She was nervous about it, but did her best as an eleven-year-old. Little did she know that she should have taken the innards out of the chicken before cooking it. Her brothers never let her forget that meal!

Aunt Clara, one of Mom's aunts, wanted my mother to become the organist at their little church, St. Anne's, in Naytahwaush. She paid the nuns at the boarding school for her piano lessons. Despite months of lessons, my mother was not getting more proficient. Finally, her piano teacher caught on and realized why her student was not progressing. My mother did not enjoy playing the piano, and she had been reading books instead of practicing.

In those days, students took state board tests in seventh grade to determine how proficient they were in their studies. Because Mom had such excellent test results in math and English, she skipped eighth grade. Since the boarding school was only for grades one through eight, Mom left boarding school and attended the public high school in Mahnomen. During her high school years, she roomed with relatives in Mahnomen, since her father lived twenty-five miles away, too far for her to commute each day to and from school.

It was some time during Mom's high school years that she decided to change the spelling of her last name from LaVoi to LaVoy. The original French spelling was DeLavoye which then had variations of Lavoie and LaVoi. I don't know how or why Mom decided to change the spelling; her family spells it with a "y" to this day, but my grandfather's brothers in the area kept the LaVoi spelling.

After high school, Mom attended Moorhead Normal School about eighty miles west of Naytahwaush. A person needed to be in Normal School for two years to qualify as a teacher. If the candidate promised to teach in Minnesota for two years, tuition would be free.

My Mom graduating from Moorhead Normal School.

Mom was nineteen when she started her first teaching job in Naytahwaush, where she taught students almost as old as she was. Suffering many challenges and difficulties, she wanted to give up teaching. Her father didn't want this to happen. He used his influence and helped her to find another place to teach.

She accepted a teaching position in a one-room rural school near Waubun, about twenty-five miles from her father's home. While teaching there, she boarded with the Barta family near the school. It was during this time that she began to date my dad.

The Ruhmreich Genealogy

My dad's heritage was Czech, with Bohemian origins. His mother, Barbara Tupa (1884-1959), was born in Veseleyville, ND. Her parents were from Bohemia. My grandfather, John K. Rumreich (1882-1957), came from a family of thirteen and was the sixth of nine surviving children. He was the first Rumreich to be born on American soil. His parents and older siblings had emigrated from Bohemia to Pisek in 1880. His father, Frank Paul Rumreich (1845-1909), was one of the first settlers to arrive from Europe to found the town of Pisek, North Dakota, where my father was born.

To give an example of my great-grandfather's business prowess, he applied under the Timber Cultural Act of 1873 of the Western Prairies Deed from President William McKinley. The town of Pisek was virtually a prairie and had no trees. If one planted 40 acres of trees on 160 acres of land, he would, in the end, receive a grant and deed for the 160 acres. Frank received this grant in 1898 and a railroad grant to buy another 160 acres. It was this latter grant of land that he donated to create the town of Pisek. He became the town's first mayor that same year.

Frank was a mechanical engineer and a versatile man interested in business. He established the first hardware store and lumber yard in Pisek. A devout Catholic, he commissioned Alfons Mucha in Bohemia to paint a picture combining images of St. Cyril and Methodius for the local church. These two saints had brought Christianity to the Czech lands in the ninth century. Marie Patocka, his sister, brought the painting when she and her family sailed to the USA. They placed it in the Catholic church in Pisek, which was named St. John Nepomucene, in honor of the patron saint of Bohemia.

After marrying Barbara Tupa in Pisek and having two children, my grandfather, John K Rumreich, moved to Mahnomen, Minnesota, in 1909. In Mahnomen, my grandfather farmed and operated a farm implement and hardware business. He also served as Mahnomen's mayor in 1915 and 1916. During their married life, John K. and my grandmother had seven children. It is interesting to note that they chose to name each child after the Saint of the day on which they were born: Theophil (1906), Aloysius (1907), Louise (1909), Clara (1912), Marcella (1915), Mildred (1918) and Irene (1924).

Grandpa and Grandma Rumreich in front of the implement store.

Over the next six years, three of my grandfather's brothers moved to Mahnomen. His brother Erhart (Doc) had been mayor in Pisek and had a successful medical practice when he moved to Mahnomen. Doc served as coroner of Mahnomen County from 1926-46.

Frank, his older brother, came in 1915 with his wife and six children. He opened a grocery store with Frank A. Bastyr in a building owned by my grandfather. His wife, Mary, died in 1919. When Frank died three years later, Doc and his wife Stacie took the children and raised them as their own.

The youngest brother, Cyril, became an agent and telegrapher for the railroad. These four men and their families became a part of the fabric of Mahnomen over the years.

My father, Aloysius Rumreich, inherited the gypsy spirit and was a true Bohemian. He became known as Alois, and in later years, known to all as Bo (short for Bohunk). My dad lived with his parents near Mahnomen and helped them farm. Later, he worked in his father's implement shop and earned a dollar a week.

In high school, Dad became a star basketball player. When he was a senior, he ran away from home to Butte, Montana, riding on boxcar trains. Dad claims this included riding on top of trains, in the blinds, on the tender, and underneath during that 950-mile trek. He was a talented person who could successfully do whatever he set his mind to do. A man with a great sense of humor, he called himself a "Jack-of-all-trades." His goal was to become a businessman when he grew up.

After returning home from his gypsy wanderings, Dad worked for his father and lived with his parents again. Even though he had attended Mahnomen High School when my mother was there, he was two years older than she and never dated her. Years later, he double-dated with his good friend, Matt Blaeser, who went with a young woman named Dorothy Neubert. Dorothy was Mom's best friend in high school. She and Mom accepted the double date with Matt and my dad. That began the courtship of my parents.

Since Mom was teaching in the rural school, Dad drove to Barta's home each time to pick her up for a date. She claimed that she could hear him coming miles before he appeared in his Model-T Ford. After a few years of dating, he popped the question and asked her to marry him. But, this was a big problem for his parents: She was not Czech. Czech people needed to marry Czech people.

Because she was an Indian, Mom was not deemed acceptable to Dad's parents. It is interesting to note that my mother's complexion did not reflect the dark, Native coloring. Instead, she was very fair-skinned and did not look Indian. The irony of the situation was that my dad's skin color was dark, and he was often mistaken for an Indian, even though he had no Indian heritage. Dad later shared stories of how he, not Mom, was refused alcohol in a few bars because they thought he was an Indian.

Mom and Dad's wedding day, 1935.

Despite his parents' disapproval, my parents were married at St. Anne's Church in Naytahwaush on June 3, 1935, with only close relatives and friends attending. Nip (Mom's brother) and Clara (Dad's sister) were their attendants. They went to Winnipeg, Canada, and a few places in North Dakota for their honeymoon.

After their marriage, Mom and Dad lived in a farmhouse located about a mile outside of Mahnomen, owned by Dad's parents. Dad purchased a small bar/café in Mahnomen. It was a law that married women were not allowed to teach at that time, so Mom—who had taught for seven years—had to quit teaching. She then worked with my dad in their café/bar.

It took time before my dad's parents accepted Mom, but I learned that she became their favorite. Dad's parents discovered her exceptional qualities and realized her asset to the family. Years later, Grandma Rumreich told Mom that she was like her real daughter.

Early Years of My Parent's Marriage

On March 26, 1938, my sister, Floreen, was born at the White Earth Indian Hospital in White Earth, MN. Mom was pregnant again two years later, but it was a difficult pregnancy. Her good friend, Claudia Rodwell, worked as a nurse at the Cass Lake Indian Hospital, located seventy miles from Mahnomen. She told Mom that it would be safer to give birth at Cass Lake rather than White Earth hospital, in case there were complications. Besides that, Claudia would assist her before and after her baby's arrival.

Flo and I by the lake.

On June 7, 1940, I was born in the Cass Lake Indian Hospital. Because it was such a long birthing process that required so much ether, both Mom and I almost died during childbirth. The doctor informed Mom she would never be able to have another child. Claudia carefully monitored both of us during the extended hospital stay and kept us at her home until she felt we were ready to return to Mahnomen.

Born at 7:00 that morning of June 7, I weighed seven pounds, and our hospital room was Room 7. Not only that, but I learned that I was the seventh grandchild on both sides of the family! If one believes in lucky sevens, that number played a vital role in my birth.

Another exciting thing was that I frightened my mother when I opened my eyes for the first time. One eye was a bright blue, and the other was dark brown! My eyes created an astounding contrast to the stark white blankets enfolding me. From the start, I was the baby who needed lots of cuddling and closeness, the opposite of my sister. Floreen had been independent since the beginning of her life, and she did not need or want to cuddle.

When I was one year old, Aunt Clara Fairbanks, the Postmistress in Naytahwaush, told my mother that she was retiring. A few years before, she had offered her local village store to my mother's brother, Uncle Howard. Now she was ready to give up the Post Office and asked if my mother would assume that position. Becoming a postmistress required taking a Civil Service exam and learning the rules and regulations of the office.

My parents discussed this possibility. They realized that owning a bar/café was not the best environment to raise children. Being Postmistress would be year-round employment for Mom. Dad would try to find local work. It seemed like a good opportunity for them. The answer to Aunt Clara was, "Yes, we want to do this."

In 1941 they sold the café and moved to Naytahwaush. They lived in the apartment above the village store. While assisting Aunt Clara in the Post Office, Mom learned the ins and outs of being a postmistress. She studied, took the Civil Service exam, and in 1943 received the official document to make her the new Postmaster.

The official statement read:

Frank C. Walker,

Postmaster General of the United States of America:

To all To Whom These present shall Come, Greeting:

Know ye, That, reposing special trust and confidence in the intelligence, diligence, and discretion of Philomene A. Rumreich, I have appointed and do commission her Postmaster at Naytahwaush, in the county of Mahnomen, State of Minnesota, and do authorize and empower her to execute and fulfill the duties of that office according to the laws of the United States and the regulations of the Post Office Department and to have and to hold the said office with all the rights and emoluments thereunto legally appertaining during the pleasure of the Postmaster-General of the United States.

In testimony whereof, I have hereunto set my hand, and caused the Seal of the Post-office Department to be affixed, at the city of Washington, the second day of February, in the year of our Lord, one thousand nine hundred and forty-three and of the Independence of the United States of America the one hundred and sixty-seventh.

While Mom was working with her, Aunt Clara purchased a small four-room home for Mom and Dad, just up the hill from Uncle Howard's store. Dad built two additional rooms that faced the road, which became the Post Office and a small lobby for people to gather while waiting for their mail. The door from the living room opened into the Post Office. My parents now owned their first home, small

My parents first home in Naytahwaush.

though it was. Having the post office connected to their home was ideal for Mom to work while raising their family.

Because there was not much work available in the village, Dad ventured with his friend, Oscar Lee, to Alaska in 1942 to help build the 1,600 mile Alaskan highway. Eleven thousand soldiers and 7,500 civilians were assigned to build a road connecting the string of World War II airfields that dotted the Alaskan coast from Edmonton to Fairbanks.

Because of weather conditions and the lay of the land, the men could complete only six miles of the highway a day. With no curves or grades, the road design wound through the subarctic forest. The road was completed in eight months and six days, a fantastic feat of hard work and sacrifice, despite all obstacles.

While Dad was in Alaska, unlike my independent sister, I became a "mama's baby" and cried whenever I was not near her side. Because I was almost two, Dad's Mother decided it was time to end this behavior. Grandma Rumreich took me for a weekend visit to her home in Mahnomen, a town about twenty miles away. That visit did not last for even a day. Grandma quickly returned me to Mom. Shaking her head, she asked, "What on earth is going to become of this crybaby?"

When Dad returned home at the end of 1942, he thought it would be great to surprise us. One day, a man with a shaggy beard and scraggly clothing knocked at the door. Mom answered it. I was clinging to her dress and took one look at this scary creature. Letting out blood-curdling screams, I ran into the other room. How was I to know that this was my dad? Even after he had cleaned up, shaved, and put on different clothes, it took a long time before I let him hold me in his arms.

After being home for less than a year after his Alaskan adventure, Dad decided to join the Navy to fight for his country during WWII. He enlisted even though he was married with a family. In 1944, they sent him to the South Pacific Finschafen in Papua, New Guinea, as a Seabee. The Navy Seabees constructed naval bases with miles of roadway and airstrips on the island.

The earliest Seabees were under the leadership of the Navy's Civil Engineer Corps. Because of an emphasis on experience and skill rather than physical standards, the average age of Seabees was 37. Dad was that age when he enlisted. The motto of the Seabees was

"Construimus, Batuimus" ("We Build, We Fight"). Dad stayed until the war ended in 1945.

In the meantime, Mom was left alone once again with two children to raise. The positive side was that she could work within her own home. Another positive aspect was that she had family members all within walking distance. Uncle Howard's house was a "hop, skip, and a jump" away from ours, as was the general store he ran.

Dad as a Navy man.

Across the street from the store were the homes of Aunt Mary Jane and Uncle John Terway, and right next to their home was Aunt Clara Fairbank's home. Down the dirt road from them was Grandpa LaVoy's home, where Uncle Sid and Aunt Gerda lived so they could take care of Grandpa. Living in such proximity, each family automatically knew when to step up to the plate to help each other.

Maintaining a home at this time was difficult. The village homes had no electricity or running water. At the bottom of the hill, between our home and Uncle Howard's house and store, was a running well for our water supply. That meant hauling pails of water up the hill to our house for drinking, cooking, and bathing. The kitchen wood stove had a reservoir on its side to heat the water for all our needs. Because winters were long and cold, Mom hired village men to supply sufficient wood to heat both the kitchen and living room stoves.

Grandpa Dick and my cousin, Sid.

My early childhood memories are sparse. Here are two of them:

When the Mail Came

There were few cars in those days, so most everyone in our little Indian village walked to the post office at noontime, Monday through Saturday. They hoped that Ernie Kreysha, our mailman from Mahnomen, might have brought them some mail or the latest catalog from Sears Roebuck or Montgomery Ward. Coming to get their mail gave them a chance to mingle and talk in the lobby with other villagers while my Mom distributed the mail into their mailboxes.

Mom told Flo (the name everyone called Floreen) and me (Vonnie) never to put a foot inside the post office during mail time. Ernie always arrived with the mail just at noon. After he came, Mom distributed the new mail and organized the outgoing mail. She tied all the first class, three-cent envelopes, and penny postcards in separate bundles with rubber bands. Mom stamped each letter or package with a rubber stamper that said Naytahwaush, Minnesota, with its date and year. (When I turned five in June of 1945, if I had been a good little girl, I could help Mom change the date on that rubber stamper every morning before the post office opened.)

After Mom bundled the mail, Ernie placed the first-class mail in one canvas bag and packages in another. If someone needed a ride to Mahnomen, he acted as a taxi. It cost fifty cents to ride with him.

After Ernie left, Mom opened the sliding window partition that divided the lobby and post office. She was then ready to help any villagers who needed assistance. Many would say to Mom, "Phil, I forgot my mailbox key" or "Phil, I lost my mailbox key again." Mom would smile and patiently remove the mail from their boxes and hand it over the counter. One time she kept a box of peeping baby chicks for an extra day until the family finished building the chicken coop! They knew she would even keep packages for them in our small home during the Christmas season when they had no place in their homes to hide them.

Grandpa walked up the hill every day to get his mail. When I turned five years old, my Mom told me I was big enough to have a noontime job of entertaining Grandpa when he came to wait for the mail in our living room. Every noon when the clock struck twelve, my seventy-year-old Grandpa opened our squeaky screen door. He was never late. I was waiting and excited to take care of him.

Grandpa strolled into our living room and plopped down on his favorite green rocker near the post office door. I ran to get my favorite book Grandpa had given me for my birthday the previous month. As I jumped into his inviting lap, I asked him if he could read it without my help this time. The book was called *Who Am I?* Even I recognized most of those words.

Even though he could read, he'd say, "Maybe next week, my girl. Let's see now. What was the name of this book?"

"Oh, Grandpa," I giggled, "It's *Who Am I?*" I just couldn't understand why Grandpa always needed my help.

Wednesday was my favorite day of the week that summer because Grandpa and I decided that would be his beauty parlor time with me. After all, Mom had told me to take good care of him. I wanted to be the best helper she ever had.

On Wednesdays, when the clock struck twelve, I grabbed the chipped white basin and skipped down the hill to meet the best Grandpa in the world. Grandpa waited for me by the flowing well at the bottom, a stone's throw from our house. I placed the basin near the curved pipe, bringing constant, icy-cold water right up from the ground. When the basin was half-full, Grandpa reached for it, balanced the basin under his one arm, and held out his other hand for mine. I tried to match my footsteps with his as we walked up the hill toward my kitchen door.

When we reached the rickety stand outside our back door, Grandpa stopped. He gently placed the basin of ice-cold water on it. Resting his huge hands on the rim, Grandpa bent over so that his head was near the water. He shivered as I poured the water over the three strands of white hair on top of his almost-bald head.

"Ooh, Vonnie, that's almost as cold as Paul Bunyan's drinking water!" he sputtered. "Hurry up, or my hair might freeze and turn into icicles and break off. Then you won't have any hair to wash and curl."

Grandpa and I giggled as I finished shampooing and rinsing his icy head. I ran inside to get a dry towel and hurried back to very carefully dry the three "icicles." We walked inside to his favorite rocker. As part of our Wednesday ritual, Grandpa bent his head toward me. I twirled the three white strands into a circle. Then, very gently, I inserted one of my Mom's bobby pins through his new curl.

"Now, Grandpa, time for my book and another Paul Bunyan story. Was he so big that his footsteps made our lakes and that he used trees for toothpicks?"

"First, we'll read your book, and then I have a story about how Paul Bunyan made pancakes for his logging friends. Let's see, what was the name of our book?"

"Oh, Grandpa!" I giggled. "It's *Who Am I?*"

"Oh, yes!" Then Grandpa started to read my riddle book: "I say, 'Moo, moo. I am black and white. I give milk. Who am I?"

Grandpa looked quizzically at me, and I squealed, "It's a cow, Grandpa! It's a cow!"

Grandpa finished our book. Then he began our new Paul Bunyan tale with a twinkle in his eye. Just as he started the part about the griddle being as big as North Twin Lake, Mom walked into our living room with his mail. Grandpa said, "Well, my girl, we'll finish that story tomorrow when I come for my mail. Let's see if my curl is dry and ready."

Mom admired his new curl and told me I had done an excellent job. As Grandpa slowly rose from the rocker, his gold pocket watch with its unique gold chain slipped out. Grandpa always let me press the knob and watch the gold cover open to display the numbers. Then I could put it to my ear and listen to its tick-tocks. "What time is it, my girl?" he asked.

"The big hand is on the six, and the little hand is between the twelve and the one."

"Aaah, yes, time for me to go home and have some lunch." As he tucked his gold watch back into its special pocket, he gave me a huge bear hug. I knew I never wanted this summer to end because I would have to go to first grade every weekday in the fall. Who would be there to take care of Grandpa when the mail came?

Sharon (right) and I were not happy with the teddy bear.

Playing With Matches

My cousin, Sharon, and I were like twin sisters. We were only three months apart in age and inseparable since birth. We often watched our parents use matches to light the wood stoves and the bonfires for roasting marshmallows. When we were both about five years old, we thought: "Wouldn't it be fun to do that by ourselves?"

First, we needed to get the matches. Sharon knew just where her Mom kept them on the second shelf in the kitchen cupboard. Why not use the step stool and pretend we were looking for peanut butter if we got caught?

We quietly snuck into her kitchen and did not let the screen door make a noise as we tiptoed like pretend burglars. The scraping of the step stool legs as we pushed it up to the cupboard caused Aunt Ruby to call out from another room, "What are you girls doing now?"

"Oh, we're just getting the peanut butter down to make some sandwiches. We promise not to mess up the kitchen. We can do it by ourselves."

With that, Sharon grabbed the box of stick matches, and we rushed out of the kitchen. I had found a bag of marshmallows at my place, so we were all set. The old garage building between our homes and the store was perfect for building our first bonfire. It had lots of old egg crates and newspapers piled in one corner. We wouldn't even have to use chopped wood to start the fire.

The two sticks we found in the woods behind my house would be perfect for roasting our marshmallows. After Sharon struck the first match, a small flame darted into view. With the second match, the fire grew higher. At that moment, my Mom happened to be walking from our house down to the flowing well to get water.

We had accidentally left the door open in the garage and were giggling excitedly to see our bonfire greedily devouring more egg crates. Sharon and I looked on in awe as the flames danced and tried to ignite more containers and newspapers.

My mother's sudden screams of, "What on earth are you two doing in that garage? GET OUT!!" brought Aunt Ruby running from her house, and the two of them rushed in to grab us out of the building. Then they both raced to the flowing well to fill buckets with water and managed to dowse the flames before they leaped out of control.

The next thing I knew, Aunt Ruby grabbed Sharon and marched her to their house while my Mom grabbed me and pulled me to ours. Both our Moms were crying and shouting at us and asking what had made us try to build a fire? Didn't we know how dangerous fire was? What were we thinking?

My Mom seldom paddled me, but she found her hairbrush at that moment and started to spank my butt uncontrollably. All the while, Mom cried, saying how we could have quickly died in that fire.

"But, Mom, we just wanted to roast some marshmallows and make our fire," I cried hysterically. More brush strokes on my behind and reprimands from my Mom made me even more aware of the disaster we could have caused.

Little did I know that Mom and Aunt Ruby had vivid memories of four years earlier when two of my cousins had played with fire in the woods, and one had died from extensive burns.

We never played with matches again!

Cousins (left to right) Sharon, John, and Me.

Chapter Two

My Home and Early Years

HOME: A place that feels like a tight hug: Where time stands
still for just a moment, where the noise of the outside world is
blocked out and where you can breathe it all out after being
tense all day. From the moment you enter the door, you know
you are safe, you are warm, and you are loved.
(Author unknown)

My Home

As kids, we were living in Naytahwaush in the 1940s and
1950s. Those were the best of times and the worst of times,
depending on our conduct and demeanor. We had first- and
second-generation aunts and uncles all living a stone's throw away.
They managed to keep close track of our coming and goings.

Everyone in our village (all two hundred and fifty of them)
knew everyone, so gossip spread as quickly as the real stuff. Since
biking and walking were how we kids got around the town, I think
the best way to introduce my village is to use those transportation
methods. Hop on my bike with me as we ride the dirt roads to check
out what happened in those years.

Let's start with my home since it was essential in my life. Our
small, four-room home consisted of two bedrooms, a living room,
and a tiny kitchen containing a wood stove, a small table, an icebox,
and cupboards. (I'm not counting the two adjacent rooms of the
Post-Office and lobby.)

Our life revolved around the four seasons, each requiring and
offering different opportunities for work and play. The house win-

dows needed screens for the summer and storm windows in the winter.

Because Dad was away doing road construction work in Montana, Wyoming, and South Dakota during the summer and fall months, Mom hired a local handyman, Bill Littlewolf, to do jobs for her. Since Uncle Howard was known for his teasing, he told me that Bill was now my new Daddy.

I remember getting so angry that I cried and rushed home to Mom, wanting to know where my real Daddy was. Why did Bill Littlewolf have to come to change our window screens? Mom hugged me and said that Uncle Howard was teasing. She reassured me that my Daddy was away working on road construction jobs to earn more money for our family. I immediately ran to tell Uncle Howard so he would know where my real Daddy was!

Our Kitchen

Every Saturday night, we had a bath ritual. Mom brought the grey metal washtub she used every Monday for washing clothes into the kitchen. The tub was square and stood about two feet tall. Since we had no running water, we helped haul water from the flowing well for our special weekly cleansing. Then Mom heated buckets of water on the stove to have warm bath water. She placed the tub near the woodstove as another way to keep the water warm while we bathed.

Flo, being the oldest, got first dibs and crawled into the tub for her bath. Since we both wore long braids, Mom would undo our braids and include a shampoo. I was the second one to be bathed. That meant adding a bit more hot water to the tub and a bit more soap. Why did Flo always get to be first? I wished I were the oldest every Saturday night. I never once heard Mom complain, even though she was the last one in the tub to get her weekly bath!

For special occasions, instead of braiding our hair after our bath, Mom would get out strips of rags and use them to wrap around sections of our hair to make "curls." This procedure meant sleeping on layers of uncomfortable twirled rags during the night, just to have curled hair the following day.

When we were all bundled up in warm pajamas and ready for bed, Mom read bedtime stories to us. We snuggled next to her as she sat near the kerosene lamp that shed light on the book's pages. After we were tucked safely in the bed that we shared, Mom took her bath. The last part of the ritual required her to laboriously carry one bucketful of bathwater after another to throw outside the house. No matter how cold the temperature was, this chore was necessary. Before she went to bed in wintertime, Mom stoked and refilled the wood stove so we wouldn't freeze during the night.

Our icebox with space for ice block on the left.

Located in the corner near the door leading outside was our icebox. It had a latched opening space on the left side with a metal rack to hold the block of ice. A drainage hole with a tube on the shelf allowed the melted ice to drain into a container below. The right side of the icebox had shelves to place food that needed cooling. Because we had no electricity, this was the standard refrigeration method.

So, where did we get the ice blocks? Some men in the village went out in the winter on North Twin Lake to cut ice blocks into a size that fit one's icebox. These ice blocks were stored in a huge shed in the village and covered with sawdust to keep the ice from melting in the summer. The men who sold the ice brought us a new block whenever we needed one.

Hauling the ice blocks and storing in shed.

Another way we had for preserving food was to can it. The canning process involved placing foods in jars and heating them in water kettles to a specific temperature to destroy the microorganisms that cause food to spoil.

In the summer months, our kitchen was a beehive of activity preparing foods for the winter. During the height of the season, Mom bought crates of peaches and pears. She sterilized quart jars, cut the fruit into quarters, and placed them into the jars. After adding some sugared water to cover the fruit, Mom put a sterilized lid on top of each jar. A round metal screw band tightened the seal before being placed in the canner for the required time. After taking them from the canner, Mom put the jars on a flat surface. Shortly after that, we would hear "ping, ping, ping"—the sound of the little round button in the center of the lid sealing the contents. Mom also had a big pressure cooker needed for preserving chicken and venison.

Every year we had a massive garden behind our house that contained vegetables we ate during the summer and canned for the winter months. As each garden vegetable ripened, Mom canned them. Gardens were a must for all families in our village, and tending the garden became a family affair. We all were involved in the planting, weeding, and harvesting.

My cousin, Ruth, and I picking beans in our garden.

I remember how proud I was to show Mom and Dad how carefully I had hoed in between the rows and then raked the soil to look pristine. To thin the radishes and carrots was an art to learn and master. It meant pulling out extra little seedlings so that we would have large, rather than skinny, little tubers to eat. Fresh peas and carrots were tasty treats. Our garden had peas, beans, carrots, corn, and beets. Cucumbers became pickles of every variety, and cabbage became sauerkraut to enjoy all winter.

We kids enjoyed going into the woods in the summer to pick wild berries, especially chokecherries and pin-cherries that Mom made into jellies and syrups. Mom and Dad created picking containers for us from plastic and tin pails. Dad drilled holes into the buckets for adding handles. We then wore belts around our waists to carry the buckets. When we filled the buckets to the brim, we walked home, dumped out the berries, and headed back to pick more.

After we cleaned the berries, Mom added water to cover them and brought the liquid to a boil. She then strained the berries, measured the number of cups of juice, and added sugar and some pectin. This mixture boiled until it became thick. Mom poured the hot liquid into sterilized jars of all shapes and sizes. To seal the jars, she melted paraffin blocks to pour over the top of the jelly. We screwed lids on the containers

Me standing in Aunt Ruby's garden.

when the wax solidified, and placed them in the cellar after cooling. If there wasn't enough pectin in it for thick jelly, it became syrup for our pancakes. These jellies and syrups were incredibly delicious on Mom's homemade bread and pancakes. Store-bought jelly and syrup were too expensive and not as tasty.

Because our house was so small, Mom needed a place to store all the canned goods. There was a primitive root cellar underneath the kitchen area. When Dad put in new kitchen linoleum, he cut a 3x6 section to fit the cellar opening. He glued the linoleum onto a wooden frame that was the size of the hole and added a strong metal ring to fit securely and flatly in an indentation on the top. That ring made it easier to lift it from the floor, but it was necessary to lift the whole heavy frame and put it aside whenever someone went down into the cellar. It was usually a two-person effort to pull it up and place the frame back on the floor.

Dad built sturdy wooden steps to descend into the cellar and created wooden shelves on both sides of the dirt-covered walls for the jars of canned goods. The sandy floor was an excellent place to keep the potatoes, squash, onions, and carrots fresh during winter.

I never wanted to go down into the spooky, dark cellar, even though I had a flashlight to help guide the way. The musty smell of damp sand crept into my nostrils, and I was afraid of what I might see when I went down there. It was always comforting to have someone else say they would go down to get food from the cellar!

There was a cupboard along the inside kitchen wall for the dishes Underneath was our wood cooking stove, some counter space, and the water pail that held our drinking water. We had a dipper in the bucket, and everyone drank water from the same dipper without ever wondering about germs! On Saturday nights, Mom placed a clean dishcloth over the top of it to remind us that no one was to drink water after going to bed. A Catholic rule was that people needed to abstain from eating and drinking after midnight to receive Communion at Sunday morning Mass.

Saturday was Mom's bread-baking day. The smell of bread baking was always a Saturday aroma in our house and one that still clings to me and makes me nostalgic. Before forming the dough into rolls and loaves, Mom sliced off a small section, formed it into a circle with a hole in the middle, and then fried it in a skillet that contained a bit of hot fat. When the dough was brown on one side, she turned it to brown the other side. We called it "squaw bread" and ate it with margarine and Karo syrup. It was our Saturday noon lunch.

We loved to watch the oleo melt on the warm bread just out of the oven. Since butter was expensive, we bought plastic oleo bags filled with a white lard-like mixture. In the middle was an enclosed circle that contained red food coloring. The coloring reacted with the lard mixture and turned yellow as you kneaded it. It was fun to push on the circle to squeeze the streaks of red color dye that squirted out in veins across the white gelatinous mass.

Mom warned us to be careful so the bag would not break. Our job was to squeeze the mixture until it was a uniform yellow—woe to the person who squeezed too hard and broke the bag. It was a feeling of great pride when the bag magically turned buttercup yellow color, with no white streaks. Mission accomplished. We added Mom's homemade jelly on top of the newly created oleo on the warm, fresh bread and asked for seconds!

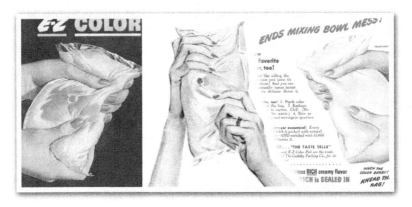

Creating yellow oleo!

Dad grew up with unique Bohemian breads that he loved. Mom wanted to please him and learned how to make those special rolls from his mother. The rohlíkies were crescent-shaped rolls topped with poppy seeds. Dad loved crispy dark brown tops and bottoms, so Mom always baked his longer. Kolaches were square-shaped rolls filled with different fruit fillings such as prunes, ground poppy seeds, apricots, or a unique cottage cheese filling. Besides rohlikies and kolaches, Mom made either cinnamon or caramel rolls and always loaves of crusty, white bread for sandwiches every week.

Our meals were plain but substantial. The pressure cooker was the essential cooking pot in the house because it helped to tenderize the tough meat and cook delicious soups. Dad loved lentil soup with lots of garlic and homemade noodles. It often became our Friday supper meal.

Because we were Catholic and could not eat meat on Fridays, Mom tried to be creative and serve various meatless meals. She created a white rice dish made with milk in the winter. It slowly cooked in a cast-iron skillet for hours—or so it seemed to our eager bellies. When ready, she placed a huge dollop on our plates. Immediately, we added a massive glob of oleo and lots of sugar and cinnamon. My favorite Friday supper meal! Who can forget Mom's homemade tomato soup in which she used whole, canned tomatoes that she added to a tasty milk base?

We had fresh lake fish on Fridays or sometimes our favorite potato pancakes if we were lucky. These pancakes required hours of grating raw potatoes on a hand grater. Often there was a pink hue to the pancakes because a finger would accidentally get scraped along with the potato.

After mixing the grated potatoes with a bit of salt and flour, Mom took a large spoonful and carefully spread it thinly on a hot, greased iron skillet. When the thin pancake bubbled up on the edges, she carefully turned it over to brown on the other side. Flo and I stood close to the stove, mouths watering in anticipation to see who would get the first potato pancake hot off the skillet.

After getting a freshly fried pancake put on our plate, we rushed back to the table, placed a pat of oleo on the pancake, and watched it melt. Next, we carefully rolled the pancake into a cigar shape, bit into the mouth-watering pancake, devoured it quickly, and returned to the stove for our next one.

Once a month, every family in the village received government food commodities at the community hall. These consisted of cheese, dried milk, flour, powdered eggs, peanut butter, and sometimes canned vegetables. Mom used the milk, flour, and eggs in her baking, and we all loved to smear the peanut butter on her freshly baked bread. We topped it with homemade jelly for our favorite almost daily peanut butter and jelly sandwiches!

I remember when we got a case of canned peas from the commodities. Mom opened the can and saw what looked like shards of glass on the top. She immediately rushed over to the commodity center to warn everyone. Was someone trying to eradicate the Indians again? A false alarm, but a story to live on in the history of government commodity stories! It turned out that the glass shards were crystalized salt granules that disappeared once the peas were heated.

Bedrooms

The bedroom next to the kitchen was where Flo and I shared a bed. My feet were always cold. In exchange for warming my icy feet on her warm legs, I had to scratch Flo's back every night. Then it got to the point where Flo expected me to create designs on her back while rubbing it. She claimed that I twirled her hair when I was sleeping, so she deserved special treatment in return for that discomfort. A small price to pay for warm feet!

When Flo stayed overnight with some of her friends, I could invite Sharon to sleep at my house. Often, when we giggled way beyond our bedtime hour, Dad yelled out his warning: "Girls, it's time to go to sleep. If I have to get up one more time, I'll use my strap!"

As soon as we heard his footsteps approaching, we jumped up to get his Navy strap out of the cupboard and quickly hid it under the mattress. He never once used it, but we wanted to have it hidden, just in case. Our muffled giggles were a bit quieter after several warnings.

Our parent's small bedroom was located right off our living/ dining room. It had room for a bed, dresser, hamper, and clothes closet. Their bedroom and ours each had a holy water font placed by the door. Mom kept them filled with water from Holy Week so she could bless us with the holy water each night when we knelt by our beds to say our prayers and ask God to bless everyone and be thankful for the day. We always ended with this prayer to our Guardian Angel:

"Angel of God, My Guardian dear, to whom God's love commits me here. Ever this night be at my side, to light to guard, to rule and guide. Amen"

There was also a crucifix in each bedroom with braided, blessed palms placed behind them. We received these palms at church every year on Palm Sunday. After Mass on Palm Sunday, Mom showed us how to braid the long narrow branches into unique designs, an art she learned in boarding school. As she replaced the old palms with the new ones, Mom explained that she'd give the priest last year's blessed palms. He used ashes from these burned palms to bless our foreheads the following year on Ash Wednesday.

No Inside Bathrooms

Because we had no running water, there was no bathroom inside our home. Winters were cold and harsh, so it was necessary to have a pot in each bedroom just in case we needed to pee during the night. That also meant we had the chore of going outside each morning to carry the bucket and empty it in the outhouse.

Having an outhouse was common in our little Indian village. My family didn't have a specific name for our sturdy outhouse or even a crescent moon to decorate it. Thankfully, Dad added a latch on the door for our privacy. Our outhouse was far enough away from our house to offset its smells and flies as it was located way behind the clothesline.

In the outhouse, shafts of light seeped through the cracks of the roughly hewn two-by-four walls. Spiders built their webs in the corners and caught flies in them. Some air entered from openings where the roof joined the walls, making it almost bearable when one had to sit for a while.

Comfort was not the concept behind the outhouse, especially during the winter months. That two-holed refuge, always stocked with catalogs that served a dual purpose as toilet paper or reading material. If you wanted to sit for a while or were trying to avoid certain household chores, you always had the catalogs to peruse. If you alternated between plugging your nose and not breathing for thirty counts, you could read quite a few pages in the Sears and Roebuck or Montgomery Ward catalogs. And tear out the "I Wish" collection of pictures for Christmas.

We kids were thrilled when our parents invested in a chemical toilet. After placing it in the corner of our bedroom, they added a curtain for privacy. The downside of having it in our bedroom was the constant smell of Lysol that permeated the area. On the upside, it was far better than having to run outside to the outhouse, especially in the cold of winter. It certainly was much more convenient and sanitary.

Living Room

In the evenings, we sat around our battery-operated radio situated in the corner of our living room and listened to radio programs. Some favorites were Amos and Andy, Fibber McGee and Molly, Green Hornet, Baby Snooks, and The Lone Ranger.

Under the radio, the console's lower section had a small drawer with a handle. One day when I opened the door, I found it empty. Right then and there, I decided that this space would be a perfect hiding place for my popsicle wrapper collection. I discovered that if you collected fifty wrappers, you could send them to the address on the wrapper and get a prize. I begged my friends to give me their wrappers for my collection and promised to show them the award when it arrived.

One day before I could collect fifty of them, Mom noticed a trail of ants coming out of the console door. She jumped up, opened the door, and discovered my popsicle wrappers swarming with

Console radio similar to the one we had, minus the bottom drawer!

ants. My collection immediately ended up outside in the burning barrel as my hopes of getting that special prize went up in flames. In tears, I spent the subsequent half-hour scrubbing and cleaning the little hideaway until there were no more traces of sweetness or ants or any hope of getting my prize.

Since we did not have electricity in those early childhood years, we had to use flat-wick kerosene lamps as our light source when the sun went down. The glass globes became blackened from the soot of the kerosene flame and required regular cleaning. Despite the poor lighting, we always gathered together to read or play games in the evenings.

When we got Aladdin lamps, they gave brighter light equal to ten flat-wick lamps or a light similar to sixty candlepower. The light was mellower and easier on the eye, and the lamps were easier to keep clean with no smoke, odor, or need for constantly pumping the wick. We kids were never allowed to clean the fragile glass globes or carry the lit lamps from one place to another.

REA (Rural Electrification Administration) began in the 1930s, but it did not reach our reservation until the mid- and late-1940s. Before that happened, Dad hooked up a gas generator in the outside shed up on the hill. Being a "jack of all trades," he cleverly rigged wires from the shed to our house, which gave us sporadic electricity. By the time I was nine, we had actual electricity, but Dad kept the generator for emergencies when the electricity from REA failed us.

Kerosene lamp with a flickering light of a flat wick oil

Aladdin lamp with a non flickering light and round wick.

The Post Office in Our Home

The Post Office was connected to our living room by an inside door. Inside the post office—which was about eight foot by ten foot (lobby was about the same size)—was a small table near the lobby door for the mailman to work at. Next to that was Mom's roll-top desk with drawers and a place for her special adding machine. Every day when the post office hours were over, Mom dutifully counted all the money and stamps to make sure that everything tallied correctly. Flo and I knew this was a time to never disturb her. We waited patiently while we listened to the clicking sounds of her old fashioned adding machine that tabulated the day's monetary accounts. Disturbing Mom could bring on one of her multiple migraine headaches. Whenever the Post Office inspector was due, we knew that Mom always worried that he might find a mistake in her records so at those times, we tread lightly and stayed out of her way. We didn't want Mom to get sick with a migraine.

The post office at noontime became the busiest place in the village, especially at the first of the month when all the government checks arrived. The lobby was divided from the post office area by a wall of mailboxes that butted up to a 4x4 opening we called the mail window. It had a moveable partition that could be closed while Mom distributed the daily mail. Next to the mail window was a door leading into the lobby that the mailman used when he brought the mail. In this way, the mailman did not have to enter our home. Most people purchased box rentals but many just had General Delivery, so Mom had to literally hand them their mail. In my early years, stamps cost three cents and postcards cost a penny.

In the summers, when Flo and I were old enough to read, Mom let us help in the Post Office, but never at noon time. "Hey, Mom," I asked one day. "Can I stamp all the letters and postcards?" The answer was, "If you make sure that the correct date is on the stamper," she replied, "But show it to me before you start stamping." The rubber hand stamp had the dates for the year, month, and day as well as the words: "Naytahwaush, MN." on it. It had removable pieces so that you changed the numbers for each day and month as well as year. Mom showed us how to ink the stamp pad and then carefully stamp each letter or postcard after inking the stamp pad each time.

I hoped there would be lots of postcards this one Monday because my friends all were listening on the radio to the station that told its listeners to send in a postcard requesting a certain song for a special person they wanted it played for. To have one's postcard read over the radio was like becoming famous. The announcer would say, "And here is a request to play, 'Don't Be Cruel,' by Elvis Presley for

Joanne from *You-know-who*." No one ever wanted to sign their name to the request for fear they would get teased.

There were always postcards every week with the word game puzzle cut out and pasted on the card in hopes to be the monetary winner of big prize money offered to the person who first correctly solved the puzzle. Even though Mom told me not to ever READ the cards, how could one resist not doing that?

Since this was the era in which many people in the village did not have bank accounts, they came to the Post Office to purchase money orders as the payment to purchase orders in the mail.

Flo and I posing with new outfits.

Changes in Our Household

When I was about nine, Dad and Mom decided to build an addition to our tiny house. It was for a new post office and lobby extension that would make an L-shape to our home. Flo and I were so excited because that meant we would have two extra rooms for living space. The old lobby became a bedroom for Flo and me, the post office area became our living room, the former living room became our dining room, and our bedroom became the new bathroom and laundry room.

Mom had an old Singer sewing machine in the living room. She used it to mend clothes and household articles such as sheets and towels, but because she was not a seamstress, she had others make our clothes. Nothing ever went to waste. Mom decided that Dad's old Navy outfits could be used to make clothes for Flo and myself. We ended up with capes, coats, and look-alike Navy outfits.

Flo and I proudly displaying Navy outfits.

Having electricity and running water created many changes for us and our home. Our kitchen took on a whole new, modern look. They replaced the wood stove with a gas stove, and a gas refrigerator replaced the old icebox. We now had a white-enameled sink between the stove and refrigerator with a double-sided counter and shelving beneath. An oil heater replaced the wood stove in the living room. The room next to the kitchen became our bathroom, complete with a tub, toilet, and sink. Our tiny four-room home became a six-room home with space we had never dreamed we would have. But the best part was that we had indoor plumbing and electricity!

Mom had not been well for a while, and the doctors on the reservation could not figure out why. She had a growth in her abdomen that the reservation doctors diagnosed as a tumor. They sent her to specialists in the Twin Cities (a metropolis about five hours away) for further study.

After a series of tests, the Twin Cities doctor told Mom that the "tumor" had a heartbeat! Because Mom was told she could never have any more children after my birth, it was a shock to everyone—Mom was expecting a baby in the middle of November, that year of 1949! Our family was expanding, as well as our house!

My sister was born November 13 at the Mahnomen Hospital, run by the Benedictine nuns whose Motherhouse was in Crookston, Minnesota, about fifty miles from Mahnomen. It so happened that Grandpa LaVoy, suffering from blood clots in his left leg, was hospitalized there when Mom gave birth to her baby girl.

When Mom brought his latest grandchild to him, she told Grandpa that the baby's name would be Nancy. "Oh, no, Philomene!" he cried. "You can't name her after the horse I never could manage to train. She is such a beautiful baby girl. She cannot have that name!"

Mom and Dad had no other name for their new girl. Sister Albertine happened to be the nurse in Grandpa's room at that time, and she heard what Grandpa said. Immediately, Sister Albertine asked, "Why not name her Mary after the Mother of Jesus and Ann after the Mother of Mary? Her name could be Mary Ann."

Grandpa nodded and smiled happily when my parents agreed. Besides, St. Anne was the patron saint of the French, and the name of our local church which Grandpa had helped build. Shortly after her birth, Grandpa had to have his leg amputated because gangrene set in. He could never come home from the hospital after that, and he died on February 16, 1950.

Grandpa's legend lives on as a man who loved being with people (especially his grandkids), a man who loved animals, and a man who was the most fantastic storyteller of the village. We all remember and visualize him lighting up his favorite pipe before settling in to tell a joke or two plus a story that kept everyone mesmerized.

Our new baby sister, Mary Ann.

New addition to our home, from the front.

Car and the new addition to our home, from the back.

Chores and Seasonal Memories

Mondays were laundry days. When Mom was ill, she asked Lizzie Roy to do our laundry before our sister was born. Lizzie lived about a mile from our home, so Mom reluctantly got behind the steering wheel of our old Chevy twice a week to drive to Lizzie's home—one day to bring the laundry and the other day to pick it up.

Mom was a terrible driver, and Lizzie's home was on top of a steep hill. Flo and I reluctantly got in the back seat every time with the basket of laundry between us. We hated that drive to and from Lizzie's because Mom had no place to turn the car around on top of the hill and had to back down to the main road. With a few close misses of almost driving into the steep ditch, Flo and I cried and screamed, begging Mom to be careful. I often wondered why Mom did not just leave us at home. Her nerves were frayed enough. We only added to her nervousness and feelings of incompetence when driving the car. The only help we were was to lift the laundry basket in and out of the vehicle.

It was a great relief when Mom could do our laundry again. We had no clothes dryer except the sun and wind in the summer and the warmth of the house in the winter. In the summertime, Flo and I

42

helped hang the clothes on the clotheslines in our back yard. The smell of freshly dried clothes in the summer was stark contrast to the damp garments drying on the wooden racks in the living room during the winter months.

Laundry day with the wringer washing machine.

Every fall, we had a chicken day. Dad bought at least two dozen live chickens from a farmer and brought them home to slaughter. Dad placed a tree stump in our backyard to use as a chopping block. One by one, he chopped the heads off those cackling hens with his ax. As soon as he decapitated one, he threw it on the lawn. We then had twenty-four headless chickens flopping around before they became silent.

Next, Dad took a chicken by its legs and dowsed it in a pail of scalding water. Then he hung it by one of its legs on a piece of clothesline rope attached to a tree branch near the outhouse. Plucking the feathers was the next step of the operation. He then gutted the plucked chicken outside before bringing it into the kitchen sink to be washed and cleaned.

The stubborn pinfeathers that didn't come off got singed when Mom held the chicken over the low gas flame of the stove. The chickens were cut up into smaller pieces, cleaned again, and placed in quart canning jars. Mom added liquid and seasoning, sealed the jars with lids and screw tops, and then put them in the pressure canning container. After the jars had been pressure-cooked for over an hour, they were removed, allowed to cool, and then found their home on the cellar shelves until needed.

Mary Ann enjoying a swim in the laundry tub.

We often had cousins and friends over to play games on weekend evenings during the long winter months. When Mary Ann was still a baby, I remember each of us taking turns pushing her buggy back and forth to keep her sleeping and content while we played games. Canasta was our favorite card game that sometimes took hours to finish. Monopoly, Sorry, Chinese Checkers, and Parchesi were other board games that we played. The one we chose depended on how many kids were seated around our dining room table. Popcorn was a favorite snack, as were jars of dill pickles, assuming we could find someone who dared to go down to get them from the dark cellar.

HOLIDAY MEMORIES

Christmas

A big, white-latticed, wooden clothes hamper with no top was in the corner of my parent's bedroom. On Christmas Eve, it became the perfect hiding place where Flo and I eagerly awaited the coming of Santa. Mom sat on the bed, telling us to be very quiet and listen for Santa's arrival.

With trembling bodies, we hid and waited for the "Ho, Ho, Ho" of Santa's voice. Then we listened for his footsteps and the sound of packages placed under the tree. After we heard Santa wish everyone a "Merry Christmas," the back door slammed. Mom gave us the signal to jump out of the hamper. We ran into the living room to discover Santa's treasures that he had left behind. Mysteriously, our Dad soon appeared from outside. We felt sorry that he had missed Santa, but he needed to help a neighbor in distress when Santa came. Dad rubbed his cold hands together, shivered, and said it was freezing outside. We hugged him and hoped he wouldn't miss Santa next year.

The next part of the ritual found Dad settling into his favorite chair near the Christmas tree. A stand, placed next to the chair, had a bowl of nuts and a tray of homemade Christmas candy. Dad took his sweet time sampling some of the candy and cracking nuts until we couldn't stand it any longer.

"Dad, when can we open the presents that Santa brought us?"

He looked surprised and innocently looked under the tree and pretended to be amazed at the wrapped gifts. Next, Mom handed him the opened Bible that told the story of the first Christmas. It seemed like the story got longer each year. After reading, Dad handed out the gifts one by one. Each year there would be one big gift for each of us, plus smaller, practical gifts such as articles of underwear.

Having a variety of Christmas candy and cookies was always a must for the season. Making fudge, penuche, divinity, and peanut brittle became a family tradition. As a little girl, I shucked the peanuts and helped measure some of the ingredients. We had cookie cutter shapes to cut the cookie dough into figures of a star, Santa Claus, angels, and Christmas tree shapes. Flo and I loved decorating the sugar cookies with frosting and adding the colored sprinkles. There were always little scraps of dough to slyly sample. Then there was the frosting on the spoons and bowl to lick when we finished.

Every Christmas Eve followed a definite pattern. Santa always came to our house first, and then he flew over to Uncle Howard's home. I could never figure out why Santa waited until morning to go to Uncle Sid's house. After all, their house was just down the road from ours. Why did he make two different trips? It was a mystery I never solved until my later years!

Every Christmas Eve before midnight Mass, our family joined the Catholic villagers for Christmas caroling. After Mass, it was customary to have our families get together at one of our homes to enjoy a midnight spread of food and drinks.

Easter

Ash Wednesday was not a day I enjoyed because it marked the beginning of Lent. We had to do penance during those forty days before Easter, such as giving up something we liked. I knew that giving up liver would not fit into that category, so candy it was! My secret plan was that if anyone gave me some candy, I'd put it in a container to save until Lent was over.

Holy Week meant going to church a lot for prolonged services. On Holy Thursday, the priest asked twelve men to come to the altar so he could wash their feet as Jesus had for his apostles. One Holy Thursday, only eleven showed up, so Father chose a boy from the pews to be the twelfth disciple. I giggled when I saw the boy take off his sock and put his dirty foot in the clean water. I thought that Father should have washed both feet of that kid, but he didn't.

Good Friday was designated as a quiet day to remember the suffering that Jesus had done for us. Mom told us that we had to be silent from noon until three with no talking and no radio or music. Those were three long hours that never seemed to end. Later in the evening, we had to go to church for solemn, quiet services.

It was always so mournful at church on Good Friday with no organ music. As a child, I never could figure out why we all got in a long line in the church aisle to kiss the feet of Jesus on the crucifix. "This is the wood of the cross, on which hung the Savior of the world," said the priest as we kissed the feet and returned silently to our pew. After each person kissed the feet on the cross, the priest wiped the area with a cloth. Another thing I remember was the priest going around the church with special prayers and kneeling at each of the twelve Stations of the Cross. It seemed so sad and long.

On Holy Saturday, when Lent was officially over, my prized container of hoarded candy came out, and the candy feast began. The real sacrifice would have been to give the candy to others, but I hadn't reached that pinnacle of penance at that time of my life.

We returned to church for the most prolonged ritual that never seemed to end in the evening. When we sang the litany of the saints, I never realized how many there were and hoped no one else would join the ranks of sainthood.

Flo and I woke up early every Easter Sunday to find our Easter baskets hidden by the Easter Bunny. If we found each other's basket, we were not to tell. Sometimes, the Easter Bunny hid the baskets too well, and there were tears and pleas for help. This tradition continued all through high school. Our goal was to find our baskets before going to Easter Sunday services.

Since it was the era that required females to cover their heads in church, it became customary to acquire a new hat every Easter. We also bought new clothing for the occasion. Going to Easter Sunday Mass was almost like a fashion show. We wanted to see what new outfits everyone wore. Somehow, I missed the real meaning of Easter!

County Fair

Sharon and I, as fourth graders, had saved our money to buy something special from the Sears Roebuck catalog for the Mahnomen County Fair. Poring over all the choices, we decided that twin dresses would be a unique way to mark the occasion.

We finally agreed that the lime green, bibbed dress with a cute set of ruffles was our absolute favorite. Then we spied some huarache sandals on sale at a price we could afford. We decided they would be perfect to complete our outfit.

After ordering our shoes and dresses, we played the waiting game for their arrival. After asking Mom every day if our package had come, our two parcels arrived two weeks later. Mom held her nose as she handed us the first of our long-awaited purchases. Whew! Why did that package stink so badly? We opened the smelly package to find our unique on-sale leather sandals reeking like the rotting dead fish that sometimes washed ashore in our lake.

"Get those shoes out of the house and put them someplace in the sun," Mom said and quickly went back to finishing the noon mail distribution.

Sharon and I were on the verge of tears as we hung our new smelly shoes on the clothesline. We surely couldn't wear those smelly things and didn't even know if they fit. Maybe when the smell died down a bit, we might be able to try them on.

Oh, no! What if something was wrong with our dresses too? Tearing open the next package, two green bundles fell out. At least they didn't smell, even though they may have been in the same mailbag. Running into the bedroom, we shed our tops and shorts and tried on our brand new dresses. Helping each other button up the back and tie the sashes, we rushed out to show off for my Mom even though it was mail time. She nodded and smiled and said she would admire them after the mail rush.

"Go and show them to your Aunt Ruby," she said to get rid of her two giggling, excited girls. Getting a new outfit was a celebration day, so we proudly marched over to Sharon's house to twirl and dance around in our gorgeous green dresses. The shoes never lost their dead fishy smell but, since hope springs eternal, we kept hoping they would. One definite place we were not permitted to wear them was to church. Mom said the smell would drive everyone out of the building.

HEALTH PROBLEMS AND CHALLENGES

Iron Deficiency

Miss Northrup, our village nurse, was practically like a doctor and took care of us on all the other days the reservation doctor was not there. We all loved her because she was such a gentle and caring nurse. When Ms. Northrup retired, we got

48

crabby Ms. Stoltz, who used to be an army nurse. She LOVED to give shots with dull needles. Just ask me because I had to get a liver shot from her for iron deficiency every week.

"Why do I always have to get iron shots, and Flo doesn't, Mom?" Flo never seemed to have horrible things happen to her. Why always me?

"Well, she's not anemic. You just happen to have low iron in your blood. The shots will make you healthier. If you would eat more liver and spinach, you'd be stronger faster."

Mom would then go into the long explanation of why I needed to eat food that would build up the iron in my blood. She would go on and on about the necessity of eating lots of liver. Liver was my least favorite food. No matter how big of a piece of bread I would bury it in, the smell, taste, and texture of the grey chunk of liver made my stomach roll over and over. I tried washing it down with big gulps of milk. Nothing worked. I HATED liver nights which meant being at the table forever. It was the rule that I had to eat the piece of liver before I left the table.

Every Friday after school was "Iron Shot Day." Mom sent me across the road to the clinic. There I knew the iron-fisted, non-smiling Ms. Stoltz was armed and waiting.

"Look the other way, and it won't hurt so much," she muttered as she stabbed my arm with the small, dull machete needle.

After she yanked out the needle, she'd swab the blood running down my arm with a cotton ball. As she plastered on the band-aid, she looked crossly at me (the scaredy-cat anemic girl) and asked, "By the way, how are the pinworms?" That was another part of my life that made me mad. Why did she have to bring that up every week when I came for my dreaded iron shot?

Pinworms

Each night just before I fell asleep, the pinworm routine happened. I heard Mom's slippers approaching the bedroom that I shared with Flo. The bedroom door squeaked as she pushed it open. The small beam of the flashlight meant it was pinworm patrol time. I always squeezed my eyes shut so Mom would think I didn't know she was there. After lifting the covers, she pulled up my nightgown, pointed the flashlight beam on my butt to see if those thread-like worms were crawling out like they did every night. Yuck! When would this ever end?

"Mom, why doesn't Flo have to have an enema every other night just like I do?" I asked every time Mom brought out the enema bag. Mom gave me one of her "I am so sorry" looks. She told me that I wouldn't have to have enemas as soon as the pinworms disappeared. Flo, just two years older than I, always seemed to be the picture of health.

"Who invented pinworms anyway? Why do I have them? Do they come with being six years old?"

"Well, Vonnie, (somehow my family and friends started calling me "Vonnie" and to this day they still call me by this name) lots of kids get pinworms, and I keep telling you not to bite your nails and to be sure to wash your hands lots of times. The pinworms will go away with the medicine and the enemas. I promise."

One morning after a multitude of months, Mom smiled triumphantly and said, "No more enemas—no more pinworms!"

Head Lice

As if having pinworms and iron shots weren't enough, I managed to end up with head lice. Mom decided that it would be the most effortless hairstyle for my sister and me if we had braids during grade school. That meant we did not have to pay for haircuts, and Mom knew how to braid our hair. She said that braids always looked neat and would not have hair hanging in our eyes. I liked having braids but did not enjoy sitting patiently while Mom braided them each morning before school. Mom let us have "bangs" a few times because she could cut those herself.

One Saturday night, just before I jumped in the washtub for my weekly bath, I said, "Mom, why does my head itch so much? Flo, does your head itch?"

Mom came over to me, looked carefully under my braids, and said, "Oh, no, Vonnie, you have nits and head lice. Have you been putting your head close to other kids? Has your teacher said anything about head lice to the class?"

"Well, they sent Isabel to the nurse and told us to have our moms check our heads when we got home. I forgot to tell you but just remembered now because my head itched."

"That explains it. Let's undo your braids. Then we need to get the kerosene and wash your hair with that to kill those head lice."

"Kerosene is what we put in our lamps, Mom," I complained. "It stinks. I don't want my hair to smell like kerosene. Please, Mom, don't."

Mom insisted that kerosene was the only sure, quick way to kill the lice. She said she would wash my hair with shampoo afterward to remove the kerosene smell.

"Just be sure to keep your eyes closed tight, and this will be over before you know it," consoled Mom.

My sore arm from the iron shots took second place in my thoughts as I bent my head over the basin. I tried not to breathe the kerosene fumes that filled the air surrounding my head. Crying, I shivered and planned revenge on Isabel and her crawling head lice.

After Mom washed my hair with kerosene, she scrubbed and scrubbed it with shampoo. Then it was my turn for the Saturday tub bath. My bathwater had cooled down by the time Mom finished the kerosene shampooing. Mom added more hot water while my thoughts raced wildly in my sore scalp. On Monday, I would ask to sit at another desk because Isabel's desk was in front of mine. Her braids must have swished around and touched mine when I wasn't looking. Because of Isabel, I had become a member of the nit and lice patrol. It hadn't been very long since I had just escaped from the pinworm patrol.

What did other kids do for fun?

Chapter Three

Uncle Howard and Aunt Ruby's Home and Store

*I want to turn the clock back to
when people lived in small villages
and took care of each other.*
Pete Seeger

Uncle Howard and Aunt Ruby's House

Let's walk over to Uncle Howard and Aunt Ruby's house because it's only a stone's throw away from my home. Uncle Howard was Mom's baby brother, and he and Aunt Ruby had four kids: Don, Dick, Sharon, and Linda. The boys were several years older than Sharon, and Linda was four years younger than we were.

On our walk over, I think we should stop and check out Sharon's playhouse first. It was right between our houses and was a second home for Sharon and me because we spent so much of our time playing inside with our dolls.

Her playhouse was a triangular-shaped, white-sided building with a blue-shingled rooftop that made me think it was a former chicken coop. The slanted roof made the inside cozy, but we could still stand tall without touching the ceiling. The back wall had a window curtained with material left over from Aunt Ruby's sewing projects. The table and chairs took up most of the room.

The playhouse became perfect for our embroidery club, and our secret meetings. We did allow our cousin Johnny to join us. He wanted to be a part of our embroidery club, but he was the ONLY

Sharon, Linda, Aunt Ruby, and Uncle Howard.

boy allowed inside. Johnny liked being with us, and he never got mad when we told him we were the bosses. He always did what we told him to do, no matter how hard it was. When we played house, he became the Daddy. Sharon became Veronica after a movie queen, but I chose Victoria after the real queen of England. The playhouse never lost its magic as a special place to enter our imaginary play world.

Located right next to the playhouse was Aunt Ruby's enormous garden. On the other side was their two-story, four-bedroom house with a huge basement. Their dining room was big enough for a huge table, a built-in cabinet for fancy dishes, and even the little tea set that Sharon bought her Mom from the Sears Roebuck catalog. When Sharon ordered it, she thought it was a grown-up tea set, so it was quite a surprise when it arrived. It was a doll's tea service size, but Aunt Ruby still proudly displayed the tea set beside her fine china.

There was an archway through which you could walk into their living room. It seemed that Uncle Howard's family always bought the bigger and better in everything and always got it before anyone else in the village. According to Aunt Ruby, this was either a blessing or a curse—especially when they were the first family to purchase a television.

The summer they bought the TV, every night after supper a line of eager cousins formed outside their door, hoping Aunt Ruby would say we could come in and watch TV for a little while. Besides their four kids, there were always at least six cousins and a few strays who managed to pretend they belonged to the LaVoy clan. We promised to behave and not talk so we could keep coming back to watch the miracle of moving pictures on the black and white screen.

Having her living room floor littered with kids' bodies on their tummies, resting on their elbows, and peering intently at the magic box was in stark contrast to the loud laughter and screams when we played games in their big outdoor yard. When September and school rolled around, TV was off-limits during the week.

Sharon and I decided to make and sell popcorn at the summer baseball games and Friday night movies at the community hall. We set up a credit plan with Uncle Howard at the store to purchase the popcorn, oil, salt, and paper bags. We used Aunt Ruby's popcorn popper and found a table in the basement to set up our popcorn shop. Their big basement was an ideal place for our new venture.

We could always count on movie nights to sell our popcorn, but when rain caused the cancellation of the Sunday games, we had to be creative in thinking of other ways to market our popcorn. It helped that we worked in the store and could sell it at a discount price during the week. We had invested our money in this popcorn enterprise and did not want to face bankruptcy.

Uncle Howard's Store

Let's walk a very short distance from Uncle Howard's house and go down the hill, past the running well, to enter their store. Located in the middle of the village with the main dirt road passing right in front of it, the store was the focal point of Naytahwaush. Uncle Howard sold everything from soup to nuts and managed to meet almost all the village's needs.

The porch in the front of the store was a gathering place for people to sit and share neighborhood gossip or the latest stories of the village. They sipped a bottle of pop or chewed some treat they purchased as they sat and talked. Everyone knew they must return their empty glass bottle to the pop crate near the pop cooler. That way, no one had to pay extra for the bottle. (Recycling even then!)

Me, sitting in front of Uncle Howard's store petting a stray cat.

Inside the store, there were treasures for every age. Different counters divided the store into food, clothing, or hardware, and every wall had shelves displaying goods to buy. My favorite place in the store was the glass-framed candy counter located to the right of the front entrance. It showcased rows and rows of penny candy and some nickel candy bars. Even the youngest kid, with a penny tightly grasped in his sweaty little palm, could enter and leave with a smile as he chewed his favorite piece of penny candy.

Next to the candy counter was a small freezer with see-through glass top covers to show the ice cream inside. The bread and baked goods counter was next with rows of Holsum bread and products. On the counter next to the bread were clear plastic cookie jars with screw-on lids so that you could buy one cookie at a time.

The main counter had an adding machine to calculate the purchases. Underneath that were drawers containing the charge booklets arranged alphabetically. Very few people had cash, so every item they purchased had to be written down in their booklet with its cost. Toward the end of the month, we used the adding machine constantly to tabulate each family's amount due for that month. When the social security and other checks came in the mail, everyone knew they first had to cash their check at the store to pay their monthly bills. My Uncle knew everyone, and no one could escape without paying.

In the very middle of the store was an icebox for cold drinks such as milk, pop, and non-alcoholic malt beer. My favorite pop was crème soda. I always saved my pennies for that sugar-sweetened drink.

The meat counter was directly in the back of the store with a glass front to display the latest shipment of meat. Next to it was the meat slicer for slicing bologna, bacon, or cheese. On the counter shelves to the left of the meat counter were cooking utensils of all kinds, and handy tools and supplies needed around the house.

Uncle Howard built an extension to the store to accommodate clothing and personal needs or wants—even cheap jewelry. One wall of shelves contained household and cleaning products and medical supplies.

Toward the store's back was a floor-to-ceiling wooden pillar supporting the shelving that extended a few feet from the ceiling, displaying toilet paper rolls and boxes of Kotex feminine products. Because the shelf was so high up, a person had to take the broomstick that had a nail drilled in at one end to stab the Kotex or toilet paper to get it down. On the opposite side of this wooden pillar hung the only telephone in the village.

My Mom told me to go down to the store one day to get some Kotex. I did not want to, but she insisted. My Dad happened to be sick that day, so that he couldn't. Blushing, I found the broomstick, tried to stab the box but couldn't quite reach it.

"What's wrong, my girl?" Uncle Howard asked in a teasing voice. I was so embarrassed that I told him my Dad was sick, so I had to come to the store.

"Oh, I hope your Dad is feeling better, but I don't know if that box will help!" he teased.

I could not get out of the store fast enough and told Mom that I would never buy Kotex at the store ever again!

Since the telephone was on a party line, each phone had a specific number of rings. Three short and two long rings meant it was Uncle Howard's number. Uncle Howard would rush over and pick up the long, black-handled receiver and yell into the voice box when he heard that combination of rings. The audio reception was always bad due to our far away location. Usually, the phone calls were the bearers of bad news, but sometimes it was a happy event.

The telephone in Uncle Howard's store.

"Hey, Uncle Howard, when can I have my turn to take the next phone message to someone?" I hopefully asked when I was at the store buying a piece of penny candy. I had my bike, and at the age of seven, I was sure I could take the responsibility of being a phone messenger.

"Well, my girl, if you are in the store the next time the phone rings and I need to send a message, I will let you deliver it. I think you are big enough now," he replied.

I could hardly wait for my turn and hung around the store just in case. Uncle Howard paid us a whole nickel to relay the message since he could not leave the store. He never lacked a volunteer to do this crucial, paying job.

Memories of Working in the Store

A few days before summer vacation at the end of our sixth grade, Sharon and I were in a pickle. We had spent hours trying to think of ways to earn money. We wanted money to buy new clothes, go to the County Fair, have some money to save, and spend money on summer treats.

One afternoon when I was walking down to the store, Sharon came charging out her door, yelling at me. "Guess what, Vonnie?"

Sharon jumped up and down excitedly as she exclaimed, "Dad says he might hire us to work in the store this summer! What do you think of that?"

I could hardly believe my ears. This was too good to be true. "Wow, when can we start? I'll ask Mom, but I'm sure if I promise to still help around the house, she'll say it's OK."

"Dad wants to talk with us this afternoon, and he wants us to start right away because he needs two helpers," she continued. "Can you believe that he's chosen us to be those helpers? Go ask your Mom and meet me in the playhouse after lunch."

I ran up the hill to my house and found Mom making fried egg sandwiches for our Saturday lunch.

"Mom, guess what? Uncle Howard wants to hire Sharon and me to work in the store this summer. Can I, please? Honest, I will help you with household chores before or after work and when he doesn't want us there. Please, Mom, please?" I begged.

Mom finished frying the eggs and put them between two slices of her homemade bread. She cut each sandwich in half and told me to come and sit down at the table. I got the catsup out of the icebox, poured us each a glass of milk, and joined Mom.

"Now, tell me what this is all about. My brother is well known for his stories, and this might be one of his jokes to see how you will react," responded Mom with a twinkle in her eyes.

"Well, Don and Dick are too busy with sports and other jobs, and Uncle Howard needs two dependable workers," I babbled excitedly. "Oh, Mom, I could earn my own money and pay for many things I need or want. Then I wouldn't have to be asking you all the time. Just think of it, my own real money that I earned!" I hopefully continued.

"So, just how much money will you be making?" Mom asked.

"I don't know, but Uncle Howard wants to talk to both of us this afternoon, and I can ask him. No matter how much it is, it would help if I could earn money this summer, right?" I asked.

Mom studied my eager face, put her hand on my shoulder, and said, "You talk with your Uncle Howard and let me know. We could work something out with house chores on the side. You're eleven years old, and I think taking on the responsibility of working in the store this summer would be good for you."

I jumped up, gave Mom a huge hug, kissed her on the cheek, and said, "You are the BEST Mom in the world! I promise to work hard both in the store and here in our house. Promise, Mom!"

So that Mom would know for sure that her daughter was the best worker ever, I told her I would wash the lunch dishes before I talked with Sharon and Uncle Howard. Mom's special "Vonnie, I'm-proud-of–you smile" made me feel like the luckiest girl in the world to have a mother like mine, plus a job for the summer working in the store. Who could want anything more?

After finishing the dishes, I ran to meet Sharon, and we walked hand in hand down the hill to the store, ready for our first job interview. Aunt Ruby said she would work in the store while Uncle Howard talked with us.

"Well, my girls, are you ready to become summer clerks in our store?" he asked. "I would expect you to be very polite to all our customers. You will have to help with whatever jobs are needed each day. If you do your work to my satisfaction, I think I could pay you twelve dollars a week for six days of work."

Twelve dollars a week! I could hardly believe my ears. Were we worth that much to Uncle Howard? Oh, wait until I tell Mom about all the money I would be earning. She wouldn't believe it, I was sure.

Uncle Howard continued, "Each day, I will explain what work you are to do and how to do it. There are many responsibilities in running a general store like this. I'm sure you two girls will do well and try your hardest. I expect you to start at 9:00 every morning from Monday through Saturday."

He continued, "Aunt Ruby will prepare lunch for you each day. You can have a half-hour to eat lunch and work until 5:00 when I close the store. Are you ready to start on Monday?"

"Will Aunt Ruby be working in the store with us?" I asked because there were many times that I didn't seem to please her.

"No, we talked it over, and she wants to be able to have a larger garden this summer and will be busy with that, as well as her usual household chores. It will be a nice break for her, and she will help us whenever we might need her."

I eagerly nodded and gave Uncle Howard a big hug, relieved that I would not have to be under Aunt Ruby's watchful eye. I said I would try to be the best helper he ever had. Sharon did the same, and we jumped up and down, yelling, "We've got a job! We've got a job!" Monday seemed too far away. I was going to earn twelve dollars a week!

Monday morning finally came. I got up before Mom woke me, made my breakfast, did the dishes, and looked at the clock. With a half-hour to go, I asked Mom what chores I could do around the house before starting my real job.

Me entering my place of employment.

Monday was the Holsum Bread truck day, and Uncle Howard introduced Sharon and me to Buddy. He told us to watch how Buddy stacked the new bread on the bread racks. Buddy placed the older bread up front. Most families in our little village baked their bread, but the white mushy store-bought bread was always a treat for everyone.

Buddy showed us the particular area where he placed the Twinkies, Ding Dongs, Ho Ho's, Snoballs, fruit pies, and cupcakes. My mouth watered, looking at all those yummy treats. I decided I might splurge and buy one when I got my first week's pay. Buddy must have seen us eyeing his baked goods because he decided that Sharon and I could sample one of them.

He said, "I think you girls will be better salespersons if you have sampled some of the products. Then you can tell your customers how delicious they are."

This new job already had a fantastic benefit. We could sample some of the products. We heartily agreed with Buddy, and I had my first taste of Twinkies. The taste of that marshmallow treat remained my favorite forever. I wondered what the next truck would bring.

Tuesday was Meat Day. That meant Uncle Howard got in his pickup early every Tuesday morning to drive the twenty-five miles to Mahnomen to be there when the Sioux Railroad train pulled into the station. It carried the beef and pork quarters and the big chunks of cold cuts and slabs of bacon with the rind still on it. He brought all these bulk meats back to the store.

The back room of the general store had meat cleavers and a special meat board for cutting up the meat. Uncle Howard became the butcher cutting the quarters into pieces that his customers would buy. He knew that boiling beef was the most popular cut that people bought.

Sharon and I learned how to run the meat slicer to cut the meat to each customer's desired thickness. Sliced fingers were not to be a part of the meat offerings! I prayed that no one would want bacon that first week!

The Young's candy truck drove up for its weekly delivery on Wednesday. Steve, the candy man, arrived with a big smile on his face as he offered samples for the new store clerks. Sharon and I couldn't wait to try them. Uncle Howard told us we had to wait until after lunch for those treats.

After Steve checked the list of needed candy supplies, he disappeared into his truck. When he returned, he had boxes of Necco wafers, Bazooka gum, Neapolitan coconut bars, Bit O-Honey bars, Jujubes, Licorice pipes and wheels, and the orange Circus Peanuts, as well as Snap licorice boxes. Our job was to display the new candies so that customers noticed them.

Steve told us we might need more Tootsie Pops, Smarties, Red Hots, Root Beer Barrels, and Candy cigarettes next week. "It all depends on how well you girls work the candy counter!" Steve warned. "Let's see what great salespeople you are! See you next week!"

Wednesday was the truck day for bringing milk, pop, and non-alcoholic malt beer. The milkman quickly arranged the different containers in the cooler as the liquids must stay cold. Uncle Howard explained that the cover of the cooler needed to remain closed at all times. It was part of our job to check it periodically to ensure the last customer had closed it.

One time Sharon and I found a supply of popsicle sticks in a box. We had the bright idea of making frozen candy bars to sell. After inserting a stick into each bar, we placed them in the ice cream freezer. When people came in, we advertised our new frozen treat. They became the new favorite. Uncle Howard proudly smiled at the latest sales success of his new helpers.

On Thursday, the general merchandise truck arrived. This truck brought clothing, pots and pans, medical supplies, building supplies, and anything that wasn't edible. Sharon and I had to keep a check-off list for items getting low in stock so Uncle Howard would know what to order each week.

Friday was a food truck day, the biggest day of the week. We opened all the new canned and packaged food boxes and stacked them on the shelves. Uncle Howard showed us how to put the more recent merchandise in the back, with the oldest up toward the front.

Sharon and I were so busy that we hardly had time to come up for air to wait on customers. Not only did we have to stack the shelves, but we also dusted the shelves and the tops of cans and boxes. If the store got too busy on Fridays, Uncle Howard called one of us to leave our stacking shelves and help him. We saved all the empty boxes and put them in the backroom for packing big food orders for customers.

Saturday was always the busiest day. Everyone in the village needed to get all their supplies for the weekend. We were constantly cleaning the front of the candy counter. Kids made marks with their dirty fingers as they pointed to each penny candy they wanted. Uncle Howard insisted on keeping his store neat and clean.

The best store clerks ever! Sharon (left) and me.

Sharon and I were there to prove to him that we could do just that. Every day after closing, we swept the wooden floor. We used a special reddish-yellow sawdust compound sprinkled on the wooden floor before cleaning it to prevent lots of dust. It also gave a shiny, moist covering to the floor.

Toward the end of each month, some families had to be limited to what they bought. Uncle Howard knew how much their monthly check would be, so they needed to stay within their allotment.

One day, I heard Uncle Howard say to this little kid who had brought in his mother's grocery list, "Tell your mother that I am not selling you a box of Corn Flakes. Your bill for this month is higher than it should be. This oatmeal will last longer" He continued: "No, you can't get any candy either. Tell your mother to come to see me if she has any problems."

Uncle Howard showed us how to use the adding machine to total the monthly bills for each family when we had any free time. We had learned how to enter items neatly and legibly in their charge books to avoid any mistakes. If we were unsure of the person who asked to charge for their family, we must ask Uncle Howard. He determined if they could charge items or not.

My Uncle was a strict but fair businessman who helped many families live within their means. They knew him well. Since Uncle Howard spoke the Ojibwe language, even the village elders could communicate.

Uncle Howard often used a barter system when people were in real need. He encouraged them to live off the land as much as possible as their ancestors had done. Since everyone had gardens, no one went hungry.

Because Uncle Howard always enjoyed teasing people, Sharon and I were often at his mercy. Two old bachelors in the village became his targets to tease us.

Whenever Mickey G. entered the store, Uncle Howard and Sharon disappeared so that I had to wait on him. I dreaded the days when his old pickup drove up in front of the store. He owned a resort about ten miles away on an isolated lake. It always seemed like he had a never-ending list of needed items whenever he came in.

Mickey was very fussy about the way he wanted his bacon sliced. Bacon was hard enough to cut with the rind on it, but he insisted that I first cut off the rind before slicing it on the machine. Then he would stand and watch with narrowed eyes as I tried to cut the peel off carefully. For me to slice that slippery chunk of bacon without the rind was almost impossible to keep it even. Cutting every piece of bacon was torture.

Uncle Howard told me to keep smiling and remember that the customer was always right! He also told me I had to weigh the rind with the cut slices as that was no more than fair. Having to pay for the rind did not please Mickey. He often asked if I held my hand on the scale when I weighed the sliced bacon and the rind. I could hear muffled giggles from the back of the store whenever he asked me that. I knew Sharon and Uncle Howard were watching me as I tried my very best to be polite to my customer.

Eddy B. was Sharon's nemesis. I gladly went with Uncle Howard to work in the back of the store whenever he arrived. Eddy was not the most kempt man, and Sharon couldn't stand him. He took his sweet time in deciding what he wanted. Then he would change his mind and often end up with his first choice. It was difficult to control my giggles as I saw the pained look on Sharon's face the multiple times Eddy tried to make up his mind. I assured Sharon that Eddy never asked her to cut bacon without the rind!

Because Uncle Howard was quite the businessman, he let George Norris, our village barber, set up his barbershop in the store's basement. When people got haircuts, it brought business to the store as well. People always stopped to buy something after their haircut.

One day, Sharon and I decided to let George cut our hair since he was right there in the store. We gave up our pigtails and came out looking like every other George Norris customer with short—really short—clipped hair. We decided that we looked like the Bobbsey Twins, so Uncle Howard said we should start dressing alike and be the main attraction for the store. We were embarrassed and upset when our parish priest, Father Andrew, came into the store and asked what lawnmower had run over our heads! I never did like that priest.

Every January, Uncle Howard did an inventory of all the goods in the store. George helped out during those busy times, so Sharon and I thought we would have fun teasing him. We held up various underwear items such as snuggies of all sizes and asked George what size he thought we should categorize them for the inventory. George tried to ignore us as he ducked his blushing face behind another counter.

On the last weekend of every July, our Catholic Church, St. Anne's, put on a big bazaar and dinner. Sharon and I asked Uncle Howard if we could please advertise this in the store. He agreed. Little did he know that we planned to wear our Indian jingle dresses to do that.

We made cardboard signs advertising the bazaar and dinner on the front and back of our dresses. All day, with every step we took, our jingles jingled noisily, nonstop. Uncle Howard's migraine headache had set in full force by noon of the second day. He had to go home to rest. When he returned, he announced that the jingle-dresses had to go. We would have to find another source of advertising, preferably a quiet one!

My Indian jingle dress 70 years later.

Toward the end of the summer, Uncle Howard decided we were doing so well that we could try ordering some supplies. The general merchandise vendor told us he had a special on Sweetheart Soap. Since it was such a good deal, we decided to order three cases.

Palmolive soap had always been the big seller. Sharon and I thought of the profit we could make for the store if we sold Sweetheart Soap for the same price as Palmolive. We could make fifteen cents on every bar!

Beaming with pride, we shared our good idea with Uncle Howard when he got back to the store. He looked at us with a surprised look and said, "Do you know how hard it is to sell a new product when people always buy the same brand all the time? You two need to sell every one of those Sweetheart Soap bars before the end of the summer, or I will dock it from your pay!"

We now directed our new advertising campaign by asking every customer that came in if they would like to try this fantastic new Sweetheart Soap. We each bought a bar to personally share how wonderful it was and how great it smelled. It took all summer to sell the three cases—a lesson learned and a mistake we never repeated: Be careful of the amount when you order!

At the end of that summer, Uncle Howard rewarded each of us with a FREE bar of Sweetheart Soap that he had removed from one of the cases. He told us we were the best workers he had ever had. Would we be willing to be his store clerks the following summer?

Since we would be twelve, maybe our weekly pay could be bumped up to thirteen dollars a week with some Sweetheart soap as a bonus? He didn't have to ask twice.

Cousin John and a friend, Joanne, posing in front of Uncle Howard's store.

Chapter Four

Other Relative's Homes

Not everyone is lucky enough to have such Uncles and Aunts in
their lives who are next to parents but I was definitely blessed
with them...
Lyric from an Unknown Source

Great Aunt Clara's House

I f we walk across the street from the store, we can visit the home
of my great-aunt Clara Fairbanks, the sister of Mom's mother. I
learned that Aunt Clara had been a very sharp, business-minded,
independent woman ahead of her times. When I was a kid, she was
in her seventies and forgetful.

She had been married to Uncle Willie, who died before we kids
were born. I guess he had been quite the character, a dashing good-
looking man who wore long fur coats, a fur hat, and smoked cigars.
Alcohol, gambling, and women were his specialty, so we heard. After
he died, Aunt Clara never remarried, remaining childless and a spin-
ster for the rest of her life.

Aunt Clara lived in a large, white, wooden-framed structure big
enough for a large family, though she lived alone. Whenever we visited her, she always had a piece of candy or a cookie to share. One of
her legs was stiff, so she used a beautifully carved, willow cane to
help her walk. She'd slowly get off her chair, grasp her cane and limp
to her candy jar.

Aunt Clara always wore cotton house dresses and was as neat
as a pin. She wore her hair in a braided bun on the back of her head.
It had many shades of white, gray, and even some yellow streaks

peeking out. Never having any children of her own, she looked forward to our pop-in visits, but would put up with no nonsense.

Her favorite pastime was cheating while playing Solitaire games. To this day, I can still hear her sing-song melody of "Tu, di, doo, doo, doo" as she cleverly manipulated the cards to win every game. All the while she was cheating, her one good foot kept the beat of her little ditty that never contained words, just the syllabic chant that became etched into each of our memories forever.

When Aunt Clara began to grow senile in her older years, Mom decided that Flo and I should take turns sleeping at her home during the nighttime to keep her company and protect her. We soon realized that she was frightened by thunderstorms because, at the sight of dark clouds in the sky, she kept repeating: "I hope we don't get a bad storm tonight. Pray that there's no thunder and lightning, my dear."

At the first sound of thunder following the lightning, we had to follow her into her bedroom. We then sat on her bed and began to pray the rosary. If the storm got worse, we knew that she would have us in her closet to wait out the storm. Somehow, she thought her closet was the safest place to ride out a storm. She always had a flashlight by the side of her bed to be our protector if the lights went out.

I prayed each time it was my turn to stay with Aunt Clara that we would have good weather. I remember glancing at the threatening thunderstorm clouds one day and running into our house yelling, "Mom, Mom, it's Flo's night to stay with Aunt Clara, isn't it?"

Today was not my lucky day. It was my turn. Reluctantly walking over for my night's duty, I prayed again for clear weather. No such luck. I awakened with loud claps of thunder and a flashlight beaming into my face.

"Wake up, dearie, we need to sit in the closet until the storm is over," she nervously said in a loud whisper. I knew better than to argue and try to change the storm routine. We sat huddled in her tiny closet until the storm passed. Then Aunt Clara asked if I would sleep with her just perchance the storm returned. She didn't want me to be frightened! I kept wondering why I always seemed to be blessed with the stormy nights at Aunt Clara's.

The good thing about sleeping over was having supper with Aunt Clara. She always wanted to have us share some of her homemade hash that was her specialty. It contained secret ingredients of different herbs. I always asked for toast to use her unique two-sided toaster with sides to pull down to insert each piece of bread.

Aunt Clara warned me to watch the bread closely to ensure it didn't burn. I always quickly grabbed the toaster handle and turned the bread to toast on the other side as soon as I smelled the toast. Then I hurried to do the same for the piece of bread on the other side of the toaster. All the while, Aunt Clara hummed her little tune and hobbled around to take care of the finishing touches of her famous hash. She loved hot tea, so we learned to drink it with her as she let us add lots of milk and sugar.

A flip side toaster like Aunt Clara's.

After supper, I watched Aunt Clara cheat again at her nightly solitaire games that she won every time. When it was time to go to bed, Aunt Clara picked up her willow cane and hobbled to her bedroom for her nightly rituals. She always let me join her.

These rituals included donning her long, white nightgown and then taking the big, curved bobby pins out of her braided pug on the back of her head. It was fascinating to watch as her long hair unfolded and hung almost to her waist. She then carefully brushed the yellow-white strands with a beautiful pearl-backed hairbrush.

In my imagination, she became transformed into a fairytale queen without her braided crown. With each brushstroke, she hummed a quirky little tune. Next, she removed her teeth and placed them in a particular glass water container. Finally, she slowly leaned back, tucked her good leg first underneath the covers, and then tugged at the stiff leg to do the same. When she finished this last part of her nightly routine, it was time to recite the rosary. Completing that, I walked to my bedroom in the next room. Then, my nightly routine was to kneel beside my bed and say a quick prayer to God, begging for a peaceful night of no thunderstorms.

Great-Uncle John and Aunt Mary Jane's Home

Next door to Aunt Clara lived our great-uncle John and his wife, Aunt Mary Jane. Their house seemed so tiny after being at Aunt Clara's home. As a kid, I often wondered why they didn't switch places since two people lived here and Aunt Clara lived all alone.

Aunt Mary Jane never complained about anything and had an aura of dignity and serenity about her. Her parlor begged a quietness and reverence that matched her personality. It made me want to tiptoe and whisper. Nothing was ever out of place. I felt like I was entering a different world filled with untold secrets.

She and Uncle John had lost a baby in childbirth and never had another. They loved children but expected us to listen and show our best manners while visiting. When we kids stopped by, Aunt Mary Jane invited us to come in and have one of the white peppermint candies that she kept in her special candy dish.

If we promised to be very careful, she let us look into her magic stereoscope and see a world we had never visited. As she tatted (a technique using a little hand shuttle and thread to make lace from a series of knots and loops for edging, as well as for doilies and collars), we spent hours looking at black and white pictures that came alive in her magic machine. We saw the Eiffel Tower, the Great

Stereoscope similar to Aunt Mary Jane's.

Wall of China, and exotic places we never dreamed existed.

Aunt Mary Jane was the most gentle and prim woman I have ever known. She contracted tuberculosis years before I was born and had spent time in the sanatorium to get cured. Her trademark was the snow-white hanky that matched her perfectly coifed, snow-white hair tied up with braids. This hanky served a dual purpose: to cover her mouth whenever she coughed and to hold the small coins carefully knotted at one end. She would often stop in the store to buy her favorite candy or her favorite sugar cookie and use the coins from her hanky to pay for them.

Aunt Mary Jane insisted on keeping her charge book from Uncle Howard's store in her home. She made her daily trip to the store after she had gone to our house to pick up her mail. Once a month, she brought in her book to pay her bill that she already had added up to show what she owed. Uncle Howard never doubted her accuracy!

Uncle John loved to sit on the 2x4 bench in front of his small, white-sided house and whittle figures with his sharp knife. We liked it when he showed us how to skin bullhead fish he caught in the lake nearby. After placing the bullhead on the grass, Uncle John pounded a long nail into its head behind the gills. With a quick turn of his hand, he cut across the top layer of skin with his sharp knife. Then, he pulled the skin off with his pliers, and it became skinless in a flash. It was like magic, and we stood mesmerized as Uncle John quickly cleaned his mess of fish for dinner.

In the summer, Uncle John practically lived in his garden, where no weeds were allowed. He planted lots of potato plants and gave us kids a nickel if we picked the potato bugs from the plants.

To do that, Uncle John gave us each a clean, used tin can that contained soapy water. He showed us exactly how to remove the potato bugs without harming the plants. We then became potato bug detectives in his garden and worked hard to find as many as possible. After inspecting our tin cans, he smiled and beckoned us to follow him in his striped bibbed overalls to the side door.

He kept a jar of coins in the house and took his time looking for just the suitable nickel to give us. We thanked him and rushed across the road to Uncle Howard's store to spend a long time looking for our favorite penny candies. We quickly ate up our wages, unless we chose to buy a Sugar Daddy sucker that would last for at least an hour if we sucked on it slowly.

We always begged Uncle John to show us how he sharpened his knives and scythe. Situated by their side door stood a big rounded grinding stone balanced on a wooden structure. It had a seat for our uncle to sit on and pedals for his feet to make the grinder move in circles. Uncle John poured some water on the stone and started pedaling as we watched. He put the side of the knife on the wet stone to sharpen it. Everyone knew that he always had the sharpest knives in the village.

I think Mom forgot Uncle John would sharpen our knives too, if we asked him, because the knives in our house were always dull. (A trait and tradition from Mom that I manage to have continued for posterity's sake.)

Uncle John's knife sharpener resembled
this one.

Grandpa, Uncle Sid ,and Aunt Gerda's Home

If we bike down the dirt road past Aunt Clara's house, we can see the Episcopalian church cemetery on the left, a pasture, and a big garden. Next to the garden is the large two-storied, white-board house where Grandpa lived with Uncle Sid, Aunt Gerda, and their children: Jeanette, John, Ruth, Rita, Sidney James, and Roy Allen. It is the house in which Mom grew up. When Uncle Sid got married, he said he and Aunt Gerda would live there and care for Grandpa.

There was an oversized screened porch covering the entire front of the house. Inside were two living rooms, two bedrooms downstairs, and a massive kitchen with a big dining room table. The table was big enough for the whole family and Grandpa to sit around for their meals. Upstairs there were big bedrooms where all the kids slept.

A big wood box filled with wood chunks for heating their cooking stove was in one kitchen corner. The milk separator and a porch leading to the outside were in the other corner. Outside was a barn for the horses and cows and a chicken coop.

I remember sitting on the edge of the wood-box, wishing to eat supper with the big family. After many attempts to eat at each other's homes, our parents said we could sit, wait, and wish, but not eat except for special occasions. We needed to eat at our own home first. After eating and doing the dishes, we could go out and play with our cousins.

We all knew which days were bread days at each home. It just so happened that we kids managed to be at that home just as the fresh rolls came out of the oven. No Mom ever refused us a taste of warm fresh bread covered with melted butter!

There were several patches of rhubarb near Uncle Sid's garden. We kids would get a salt shaker and run to pick a stalk of ripe rhubarb. After breaking off the big leaf, we put it on our heads as our sun hat. Then we peeled the rhubarb stalk, poured salt on it, and then sat down in the field to eat our snack.

After eating, we ran around to see how long we could keep our leaf hats on before they fell off. Sometimes, we kept the stalk on the rhubarb and played like they were our umbrellas to keep out the sun or rain. Of course, we also picked rhubarb for our Moms to make rhubarb sauce, cake, or pie.

Since John was born the same year as Sharon and I, we mostly played with him at their house. Sometimes Ruth, who was two years younger, would join us.

Uncle Sid was short of stature and had the nickname of Shorty. I remember one time when we were having a family get-together at our house. All the men gathered in our tiny kitchen for a drink. When I entered the crowded kitchen, I had to walk in front of Uncle Sid to get to my bedroom. "Excuse me, Shorty," I said, tring to be cute and get some attention.

That was the WRONG thing to say! My Dad grabbed my arm and angrily said, "Little girl, you must respect your elders and NEVER call them anything except their real name. His name is Uncle Sid. You apologize right now and NEVER be disrespectful again. Do you understand?"

Crying, I hugged Uncle Sid and told him I was so sorry and that I would never do it again. (It is a custom that I engrained in my children and grandchildren to this day, to respect their elders and use the words of Aunt and Uncle before their names!) It was a lesson I learned that day and never forgot!

Uncle Sid was the community custodian and took care of all the community buildings: four school buildings, the village clinic, and the village hall. Being a quiet man, he never complained and never called attention to himself. I learned later that Uncle Sid often worked until the late hours of the night. Since all of the community buildings were heated with wood stoves, he had to get up by 4:30 in the winter mornings so the buildings would be warm by the time people came to work. He wore out his short legs as he faithfully worked all his life being there for others in the village.

Uncle Sid never asked for a raise in his paycheck. When Mom was on the School Board, she demanded that they increase his wages because he would never ask for one. While he worked so hard for the community, Aunt Gerda selflessly worked at their home taking care of Grandpa and his needs, as well as the needs of their seven children. (She lost two at childbirth, and one son died in a fire accident). Later on, she even took care of our Aunt Clara too!

Grandpa had a car with a rumble seat in the back. We all envied Uncle Sid and Aunt Gerda's kids as they got to ride in it the most whenever Grandpa went somewhere. It was always a special treat to go down to visit Grandpa. He would slowly take out his pipe and tap its head onto the tall ashtray that stood next to his rocking chair. Then with a twinkle in his eye, he would take out his tobacco pouch, unzip it, and tamp the tobacco into the pipe. Next, he took a match, lit the tobacco, and took some satisfying puffs before he started to rock back and forth.

Looking around at all of us kids seated on the floor eagerly leaning forward, ready to listen, he would smile and slowly start to share whatever story or tall tale he knew would keep us mesmerized for long periods. Grandpa had to be the best storyteller ever. He always had an adventure or two to share with us.

Me sitting outside the screened porch at
Grandpa's house.

Chapter Five

Village School Buildings

> The mediocre teacher tells,
> The good teacher explains,
> The superior teacher demonstrates.
> The great teacher inspires.
> **William Arthur Ward**

Multiple School Buildings

When I was going to school, we had all Indian kids but never an Indian teacher. Our skin colors varied from white to dark brown, and the idea of being Indian seldom came into my head during those elementary years. We were all just kids. Because Dad was a white man, we lived a non-traditional lifestyle. Our family took part in community pow-wow dances and celebrations, but did not practice the Indian way of living.

Instead of getting on our bikes, we could easily walk from my house across the road to the school buildings.

When I started school at the age of six, there were four separate buildings for the elementary grades. We did not have such a thing as kindergarten, so my first chance to attend school was when I turned six and entered first grade. The first- and second-grade classrooms shared a building with two different entrances. This building was across the road from the general store.

My first-grade teacher, Mrs. Gilbert Tviet, became the most memorable teacher in all my years of education. Since our home was

First grade class, with Mrs. Tviet.
(I'm second from the right on the back row.)

just across the road from the first-grade building, my Mom told me I could help her anytime she might need me. My world now revolved around first-grade adventures and my home. The world of books and love of learning exploded, as did my latest emotional decision that I would grow up to be a teacher.

Mrs. Tveit showed me how to make worksheets for our class using a pan of gelatin. Making copies of our worksheets for the next day was one of my favorite jobs. I knew that when I got to be a teacher, I would let my first graders help me just like this.

One afternoon, as I carefully wet the clear, hardened gelatin in the 12"x16" cookie sheet pan with my dripping sponge, I wondered what Mrs. Tviet wanted me to copy for her this time.

"Mrs. Tviet, if I am careful and do a good job like I did yesterday, can I do two sets of papers today?" I wistfully asked.

Mrs. Tviet glanced over, smiled, and assured me that I certainly could if I had the time to help her. She came over and helped me carefully place the master carbon copy on the gel pad. She reminded me to gently smooth it out to each corner and then pull it back off the gelatin. There, on the gel, just like magic, appeared a copy of our reading worksheet for tomorrow.

"Now, Yvonne, remember always to take a clean sheet of paper and put the corners down first. Smooth out each piece of paper to get all the words before removing them from the gel pan. You did it so well yesterday, and I know you can do the same today. I appreciate having a first-grade helper like you," she said in her gentle voice. She smiled, returned to her desk, and began correcting our papers.

I watched her every move, nodded, then carefully placed the blank sheet of paper on the gel. After I did swishing motions back and forth, back and forth, I gently took one edge and carefully pulled it toward me. Magic happened again: The blank page now had become a ditto copy of the master copy. I needed to quickly put on the next blank sheet and make a copy for each of my classmates—all twenty-six of us. I didn't care if the other kids called me teacher's pet because I was learning to be a teacher.

Even though I wasn't very good at phonics, I was good at making copies of the phonics sheets. Phonics, yuck! Why couldn't we just read? Those funny letter sounds didn't make sense all by themselves. But I wouldn't tell Mrs. Tviet because she might not let me help her every day after school. These phonics papers gave me a C on my report card. All the other marks were A's and B's. Maybe if I kept making these phonics worksheets, I'd get better and get rid of that nasty C. First grade was perfect, except for phonics!

My favorite time of the school day was when Mrs. Tviet read to us. We left the world of worksheets and entered into the world of imagination. Our Dick and Jane books with silly sentences like, "See Dick run. Run, Dick, run. See Spot play. Play, Spot, play," paled in comparison with the words as she read about the lives of children so different than ours. I remember the books about Eddie and Betsy, written by Carolyn Haywood. Mrs. Tviet must also have enjoyed them; she read the whole series to us.

At Christmas time, every class in the school put on a play for the village. I cried when Sharon got the role of Mrs. Santa Claus. I wanted to be Mrs. Santa Claus so much, but Mrs. Tviet said I would make a good maid for Mrs. Santa. Orvie, a chubby boy in our class, got to be Mr. Santa.

So that we would present the best Christmas play in all the school, I asked everyone to come and practice our parts in my house.

Even though I couldn't be the star player, I wanted our play to be the best.

Most of the teachers who taught at our school lived in other communities as there were few places for them to live in the village. Our principal, who lived in part of the community clinic, was one exception. Some teachers lived over forty miles away. These dedicated educators drove to school every day, even in the harsh winter weather with bad roads.

Mrs. Tviet liked Sharon and me a lot because she invited the two of us to come and visit her for a weekend at her home in Mahnomen. We couldn't believe it. She said we could ride home with her on Friday after school and return on Monday morning.

Mrs. Tviet told us that she lived alone with her husband and that he wanted to meet us because she had told him lots of stories about us. We couldn't wait to meet him or see her house. After getting permission from our parents, they warned us to be on our absolute best behavior and be very respectful.

Her husband was called Tiny, but he certainly was not tiny. He met us at the door. We stood on our tiptoes to look up at a very tall man towering over us with a welcoming, hearty, giant-like laugh. After showing us our bedroom, Mrs. Tviet told us that Tiny would entertain us as she prepared supper. His eyes twinkled behind his spectacles as he told us one story after another that made us giggle uncontrollably. Mrs. Tviet watched and smiled as Sharon and I begged him for "just one more story, please?" He was a great storyteller, just like our Grandpa.

It was so strange to be in our favorite teacher's home and stay overnight. We pretended we were her girls and basked in the attention paid to us by both of them. We were SO lucky to be honored like this, but decided not to tell the other first graders. They might get jealous.

(Years later, when we were in our thirties, Mrs. Tviet invited us for a visit. When Sharon and I stopped to see her, she was still the wonderful woman we remembered from first grade. Mrs. Tviet had kept track of many of her students from Naytahwaush in a unique album. She brought out her album with the notes, newspaper clippings, photos, and other memorabilia she had collected about her former students. There were articles about students who had entered the military, graduated from college, and even clipped an article about one of our classmates who ended up in prison! Her gentleness and lovely smile will remain a fixture in my mind and heart forever. She was a living example of a teacher who truly loved her work and her students.)

Second grade does not evoke any special memories, but I remember my teacher, Mrs. Hauge, as pleasant, strict, and stout. She paled compared to Mrs. Tviet, whom I still stopped to visit every day to see if she needed any help after school.

The third grade brought Mrs. Stone as our teacher. Third graders had a separate building behind the Episcopal Church. It was as if we had our private school, separated from the other school buildings. Tucked away in the woods, we had our playground and only third graders to play with during recess and lunchtime.

One day, while we girls were playing hopscotch using colored pieces of glass as our markers, a new student appeared on our playground. This new boy was the tallest third grader I had ever seen, and he had the friendliest smile. He watched us girls play hopscotch. I giggled and showed off whenever he got near our hopscotch area. Russell immediately became my reason for becoming the best hopscotcher there ever was on Earth.

Reproduction of a classroom with runner desk and wood stove.

Of course, I wasn't the only girl he noticed. He began to pay attention to one of my best friends, Maxine. With crushed hopes, I decided to get his attention by becoming the best reader in the class to outsmart Maxine.

Mrs. Stone introduced a new strategy for students reading aloud to the rest of the class. She called on one student to read aloud while the rest of us followed the words closely in our books, hoping that the person reading aloud would make a mistake. We jumped up beside our desk to tell the error if they did. The first person to notice the mistake could then read aloud until they read the wrong word. I always hoped I could be the one to discover Maxine's error. Then Russell might pay more attention to me, not her. Even though I felt I was a better reader than Maxine, it did not win me the special attention of that tallest boy in our grade.

Gladys Stone was a very prim and proper woman who always wore bright red lipstick, and her hair was always carefully coifed. Since she was a close friend of Sharon's parents, I often saw her all dressed up to go to dances with them. It was challenging to think of my teacher going out drinking and dancing—after all, she was a teacher!

She lived above Uncle Howard's general store in an apartment with her son, Donnie. Mrs. Stone's son was in high school and a good friend of Sharon's brothers. I always wondered where her husband was, but one day I heard Aunt Ruby tell Mom that he was in Saudi Arabia with the oil wells. I knew Sharon had a crush on Donnie, but that was our secret, and we never told anyone else.

The fourth-grade building shared a building with other upper grades, and all students shared two outhouses at the edge of the playground close to the woods. One was for the boys and one for the girls. These outhouses often became an escape for some students during school hours to avoid classes. Some of the kids used the outhouses as a refuge during recess when other kids picked on them or teased them unmercifully.

Orvie, the famous Santa from first grade, got tired of other people calling him Fatso, so he decided that I should become the fourth-grade target for teasing one day. I had never thought that the bump on my broken nose would become the cause of such hurtful teasing and humiliation.

To begin with, Orvie and his friends started calling me Dick Tracy, the name of a hook-nosed man in the comic books. Since I had two different colored eyes, one a bold blue and the other a dark brown, my eyes became the next target for their teasing. The boys taunted me, saying that only cats had two different colored eyes. So my next nickname became Cat Eyes. As if that weren't bad enough, they added Teacher's Pet to the name-calling since I often stayed after school to help our fourth-grade teacher, Mrs. Bisson.

We seldom received new clothes, so it was extra special when my cousin gave me a brown woolen cap with brightly variegated colors embroidered on it. The colorful cap was divided into shell sections like a turtle's back. Flaps covered my ears to keep them toasty warm. Proud as a peacock, I flaunted my cap at recess on the playground. All the kids knew how unique that cap was because I told the class that it was my first new cap, not a hand-me-down like all my other clothes.

One day at recess, Orvie started teasing me about my cap.

"Turtlehead, turtlehead!" shouted Orvie and his friends as we girls played on the steel-pipe monkey bars.

"Can't catch us, can't catch us!" he and the other boys yelled. Instead of following my mother's advice to ignore anybody who teased me, I chased after them but had forgotten to tie my hat on tightly. "Turtlehead! Slow like a turtle!"

When I finally caught up to Orvie, he grabbed my hat, put it on a stick, and ran with it toward the school outhouses. Racing after him, I tried to catch him. Seeing that the school outhouses were occupied, Orvie turned and ran in the opposite direction. He headed toward my house, darted across the road, making a beeline for our outhouse.

"NO, don't you dare!" I screamed as he rushed to open the outhouse door. Orvie dropped my precious turtle cap into one of the holes.

"Ha, ha, now your hat will be browner than ever. Ha, ha," Orvie yelled as he dropped the stick and raced back across the road to the playground.

"No, no, no! " I cried hysterically. How could he be so mean? What could I do? All I could think of was where my turtle cap was and how could I ever get it back? Near the door of the outhouse, I saw the stick he had dropped.

I quickly picked up the stick, opened the outhouse door, held my breath, and peered down the holes. There it was—my cap with its bright colors shining deep below. Sobbing, I pushed the stick into the hole and repeatedly tried to hook it.

Finally, I hooked it and slowly pulled my cap up through the hole. Phew! I opened the door, dropped it on the ground, and went crying to Mom. Between sobs and gulps, I told Mom what Orvie had done. She put her arms around me and let me cry. When my sobs subsided, she went outside with me to see my cap.

"Vonnie, we can't save the cap. It's wool and would shrink if we washed it, and the smell will never leave it. I think you, Orvie, his mother, and I need to talk," Mom said. "At 5:00, when I close the post office, you and I will walk up the road to their house. We'll get things settled once and for all. This teasing can't go on, she continued, shaking her head.

Orvie promised to stop teasing me if kids would stop calling him Fatso. I promised to help if he stopped teasing me. We could talk to Mrs. Bisson about it. The teasing stopped, but I never wore my precious wool turtle cap again—the outhouse reclaimed its prize. To this day, turtles have a special place in my heart, but not on my head.

My favorite memory of fourth grade was after lunch when Mrs. Bisson walked to her desk and picked up a book to read to us. She must have loved horses, because she read the whole series of *My Friend Flicka*. I didn't have a horse, but the story captivated my interests and dreams. Maybe someday I would have a horse like Flicka.

Every suppertime, I shared what had happened to Flicka that day with my family. Then I talked incessantly about how great it would be to have a horse. One afternoon, Mom had to drive to the Ranch for some errands. She took me along, and I couldn't believe my eyes. There were horses there—one was even saddled up and giving rides to people.

The horse looked gigantic, and I was scared. I had pictured Flicka so differently in my mind. The rancher asked if I wanted to try riding his horse. Here was my chance, but I was so scared. After much encouragement, he helped me get up on the saddled horse. Just at that moment, a loud sound frightened the horse. He reared up. I screamed and fell off the startled horse. Crying, I ran to find my mother with nothing hurt except my pride. I decided to just read about horses, not ride them from that day on.

For Valentine's Day, Mrs. Bisson decided we should make our own Valentine cards to give to classmates, rather than buy them. She also announced a contest to see whose card was the most creative. I so wanted to win and tried to think of a unique design. It was the era of paper doilies, but I needed something to make my cards stand out.

Mom had bought red gumdrop candies for our Valentine's Day treat. Looking at my white doily and the red gumdrops gave me an idea. I could glue my red gumdrops on a heart-shaped doily with a red heart background. It meant giving up my share of gumdrops for eating, but maybe I might win the prize for being so original.

Mrs. Bisson mounted all the entries on the bulletin boards above the chalkboards. One of the other teachers was to judge them. The day of judging arrived. I could hardly wait to find out if my Valentine card won. How disappointing to discover that Patsy won with her remarkable, intricate, woven paper designs on her Valentine. Holding back tears, I took my Valentine down, ran home, and cut off the tops of the gumdrops. At least I could eat part of my defeat!

Fifth grade lacked special memories, and I can't even remember our teacher's name. I have report cards from all the other grades, but not the fifth grade. I know I didn't skip any grades, so that must have been a year of little consequence in my life.

New School Building

The school board worked very hard for years to get a new school. When I was in sixth grade, in October of 1951, we moved to a new, two-story, brick building about three blocks away. It cost $212,000, but the federal and state government helped pay for it. Because Harold Emerson, an Ojibwe elder, and Adele Northrup, the community nurse, had worked so hard to help the community, the school board decided to name it: The Northrup Emerson School.

It was like entering into a new world. As we toured our new place of learning, our eyes became wider and wider. We had never experienced such luxury and space before. Our teacher, Mrs. Bisek, explained that now we had a science room, a home economics room, and even a room just for the library. The smiling cooks greeted us as they worked in their sparkling new kitchen. They had never before worked in such a massive kitchen equipped with the latest appliances and spacious cupboards.

Each classroom had a wall of windows to bring the outside into view. Brand new blackboards lined the front of the room, eagerly waiting to be marked up and to become a vital tool in our learning process. We had closets to hold our coats and belongings in the back of the room. On the fourth wall were shelves for our books and materials.

The new school had separate desks for each of us with moveable tops, showing lots of space underneath to hold our books and writing supplies. The seats even looked comfortable!

Our old desks had been attached to a board that connected a whole row of desks. They were only big enough to hold a few books and were difficult to remove whatever was inside.

Everything smelled so new. The shiny, waxed linoleum floors shone so that you could almost see your reflection. Walking up concrete steps to get from one floor of classrooms to another was a new experience. It seemed so strange having all grades together in one building. We had so much space to roam around and still be in the same building. Even the principal had his own office space.

There were separate boy and girl bathrooms. Not having to use the outdoor outhouse was pure luxury. But then, this new school even had showers! Taking a shower became mandatory after physical education classes. Many students still did not have running water or electricity in their homes, so this new experience was scary and unknown for them.

Taking a shower also meant we had to undress in front of other girls to get into the shower. Our modesty ruled big time, so lots of girls just turned on the water and pretended they had showered. They did not want to undress in public. Sometimes a woman teacher unexpectedly came in to supervise. Someone must have snitched on us. The teacher waited until everyone got in the shower.

Since the auditorium/cafeteria space was large enough for all the grades to gather together, Mr. Searles decided that all students would join every Friday afternoon for a sing-along. He seated himself at the piano on the stage as we learned to sing ballads and songs.

We sang "Old Black Joe," "Swanee River," "Clementine," as well as holiday and national anthems. He expected every student to sing along and pay attention.

Besides being in a brand new building, sixth grade was an exciting year because Mrs. Bisek, our teacher, explained that we would be doing a year-long study of our village, Naytahwaush. We sixth graders became researchers and reporters interviewing the elders and other important people in the town. Many of the elders came to our classroom to share their stories. We went in small groups with Mrs. Bisek to interview people that couldn't come to our classroom. Since this was the first time any class was involved in such a project, the local villagers showed great interest and enthusiasm.

Since they named our school after both Mr. Emerson and Ms. Northrup, we wanted to make sure that we spent time learning more about them and what they did for our village.

Mr. Harold Emerson was one of the elders who helped us obtain historical documents. He told us that his teacher could not pronounce his Ojibwe name (May-zhuc-e-be-nais), so the teacher decided to call him Harold Emerson, the name we all knew him as.

Mr. Emerson was a former game warden, wild rice director, and the first notary public in Naytahwaush. Currently, he was a member of the School Board, Draft Board, and the Indian Council. He wanted our history booklet to contain copies of actual historical documents. That is why our final booklet included many originals. It even had a copy of the original paper inviting the Otter Tail Band of Pillager Chippewa to share our White Earth Reservation land with equal rights on July 6, 1872. (See Appendix C.)

Miss Adele Northrup, a nurse who came to the reservation in 1936, was known simply as "the Nurse" to many. She was a friend to all, took a great interest in community affairs, and was very active in the Episcopal Church.

Completing our research, volunteers offered to type the document. Mrs. Bisek explained that our booklet needed drawings added to make it more visual for our readers. We students entered pictures to show the old store and post office, the current store, the old school buildings, and our new school. A committee chose the best drawings for the booklet.

Each student in our class became responsible for making cardboard covers with artistic designs on the front cover. Since cardboard was expensive, we recycled pieces from whatever sources we could find, such as cardboard signs used for advertisements. Churches saved cardboard for us, and we kids were like scavengers hunting down any place that might have suitable cardboard. Mrs. Bisek even had people from her town of Mahnomen save cardboard for the covers.

After cutting the cardboard pieces to the correct size, we covered them with brown paper. We printed the title: History of Naytahwaush on the cover and then drew pictures of Native scenes using crayons. (In the back of this book, I have included a copy of our booklet.) I still have my original copy that holds a place of honor among my library books.

Seventh grade gave us a man teacher, Mr. Miller, whose lackadaisical ways did not make learning challenging or fun. He certainly was not my favorite teacher.

In October of that year 1952, I became very sick. Mom couldn't figure out the cause of my illness, and even the school nurse was baffled.

After I was home in bed for several days, Flo came home from high school with some news. She told Mom that they had been discussing the epidemic of polio sweeping the country Symptoms were fever, aches, and one of the significant symptoms was the stiffness of the neck and back. Mom and Flo rushed into my bedroom.

"Vonnie," Mom asked, "Can you touch your chin to your chest?" Not being able to do that movement, and knowing I had a high fever and an aching body, Mom immediately called the doctor in Mahnomen. He said I needed to be taken to their hospital right away to get a sample of my spinal fluid. That would determine whether or not I had the poliovirus.

I can still picture that long needle the doctor took from the shelf. He told me to hug my knees and curl up in a ball so that the needle prick would not be so painful. Crying and scared, they placed me on the long table in the office. Shutting my eyes, awaiting the jab of the ruler-length needle, I whimpered. The excruciating pain and extracting the fluid seemed to last forever. The test results came back positive. I had polio.

In 1952, the worst epidemic year, three thousand people died from polio. (Poliomyelitis (Polio) was the term used by doctors to describe the condition in which the gray (polios) anterior matter of the spinal chord (myelos) was inflamed (-itis). It was an extremely infectious disease that could invade an infected person's brain and spinal cord, causing paralysis. Until someone discovered a cure, no one had the slightest idea where "polio" had come from or why it paralyzed so many children. The majority of people who had polio never even knew it. Most of the people diagnosed recovered with little or no disability. Many people who won their battle against polio had no after-effects. Those paralyzed were left with little to help them deal with their new lot in life.)

Since polio was so infectious, the doctor asked where they could quarantine me. The Benedictine nuns told the doctor that they had a small attic room for me in their hospital. Sr. Albertine, one of the kindest nuns I ever met, volunteered to be the nurse to bring me food and watch over me as needed. There were no televisions in that attic room, but I was too tired, listless, and in pain to want to do anything but lay there. There was no cure. The doctor prescribed lots of bed rest and good nutrition.

After a week, Sr. Albertine surprised me with a huge envelope. She said I could get mail even though I could have no visitors. My classmates had each written a letter to me—all except Sandy. As I read and re-read each one, I giggled as almost every person in my class told me that Sandy had to write twenty-five sentences using the spelling words if he did not write a letter to me. Some said he didn't want me to think he liked me, so he wasn't going to write. He didn't want the other kids teasing him because he was supposedly my boyfriend at the time.

Here are a few of the actual letters sent to me by my classmates when I was quarantined with polio:

Naytahwaush, Minn.

Oct. 21, 1952

Dear Yvonne,

I'm glad to hear that you enjoy the radio. It sure seems different here without you. It just doesn't seem like you have polio.

I knew you would like Sister Albertine. Do you get any shots? Do you get them once a day?

We have to close the hall for a week on account of polio and also the bus isn't going into the football game and there is no show this week and no PtA. I wish they would have closed school.

I'm sending Maxine's letter with mine. I picked out a book for you this morning. I hope you haven't read it.

Do you like visiting hours? When I was in the hospital I didn't know what to say to the people that came visited me. Did the Sister give you and magazines to read? Can you get out of bed yet?

I'm reading one of your Mother's books. I think the name of it is "Shoulder the Sky."

I had to sing in the choir again on Sunday at Rosary.

Noreen is not flirting with Sandy too much. Maybe she's going to let you have him since you're sick. Maxine is afraid Noreen may start flirting with Jimmy. That's all Jimmy and Maxine do is smile at each other.

Maxine is taking your place on the lunch committee in 4-H.

I hope you'll be able to come home soon. I went after Maxine this morning. The twins get cuter every day.

I suppose you really like the bedpans. I'm glad I didn't have to have them.

Yours truly,

Sharon LaVoy

Naytahwaush, Minn.

October 21, 1952

Dear Yvonne,

Mr. Searls told the class to each write you a letter. Sandy Turner is the only one who didn't write to you. He must be too busy with Noreen. Even Jim is writing to you, but Sandy has to write a story using his words in his spelling book.

Our class mural is coming along fine. This morning I drew a world map and traced over it with ink and it got just sloppy.

For lunch we had bean soup, cheese sandwiches, milk celery, and carrots.

Most all the girls in our room wear lipstick now. Sharon and I are the only ones who don't wear it.

I'll close now hoping you enjoy our class letters.

Love from a pal,

Maxine

P.S. Sandy is VERY lonesome.

90

Naytahwaush, Minn.
October 21, 1952

Dear Yvonne,

All the class is wrighting except Sandy. He is wrighting twenty five sentences. Sandy said he has nightmares every night after you got sick.

Boy, we sure miss you in school. We have some kind of math that sure is hard at first. Most of us got it so far though. That's all I can think to say.

Your friend,

Vernon B.

Naytahwaush, Minnesota

October 21. 1952

Dear Yvonne,

Sandy sure is feeling bad He sure hopes you get well quick. Your going to have a lot of letter writing to do. "huh"! You should have lots of fresh air and sunshine. Well your in a bad fix. I don't know what to write really.

Sincerely yours,

James Robert Landro

Naytahwaush, Minn.
Oct. 21, 1952

Dear Yvonne,

How are you feeling? I hope you get well soon. We started the class mural yesterday. We are drawing the pictures we are putting on the mural. We chose Maxine, Ernest, and Orville to do the drawing.

We made fifteen dollars and some odd cents at the pancake supper and bingo Friday night.

This isn't much to say when it comes to letter writing.

Yours sincerely,

John

Naytahwaush, Minn.

Oct. 21, 1952

Dear Yvonne,

I hope you are getting better. We all hope you will be back in school soon.

They are building a skating rink back of the new school. We hope you will be back to skate on it.

Yours truly,

Orville Turner

Naytahwaush, Minnesota

October 21, 1952

Dear Yvonne,

I still have a hard time in school. Arithmetic comes easier nowadays.

I went swimming in Pinehurst creek on Sunday. thought it would be warm was cold instead. Caught cold, stayed home on Monday. came to school on Tuesday.

Do you still have that penpal in England?

Your friend,

Myles Olson

I spent two weeks quarantined in the hospital. The only immediate effect of the disease was weakened muscles in my eyes. I had to get glasses immediately, due to poor vision. Every year I had to have a checkup to find out if there were any other after-effects. People with milder polio symptoms usually made a full recovery within one to two weeks. People whose symptoms were more severe could be weak or paralyzed for life, and some died. After recovery, a few people might develop "post-polio syndrome" as long as thirty to forty years after their initial illness. I was one of the lucky survivors who did not suffer paralysis.

Mr. Harold Searles was not only our principal but also our eighth-grade teacher. His high expectations for every student kept us striving to be the best students ever. His love of music and literature were some of the greatest gifts he bestowed on us kids. His expressive reading of Longfellow's *Evangeline* kept us mesmerized:

> This is the forest primeval. The murmuring pines and hemlocks
> Bearded with moss and in garments green, indistinct in the twilight.
> Stand like Druids of old, with voices sad and prophetic,
> Stand like harpers hoar, with beards that rest on their bosoms.
> Loud from its rocky caverns, the deep-voiced neighboring ocean
> speaks, and in accents disconsolate answers the wail of the forest...

He introduced us to Cajun music and the culture of the Acadians, a world so different from our *Song of Hiawatha*. We became acquainted with Washington Irving's *Legend of Sleepy Hollow* and *Rip Van Winkle* through the voice of this gifted, poetry-loving teacher.

Diagramming sentences in eighth grade was a daily routine. No student left Mr. Searles' class not knowing every part of speech and its placement in a sentence. When someone diagrams a sentence, they place words onto a diagram in a set pattern to better understand the sentence and the words within it. To diagram a sentence is to dissect how the words are strung together. Challenging sentences with subjunctive clauses and prepositional phrases kept us on our toes. We filled the classroom chalkboard with lines and descriptors, marking each word and phrase. I loved this daily challenge and knew I was good at it.

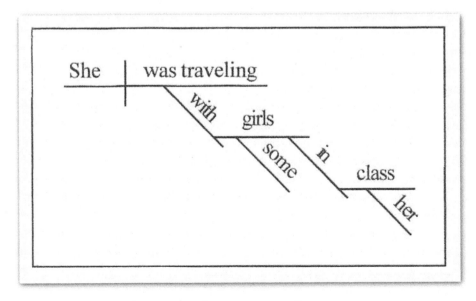

Example of a sentence diagram.

Sharon and I participating in a talent show.

Mr. Searles encouraged us to enter all kinds of contests. Maxine and I vied to participate in the Mahnomen County annual spelling bee. We both won the opportunity to attend. Maxine won! I was so disappointed, but my Mom assured me that we were both smart girls and that one does not always come out first in life.

One Friday afternoon during our weekly sing-along, I was sitting across from Jimmy Brown. Mr. Searles announced that our next song to sing was "Jimmy Cracked Corn." Jimmy Brown, who didn't like to sing, began pulling on his throat and vocal cords while rolling his eyes back into his head. He then made strange sounds and looked and sounded so funny that I laughed very loudly.

Mr. Searles stopped playing the piano in the middle of the song and said, "Yvonne, if you can't sing with us, go back to the classroom and think about music and why it is important to follow directions."

I turned beet red and couldn't believe that I was the one to get punished and not Jimmy. Embarrassed and ashamed, I rushed up the stairs to our classroom to wait for what would happen next.

When the class returned to our room from singing, I had my head down on my desk, sobbing uncontrollably. Our sing-along was always the last activity on Friday afternoons, so all my classmates came back to gather their belongings before dismissal.

Mr. Searles waited until they were gone and simply said how disappointed he was with my behavior and disrespect. It was something he did not expect from me, and he hoped I had learned my lesson. I apologized and was determined never to disappoint this great teacher ever again.

It was traditional that eighth-graders take a spring field trip with the big school bus to Duluth, Minnesota, for a two-night stay in an actual hotel. Most students had never experienced a hotel stay, so Mr. Searles tried to prepare us for this fantastic trip. He explained that we would eat in restaurants, visit the Duluth zoo and the iron ore range, and see where the vast ships came into the Lake Superior docks. It was to be the trip of a lifetime. Duluth was about two hundred miles from home, so it was a long bus ride.

Eighth grade trip. Maxine, me, and Sharon (left to right).

Elevators were a novelty that most of us had never experienced. We pushed the buttons to stop at every hotel floor along the way. It was a new game we repeatedly played while we crowded as many kids in the elevator as possible. The hotel management told our chaperones to limit the times we got on and off the elevator. Guests complained that the elevators were constantly occupied.

The late-night giggling and pillow fights, as well as trying to remember the rules for eating in a restaurant, were just part of the fun experiences of that trip. I can't remember who brought real cigarettes along, but I still have photos of us at the zoo trying to look cool with a cigarette hanging out of our mouths. I remember that most of them never were lit, but it was a daredevil thing to try without a chaperone seeing us.

Eighth grade trip, posing with the forbidden cigarettes.

Mr. Searles also believed we needed to learn proper etiquette in all aspects of our lives. Before we graduated from eighth grade, he announced that we would have a social dance. We needed to learn how to waltz, two-step, and even square dance for that event.

After teaching us how to dance in our spacious auditorium, he explained that we were to clean up and wear our best clothes for the occasion. On the night of the dance, the boys were to walk the girl to the school gym properly.

My date, Ernie, came to my house, knocked on our door, and Mom answered. His first words were, "Mrs. Rumreich, this isn't my idea, but Mr. Searles told us we had to do it. Can Vonnie come to the eighth-grade dance with me? I will have her home by 9:00 pm."

"Vonnie, your date is here," my mother called in a lilting voice. As I came to the door, embarrassed and blushing, Ernie held the door open for me, just like Mr. Searles had instructed.

Mom looked at Ernie very gravely and said, "Be sure you treat her well, and I'll be expecting her home at 9:00."

As we walked up the hill, my Dad's car suddenly appeared in front of us. Dad was always trying to be funny, so he slammed on the brakes right then and there. He jumped out of his car and demanded to know what this young man was doing with his daughter.

Mr. Searles had not prepared my date for an encounter such as this. After much stammering and stuttering and trying to explain that this was part of our school assignment, my Dad gruffly said, "She's my girl. You better be extra good to her."

The event was awkward, and the dancing was stiff and formal. We all were glad when it was over and that there was no time for a repeat as it was the end of our school year. It was also our last year of going to elementary school. Next year meant riding a bus every day to attend high school in Mahnomen.

Chapter Six

Village Community Buildings

The greatness of a community
is most accurately measured
by the compassionate actions of its members.
Coretta Scott King

Episcopal Church

G etting on our bike at my house, we can head to the Episcopal Church down the road towards the general store. The church is next to the home of Uncle John and Aunt Mary Jane.

In the 1890s, George Warmuth designed and built the church with local logs, and it was called Samuel Memorial Mission. Since there was no priest, Manny Penny, a Chippewa Indian, was the first layman stationed there.

In our day, the Episcopal Church, the Protestant Missionary Alliance, and the Catholic Church did things as a community with everyone being there for everyone else. Father Augustine, our priest, and Rev. Fritz Kramer, the Episcopalian priest, were good friends and socialized together.

It was the talk of the village when Rev. Kramer married Carol, a young Ojibwe girl from a nearby town on the reservation, who was many years younger than he.

My Uncle Howard ensured that his humor and storytelling became a part of their lives. Before the wedding, a truck pulled up to the rectory and unloaded a double-size bed. Uncle Howard noticed that from the store. When Rev. Kramer came into the store that afternoon, my Uncle grinned and coyly asked, "Hey, Rev. Kramer, are you expecting company?"

Uncle Howard teased Carol, the newlywed bride, every time she came into the store. One day when she bought some bacon, he told her always to have the bacon facing North in the pan when she cooked it as that was how Fritz liked it. Of course, Carol believed him. He always had a piece of advice for her since she was such a young bride who innocently thought he was telling the truth.

Village Hall

Located a few feet from the Episcopal Church was another village gathering place, our community hall. The hall was built in 1948 and became useful as a meeting place for the Boy and Girl Scouts, 4-H club, and the Community Council. It was used by all ages and for all social events. Before the new school was built, a hall section became the fourth-grade classroom.

The Friday night ten-cent movie in the hall was popular with everyone. Uncle Sid ran the movie projector. Most Friday nights, everyone waited in their seats patiently while he spliced the old film reels that kept breaking. Every movie started with an ongoing serial of cowboys and Indians starring Gene Autry, Roy Rogers, or the Lone Ranger and Tonto. The actual film started with the numbers 5-4-3-2-1 appearing on the screen. We kids loved shouting out each number as it appeared. Our Friday evening was complete if we had an extra dime to buy popcorn to eat during the movie. Since Sharon and I made and sold the popcorn, we always enjoyed some during the movie.

Uncle Sid arranged tables in the hall for us school kids to eat the government-provided school lunches every school day. Mary Bunker, our chief cook, knew each of us kids by name. She had the eyes of an eagle, and we were all scared of her. You ate her food and were not to complain.

The Friday scrambled commodity eggs looked like raw fish eggs. My stomach turned every time I looked at them, but I ate them unless one of the kids whispered that Mary wasn't looking. I would then make a mad dash to the slop pail. We all knew that getting caught throwing away your food was worse than trying to swallow the "fish eggs" in one gulp. Since the Catholic ruling restricted

Catholics from eating meat on Fridays, we never had meat served on that day.

Bingo nights at the community hall were popular for all ages and always drew a crowd. We kids learned how to play regular Bingo, four corners, and "X" bingo as soon as we knew our numbers. We had nickels from our allowance to pay for each game. A box of Corn Flakes, cans of Potted Meat, or cash served as some of the Bingo prizes offered. Uncle Sid arranged the furniture in the hall to match the occasion, whatever the event. He also always took care of all the cleaning after each event.

The Morgan boys, who played fiddles and guitars, provided the music for our community dances that included the waltz, two-step, polka, and even square dancing. Both kids and adults gathered together for the dances.

The broom dance was my least favorite because I did not want to get caught having to dance with some of the old guys. One person danced with a broom, and when that person dropped the broom, you had to quickly find a new partner or be stuck with the broom. I remember this one man who had lost an arm in the war and had a hook for his hand. I was scared stiff of him and ended up having to dance with him sometimes, and I didn't know what to do or how to hold that hook.

Pie and basket socials that always included dancing were also popular events at the hall. We, girls/women, decorated a box or basket for basket socials. Inside the box was a picnic lunch for two persons. We included sandwiches, potato salad, some veggies, and a dessert such as cake or cookies.

These boxes were auctioned off and sold to the highest bidder. The mystery of who would buy each basket was nerve-wracking. We girls tried to describe our basket to the boyfriend of the hour, but that didn't always work out. Many of the young guys often didn't have much money to bid.

One summer Sharon and I decided to bake a pineapple cream pie for the pie social that Friday.

"Hey, Sharon, I've never made a fruit pie like this," I said. "And Mom has always made the crusts."

"Oh, we can do it by ourselves," Sharon assured me. "After all, we've watched our Moms make pies all these years. How hard can it be?"

Sharon told me to make the crust, and she started to make the pineapple filling. We wanted these pies created without any help from our Moms.

After several attempts to roll out the pie dough and place it in the pie tins, I realized this was not easy. Part of the crust fell apart, and the pie tin looked like a patchwork quilt of stray crust pieces trying to stay connected.

"Vonnie, I'm not sure if I cooked this enough," warned Sharon. "It looks syrupy but is supposed to get thicker when it cools."

We giggled as she poured the runny pineapple mixture into the baked pie crusts.

"Now we have to make meringue, " I said. "How hard can that be to beat egg whites? I've seen Mom do it lots of times, but I'm not sure how thick they have to get."

The process of making pies was not as easy as we thought. We ended up giggling nonstop as we tried to make the top of the pastries look like the meringue our Moms made. Oh, well, the person bidding on our pies hopefully would be understanding and not upset if the pies weren't perfect.

The night of the pie social arrived. Sharon and I dressed up in our best dresses, took our pies out of the icebox, and hoped for the best. I hoped Kenny had lots of money to buy mine, but that didn't happen.

This older man bid lots of money because the meringue looked beautiful. When I cut the pie, it was all soupy and runny. I was so embarrassed, as was Sharon. We looked at each other, quickly excused ourselves, and ran home giggling. We were too embarrassed to stay for the dance!

We had talent shows in the hall at different times of the year. I can still remember one year when I decided to act out the poem:

Little Orphant Annie
by James Whitcomb Riley:

Little Orphant Annie's come to our house to stay, An' wash the cups and saucers up, an' brush the crumbs away, An' shoo the chickens off the porch, an' dust the hearth, an' sweep, An' make the fire, an' bake the bread, an' earn her board-an'-keep; An' all us other children, when the supper things is done, We set around the kitchen fire an' has the mostest fun A-list'nin' to the witch-tales 'at Annie tells about, An' the Gobble-uns 'at gits you Ef youDon't Watch-Out!

Once they was a little boy wouldn't say his prayers,— So when he went to bed at night, away upstairs, His Mammy heerd him holler, an' his Daddy heerd him bawl, An' when they turn't the kivvers down, he wasn't there at all! An' they seeked him in the rafter-room, an' cubby-hole, an' press, An' seeked him up the chimbly-flue, an' everywhere, I guess; But all they ever found was thist his pants an' roundabout— An' the Gobble-uns'll git you Ef youDon't WatchOut!

An' one time a little girl 'ud allus laugh an' grin, An' make fun of everyone, an' all her blood an' kin; An' onc't, when they was "company," an' ole folks was there, She mocked 'em an' shocked 'em, an' said she didn't care! An' thist as she kicked her heels, an' turned to run an' hide, They was two great big Black Things a-standin' by her side, An' they snatched her through the ceilin' 'fore she knowed what she's about! An' the Gobble-uns'll git you Ef youDon't WatchOut!

An' little Orphant Annie says when the blaze is blue, An' the lamp-wick sputters, an' the wind goes woo-oo! An' you hear the crickets quit, an' the moon is gray, An' the lightnin'-bugs in dew is all squenched away,— You better mind yer parents, an' yer teachers fond an' dear, An' cherish them 'at loves you, an' dry the orphant's tear, An' he'p the pore an' needy ones 'at clusters all about, Er the Gobble-uns'll git you Ef youDon't WatchOut!

Since I was forever reciting the poem day and night that summer, Mom must have had the entire poem memorized too. She helped me work out the right actions to accompany the words. My Little Orphant Annie costume was a black dress, white apron, and a white gathered cap on my head. I held a broom while performing the actions for the poem and completed the look of the little orphan by going barefoot. By the end of the talent show, that broom needed replacement!

I can still visualize performing the poem and almost jumping into the audience. I attempted to scare everyone with my loud goblin imitation voice: "An' the Gobble-uns'll git you Ef you Don't Watch Out!" It was such fun to see the audience react and cringe with fright, so each time I said that phrase, my voice got louder and more frightening. Then and there, I decided I liked being in front of audiences.

Community Clinic

The community clinic building had three rooms and was just a stone's throw east of the Community Hall. One large room was the clinic office and waiting room. The other two rooms of the building contained an apartment for the principal and his office. Because our playground was so near the clinic, we never worried about getting hurt. Ms. Northrup, the nurse, was just next to us, always ready to help us.

On Wednesdays, Clinic Day, the doctor from White Earth came to work with patients. Clinic visits did not cost any money because they were part of the Indian Government Services. Since doctors were scarce in those days, we shared a doctor with other towns on the reservation. Miss Northrup, our nurse, was practically like a doctor and took care of us the other days of the week. We traveled to White Earth hospital about fifteen miles away if we needed hospitalization.

Fire Station and Game Warden's home

If we pedal hard on our bikes, we can get to the top of the hill from the clinic. On the right side of the road is a big log cabin home where the Goodwins lived. George Goodwin was the fire ranger, so his home and surrounding buildings had special equipment for his work.

The buildings near Goodwin's home stored the fire truck and fire equipment. One of the buildings had space for the toboggans that belonged to the community recreation service. During the winter, we started at Goodwin's home on the top of the hill. Several kids jumped on the community toboggans, held onto the person's legs in front, and went crashing down the descent, hoping to reach the frozen lake below. When there were too many kids, we slid on big pieces of cardboard. The sledders tried to stay out of the way of the toboggans and other sleds. A big light pole near the buildings cast light on the hill and made it possible for us to go sliding in the nights after supper.

We kids discovered a lookout tower for the fire station deep in the woods. It was about a fifteen-minute bike ride away from our house. Our parents told us not to climb the tower because many wooden steps had rotted. That made it all the more tempting to bike there and dare each other to climb to the top. Luckily none of us fell in our attempts.

It was scary looking down as we climbed the tower. Once we finally made it to the top, it was like being on top of a mountain. We could see for miles. We pretended we were fire rangers searching the area for smoke signals that we never saw. If we had, I wonder what the consequences of climbing the tower would have been. Our search for adventure never waned, even though we had some scary moments when our feet slipped through the broken slats or when pieces of a step broke.

St. Anne's Catholic Church

We get on our bikes from Goodwin's house and ride on the trail that meanders through the woods. If we follow the tree-rooted paths, we can easily reach the white-steepled Catholic church of St. Anne's.

The Benedictine abbot from St. John's monastery in St. Cloud visited our reservation in 1869. He sent Fr. Aloysius as the first priest to make a call at Naytahwaush in 1916. He celebrated the first Mass in Grandpa LaVoy's home. The person responsible for getting a priest for the village was Aunt Clara Fairbanks, and the people built St. Anne's church in 1917.

Priests lived in neighboring towns until 1951 when Fr. Casimir built a rectory. Construction started in the summer of 1951, and in November of that same year, Bishop Schenk of the Crookston diocese came to bless it. The rectory was not popular with the parish members for either its cost or size. Father told the parishioners that he wanted to have the basement for catechism classes instead of using the church. He also thought there should be quarters for the pastor and a housekeeper, guests, and space for his office. Father Casimir didn't have much time to enjoy it. In November of that same year, Father Augustine arrived with his mother to enjoy the new quarters.

In those days, the priest never locked the church doors. We kids could enter at any time but knew we had to be quiet and respectful whenever we were within the silent realms of the empty church. Serenity and peacefulness overpowered me whenever I stopped in by myself. The central part of the church had rows of pews and in the middle between the benches was a thinly-grooved, black rubber runner going all the way down the aisle to the altar. Native wood planks on the walls surrounded the altar to create a feeling of nature, joining the sacredness of the liturgies performed in the sanctuary. A communion rail separated the altar space from the congregation. A statue of St. Anne with the Blessed Mother graced the area next to the sanctuary, while plaster icons showing the Way of the Cross adorned the side walls. The choir loft, located in the back of the church, had steep, curving wooden steps to the top.

Experiences at St. Anne's Church

Before the parishioners built the rectory, we Catholic kids had religion classes in the church. All elementary students were released from public school every Wednesday afternoon for an hour to attend catechism classes. I distinctly remember Father Francis, who taught using the conservative Baltimore catechism, which ruled the scene as our portal for learning about God. He had a short fuse for any misbehaving students who did not pay attention or know the answers to his questions.

The questions he drilled us on from the Blue and Green Baltimore catechisms remain forever imprinted in my mind:

"Who made you?"

"God made me."

"Who is God?"

"God is a Supreme Being who made all things."

Religion classes consisted of rote questions and memorized answers.

I can still visualize the page in the catechism that had a picture of two milk bottles. One had a few black spots that stood for venial sins, and the other was all black representing mortal sins. (See photo.)

#53. Question: How many kinds of actual sin are there?

Answer: *There are two kinds of actual sin—mortal and venial.*

#54. Question: What is a mortal sin?

Answer: *Mortal sin is a grievous offense against the law of God.*

57. Question: What is venial sin?

Answer: *Venial sin is a slight offense against the law of God in matters of less importance, or in matters of great importance, it is an an offense committed without sufficient reflection or full consent of the will.*

#59. Question: Which are the chief sources of sin?

Answer: *The chief sources of sin are seven: Pride, Covetousness, Lust, Anger, Gluttony, Envy, and Sloth; and they are commonly called capital sins.*

We certainly had no idea of the meaning behind the answers but needed to memorize them. Anyone not paying attention or goofing around spent that hour kneeling on the thinly-grooved, black rubber runner!

When the nuns came in the summer to teach catechism, they told us about saving souls on All Souls Day, November 2nd. They explained that each time a person entered the church, one must recite three Our Fathers, three Hail Mary's, and three Glory Be's to release a soul from Purgatory. A person had to go outside the church, come back in, and repeat this performance for each soul to get from Purgatory to heaven. We couldn't remember which nun had told us this, but we firmly believed it.

On All Soul's Day, Sharon and I decided to race and see who could save the most souls in the cold of the winter. We ran to St. Anne's church, opened the door, raced through the obligatory prayers, and then raced outside only to race back in to save another soul.

For many years we repeated this performance, convinced that we were the most fantastic Purgatory releasers of all times. Sharon and I repeated this process until we got tired but felt incredibly proud of ourselves. We counted to see who had saved the most souls and prided ourselves in each saving more than twenty. We could hardly wait until the next All Soul's Day to help all those other poor souls stuck in Purgatory that we hadn't been able to take care of that year.

The Story of How St. Anne Got a New Organist

Pianos and Pump Organs

On a warm July afternoon, Sharon and I were picking chokecherries in the woods behind my house during the summer of our sixth-grade year. As we gathered berries, Sharon leaned over and said, "Guess what? Mom got the idea that I should learn how to play the piano. I don't dare tell her, but I don't want to learn. She told me that I needed to get an education in music and learn how to play. Oh, Vonnie, I like to sing, but I sure don't want to learn how to play the piano!"

As Sharon shared her secret with me, my heart fell to my knees, and I almost spilled my pail of chokecherries. How come Sharon always got everything, and I didn't?

She continued, "Dad has to go and get the piano tomorrow because she already paid for it. She thinks she always knows best for everyone and everything in our house—even what my Dad should say and do!"

I had wanted a piano for two years and asked Mom repeatedly if we could buy one. The answer was always, "Vonnie, pianos cost money, and we don't have that kind of money."

Now, Aunt Ruby had gone and bought Sharon a piano, and she didn't even want one. How come life was so unfair? The unfairness of life became too real the next day when I hung the panties and bras on the inside lines behind the sheets. I heard a truck and saw the piano that should be in my house, not Sharon's.

"I have to run over to Sharon's place right now!" I yelled to my Mom as she put the last piece of clothing through the washer wringer. I didn't even wait for her response.

Uncle Howard and three other men lifted the shiny black piano from the truck bed. Aunt Ruby eagerly held the screen door open, ushering in Sharon's new musical career.

"Where is Sharon?" I asked my smugly-smiling Aunt Ruby.

"Oh, I'm sure she is anxiously awaiting her new piano in the living room. Watch out now, and don't get in the way!"

I watched with longing eyes as they carried the piano into the wrong house. As soon as the door closed behind the men, I re-opened it and quickly followed to watch what would happen next. I made sure I was not in the way.

According to Aunt Ruby, the east wall was just the right spot. Once the piano was in position, she pulled out the piano bench and told Sharon to sit down and see what fun it would be to play.

"I don't know how, Mother!"

"Of course, you do. Everybody knows how to play Chopsticks. This week, you will start taking weekly piano lessons from Ms. Elverum in the Gospel Missionary Church. Not only is she a preacher, but she can play the piano, too. She is going to get you started. Later, when you get more advanced, we will find a better teacher for you," promised Aunt Ruby.

"Since it's close by, you can walk to lessons," Aunt Ruby just kept talking and talking. "And even though we are Catholic, Ms. Elverum says that doesn't matter. She won't be trying to convert you, just teach you piano."

My fingers were itching to try out some sounds, but this was Sharon's piano, not mine. Aunt Ruby certainly wasn't waiting to hear from me, just Sharon. Sharon reluctantly sat down on the shiny black piano bench fighting back her tears. Her version of Chopsticks was definitely choppy.

"I think you can be our next St. Anne's organist if you practice hard enough!" Aunt Ruby continued.

I wasn't so sure. Not able to stand there and not try out the piano, I ran back home. "Mom, I have an idea. Why can't I take piano lessons like Sharon? I could ask Aunt Ruby to practice on their piano."

"Vonnie, we can't afford a piano or lessons. You will just have to think of something else to do with your time." Mom rolled her eyes, shook her head, and handed me the unfinished wash to hang on the line. "And we most definitely are not going to ask your Aunt Ruby to use their piano!"

Sharon spent a miserable summer forced to practice every day, and I spent a miserable summer wanting to have a piano. Every week Sharon reluctantly walked up the hill for her lessons. She told me that Ms. Elverum was not too pleased with her progress, and maybe her mother would let her stop lessons since she was still in the Schaum A book, despite all those piano lessons.

Sometimes when Sharon was practicing, I would stand and watch and wish I were Sharon. No matter how many times I asked my Mom and Dad, the answer was always the same, "No, Vonnie, we're sorry, but pianos and lessons take money, and we don't have the money."

I searched the ad sections in our weekly Mahnomen Pioneer newspaper all that summer. One week before school began, I found an ad showing a piano for sale for $75.00 in a neighboring town.

I immediately said, "Mom and Dad, look, there's a piano for sale. Can't we buy this one? It's cheap, right? I've saved my money from working in the store all summer and have $50. There's a phone number to call. Please, can we use the phone in the store and call? Could we see if the piano is still for sale and try to get it cheaper than $75? Please?"

The following week, Dad got several muscled men in the village to help him carry a gigantic, blond upright piano into our living room. Because our living room was so small, it could fit only by the

My sister, Mary Ann, and Cousin Roy by my
piano.

wall facing the post office. I heard my Dad mutter, "She'd better practice to learn how to play after all this!"

Getting a piano also meant needing money for weekly lessons, books, and a piano tuner every year. Ms. Elverum started me with Sharon's used Schaum A book, which saved us some money.

Sharon could not believe how excited I was to learn how to play and how I loved practicing on my old upright piano. We laughed to think of her small piano in their huge living room and my massive upright in our tiny living room. She hated to practice, and I couldn't wait to get better.

"My mother is going to be upset if you go faster and pass me up in the Schaum books," Sharon shared with me one day. "She told me that Betty Rodwell, our organist at St. Anne's, is graduating from high school next year. Of course, she hopes I will be far enough along to take her place. Vonnie, I don't want to be an organist, and I don't even want to play the piano!"

One day Ms. Elverum closed my piano book and announced that she would not teach me after finishing the Schaum C book. I was making significant progress, she told me, and in a few months would be beyond her ability to teach me.

"After all, I did tell your Aunt Ruby—when she insisted that I teach Sharon—that I would be willing to start lessons, but I am not a real piano teacher," she explained. "Now, Vonnie, you will soon have to find another teacher. I heard that the Catholic nuns in Mahnomen give lessons, BUT I warn you that I have heard stories about nuns and priests."

"What stories, Ms. Elverum? Nuns come every summer for two weeks to teach us catechism. They are strict but good, and I never heard any stories about them," I responded.

"They're not always good people. We Missionary Alliance preachers have heard horror stories about things they do behind people's backs." continued Ms. Elverum. "Sometimes priests, well, maybe I shouldn't tell you. Be warned that they might try to get you to become a nun and who knows what could happen to you then."

"But Ms. Elverum, Father Gus is such a good priest, and he's always there to help everyone. Why would you say such things?" I asked. "I'm going to ask Mom about what you are saying."

"No, No, this is just between the two of us, but don't say that I didn't warn you."

If I told Mom what Ms. Elverum said, I would have to quit lessons, and that would end my dreams of learning to play the piano —maybe someday becoming our next church organist.

I finished Schaum's C piano book two months later and told Mom I needed a new piano teacher. Father Gus happened to be getting his mail and heard me talking with Mom. "Well, Philomene, there is a nun in Mahnomen who teaches piano. I could see if she has any openings for Vonnie.

"Father, we don't have the money for expensive lessons. Mahnomen is twenty-five miles away. Her Dad is away doing road construction, and I'm here all alone trying to make ends meet," explained Mom. "Besides that, I only drive when I have to on these dirt roads."

Father Gus thought a bit and said he would ask the nuns to give me free lessons and teach me how to play hymns because the organist, Betty Rodwell, was leaving for college in the fall. There was currently no one to replace her.

Ever since I started piano lessons, I desired to become the next church organist. It was a fantasy that I had kept secret even from Sharon. Pushing away Ms. Elverum's warning of priests and nuns, I blurted out, "Really, Father, would you do that for me? Do you think I could get good enough to become the next organist? Oh, Mom, PLEASE, can I, can I?"

The following Tuesday after school, Father Gus drove to our house to drive me to Mahnomen for my first piano lesson from the nuns. Mom came out to his station wagon, hovering over me like a mother hen.

"Now listen to Father Gus. Are you listening carefully, Vonnie? Taking lessons from the nuns is such a special opportunity for you. Mind your manners and good luck. Thanks so much, Father!" she said as she backed away from the car. Her thoughts went back to the nuns giving her piano lessons at boarding school and how she hated piano. How ironic that her daughter was so excited to become the next church organist at St. Annes!

The half-hour drive to Mahnomen flew by as Father Gus shared how happy he was to have someone from our little Indian village who wanted to be the next organist. He told me how the nuns would help me learn the hymns and other piano pieces.

"Your teacher is Sister Florentine. She expects her students to practice hard and play well," explained Father Gus. "Since she is an expert piano teacher, you must always do as she says. I'm sure it will be different than taking lessons from Ms. Elverum."

I wondered what Father Gus knew about Ms. Elverum, and I did not want to ask. She had given me a start in piano, but she had scared me about being with the nuns. Maybe someday I might ask Father Gus about what she told me.

As we drove up to the convent, I wondered what my new piano teacher would look like or be like, other than strict. Father Gus rang the doorbell, and I took a nervous step back as it was the first time I had ever seen or heard a doorbell. In Naytahwaush, you just knocked on the door or walked into a home.

I heard a rustling of material from inside and quick, precise steps clicking on the floor. I looked up as the door opened. Sister Florentine's pale white face, wrapped in what looked like a white pleated bib, stood in the open doorway, looking stern and forbidding. So did those inquiring eyes behind her wireless rimmed glasses!

Father Gus introduced me to my new piano teacher. Sister glanced in my direction. With cold, perspiring hands, I reached my hand out. I tried to remember my manners as I nervously said, "Hello, Sister. I hope I will pass your inspection."

Sister told Father Gus to come back in an hour with a slight nod and a very tiny smirk. "I usually give half-hour lessons, but she will need extra time, and I need to teach her piano technique as well as how to play hymns on the organ."

With that, I began my Catholic training on the piano and organ. I wondered why or how Ms. Elverum could ever think nuns ever did anything wrong. Sr. Florentine seemed so holy and sinless in my eyes, even though she was strict and expected perfection. If I wanted to learn quickly, I knew I had to practice longer and harder than ever before.

I baptized my blond upright piano with holy hymns that were not always recognizable. I also confirmed it with sounds of the world and its passions, wrong notes and all. "Holy God, We Praise Thy Name" was mixed with "Seven Lonely Days Make One Lonely Week." Whenever I had a spare moment, my fingers found the keyboard.

Because we had only radio and no television, I had no great distractions. My mission was to show Mom, Dad, Father Gus, and Sister Florentine that they had not made a mistake letting me take piano lessons. Even though Sister Florentine told me my timing and sight-reading skills needed much improvement, I learned how to play the piano. Sister did admit that my will to learn was beyond her expectations.

Playing the piano was one thing, but learning to play a pump organ was another thing. Not only must I play the keys of a pump organ, but pump the pedals with my feet simultaneously. Coordination was not my strong suit, and my piano skills were minimal.

In the fall of my eighth-grade year, Betty Rodwell left for college. My musical career as a church organist began whether I was ready or not.

Since St. Anne's was now without an experienced organist, I needed to step up to the plate, and fast. The choir had been singing a capella without organ accompaniment, and they were ready for any organist.

Sister Florentine kept telling me that playing the piano was different from playing the organ. The jerky notes were supposed to become smooth on the organ—no staccatos on the hymns, just flowing melodies. If I forgot to keep pumping rhythmically, the sounds escaping from the organ were like someone gasping for breath with weird wheezing sounds.

Every day, I jumped on my bike and pedaled through the woods to our little church about five minutes from my house. I biked as fast as I could. Rooted tree branches on the path were a challenge, but I concentrated so I wouldn't have any tip-overs. The door to our little church was always open. After leaning my second-hand boys' bike near the door, I'd take the choir loft steps two at a time. I was ready to conquer the wheezy foot pedals and stubborn organ stops.

Sister had instructed me about the organ and its array of knobs called stops. I needed to pull some out and push others in to determine the sounds I needed to use for the different hymns. When the choir sang along with the organ, the sound needed to be loud. When I was to play for quiet parts of the Mass, I had to learn other stops to pull out or push in. At the same time, I had to keep my feet pumping the pedals up and down as my fingers tried to play the keys.

Often, when Father Gus saw my bike parked outside the church, he walked across the dirt road from his rectory to check on the progress of his new organist. He told me, "Vonnie, you are one dedicated young lady. I'm proud of the way you are working so hard." He said the choir members needed to be patient while I was learning the hymns. He also suggested that they sing louder and stronger while I struggled with new melodies."

I looked forward to Fr. Gus' encouraging words and thought he was the best priest any parish could have. Why had Ms. Elverum told me differently? I began to think that I might have an eighth-grade crush on this amazing man who was so kind and gentle. I knew I always looked forward to our weekly ride to Mahnomen, and no other girl had that privilege. My mind jolted back to reality.

Father Gus chuckled and continued, "Lizzie and the Graham boys have been with the choir a long time, and they will be your support system. Don't worry about making mistakes. We all do, and that's how we learn." He suggested that I ask Sister Florentine to teach me the "Immaculate Mary" hymn. Her feast day was coming up in a few days. He added that the choir could follow even if I only played the melody with one hand.

"Sure, Father, I will ask Sister at my next lesson," I replied.

Sister Florentine helped me learn the melody of four hymns. The easiest to play hymns were in the brown St. Basil Hymnal, so that hymnal and I became inseparable. Sister Florentine said it was all right to start easy, and I could advance to the blue St. Gregory Hymnal later. Since "Immaculate Mary" was in the St. Basil hymnal, she put that hymn in my small repertoire of hymns to practice.

Playing the hymns on the piano was a whole different story than playing them on the pump organ. Every day as I practiced on the organ, I sang the words of the melodies but decided it would be easier if someone else sang with me. Maybe Sharon and my sister Flo would be guinea pigs to help me prepare for Sunday's hymns.

Sharon said, "Sure. I'm so glad I don't have to be an organist, even though my mother still thinks I should be. Shoot, I'm still struggling with Schaum books with Ms. Elverum and not enjoying it one bit. Hopefully, Ms. Elverum will soon give up on me."

Flo said if Sharon would sing, she would too. Maxine, my second best friend, heard about our practices and said she would join the choir, as well as her sister Norma. With four willing singers and enough hymnals for everyone, I felt more like a real organist as we practiced together during the week.

Late in the week, Father Gus saw all our bikes parked in front of the church and walked over to see what was happening. He thought we needed a male voice to add to our all-girls choir and joined us for practice as I got ready for my Sunday debut as the new organist.

I sat on the round turntable organ bench the following Sunday, wet with sweat, trembling fingers, and shaky knees. When the bells rang to announce the start of Mass, I held up one trembling hand to direct my new choir and squeaked out the melody of "Holy God We Praise Thy Name" with my other hand on the keyboard.

I hoped that my God was a loving God who gave extraordinary strength to all beginners trying to praise His name. The Graham boys and Lizzie sang extra loud, covering up my mistakes. Their smiles of encouragement made me hopeful that one day I would be worthy of this honor of being their organist at St. Anne's Church.

At Communion time, I decided to try to play the notes of both the treble and bass clef for my new song, "Oh, Lord, I am Not Worthy." I nervously tried to keep the bellows full of air and keep both hands working together on the keyboard. Even though I felt I was not worthy of this task, the church needed an organist. Nothing could stop me from rising to this new, significant challenge.

It was a communion to remember—my first time putting both hands and feet together simultaneously. It sounded like a real hymn with the bass clef joining in. By the last stanza of the hymn, I was wringing wet. My perspiring fingers kept trying to slide off the keys as we sang the last words of the psalm: "Only say the word, and my soul shall be healed."

Lizzie, the oldest person in the choir, had certainly seen better times while singing. She gave me her tooth-missing smile and said, "It was OK, Vonnie. It can only get better!"

My new career was off to a shaky start. Hopefully, all the choir members would still be there next Sunday to drown out my mistakes and help me feel more worthy, as well as give me another chance to "Praise His Name..."

A Confessional Story in St. Anne's Church

Immaculate Mary

The old confessional was situated in the front of the church, left of the altar. The priest's section where he sat was in the sacristy behind a non-visible partition. Each penitent pulled aside the curtain, knelt on the bench, and whispered their sins to the priest. The partition made it impossible for the priest to see the person confessing. Because the confessional entry was in the front of the church, everyone could see who went to confession.

Father Gus decided it would be more private if the confessional were in the back of the church. He helped build a pine-knotted confession room to the left as one entered the church. For some reason, the door opened into the confessional rather than outward.

"Let's see if Father Gus can tell who we are when we come in the confessional," I suggested to Sharon one day. "I'll be Father, and you be the sinner."

116

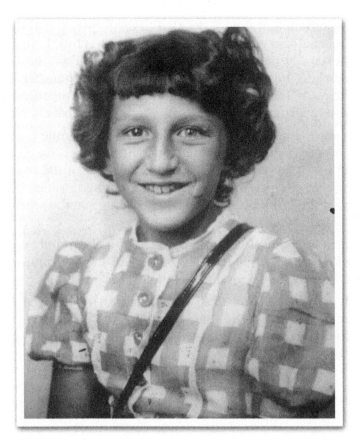

Dressed for Easter.

Checking to see that no one was in or near the church, I stepped into the confessional to sit in Father Gus' chair behind the partition. I clicked on the light switch, which showed the congregation that the priest was ready to hear confessions. Then I waited for my penitent to enter.

"CREEEEAK." (Door opens). "CREEEAK." (Door closes)

Glancing up after the second squeak, the back of Sharon's coat became quite visible to me. She tried to quickly move into the kneeling penitent position behind the partition separating priest and penitent.

"I told you!" I blurted out. "Father Gus can tell who's coming to confession. What are we going to do? I saw the back of your coat! Darn it! Why didn't they leave the old confessional in the front of the church? Father was in the sacristy, and we could slip in and out without him knowing who it was going to confession."

Father Gus knew I wore a red plaid coat, a tell-tale sign of identity when I confessed my sins. Since I made this discovery, I wished I weren't our church organist, CCD assistant, and daily mass server. (No boys came to daily Mass, so Sharon and I got to say the Latin responses and ring the bells at Consecration time.) How could I go to confession incognito with a red-checkered coat?

As I knelt in the choir loft the following Sunday morning, I examined my thirteen-year-old conscience before I went to confession. I had quarreled with my older sister—as usual—at least twenty times. The previous Saturday, I had invited kids to my house for a party when my folks were stranded in Mahnomen. (That was an actual transgression in our family rule book.) I had tasted my first real kiss with Vernon, who I had a crush on, and then I had lied about the party to my folks.

An inspirational, yet scheming, thought entered my mind as I thought about these sins. Why not wear someone else's coat when I went downstairs to confess my wrongdoings? What a brilliant incognito idea! If I did that, Father Gus wouldn't know his church organist was such a sinner, because I'd be wearing a different coat that he wouldn't recognize.

I glanced at the choir members' coats on the three wooden pews in the choir loft. There was a drab, brown coat; it was so unlike my red-checkered one. Our oldest choir member, Lizzie Roy, owned that coat, and it would be a perfect disguise.

"Hey, Lizzie," I whispered, "Can I use your coat a minute? Thanks!"

Before she had a chance to answer, I hopped quickly down the choir loft stairs. When I was on the bottom step, I discovered that no one was in the confession line. I breathed a sigh of relief. No one in the congregation had seen me in Lizzie's oversized coat to wonder why I was wearing hers.

Just before I entered the confessional, I had a horrible thought: "Oh, no, what about my voice? My sins didn't match the owner of the coat." Father Gus wouldn't recognize the coat, but the voice was something else. I had Lizzie's coat, but whose voice should I imitate with my teenage sins? What should I do? Oh, yes, if I had a horrible cold and cough, maybe Father Gus wouldn't recognize my voice.

"Bless me, Father, for I have sinned," I hoarsely whispered as if laryngitis had just set in. "My last confession was…"

I kept my voice low, coughed a little, mumbled and quickly rattled off my three sins as incognito as I could. Hey, it was working. Why had I been so worried?

"For these and all my sins (cough), I am very sorry."

"Is that all?" Father Gus inquired after a long pause.

"Yes, Father." (Cough, cough)

"For your penance, say three Our Father's, three, Hail Mary's, three Glory Be's," Father responded. "Go and sin no more."

Wow! That had worked out well, so much better than I thought it would. I quickly rose from the kneeler. In my jubilant smugness, I almost forgot to hoarsely say, "Thank You, Father." I charged for the door and couldn't wait to share my incognito success with Sharon.

As the edge of Lizzie's coat made its exit, a voice from behind the screen casually said, "By the way, Vonnie, please play Immaculate Mary for the closing hymn."

Biking with my sister, Mary Ann.

Christian Missionary Alliance Church

I f we hop on our bikes and head south from St. Anne's, we can see the Missionary Alliance Church at the end of the same block and on the same side of the road. It is across the street from the new school. The church had its beginning in 1926 when a daily vacation Bible School was conducted by two young ladies that summer. This small church has the fewest members of all the churches, but the two women preachers tried hard to increase their flock. After them, a young couple, the Pollacks, took over. They worked in our village for about five years.

During my life in the village, two single women, Miss Elverum and Miss Shields, ran the church and changed the name to Gospel Tabernacle Church. They lived in the back of the church. Neither women—one tall and the other short—played a significant role in our community. If it hadn't been for my piano lessons in the church, I would not have known what it looked like inside. It seemed so plain without statues and Stations of the Cross.

The Rest of the Village

I n 1888, our villagers changed their name from Twin Lakes to Naytahwaush in honor of Chief Naytahwaush. One of the main reasons for the change occurred because another town in southern Minnesota had the Twin Lakes name. Mail often ended up there instead, so to end this postal confusion, the village became known as Naytahwaush.

Since our village was not incorporated, it wasn't easy to know the official population. When I was growing up, about sixty families were living there.

Many homes in our village were tucked into the woods and covered with tar paper. The exterior covering was made by mixing paper or fiberglass mats with tar, which produced a waterproof material. Other homes were wood structures and varied in size and shape, depending on the size of the families. All roads in our village were dirt, with no streets. In dry weather, the dust plumes from the cars spread far and wide. During rainy seasons, deep ruts sometimes become impassable. In the winter, snowplows kept the roads open.

A tar paper house in the woods.

If we hop on our bikes, we can follow the dirt road from the village leading to North Twin Lake, and to BAB (Bare Ass Beach), a favorite hang-out during summer days. Floyd Keahna, our community recreation leader, gave us swimming lessons there. If you wanted to change into your swimsuit at BAB, there were protected, high-bush areas, but we put our swimsuits on at home most of the time and then wore our T-shirt and shorts over the suit. We biked down to the beach and always brought a salt shaker along for our swim lessons.

With lots of laughing and splashing kids surrounding him, Keahna attempted to demonstrate how to swim with our heads above the water. North Twin Lake had a weedy bottom where leeches (flattened worms) lived. He showed us how to keep our feet paddling to avoid the bottom of the lake where the leeches (called bloodsuckers) were living among the weeds and water plants.

When we inevitably failed to keep the leeches at bay, Keahna showed us how to sprinkle salt on the bloodsuckers attached to our feet after we got out of the water. (Salt causes all their cells to lose moisture, shrivel up like a raisin, and then die.) The salt made it easier to pick off the bloodsucker before it got too attached to our skin. It was just part of the routine when we went swimming at BAB. We counted it a lucky day if we could swim without having to use the salt shaker.

I learned that BAB was a favorite place for young couples to park and escape for privacy in my teenage years. Not that I speak from experience!

The dirt road that leads south from our village, toward South Twin Lakes, had a baseball field across the road from the Missionary Alliance Church. The men and older boys of the village belonged to a baseball team and had actual uniforms. They traveled to different reservation towns and had a tremendous winning reputation. We spent many Sunday afternoons going to the baseball diamond to watch them play.

The girls and women of the village had a softball team in the summertime, but we never rated uniforms. White T-shirts and jeans were our uniforms. We could practice on the baseball field when the men's team was not using it, which meant often practicing after supper until dark.

We, too, traveled to different towns to play against other all-girl teams on the reservation. We often all piled into the back of someone's pickup to ride to games. We enjoyed the wind blowing in our hair, the freedom of the outdoors surrounding us, and the bumpy roads that caused jostling and laughter.

I remember mothers on our team who were super players that put up with us neophytes as we learned how to play the different positions. Shortstop seemed to be my specialty, as I did not have the arm to throw the ball from the outfield. Our older members gave us a definite advantage for winning games.

If we bike further south on the dirt road, we pass more homes tucked in the woods along the lake. The next big building about a mile from the ball field is Kohler's tavern. One of the outdoor attractions at Kohler's was this big, black bear in a cage. I was so scared of it, but I found it fascinating to watch from a great distance. I was always afraid that it might escape from its cage, and I did not want to be anywhere near when that happened.

Kohler's tavern was a place for villagers to stop by for a few beers, learn the latest news, play the jukebox, and relax in the booths lined up around the walls. When my folks went down to the tavern, they often sat up at the bar while we kids played outside or got some money to play the jukebox.

Cats at Kohler's Tavern

When I was about eight, my Mom and Dad visited Kohler's tavern for a drink. I wandered outside to see the bear from a distance, but I got distracted by a mama cat. She was curled up nearby under an old pickup. I heard her distressed mewing and bent down to see what was wrong.

She was having babies! Mama Cat carefully licked each newborn as they kept coming. When the last tiger-striped kitten emerged, I just knew she was the one I wanted. She was so tiny, and the other baby kittens kept pushing her out of the way just because she was the smallest. Maybe I could save her. I rushed into the tavern to tell Mom and Dad about the baby kittens I had just seen being born.

"Mom, PLEASE, can I have one of the new kittens? PLEASE! You told me if I didn't fight with Flo about who was to dry or who was to wash the dishes, I could maybe get a pet someday."

Nina, the tavern owner, and Mom came outside to see the situation. Nina said they would watch the kittens and let me know when they would be ready to leave their mother. It would also depend if my folks allowed me to have a kitten. Mom had grown up on a small farm. She reminded me that animals were outside animals, no matter how attached one might get. If and when I got a pet, it must live outdoors.

When my parents drove to Kohler's several weeks later, I ran out to see how little Tiger was doing. She was so skinny and was mewing so pitifully. She kept trying to eat, but the other kittens pushed her away all the time. I just knew she needed me.

Nina came out of the tavern at that moment, and I rushed over to her. "Nina, look. The little tiger kitten is so tiny. The other kittens won't let her eat. Don't you think she needs a mother? Could I take her home with me?"

Nina looked at me, smiled, and said, "Yes, she is the runt of the litter and needs more food. You need to ask your folks." I raced back to my parents.

"Nina said I could have the tiger baby kitten because the Mama Cat isn't taking time to feed her. Honest, Mom, my little Tiger is shrinking and mews all the time. Please! I'll even do the dishes by myself every night if I can have a kitten. Pretty, please, Mom, Dad! I know I can be a good Mommy for Tiger."

Mom and Dad said they would think about it. A week later, after closing the Post Office, Mom found the car keys and said, "We have an errand to do. Get your shoes on and get in the car. We have a few places to go."

Since Dad was working out of state on a road construction job, Mom was the driver. I was always a bit anxious whenever I had to be in the car with Mom as the driver. I headed for the back seat to do my part. Mom always needed help when she backed up the car, and I was her back seat driver.

She caused the car to make the usual odd

Wondering if I would really get a kitty.

grinding-the-gears noises as she started the old grey 1935 Chevy. Reaching the pedals was an effort for my short, five-foot two-inch Mom, and she grabbed and gripped the steering wheel with white knuckles. After a few jerks and jumps, we managed to back up without hitting the clothesline pole, missing it by mere inches.

Mom continued, "Now sit back down and stop shivering. I can drive, and you don't have to be such a scaredy-cat." She then broke into laughter and said, "Speaking of cats, do you know where we are going?"

"Oh, Mom, you are the best," I cried. Going to get my kitten was what I had hoped. I triple crossed my fingers and prayed that nobody had taken Tiger.

"Mom! Where are we going to put her if she is still there? You said we couldn't have any pets in the house. Can we use a shoebox or something?"

The car jerked to a stop in from of Kohler's tavern. Before another jerk occurred, I was at the side of the shed searching for my Tiger, and she was still there!

Nina appeared with a special cage and a smile to light up the whole village. "Well, Vonnie, you must have been trying to be a good girl because the runt is now yours!"

I hugged Nina, hugged my Mom, and jumped up and down with whoops of joyous laughter. I heard myself yelling, "Oh, Tiger, you're mine, you're mine, all mine! I promise to be a good Mommy!"

Back in the car, I was mesmerized with my new pet. I didn't even notice the usual jerks and jolts as Mom tried to back up. The two miles back home took forever. My Tiger mewed and scratched on the wired cage, and Mom finally came to a not-so-gentle stop that sent both Tiger and myself bumping into the back of the front seat.

"Mom, what bowl can I use for Tiger's milk? Can I feed her right away? Where do you think is the safest place for Tiger to live? Can I go and get a box from Uncle Howard's store that has a cover so no wild animals can get her? Can we use one of our old, old towels for her to sleep on to keep warm? Oh, Mom, to think I have my very own kitty, and she's all mine!"

With a satisfied smile, my mother nodded her head and said, "Yes, to all of your endless questions. Run down the hill and ask your Uncle Howard for a box while I get the bowl and towel ready."

Before Mom could finish her sentence, I raced down the hill to tell Uncle Howard that I was now the proud Mommy of Tiger, and that I needed a big box to keep her safe.

"Uncle Howard, Uncle Howard, guess what? I have a new baby kitten, and she is all mine, and I get to keep her. Tiger needs a big box to keep her safe because Mom won't let me have any pets in the house. Do you have a box for me?"

Uncle Howard chuckled and stopped unpacking the Corn Flake boxes lined up row-by-row inside the larger shipping box. I just knew that the larger box would be perfect for Tiger's cage.

"Well, my girl, it's your lucky day. This box was just waiting for you. Hand me the Corn Flakes one-by-one, and then you can take the big box home. Be sure to have your new kitten face North, and all will be fine."

"What way is North, Uncle Howard? Why does the kitty have to face North?"

"Well, North is always the opposite of South. Face your kitty that way so the sun won't be in her eyes when she gets up in the morning. At night when the sun sets, it will not bother your kitten either. Always look to the North and put the bowl of milk there, so your kitten will know where North is. Now run along and tell your mother what I said."

I raced back up the hill to share Uncle Howard's wisdom with Mom. She came to greet me holding a chipped white bowl and old white towel. When I shared what Uncle Howard had said, Mom shook her head, smiled, and said, "Well, we'll have to see about that."

Only years later did I realize my uncle was always joking and telling people to do silly things. Of course, as a child, I truly believed everything he said.

After getting the cage set up, I tried feeding Tiger with the bottle I used to feed my doll. She started sucking right away, and Mom explained we would have to try to get her to lick the milk from the dish too.

As we watched her drink, Mom said, "Vonnie, you must always make sure that she is in her cage at noontime. Cars drive up to our house every day at mail time, and they might not see your kitty.

Several weeks went by, and I carefully put Tiger in her cage every noontime. Every day I made sure her bowl was facing North. One noon I was busy playing with Tiger when Sharon yelled that she needed my help right away. A baby bird had fallen out of its nest, and she needed me to hold it as she climbed the tree to put it back.

Just as she rescued the baby bird, I heard tire tracks and horns honking. I realized what time it was—mail time! Oh, no, I had left Tiger outside her cage. I ran as fast as I could and called Tiger's name. She was nowhere in sight.

I searched Tiger's box, called her name over and over and over, but no Tiger came. Where could she have gone? Sharon and I looked all over my yard and in the nearby woods but no Tiger. I ran into the house.

In between sobs, I told my Mom I could not find Tiger. Mom, Sharon, and I went out of the post office door to search the road in front of our home. We found Tiger stretched motionless on the driveway. One of the car tires had run her over. Mom sent Sharon and me back into the house to look for an empty shoebox in her bedroom. While we were gone, she wrapped the limp body with the old towel from the cage.

Tiger's nine lives ended in one fell swoop of a car tire. All I had left were memories of our few weeks together. Mom tried to soothe me with the words that, "accidents happen," and that, "Tiger was so tiny, the car hadn't even seen her."

We found a particular spot in the yard where Tiger liked to chase butterflies, and we dug a hole to bury her. I created a song to give her a proper burial service:

> Tiger, Tiger, burning bright,
>
> You were a special sight,
>
> my Northern light.
>
> Good night, good night,
>
> Tiger is burning bright.

Mom explained again that it was not easy to have a pet because of the post office traffic. Maybe it would be best not to have another pet. My tears, mourning, and sadness went on and on, and Mom softened.

Over the following years, I tried nine different times to raise a kitten. One time, it was a dog that killed my cat. Several deaths were a repeat of Tiger's demise. Each kitten's death involved a shoebox burial with a fitting ceremony. After the ninth shoebox burial, Mom finally said, "NO MORE!" Dad decided to get a hunting dog instead.

Pinehurst Resort

Continuing down the road from Kohler's tavern, we arrive at Pinehurst Resort situated between North and South Twin Lakes. South Twin Lake was shallow, had a sandy shore, and had no bloodsuckers! As kids, we always were happy when Mom and Dad decided to drive down to the lodge to enjoy a few beers and talk with the locals; that meant we could go swimming in South Twin.

As kids, we loved to go to Pinehurst to swim and have our parents give us money to buy ice cream or candy treats. We fed the jukebox in the middle of the lodge with extra nickels to play our favorite tunes. It was great fun dancing on the circular floor surrounding the jukebox.

As young teenagers, we often walked or hitched a ride to south Twin and then enjoyed swimming, going to the lodge, and dancing. Of course, it was primarily girls dancing together, with the jitterbug being the favorite dance.

Pinehurst Resort drew tourists from all over the state because of the great fishing on both lakes. If the North Twin were turbulent with high waves, South Twin would be calm and vice versa. It is a Fisherman's Paradise known for its Northern Pike, bass, walleye, bullhead, and sunfish, with summer and winter fishing on both lakes.

Pinehurst Lodge: Our favorite hangout for dancing.

Built by Naytahwaush natives in 1918 as an octagon roundhouse, the building was the site for powwows and movies over the years—events that brought in funds to pay for its operation.

In 1924, Ernie Miller, a local man, purchased the lodge and made improvements. Later, Uncle Howard purchased Pinehurst Resort. During my senior year of high school, Uncle Howard had my cousin Dick and his wife, Babe, run the resort. Dick and Babe bought it in 1969 and added a new bar and dining room.

In 2000, Dick's son Greg and his wife, Julie, purchased it and expanded it to sixteen updated cabins. On its hundredth anniversary in 2018, they added an outdoor patio.

When Greg and Julie retire, the resort will stay in the LaVoy family as their son Andy will become the next owner.

Chapter Seven

Other Village Activities

Children need the freedom and time to play.
Play is not a luxury.
Play is a necessity.
Kay Redfield Jamison

A s a child, it seemed like I lived two different lives because of the dramatic swing in temperature due to our local climate: Summer Yvonne and Winter Yvonne, with spring and fall sprinkled between them.

I had an old hand-me-down boy's bike that I learned to ride on. Flo decided she would teach me and told me to get on the bike one day. She gave my bike a shove and sent me off careening down the hill. Banged up knees and lots of tears were part of learning to ride a bike. We didn't care what kind of bike we had; we were thrilled that we no longer had to walk around the village but could bike anywhere we wanted. Freedom on wheels!

Berry picking—whether it was strawberries, raspberries, or blueberries—was a fun family outing on Sundays during the summer. Some Sundays, all three families (Uncle Sid's, Uncle Howard's, and our family) joined together for a day of berry picking and a picnic. The parents packed all of us kids in the back of the pickup and set off for the woods. The left-over adults squeezed into another car and followed the pickup. (There were no regulations about seat belts in those days.)

Everyone knew how important it was to pick as many berries as possible for the treats of pies, jellies, syrups, and sauces during the winter months. We ate some berries while we worked but knew we had to do our share of contributing to the family larder. Our berry picking attire consisted of long-sleeved shirts, long pants, neckerchiefs, and a wide variety of old hats to protect us from the sun. Everyone had a belt around their waist to let the berry pail hang so we could use both hands to pick berries to fill our buckets. Each time we picked berries, our parents warned us to be aware of bears, and those warnings kept us from straying too far from our parents.

As soon as we returned home, Mom placed newspapers on our Formica dining room tabletop. It was time to clean the berries, and she handed each of us a fork and a plastic container. We used the fork to carefully separate the berries from the twigs and leaves that managed to get into our pails. Strict directions to gently roll the berries into the plastic container and leave the debris on the newspaper were the first lessons to be learned.

After hours of cleaning berries, Mom decided how many became pies or sauce and jellies. We wasted nothing, and visions of homemade bread dripping with jelly kept us honest and ready to help in the picking, as well as the cleaning.

Summertime was also a time for climbing trees, playing hopscotch, marbles, and jacks. We played multiple games with jackknives. One such game was that we would take our jackknife, open one of the tips and try to flip the point of the knife from the tips of different fingers to hit targets marked on the grass. I don't remember ever getting hurt from those knife games.

There were always the games of "Ante-ante-I-over" when half of the kids would be on one side of the house and the other half on the other side. We took turns trying to throw the ball over the roof and have the other side try to catch it. "Captain, May I?" and "Red light, Green Light" were also games we played outside. The school playground across the road offered climbing poles and monkey bars.

We never seemed to tire of jumping rope, either by ourselves or with others, and we learned more jump rope rhymes every year. Two favorites were:

Ice cream soda, a cherry on the top,

who's your boyfriend/girlfriend? I forgot

A,B,C,D,E,F,G,H...

(And so on until the person gets tripped up on the rope and has to say the name of someone they know that begins with the letter.)

Teddy Bear, Teddy Bear, turn around,
Teddy Bear, Teddy Bear, touch the ground,
Teddy Bear, Teddy Bear, show your shoe,
Teddy Bear, Teddy Bear that will do!

Teddy Bear, Teddy Bear, go upstairs,
Teddy Bear, Teddy Bear, say your prayers,
Teddy Bear, Teddy Bear, turn out the lights,
Teddy Bear, Teddy Bear, say good-night!

Another fun, but frustrating, pastime was building stilts with left-over lumber pieces. Our folks found leather that they cut into strips to nail on the footrests for our shoes to fit into. The leather connected the horizontal part of the wood with the long vertical piece. We spent more time falling and repairing the broken footholds than we did walking on the stilts.

Fall was always beautiful in our village, with the trees changing to vibrant red, orange, and yellow colors among the oak and birches. There was always an abundance of acorns falling from the oak trees. One fall, Sharon, Johnny, and I heard the grown-ups saying that local farmers wanted to buy acorns to feed their pigs. That's all we needed to hear as we were always looking for ways to make some money. We got gunny sacks to hold the acorns, but first took small pails searching for oak trees in the village. We were sure that the pigs ate the acorn husks and the acorns.

Each day we would go on our acorn hunt. We decided to keep the bushel bags of acorns in Sharon's playhouse so that the squirrels and chipmunks wouldn't eat them. Imagine our disappointment to discover that the bags were filled with moldy acorns when we finally tried to sell them, shattering our dreams of filling our piggy banks.

Halloween was a time to collect candy stashes that we gleefully hoarded for the winter months, imitating the squirrels with their acorns. Going trick-or-treating meant walking around the village, knocking on doors, and holding our big paper sacks, hoping for a windfall of treats.

One Halloween—when I was just about to become a teenager—sticks out in my memory. A group of us almost-teens went to the house of our former fourth-grade teacher, Mrs. Bisson. She and her husband happened not to be home, so one of the kids said, "No treats, so let's do the trick."

We all agreed it would be such FUN to tip over their outhouse as our trick, and no one would ever know it was us! The outhouse was extremely sturdy, so we had difficulty trying to tip it over. After several efforts, we accomplished our mission. Leaving the scene, we ran as fast as we could.

The following day just happened to be a Sunday. We not-so-innocent tricksters of the night before all went to Mass and exchanged knowing glances when Mrs. Bisson and her family walked into the church. As our group huddled together, talking outside the church after Mass, we heard Mr. Bisson's announcement. "Whoever tipped our outhouse over last night will be doubly punished if it's not put back in its upright position by tonight! I know who you are, so don't play games with me!" Mrs. Bisson stood next to him and nodded in agreement.

Our group looked at each other with fear in our eyes. Who ratted on us? We started to laugh as he strode toward us. One of the boys in our group shouted out for all to hear, "Hey, that was a horrible thing, and we sure wouldn't want someone to do that to our outhouse. Come on, let's help Mr. Bisson right now. Maybe he'll even give us a treat for being so helpful."

With that, we all marched over to Bisson's house. He even helped us push his outhouse onto a standing position, but somehow he didn't offer us any treats. Did he know we were the culprits? That was the last time I ever was involved in tipping toilets as a trick on Halloween.

Winters in northern Minnesota stretched on forever, and sometimes snow arrived as early as the end of October. In winter, North Twin lake was our skating rink. Most of us had hand-me-down skates that didn't fit correctly, but at least we had skates! Some years the lake froze with a smooth surface and little snow, and those years were skating paradises. But more often, it seemed like we spent more time shoveling snow off the surface to create a place to skate than we spent actually skating.

The community built a cement stone sitting area near the lake where we could safely build a fire and warm ourselves when the cold got too much for us when sliding or skating.

Sledding with me in the front.
Linda and Rita in the back.

Spring usually arrived by May. When it was just around the corner and snow began to melt a bit, we kids scraped away small piles of snow. Then we made circles in the wet dirt to start playing marbles again. Every kid had a bag to hold their marble collection, including steelies and crockies (those giant marbles used for particular games). Each player placed one or two marbles in the center of the ring to play. Taking turns, each player knelt outside the ring and flicked their shooter marble with their thumb, trying to hit as many marbles out of the ring. If they knocked any marbles out of the ring, they kept them. Each night in the spring, Sharon and I met either at her front porch or mine with our bag of marbles, counted them, and showed off our prize winnings or tearfully mourned the loss of some favorites.

No matter the season, reading was an all-time favorite of mine. As I look back on my childhood, I realize that Mom was always an avid reader. (She kept this hobby and prolific desire for print until the day she died.) Since Dad was absent much of the time, Mom chose to snuggle up with a book every evening, even though the only light source was the kerosene lamp by her side. Mom was partially blind in one eye, but that did not stop her passion for reading.

She joined the *Reader's Digest* book club since we did not have a public library. Mom also had several magazine subscriptions as well as the weekly *Grit* newspaper. *The Grit* carried the subtitle "America's Greatest Family Newspaper." In the early 1930s, it targeted small towns and rural families with fourteen pages plus a fiction supplement. It had sections for news, women, family, comics, and stories.

Somehow Mom found out that she could order books from the Twin Cities metropolitan library. They sent lists of books, and she then ordered books for herself and me. They arrived in the mail and had a deadline for returning them. It was a free service. Mom decided which books I would most likely enjoy, so my life expanded by vicariously living the life of my book characters. I learned how to LOVE books, respect them, and talk about them with Mom. Reading became an intense bond between Mom and myself.

At other times, Mom examined the books on her bookshelf and told me she thought I was mature enough to read a particular book. How grown-up I felt! I was also given books as gifts.

I curated my collection of the *Bobbsey Twins*, a fictional series of two sets of fraternal twins—the older pair named Bert and Nan, the younger Freddie and Flossie. The other collection was *The Five Little Peppers and How They Grew*, which shared how the Peppers lived, learned, and played in their little brown house. They were poor, and Mamsie constantly worked to keep the wolf from the door, but their lives were unexpectedly happy. In later years I added the *Nancy Drew* mystery books to my collection.

Mom did not allow one type of reading in our home: the romance magazines, *True Love* or *True Confessions*. She felt these were trash, which made me curious to find out what they were. It just so happened that I discovered where I could find these magazines: My babysitting job at my fourth-grade teacher's home. Even though the Bisson's may have suspected that I was one of the trick-or-treaters who helped tip over their outhouse, she still hired me to babysit their three unruly kids.

On Friday nights, I walked over after supper to begin my night's work for the paltry sum of $1.00. After Mr. and Mrs. Bisson left for the evening, I played games with the kids and then put them to bed. One night the oldest one objected and threatened me with a butcher knife. I grabbed the knife, pulled him by the hair on his head, and fearfully pushed him into the bedroom. With a trembling voice, I threatened to tell his parents if he ever tried that again. Something inside my head said that this was not worth the dollar I earned. But since there were few babysitting jobs, and I liked the extra money, I never told my parents or Bissons about the incident.

I always washed the supper dishes and other dishes that had piled up in Bisson's the sink for several days. It seemed that Mrs. Bisson always made Spanish rice the night I babysat. The residue stuck on the plates and pans was challenging to clean. The house was always messy, so I straightened things, swept the floor, and sometimes ironed clothes. Babysitting was like being a housekeeper, too.

The Bissons loved to go dancing and drinking, so I knew they would not be back until midnight or after. After doing all the chores, I rewarded myself by reading the latest copies of *True Confessions* I found in the living room. Babysitting at Bisson's gave me a chance to guiltily be enraptured by such romantic tales forbidden in my home.

When I heard Bisson's car come up the driveway, I quickly put the magazines back where I had found them. I didn't want Mrs. Bisson to tell my mother that she had caught me reading them. If Mom discovered that, I would have my own true confession to reveal.

Chapter Eight

My Freshman Year: 1954-55

Your life is your adventure.
And the adventure ahead of you is
a journey to fulfill
your own purpose and potential.
Anonymous

High School Decisions

I n the summer of 1954, the Benedictine nuns arrived in our parish to teach two weeks of catechism classes, an annual event that we Catholic kids always enjoyed. The nuns were like black and white spiritual goddesses, arriving from an unknown world and dressed in ancient garbs. With only their faces and hands visible, they were mysterious in the sense that they didn't seem human. Layers of Cloth covered everything on their body.

We kids watched the nuns from a distance trying to figure out what made them so different from other people. Did they go to the bathroom? How did they eat with those pleats surrounding their faces? What kind of clothes did they wear when they went to bed? Of course, we were too scared to ask them. Maybe someday I would get the courage to ask: How does one get chosen to be a nun? When did that happen? Why did they become nuns?

That summer of 1954, the nun who taught us was Sr. Kathleen. When she introduced herself to us upper-grade kids that first morning of class, I immediately was struck by her freckled face and sparkling eyes. I knew she was a younger nun because she didn't have a wrinkled face like the other nun.

Sister Kathleen smiled even if we got the answer wrong. Her quiet, husky voice of encouragement made us study more than usual. Our challenge was to memorize answers to rote questions such as the following about angels from the green Baltimore Catechism:

What are Angels?

Angels are pure spirits, without bodies, having intelligence and free will.

What are good angels; what are bad angels?

The good angels are those who remained faithful to God and entered into the eternal happiness of Heaven. The bad angels are those who turned against God and were cast into Hell. These are the fallen angels or devils.

What is a guardian angel?

A guardian angel is a good angel who has been assigned to each one of us by God to watch over, lead, guide and protect each of us in all we do.

To correlate with the questions, Sister asked us to memorize a special prayer to our guardian angel:

Angel of God, my guardian dear,

To whom God's love commits me here.

Ever this day (night) be at my side,

To light, to guard, to rule, to guide. Amen.

I began wondering about my guardian angel. Were angels boys or girls? How much should I be asking them to help me? Were they like magic? In the catechism pictures, they had wings, just like they had God pictured like an older man with a white beard seated on a cloud. Was God a man?

Maybe I could ask Sister Kathleen.

Each of us got a copy of the Baltimore catechism to study, and we took it home each evening to memorize the formulaic answers to that day's lesson. Sr. Kathleen was patient even when we struggled to answer questions or recite difficult prayers by heart. Just as we had hoped, Sr. Kathleen had a supply of holy cards, scapulars, rosaries, and even plastic-framed pictures of Jesus, Mary, or the saints. She rewarded us for learning prayers and memorizing the cat-

Sr. Kathleen

echism answers. Some of us had a contest to see who could get the most prizes during the two weeks.

She won our hearts that second day of catechism when she asked to join us playing softball during our recess. No nun had ever done that. How could she play with that outfit she was wearing? Sister rolled up her sleeves, grabbed that long black piece of material hanging in the front of her, and looped it around her belt. Someone handed her the bat. She stood at home plate, with the bat poised, ready to strike the ball coming toward her.

Much to our amazement, she hit the ball with a whack and started running for first base. I never knew nuns could run so fast with those long black skirts. Sr. Kathleen sure knew how to hit that ball hard. We all clapped as she cleared third base, almost a home run. I was mesmerized. She seemed so human, even if she were a nun. Every person wanted her to be on their team during our recess times from that day on. Sister was the star player every time she came to bat, and her team always won. I wondered what made her decide to become a nun and how she learned to become such a great softball player.

We kids also looked forward to summer catechism because we could bring bag lunches even if we lived close. It was like having a fun picnic every day with our friends, rather than going home to eat. My brown paper bag lunches always had my favorite potted meat sandwiches. Every day, besides allowing me to buy my favorite pop, Mom let me buy Twinkies or other sweet treats from Uncle Howard's store. Two weeks of being spoiled with bought treats! What could be better than that?

During our catechism weeks, I played the organ every morning for Mass while the nuns directed the students as they sang the chosen hymns. I often stayed after class to practice the next day's hymns or help the nuns if they needed anything.

On Monday of the second week of summer school, when I stayed after class to help, Sr. Kathleen asked me about my high school plans. She wanted to know where I would attend high school, and I told her I would be going to the public school in Mahnomen, a town about twenty miles away.

"You are such a good student, and I have been watching how dedicated you are to play the organ and direct the choir here," she began to say. "I think you have a vocation and would make a great nun. Have you ever thought about becoming a nun?"

What? Me a nun? The thought had never crossed my mind. How could it be that I might have a vocation? Like my piano teacher Sr. Florentine, nuns were those holy creatures who seemed perfect and not exactly from this earth.

Looking at her and realizing that she was serious, I laughed nervously and said, "No." With disbelief, I went on to say, "Oh, Sister, I like boys too much, and I just started being the church organist."

I explained that Father Gus paid for my organ lessons, and I owed him so much for his generosity. He helped me become the organist, even though I had so much to learn. My church needed me, and there was no one to replace me.

"Well, I want you to think seriously about this. I think you have what it takes to be a nun." Sister went on to say that they had a high school boarding school for girls at their Motherhouse in Crookston. As an aspirant, I could attend their school and learn what it takes to be a nun. "Go home and think about it. We can talk tomorrow afternoon after class," she said.

Wow, I couldn't believe my ears. Sr. Kathleen thought I had a vocation. Wait until I tell Mom about this!

I jumped on my bike and rushed home through the wooded trails to our house. As soon as I opened the screen door, I yelled for Mom. "Guess what, Mom? You won't believe this, but Sr. Kathleen just told me that I have a vocation to be a nun. She wants me to think about it and talk with her tomorrow after class."

Mom stared at me. "Vonnie, you are just turning fourteen this summer, and that is much too young to decide what you want to be for your life's vocation," she said as she shook her head in disbelief. "Now put aside the thought, and let's get the laundry from the clothesline."

As we unhooked each clothespin from the hanging pieces of laundry, Mom continued, "Honestly, why would that nun put such thoughts into your head? If you do have a religious vocation, it will still be there when you are eighteen."

I knew Mom always seemed to know best, but maybe not this time? As we worked to get all the clothes down from the lines, Mom became silent and seemed deep in thought. I, too, was trying to figure out what this new idea of becoming a nun meant. Why me? What made Sister single me out as one capable of becoming a nun? I didn't even know how one became a nun.

Mom said it was time for her to get supper ready, so I should fold the clothes. We would talk more at supper. She didn't have Dad at home to discuss this latest wrinkle in their daughter's life. He was away in Montana doing road construction, like he did every summer. My older sister, Flo, spent the summer after her sophomore year working at an all-girls summer camp in northern Minnesota. That left Mom home alone with my little four-year-old sister, Mary Ann, and me.

During supper, Mom just pecked at her food. She wanted me to repeat precisely what Sr. Kathleen had said and how I had answered her. I told Mom it was a shock when Sister shared that I had a vocation, and I hadn't known how to answer. I told her I had never thought of being a nun, but now I was curious. "Mom, would it be all right to find out more about their school and why Sister chose me?"

"This is not something you decide overnight, Vonnie," Mom answered. "Having a religious vocation is a serious decision that needs lots of prayers and thought. The only nun in our family is a distant cousin, and I don't know her very well." Mom then told me to tell Sr. Kathleen that I was way too young for such a decision.

I lay in bed that night, wondering what it would be like to be a nun. I was so curious, now that Sister had asked me about being one. Sr. Kathleen sure was a fun nun, though the other nun seemed severe. I was glad that she wasn't the teacher of us older kids. I wondered what Sister would say when I told her Mom's response.

I waited until after class that afternoon and ran up to tell Sister what Mom had said. "Oh, no! You are not too young to think of being a nun. Tell your mom that many girls come to the convent when they are your age," Sr. Kathleen responded immediately. "Girls either come to our boarding school as aspirants (girls aspiring to be nuns) or as boarders who come just to get a great education. All girls live at the academy during the school year."

She went on to tell me that I would be one of the aspirants for the four years of high school. I would learn how to become a nun and get an excellent education during that time.

Sister continued to share more information. If I went to school at their Motherhouse, I could take piano and organ lessons from her. She also told me that there were no boys at the school, so girls could concentrate on their studies without being distracted. I knew Mom was all about getting a good education, so I could hardly wait to tell her about that part.

Finding Mom finishing up her work in the Post Office, I rushed in and said, "Mom, guess what? Sister is sure I have a vocation and told me about the special girls' boarding school. It's called Mount St. Benedict at their Motherhouse in Crookston."

Mom interrupted me to say that Crookston was over seventy miles away and that I knew nothing about going to a boarding school.

"But Mom, it would be a brand new experience. I could go there this fall to be an aspirant—those are girls who learn all about being a nun while they go to high school classes!" I continued, "I know how important getting a good education is to you, and this sounds like it would be the best. There would be no boys to distract me from my studies."

I looked at Mom's face and knew she disagreed. She explained that we could not afford a private boarding school. I was to take the idea of being a nun, tuck it into the back of my head, and make that decision when I was much older.

I went to catechism class early the next day to share what Mom had told me about our conversation. "Sister, Mom says we don't have money for me to go away to your school, and I need to wait until I graduate from high school before deciding on my vocation."

Sister smiled and said, "You can tell your Mom that we have scholarships for girls who can't afford to pay tuition, and I am certain we can give you one of those. I need to discuss this with your parents and explain what a wonderful opportunity this would be for you. Yvonne, you would be the first girl from this village to attend our boarding school and learn about becoming a nun."

Wow, I had never thought about that. I liked being first in lots of things, and this was a new chance to do that! I ran home and almost knocked Mom over as I rushed into the kitchen. "Mom, guess what? Sister Kathleen says we don't have to have the money because they have scholarships for girls like me who can't afford it. Oh, Mom, PLEASE?"

"Vonnie," Mom replied, "you are too young to leave home, and our church needs you here, not prancing away to some boarding school learning how to become a nun!" Mom went on, "I am sure that Father Gus will not approve of this either, when he finds out about the nonsense that Sr. Kathleen is filling your head with."

I then told Mom that Sister wanted to talk with her and Father Gus that evening to explain more about the school and my vocation. I said I would take care of Mary Ann and wash the dishes after supper. How I wished I could be part of the conversation, but I knew adults needed their own time and space for serious discussions.

Mom walked up to the rectory. I tried to concentrate on the dishes and taking care of Mary Ann. If I acted mature and responsible, it would prove I was ready to leave home. The idea of going away to a boarding school almost had a fairy tale ring to it, and now that the idea of becoming a nun had started to sprout in my head, I decided it must be true. God must be talking to me through the voice of Sr. Kathleen.

When Mom came in the door later that evening, I could tell by how she walked into the living room and sank into the recliner that she was not very happy. I had read a book to Mary Ann and put her to bed, so I was eager to hear what had happened at their meeting.

Mom told me that Fr. Gus was not happy with the idea of the nuns robbing him of his organist, that I was too young to decide, and that putting this becoming-a-nun idea into my head should not have happened. Mom agreed with him, and Mom shook her head and told me that this nonsense about becoming a nun had to stop.

On the last day of catechism classes, I hugged Sr. Kathleen and told her I would try to change Mom and Fr. Gus' minds. She promised to write and send more information about the school, entrance forms, and supply lists. Now all I had to do was wait and pray that this new vocation would work!

The next day after the nuns left, Father Gus came over to the choir loft when I was practicing for Sunday's Mass. "Vonnie, this is not the time to decide about your life's vocation," he began. "First, you are too young, and I am upset with Sister Kathleen for putting this idea in your head. You have your high school years to complete, and we need you as our organist. How can you even consider going along with her idea?"

"Oh, Father, I'm sorry. And I am thankful for all you've done for me, but maybe God wants me there," I tearfully responded. "I promise to pray about it and ask my Guardian Angel to help too." Why was this so complicated? Why did she even tell me I had a vocation to be a nun? Was God talking to me through her, or not?

I tried to tell Fr. Gus that Sister said she would ask permission for me to come home more frequently than the other aspirants to play the organ for the choir, and she promised to show me how to teach the choir new liturgical songs sung for feast days, but my words did not convince him.

After the two weeks of attending catechism classes, Sharon and I began our summer job working in Uncle Howard's store. We felt like seasoned store clerks. After all, this was our third summer. We spent hours talking about my wanting to go to the Mount for school. Sharon was not excited and said, "Vonnie, we have never been apart since we were babies. How can you all of a sudden decide to go away?"

I assured her that I would be home several times during the school year if I went.

"It's not the same!" she argued. "Who will sit next to me on the bus ride every day into Mahnomen? You won't be here to share my real secrets and worries. What makes you think you need to become a nun? We're having too much fun together with our friends. I don't want you to go!"

The weeks left in June were filled with work at the store, swimming, and biking. Sharon and I took long walks around the village, laughing and giggling as we shared our elementary school fun memories.

"If you go to the Mount, we won't have the fun of sharing high school memories!" Sharon yelled out. "Come on, Vonnie, don't be so stubborn. Listen to all of us and change your mind. It's not too late. You never even knew what a nun was until that nun put the silly idea into your head. I think you're selfish."

Why was this so hard, and why didn't people think this was the right thing? How would I know if I didn't go and try?

Dad came home for the Fourth of July weekend and told me it was a great honor to have a nun in the family, but he sided with Mom in her thinking. No matter how many times the rest of that summer that Fr. Gus, Mom, or Sharon tried to talk to me and dissuade me from this notion of becoming an aspirant, I didn't listen. I was sure Sr. Kathleen recognized a vocation when she saw one. The idea of being the first one to try such a venture kept entering my mind. Why not try it out and see?

One day in July, a big envelope arrived in the mail for me. It contained a shiny brochure showing photos of the Motherhouse and high school buildings, an application form, and a scholarship request. It also had a letter from Sr. Kathleen assuring me that this was an excellent once-in-a-lifetime opportunity. As I read her letter, I kept asking myself how this could be happening to me?

I gazed in wonderment at the brochure picturing a beautiful brick building surrounded by

My first view of Mount St. Benedict Monastery and Academy

trees. It looked like a fairytale castle on top of a huge hill. How romantic! I showed it to everyone and got more excited every time I told people that this was where I wanted to go to high school.

Finally, a few weeks after receiving the information—and tired of my pleas, tears, and begging—Mom reluctantly helped me apply for the scholarship and signed the consent form. She grew weary of my daily questions and excitement about the possibility of going away for school. Despite Fr. Gus's counseling and reiterating that I needed to remain at home, I kept assuring him that I could come home frequently and be a much better organist if I went away.

I kept telling myself that if I received a scholarship, it was genuinely another sign that I should become an aspirant. In August, I received my scholarship and acceptance letter, along with a list of the supplies necessary for the coming school year. Students needed to wear school uniforms that consisted of blue-pleated skirts and white long-sleeved blouses, furnished as part of my scholarship fund.

For Sunday mass, I needed to wear a modest long-sleeved dark-colored dress. I found a plain gray dress in the Sears catalog with a white Peter Pan collar. It was not anything I'd ever wear at home. It was kind of ugly, but at least we found one my size. The rules stated that students were to wear nylon stockings, not anklets. So that was another expense. I had never worn nylons, so I was excited about being old enough to wear them. I also had to get name tags to sew on all my clothes for the general laundry. The letter stated that students could wear regular clothing after school and on weekends. Wearing my jeans would make me feel more like being at home.

Even though I had a scholarship, I had not thought about all the extra money that Mom and Dad needed to spend on personal supplies and a Sunday uniform. This additional financial burden was a big commitment for them. My parents let me know that there would be no turning back now if I chose to attend Mount St. Benedict Academy. No matter what happened, I was to complete my freshman year there. They had tried to stop me, but since I insisted on becoming an aspirant, it was now my responsibility to go for the entire school year. Father Gus had also failed in his many attempts to persuade me to go to the public high school.

September came all too soon. I had spent hours sewing my black and white "Yvonne Rumreich" labels on all the clothing that would need to be laundered by the nuns. The school requested that I send my measurements to order the correct size for the uniform. I wondered what it would be like to see every student wearing the same thing every day. It was exciting to think I wouldn't have to choose what to wear each day. But I wondered if I would I get tired of the monotony of wearing the same outfits.

The day after Labor Day was my day of departure. Butterflies danced up, down, and all around in my stomach. I cried as I hugged Sharon to say my goodbye, before heading into the unknowns of boarding school. Was I ready for my new venture of learning how to become a nun?

Reality set in like a heavy chain around my heart. I realized that I was leaving everything I had known and loved behind me. What was it going to be like at this school? How could I live weeks—maybe even months at times—without seeing my parents and sisters? And then there was Sharon. Since we were born, we had never been apart, and how could I live without her daily friendship and love?

"Time to go, Vonnie," my Mom said as she gently touched my shoulder. Dad put my new suitcase in the trunk of the car, saying nothing.

"I'll write every week and let you know everything about going to Mahnomen High School," promised Sharon. "You have to write back and tell me all about your school at the nunnery."

I looked into her tearful eyes and promised, and then gave her one last hug before I got into the back seat of our car. Trying to be brave, I waved my goodbyes until I could no longer see Sharon or my two sisters waving back.

The plan was for them to stay home while Mom and Dad tried to make one last attempt on the drive to Crookston to persuade me to change my mind. Despite all his failed attempts, Fr. Gus thought my parents might be able to do that at the last minute. Even though the nuns assured him that I could come home frequently during the school year, he wondered how often that would be. It was not fair of them to deprive his parish of the only organist they had.

It was a long seventy-mile trip, and I tried to pretend that I was more excited than afraid of what lay ahead of me. Mom and Dad sat silently in the front for a long time, and Mom kept looking back to see how I was doing. I looked out the window and saw the highway sign with Crookston on it. We were almost there!

Mount St. Benedict

Dad drove up to a vast, brown brick building perched on a big hill and overlooking the city below. The stone sign in front said: Mount St. Benedict Monastery and Academy. I saw other buildings surrounding this massive structure, and lots of trees in the background. At least the trees would be a comforting familiarity. What on earth made me think I was ready for this strange and unknown territory? Biting my lip, I forced a smile and pretended I was happy to be there.

Mom and Dad turned to me and said, "Well, here is your new school and home for a year. Let's hope it is all you hoped for." My parents helped me get my suitcase out of the trunk and walked me to the front door to ring the doorbell. How strange to hear a ding-dong sound repeat itself over and over before the door opened. There in the doorway stood a nun who took one look at us and my suitcase. She asked if I was a boarder or aspirant.

I quickly blurted out that Sr. Kathleen had told me I had a vocation to be an aspirant. With that information, the nun said to come in and wait for the aspirant mistress. Looking around at the semi-dark hallway and feeling the quietness surrounding us, I wondered if this was the usual atmosphere.

Suddenly, the quiet swishing of her habit announced the nun who introduced herself as Sr. Victorine. I looked at her. She was a short, plump woman with glasses and a somewhat lovely smile.

"Do you know Sr. Kathleen?" I quickly blurted out. "She's the nun who told me I have a vocation."

It was then that her smile broadened. She assured me that she knew Sr. Kathleen very well, since they both taught music here at the academy. "I will make sure she knows you have arrived. First, I'll show you the place you'll be staying with all of the other aspirants, in the dormitory under the chapel." We followed her.

She ushered us down the stairs to the dormitory. I stared at the grey, barren concrete walls that matched the exact color of the floor. Ten beds stood stately lined up on each side of the room, each with a small dresser beside it. Sister Victorine showed me my allotted bed, dresser, and closet space.

Each bed—surrounded by four, connected poles—had white sheets tied to the poles in the middle with a plain cotton sash. She demonstrated how to untie them and pull the sheets around the bed to create privacy for sleeping. Sister Victorine then informed me that every morning, before I went upstairs for daily Mass, I needed to pull the curtains back, tie them with the sash, and make my bed neatly.

Small windows with drab white curtains lined one side of the basement dormitory to bring in some outdoor light. More beds and two doors led into the hallway on the opposite side. At the two ends of the room were tall, skinny built-in closets; one was assigned to each person to hold their belongings.

My mind wandered back to our cozy, tiny home, and to the bedroom that Flo and I shared. It had colored walls with bookshelves and colorful curtains on the windows to make our room come alive. This dorm was gloomy with a cold, lifeless feeling. Why had I told Sister Kathleen that I would come here?

I bit my lower lip, trying to appear to be brave. Glancing over, I could tell Mom and Dad were not impressed with the dormitory either. Sister led us to the recreation room that she told us the aspirants shared with the postulants. What on earth were postulants? Sister explained that postulants were young women taking the next step in becoming a nun, after being an aspirant. She further explained that many girls become postulants after Christmas in their senior year of high school.

When we entered the recreation room, I stopped in amazement as Sr. Victorine introduced us to a postulant called Miss Janice. What an ugly, black-looking outfit! She wore a black pleated uniform covered with a cape. On her head hung a black net veil that covered her forehead and hung down over her shoulders. I looked down and saw that her dress was way below her knees. Black stockings covered her legs, and she wore black, old-woman shoes. I was so busy looking at this odd uniform that I almost forgot my manners to say hello.

I must have been the first aspirant to arrive. Sister Victorine explained that she needed to greet the other aspirants and that Miss Janice would complete our school tour. Sister said farewell to my parents, and indicated she was happy to have their daughter join them as an aspirant.

My parents then asked Miss Janice what she had done before entering the convent. She shared with my folks that she had gone to college first and then decided to become a nun. Mom and Dad looked at me with an "I told you so" look, and I knew what our following conversation would be.

When we left the recreation room, I heard voices and giggles from the dormitory. I peeked my head in and waved at several girls putting down their suitcases by their beds. Miss Janice told me that I must hurry to tour the rest of the school before my parents had to leave. She said I would have a chance to meet all the aspirants in the recreation room before supper.

Miss Janice led us up the stairs to show us the chapel right above our dormitory. There was a hushed silence as we peered into the chapel, where a few nuns knelt in prayer. With a whispered voice, the postulant explained that aspirants were responsible for cleaning the chapel every day. We would be attending daily Mass and have Gregorian chant classes there, too.

As we walked along the quiet, tiled hallway from the chapel to the main school building, I became overcome by the peaceful silence. Some nuns met us on their way to the chapel and merely nodded their heads as they swished by quietly. Wow, I had never experienced such a quiet atmosphere in my life. Was this going to continue as part of my new life?

I learned that all the students would have a supervised study period in a large study hall every morning before classes started and every evening after supper; academics were the emphasis at our school. After showing us several classrooms and a small library, our guide told us that the aspirants would only be with the boarders for classes and study halls. (Boarders were the girls who came only for the excellent education and had no desire to become a nun).

The boarders had double bedrooms on the second floor above the classrooms. The school's third floor was where the nuns lived, and it was off-limits for everyone except the nuns. On the basement level was the huge recreation room for the boarders. When Miss Janice took us into the big dining hall, she explained it was for all students, but the aspirants ate separately. Next to the dining room was the nun's refectory. Beyond that were the dishwashing room, kitchen, cannery, and bakery. Feeling overwhelmed and scared but still excited about this new adventure, we left Miss Janice at the front door after thanking her for the tour.

It was time to bid farewell to Mom and Dad. I tried to put on a brave front and act as if this was not frightening to be left alone. Instead, I cried and clung to my folks.

They assured me that I needed to give this my best and reminded me that they were only a letter away. "After all, Mom runs the post office," my Dad said jokingly. He was trying so hard to make me laugh. Mom made sure I had plenty of stamps, envelopes, and stationery. She instructed me to write home at least once a week since phone calls were too expensive.

More hugs and kisses as I walked with them to the car. After watching their car disappear in the distance, I turned around to face my new way of life—the life of an aspirant, one who wanted to live the life of a nun. Did I really want to?

Feeling lost and empty, I found my way back to the dormitory, where my new suitcase sat starkly upright next to my cot. I looked around and saw no one else but heard talk from the recreation room. I quickly rushed across the hall to see who was there. It was my first introduction to the other freshman: Donna, Ruth, Corrine, Anne, and Marguerite, who looked just as out of place as I did.

We giggled nervously and started introducing ourselves. Donna and Ruth were from Callaway, only about twenty minutes from Naytahwaush! I learned that Anne and Corrine were from Shooks. I shared that my family and I picked blueberries every summer not far from where they lived.

Marguerite was from Fort Totten, ND, where she lived on a Sioux reservation. I couldn't believe how much we had in common. Marguerite and I were two Indian girls from different tribes and reservations, coming here for school as aspirants. What was her story? I wondered who had told her that she also had a vocation.

I just knew that it would be fun with my new friends as we kept interrupting each other with questions. "Why did you decide to be an aspirant? Do you think it will be hard? Have you ever been away from your family for a long time?"

Before we could answer each other's questions, Sr. Victorine appeared in the doorway. She asked us to sit down while she explained the rules and regulations of being an aspirant.

"Welcome, to the convent, girls," she started. "As an aspirant, it will be an exciting but different life. Of course, academics are key, but you will also start to learn how to be a part of convent life. Each day you will attend Mass, chant practice, spiritual reading, and have a household chore."

She explained that the boarders had different rules and regulations—and they enjoyed more freedoms—since they were not preparing to become nuns. They could go home for weekend visits, and aspirants went home only for Thanksgiving, Christmas, and Easter. However, our parents could come on certain weekends to visit us.

The town of Crookston was just down the hill. We were allowed to go there once a month, but we could not take the shortcut through the park. Indeed, we were not allowed to talk to strangers or boys. We had to remember that we were here to learn about convent life.

Every night after supper, we would have recreation time with the postulants, not the boarders. We could play board games during recreation, have discussions, play music on the phonograph, and weather permitting, we could go outside. After evening recreation, we must retire to the dormitory where there was no talking after the lights were out. If our parents sent food during the year, we needed to share it with everyone in the rec room, not in the dormitory.

We had to wear a white blouse, blue pleated skirt, and nylons each day. The uniforms were for the school day, but we could change into our regular clothes after school. The postulants had placed our uniforms on our beds while Sister talked to us. Then Sister handed each of us a square piece of white net and a bobby pin. It was our chapel veil to be worn every morning for Mass.

Since we had no gymnasium, she explained that we exercised outside with all the students in the school. In the fall and spring, we could play softball or group games. In the winter we could skate and play games in the snow. We could always walk around the grounds but had to stay within its boundaries. Miss Janet was going to be the new director of our physical education program, so there probably would be new activities.

Finally, Sr. Victorine said it would be good for the new girls to get a short tour of the grounds. She called in one of the postulants and asked her to take us. It felt so good to be out in the open air. A few of us skipped and talked as we followed Miss Eileen down a dirt road toward some farm buildings. We learned that the nuns owned a dairy farm on their property and raised some beef cattle for food.

"Do the nuns do all the farm work?" I asked.

"No, we have a refugee family from Hungary that lives in the farmhouse. The husband and wife and their older children do all the farm work. We are lucky to have them as they are such hard workers," she responded.

Along the road were huge vegetable and flower gardens. We stopped to watch in awe as a nun appeared in the vegetable garden, driving a tractor. She had an old straw hat on top of her head with a drawstring under her chin. We all giggled. Nuns driving tractors? Miss Eileen laughed and said that we had now seen the famous head gardener nun called Sr. Benigna. We would soon learn many stories about her and her love of the earth.

Further along the road, we spied some wooden beehive boxes. We all giggled again when Miss Eileen pointed out one of the nuns dressed all in white. She had a massive netting over her head and looked like a figure from outer space. We peppered the postulant with all kinds of questions. "Did the nuns ever get stung? Would we have to help her? What about helping on the farm? Did aspirants do that too?"

Miss Eileen laughed and said, "Only when you don't obey the rules!"

Back up the hill was the candle house, where nuns made candles from the beeswax. She said another day we could visit the nuns making honey and candles. Behind the candle house was a brick two-story building that looked forbidding, with big smoking pipe stacks. The laundry building had a big press and irons upstairs to press our uniforms. That building, too, Miss Eileen explained, would wait for another day to explore.

Next door was the conservatory. Since we were all expected to learn to play some instrument, Miss Eileen took the time to show us the inside of that two-storied building. There seemed no end to all the rooms with pianos and musical racks. We could walk over for our weekly piano lessons and our daily practice. I wondered if Sr. Kathleen might be there.

As we peered into one of the rooms, there she was! I ran over and almost knocked her over as I hugged her tightly. Hers was the first familiar face I had seen in this new, strange environment. She laughed and put her arms around me to welcome me. All the other girls stood with their mouths open, wondering how I knew her. Oh, it was the best gift yet. I could hardly wait to have my first piano lesson with her.

Sr. Kathleen welcomed all the other girls and told them she had taught me catechism in Naytahwaush that summer. She hoped many of them would be her new pupils, if they took piano. Miss Eileen said we had to get back for supper, so I reluctantly left Sister, but now I knew where I would see her every week for my piano lessons.

Miss Eileen pointed out the last building on our way back to the main building, the priest's house where Fr. Roger, the chaplain, lived. She explained that he was a Benedictine priest from St. John's Abbey in Collegeville, Minnesota, near St. Cloud. Father was an older priest who said Mass every day for the nuns and students, and he also taught all the religion classes for the students.

We walked to the dining room to experience our first meal. Miss Eileen led us to the aspirant's table and said we could sit at any open space with a plate and silverware. She explained that students took turns being waitresses to serve each table family style. We could eat as much as we wanted, but we must eat all the food on our plate.

Our group chose to sit next to each other. After a day of travel and touring our new surroundings, we were all so hungry. The mashed potatoes, meatloaf, and green beans tasted so good, and the chocolate cake with chocolate frosting was delicious. We could choose milk or water, and I decided on water, just like at home.

After supper, it was time to go to the recreation room. Sr. Victorine told us that everyone should go directly to the dormitory, unpack, and settle into our new spaces. The lights-out time was 9:00. We must pull the sheets around our beds and begin evening silence at that time. The morning alarm bell at 6:30 was for all to awaken, dress, make our beds, brush our teeth, and be ready to line up for chapel at 7:00. Well, I thought, I won't have to take time to choose what to wear every morning. That was one good thing about uniforms.

While we unpacked, I learned the names of the sophomore, junior, and senior aspirants. There were twelve of us living in the dorm. Bonnie, the girl on my left, was a sophomore and a cousin of Corrine. She walked over to my bed and told me to ask her any questions at any time. She knew how difficult the first few weeks might be. I liked her immediately, especially her smile and soft laughter.

After unpacking, we newbies gathered by Bonnie's bed and peppered her with questions. The tap bell rang to signal lights out, and we jumped back to our bed and drew the sheets around our beds. With some whispered "good nights," we settled down for our first night. What would tomorrow bring?

The first tap bell woke me up with a start. Too early, I thought. I rushed to the bathroom with my washcloth and toothbrush and hoped to be the first in line. The communal bathroom had three sinks, three enclosed toilets, and two showers for all of us. I needed to be fast. As I bumped into Bonnie coming into the bathroom, we giggled. I needed to ask her the best procedures for the morning routine.

Right after putting on my garter belt, I gingerly opened the package of nylons. Hoping not to cause a run in the fragile nylons, I carefully placed my toes inside the first foot, making sure the black seam was straight on the back of my leg. After doing the same with my other foot, I attached the nylons' tops to my garter belt hooks. Mission accomplished. I added my panties, bra and slip, and then my blouse. As I quickly buttoned my white blouse, it felt stiff and uncomfortable. My blue pleated skirt fit my waist just right. That meant I better not gain weight, or else I'd be in trouble trying to button it. Oops, I forgot to comb my hair. After quickly making my bed, I rushed to pull back the sheet curtains to tie them with the cloth sash.

The tap bell rang again. Just as I ran to get in line in the hall, Bonnie called out, "Yvonne, you forgot your chapel veil."

As we lined up to walk to the chapel, I thought of the picture book *Madeline*, except we weren't in France:

In an old house in Paris

That was covered in vines

Lived twelve little girls

In two straight lines.

Maybe I was the new Madeline in Minnesota?

Sr. Victorine led us into the chapel and pointed to the two pews for aspirants. After Mass, we filed out to walk to the refectory for our first breakfast: hot oatmeal, homemade bread, orange slices, homemade jelly, butter, and honey. We could talk during the meals. All the new aspirants excitedly asked the other aspirants about school routines, and they told us that we first had to go to chant class before going to study hall every morning.

After chant class, we learned that first-year students had to sit in front of the study hall at an assigned desk. When the bell rang, Sr. Austin, the principal, walked onto the raised stage and clapped her hands for silence.

"Welcome, students, to the new school year of 1954. I hope you had a good and restful summer, and are ready for concentrated study. I expect the new students to learn the rules and obey them. A handbook on each desk gives the list of class schedules for each grade and the classroom number. Upper-grade students are assigned the name of a new student to help. We expect quiet in the hallways between classes. There is time for recreation after school. Take time now to read the handbook and take your notebooks to write down your daily schedule. When the bell rings, please walk orderly to your first class. Good luck on your first day back."

I quickly looked to see my class schedule: Religion, Algebra, English, Civics, Music, and General Science. Religion was three days a week, music twice a week, but all the other classes were daily sessions. I needed to see when my piano and organ lessons began with Sr. Kathleen. I couldn't wait to be with her again, since she was such a fun nun.

Classes went on until noon. When the bell rang for lunch, I was starved. Students, assigned as servers, delivered bowls of food to each table for each meal. After each meal, we scraped food scraps into a bucket, then stacked our plates on a long table. There was a dishwashing room with a dishwasher and dryer for the nuns' and students' dishes. I learned that students who needed monetary assistance were assigned jobs to help pay for their tuition. Some were servers, some dishwashers, some house cleaners.

By the end of that first day, I had learned the names of my teachers: Sr. Aquina for algebra, Sr. Basil for English, Sr. Josepha for Civics, and Sr. Cyprian for general science. Would I ever learn those odd names? If they were all saint names, there were lots of odd-named saints! Some nuns had male names, and I would never want that. Sr. Kathleen was a girl's name; it had such a nice ring to it, compared to the other nuns' names.

After classes, we walked down to the refectory to get a snack. On the serving table were pans of giant-sized peanut butter cookies and pitchers of cold milk. Mmmmm. Even before I met her, I liked Sr. Christina, the baker nun. What a treat after an exhausting first day of classes.

Next came spiritual reading at 4:30, followed by a study hall session. After supper, we had another study session followed by recreation. Sr. Victorine told us we could play board games, talk among ourselves, or do creative art projects. At 8:30, we prepared for bed, and 9:00 was lights out with no further talking.

During that first week the following routine became a part of our Monday through Friday life's pattern:

6:30 Rise

7:00 Mass

7:30 Breakfast

8:00 Chant class/Assigned chores

8:45 Study Hall for Morning Meetings

9:00 Classes

12:00 Lunch

1:00 Classes

3:00 Snacks in refectory

3:30 Outdoor sports

4:30 Spiritual Reading

5:00 Study time in the study hall

6:00 Supper

6:30 Study time in the study hall

7:30 Recreation

8:30 Prep for bed (Baths etc.)

9:00 Lights out

Friday evenings had a slight change for recreation. Sr. Victorine told us we could go to the boarder's recreation room to watch a movie. How exciting to have more time with the boarders. They offered us popcorn, and we could sit wherever we wanted!

On Saturdays, we slept until 7:00. Mass, breakfast, and chant class were the same as weekdays. Our chores required more thorough cleaning. The rest of the day, we were free to do our laundry, write letters, study, or relax until the evening study hall.

On Sunday, we slept again until 7:00. I was excited to wear my Sunday uniform and my new dress shoes. Since my dress was partly wool, I soon discovered it was itchy and too warm. It caused me to sweat so much that I ended up with tell-tale perspiration rings under my armpits. My excitement turned to embarrassment. Now I began to question why we had to wear Sunday uniform dresses? Who made up all these silly rules anyway? I could hardly wait until Mass was over to take off this uncomfortable dress.

After breakfast, we spent the rest of the day doing what we wanted until evening study hall. It felt so freeing to have some time on our own.

My first week patterned the weeks to come: Regimented during the week, with some free time on weekends. On the bright side, I LOVED the challenging high school classes offered and looked forward to my piano lessons with Sr. Kathleen. Besides piano, she gave me weekly organ lessons to learn new hymns to teach the choir back home.

In October, Father Gus wrote and reminded the nuns that since they had stolen his organist, they had promised I could come home more frequently than other aspirants. Since it was for the "church," the nuns agreed. Sr. Victorine called me into her office to say I could go home during MEA vacation, but the other aspirants could not. She explained to the other aspirants why I had this privilege. It made me feel special, but I did not want my fellow aspirants mad at me. When we were by ourselves, I told them the whole story. I promised I would bring back some baked goodies and treats.

Because of this privilege, I practiced harder than ever on the hymns. Father Gus arrived on Wednesday afternoon to pick me up. My stomach was doing flip-flops. It was six weeks since I had been home, and now I would have four days to be with my family and friends. As I babbled on and on about all my new experiences, Father listened patiently. He still didn't seem convinced that I had made the right choice.

He told me that he had arranged choir practices for Friday and Saturday nights. I said that I was excited to show off my new organ skills, and to be with the choir again. I hoped the choir would not be angry that I had left them to go to boarding school. I knew that I had to prove that I had made the right choice. Right now, I could hardly wait to get home.

Just seeing the post office made my heart pound so fast that I could almost hear it. "Oh, Fr. Gus, how can I ever thank you for driving me home and making sure the nuns kept their promise?" I blurted out. "You are the best!" As he helped me get my suitcase, I turned and hugged him in thanks. He reluctantly smiled as I went running into the house, yelling, "I'm home! I'm home!"

Before I could turn around, Sharon rushed to our house, and we laughed and hugged as if I had been gone for years. Oh, it was so good to be home!

Those four days flew by faster than a blink of the eye. The choir was happy to have me back and worked hard to learn two new hymns. They sang their hearts out on Sunday morning.

Sunday afternoon came too soon. Fr. Gus drove up to the house. Mom, Dad, Flo, Mary Ann, and Sharon lined up to hug me and say their goodbyes. I told them that Thanksgiving would soon be here, and I'd be back home. With tears in my eyes, I climbed into the front seat of Father's car and waved another goodby. My stomach was turning. Father took one look at my distress and set off down the road. His organist was not as strong as she pretended to be. Thanksgiving seemed ages away.

As soon as I got back, the aspirants rushed over to see what baked goodies I had brought back. The Rice Krispie treats disappeared in a flash as everyone started talking at once, asking what I did besides playing the organ at church. Instead of being envious, they seemed happy for my chance to go home. After all, it meant homemade goodies for all to enjoy.

The weeks until Thanksgiving vacation went by rather quickly. There was a weekly laundry routine, and we placed our soiled clothes in a laundry bag and took them over to the laundry to be washed by the nuns. Weekends were our designated times to walk over to the laundry to iron and press our clean clothes. I learned that wearing my white uniform blouse until the cuffs and collars took on tell-tale grayish signs before sending them to the laundry kept my ironing to a minimum.

Next to our dormitory was a "slop" sink, a place to wash any personal clothing not laundered by the nuns, such as our nylons. Since nylons were expensive, I tried to be very careful to prevent snags and runs in mine. Despite that, it didn't take long before runs with huge holes appeared. Every student had the same problem.

Fortunately, the senior aspirants shared a tip that came in handy.

They told us there was a solution when most of our nylons became filled with many "runs" and holes. We should buy a black eyebrow pencil. Instead of wearing nylons, we could help one another draw a dark line down the back of each of our legs to make it look like a seam. What a money-saving idea! They warned us to save a good pair of nylons for Sundays, our dress-up day.

One Monday morning in early November, as we walked into chapel for Mass, Sister Austin stood at the chapel entrance for nylon inspection. She made all of us with eyebrow-lined legs go back to our dorm and put on real nylons! I certainly thought our legs with our black lines looked a whole lot better than legs showing lots of holes and runs. My thoughts did not match those of Sr. Austin's! We all wondered how she became aware of our eyebrow pencil scheme. Did she have x-ray vision?

Our classes kept us busy studying for daily sessions and multiple tests for each subject. At my weekly piano and organ lesson from Sr. Kathleen, she always had words of encouragement and spent extra time finding out how I was doing in my classes and adjusting to boarding school life. Even though I had difficulty with the timing in some of my piano and organ pieces, she never scolded me. She encouraged me to use the metronome. Because I always wanted to please her, I practiced doubly hard by practicing extra hours.

During one of our religion classes, Fr. Roger decided to put the fear of God's wrath in us by giving us strict rules of behavior if and when we were around boys. It was the first time I had heard about "petting." He shared what kissing could lead to if you were a "loose girl" and did not command respect from a boy. We must not let boys ever try to touch our breasts. My parents never broached these topics, and I felt flushed and embarrassed. Why didn't Mom ever tell me about this?

At another class, shortly after that, Father asked us to take a formal oath of sobriety called, "The Pledge." The pledge meant that I would not drink any alcohol until I was eighteen. I decided if I was going to be a nun, I should do it. This class left me wondering what else I would learn in religion class! I thought religion classes would only be about learning more catechism like the Baltimore Catechism classes in grade school. I could hardly wait until my next home visit to share all this information with Sharon.

What about our evenings? After recreation, we were supposed to go to our cell, pull the curtain sheets around our bed area, and go to bed. When the tap bell rang, it meant lights out and keeping quiet for the night. How do teenage girls keep those rules every night? Sometimes we quietly tiptoed into one another's cell, sat on the beds, and tried to whisper. It always ended up with one of us giggling out loud. The giggling led to Sr. Victorine coming into the dorm, admonishing us and reminding us that following rules was fundamental in learning to become a nun.

Since we were aspirants, we should have been exemplary girls. Sometimes the temptation to perform pranks on the quieter, shy aspirants was too tempting. We bold, mischievous aspirants often hid their garter belts under someone else's pillow or bed. Since most of us had only one garter belt, this caused panic as we all needed it to hold up our nylon stockings. Throwing someone's panties up in the air to get caught on the rough speckled plaster was another prank.

Bonnie, my sophomore friend, taught us how to "french sheet" a bed. She showed us how to take the top sheet and fold it in half. We then tucked it in on the sides and put the covers back over it. When the person got into bed, their feet got caught in the half-tucked sheet, resulting in cries of distress.

At times like that, we culprits ended up having to march out into the hallway for some penance. Our aspirant mistress had us kneel on the floor, raise our arms as Jesus did on the cross, and recite the rosary or other prayers. Getting caught eating food in our cells also called for disciplinary action. Most of us chose not to share the sweets we got from home with everyone, which meant sharing in secret at night with a chosen few after the lights were out. Once again, if we got caught, we were marched into the hallway to kneel with outstretched arms asking forgiveness for our misdeeds. Rule breakers needed to repent. Why didn't we just share with everyone and not break the rules? I guess we enjoyed the suspense and excitement of seeing how many times we could avoid getting caught.

Since Mom had given me lots of writing materials and stamps, I wrote letters frequently. During my freshman year, I learned that our correspondence and letters had to be left unsealed, no matter whom we sent them to. Our incoming mail was slit open, even our letters from home. We never knew if the nun who opened the mail had read the contents or not.

I got so excited when a letter from Kenny arrived. He was the only boy who dared to write me. Of course, I answered his letter as I wanted to know what he had been doing and how much he missed me.

After several letters back and forth between us, Sr. Victorine called me into her office to discuss this interchange. "Yvonne, I would like you to explain why you are writing to this boy. Don't you know that nuns do not have boyfriends? What is your intention?"

"Sister, he is just a good friend of mine." I innocently answered. "My Dad works with his Dad on road construction. I like him because he tells me about things my classmates are doing when I'm not there." I didn't want her to know that Kenny had a crush on me since seventh grade.

"Well, Yvonne, you need to give this lots of thought and prayers. Do you want to be a nun or not? You can get news from girls, not boys. Tell him not to write anymore."

I left her office crushed and thought this was being too strict. After all, I was only a freshman and didn't see any harm in getting letters from Kenny. Oh my, every time I turned around, there seemed to be another rule imposed on me.

Friday night movies remained the weekend entertainment. Sister Austin, our principal, always ran the projector. She must have previewed the film first because she had a piece of 6x6 inch cardboard that she placed in front of the projector lens whenever anyone kissed. I marveled at her precision of knowing when to use that piece of cardboard!

Christmas holidays were around the corner. Father Gus sent another letter to remind the nuns of their promise to allow me extra days to help his choir for Christmas liturgies. I jumped up and down for joy because he persuaded them to let me go home on Friday afternoon, December 17. Oh, to have from December 17 until January 2 at home was the best Christmas gift ever. It would give me a whole week to work with the choir preparing for Christmas. Sr. Kathleen helped me choose appropriate carols for a Nativity play I was creating for Christmas Eve. She also worked with me to select Biblical passages to tell the Nativity story.

Fr. Gus came to the Mount to pick me up after classes on December 17, a Friday afternoon. The other aspirants said they wished they were the organist in their parish so that they could have extra vacation days as I had. I did feel privileged and unique. I hugged Bonnie, Ruth, and Donna and wished everyone a Merry Christmas. It would be wonderful to be back home to enjoy my family and Mom's meals and no bells to regulate my life.

The choir was very willing to meet several times that week to practice for Christmas liturgies and the Nativity play. I set a time to meet with my friends to explain the roles. Before meeting with the others, I asked Sharon to be the narrator. At our first meeting, each person chose which part they wanted: shepherds, angels, wise men, Mary, or Joseph. They were even willing to practice every day.

Their Moms helped make simple costumes. Gunny sacks made great costumes for the shepherds. Branches from the nearby woods became their crooks, while ropes tied around old dishtowels were their head coverings. For the wise men, they made cardboard crowns covered with tin foil. Bathrobes became their royal robes - much nobler than the gunny sack shepherds! I wanted my five-year-old sister, Mary Ann, to be the little angel by the crib scene. She was delighted. The biggest challenge was how to make her wings. Dads worked together to build the props needed for the manger scene in front of the altar. Working together was indeed a community effort. I kept thinking that this play was my special gift to our church community. I needed to let them know I was sorry I had left them without an organist.

Father Gus told the congregation to come early on Christmas Eve for a special treat. The eve of Christmas arrived. The church was packed by 10:30 p.m. The choir burst into song with Silent Night, and the church lights dimmed. Lights in the sanctuary came on to illuminate Mary and Joseph with the baby Jesus in the manger. As the angel came gliding onto the scene, she proudly proclaimed to all: "Behold, onto you this day is born..." After her message, the choir joyfully sang, "Hark the Herald Angels Sing." During that song, my little sister came walking down the church aisle proudly, displaying her wings for all to see.

When the shepherds followed, the choir sang, "While Shepherds Watched their Flocks." Next, the three kings royally walked down the aisle to the tune of "We Three Kings." We closed the play with "Joy to the World." Everyone in the church stood up to applaud. The proud actors took a bow. Lights went back on, and all in the play helped remove the props while the choir hummed, "Silent Night." In his homily, Father Gus said he hoped we had started a new tradition for Christmas Eve.

After Midnight Mass, we had the traditional family get-together feast with our extended family: Uncle Howard and Aunt Ruby with their children—Don, Dick, Sharon, and Linda—as well as Uncle Sid and Aunt Gerda with their children—Jeanette, John, Ruth, Rita, Sidney James, and Roy. Each year our families rotated homes for the celebration, and each family brought different foods to share. Since all three families were within walking distance from one another, this posed no problem for traveling.

Our two-week vacation cemented my friendship with Sharon even more deeply. Sharing our teenage stories and secrets kept us up late many nights. On January 2, it was once again a time for tears as I hugged Sharon goodby.

My family decided to drive me back to the Mount with a stopover at Dad's sister, Aunt Lou, and her husband, Uncle Albin's, home. They lived on a farm on the way to Crookston. Aunt Lou loved to cook and bake, so we kids always begged to visit her. She insisted on preparing a box of Christmas candy and baked goods to take to school. How could I say no? I would be the most popular aspirant in the dorm!

Mom gave me a calendar journal at Christmas, and it had a half-page for each day of the year for 1955. She told me that writing each day would be a great way to remember my first year at boarding school. I thought that was a super idea and promised myself to do just that. (This journal is still with me. I find it hilarious that I needed to sign my name every day. Here are a few of the entries. The brackets are things I have added to clarify my entries.)

Tuesday, January 11

Dear Diary, I played a game called Heaven and Hell. I never got to Heaven! Sob! Oh, well, I hope to someday!

(Heaven vs. Hell Card game: Two sides use their Demons/Angels to influence people to corrupt or recruit their souls for the battle between Heaven and Hell. The Angels/Demons you control are called minions and can use indirect influence cards to modify the Virtue or Sin status of a soul. Each soul has a value and a Virtue/Sin state. The higher the virtue the easier it is for Heaven to obtain his soul; the higher the sin, the easier it is for Hell. The soul's worth is a measure of the resources you will gain from obtaining soul tokens.)

Ruth and Corrine are giggling, and Ruth is giggling even more. Georgia's telling us SH! But everything else is ok. Bye. Yvonne

Wednesday, February 10:

Today we had our science test and boy, it wasn't easy! I prayed enough to all the saints in Heaven, especially St. Scholastica as it's her name day. We got holy cards at our places today. I went over to the candle house and bought a valentine's candle. Plan to send it home when I get time! Lazily yours, YR

Saturday, February 12

Dear Diary, We had a party tonight.[An against-the-rules dorm party] Ruth, Corrine, Bonnie, and I. We cut Corrine's hair and it's just crooked. We have a comforter on the floor and Ruth put the candy where she cut her toenails! We have potato chips, pop, and candy. Ruth just stuck her foot in my face, so I'd better close. YR

Tuesday, February 15

Dear Diary,

We have school today but our retreat starts tonight. I wonder if I'll be able to keep silent! It surely is going to be hard for me.

We had our first conference tonight and he surely is a good speaker. Here is the theme of our retreat:

Jesus, help me to detest sin always and

Jesus, help me to run away from sin always.

Jesus help me to delight in virtue always and

Jesus, help me to practice virtue always.   YR

Wednesday, February 16

Well, I started to say something about 3 or 4 times today! It certainly is hard for me to keep quiet, but with God's grace, I hope to keep my silence. I have a notebook where I keep all my notes on the conferences. He gives such good talks! YR

Thursday, February 17

Dear Diary,

Second day of retreat, and it wasn't as hard to keep quiet, but I whispered real loud, "Donna!" I really enjoy retreat as we have such a wonderful Retreat master. he really makes a person think. YR

Friday, February 18

Dear Diary,

Well, retreat closed at supper and boy was it noisy in there. We hadn't talked for so long that I almost forgot how! Ha, Not really. Tomorrow is Saturday and another weekend so I'll be seeing you. Yvonne

Tuesday, February 22

Dear Diary,

We had a Mardi Gras Party tonight, and it was the most fun I've had since I've been here. We had a four-piece orchestra - two young men from the AC (Agricultural College) and two older men. The young guys were real cute! Ahem! It surely was nice. I like to dance to that music. Donna and I really cut the rug tonight. I'm still busy. I mean dizzy! Ha. Not from the punch either.

Well, here's signing off for a tired little girl. Hope I have pleasant dreams! Ha. Yvonne

Wednesday, February 23

Dear Diary,

Lent started, so I've made quite a few resolutions. I hope I keep them. I made a resolution to only eat one piece of bread a day. Probably I'll lose a few pounds! YR

Thursday, February 24

Dear Diary,

It certainly was hard to pass up the dessert today. I'll see how much willpower I have. YR

Friday, March 25

Dear Diary,

I received a letter from Father Augustine and I surely was glad to hear from him. He wants me to come home a few days before Palm Sunday. Hope I can!! The nuns promised, so they better let me. YR

Sunday, March 27

Dear Diary, I finished the "Lady of the Lake" booklet in Sr. Basil's English class. She asked us to summarize each of the cantos in a creative way. Boy, was that ever a lot of work! [The "Lady of the Lake" was an epic love poem in six cantos by Sir Walter Scott, published in 1810. I'm sure we did not understand it, BUT it was a piece of great literature that Sister felt we needed to read].

We stayed from the show and we really had fun hiding garter belts. We put JoAnne's under Dianne's pillow and she just about collapsed when she found it. Ha. Ruth cried about hers, so it was quite a night.

Tuesday, March 29

Dear Diary,

I received a letter from Mom, and Sr. Austin got one too. I CAN go home on Friday. I can hardly wait!! I really have been busy practicing hymns for Palm Sunday and Holy Week. Floreen went with Aunt Ruby shopping and got a new coat on Saturday.

Thursday, March 31

Dear Diary,

Tomorrow I am going home! I can hardly wait. The other kids go home on Wednesday of Holy Week. I'm lucky huh? I have to play the organ. April Fool's Day tomorrow, and I suppose I'll really get fooled. Tonight I got fooled too! Well, bye, YR

Friday, April 1

Dear Diary,

I came home today and was it ever nice to see our place again! Three whole months since I've seen it.

We had Mass tonight and it surely was hard to play. After practice, we had a lot of fun. Maxine, Sharon, JoAnne, Ardyce, Kenny, Orville, and Vernon and I walked around the block a couple of times. Really had fun! Wow! Your awful writer, YR

Saturday, April 2

Dear Diary,

We went for a walk tonight. We ended up down at the park! In the end Sharon and Orville and Kenny and I were the only ones left. We didn't do anything. Shucks! We really had fun at the last. They wanted us to walk around the block but we didn't. I went and slept with Sharon. Your boy-crazy kid. YR

Thursday, April 7

Dear Diary,

We had church tonight and Sharon and I started BEFORE and AFTER Holy Hour to practice with Father Augustine. We told him that we could hear him during confessions and we had fun showing him! After that, we met Bobby, JoAnne, Martin, and Orvie and talked to

Bobby and Orvie. We surely had a lot of fun. JoAnne and Martin were together. Happily yours. Yvonne

Friday, April 8

Dear Diary,

We had church services tonight. It was real nice as Father Augustine made it look like Calvary and he put out ALL the lights and gave a sermon. I think it was real nice.

We went to bed and didn't watch TV. I kept quiet for THREE hours today for our Lord. Yvonne

Sunday, April 10 (Easter vacation at home)

Dear Diary,

I went to the show "Seven Brides for Seven Brothers". It was pretty good. An A-2 movie. We had a party at my house and Mom and Dad didn't know about it.[They had gone to Mahnomen to visit Dad's family and play cards and wouldn't be home until around midnight.]

I went with Vernon and he kissed me three times. First time I was ever kissed by a guy. Nothing to it! Ha, Ha. Kenny got mad, but he wasn't after a while. He talked to Maxine, Sharon and me till 11:15. We really had fun. I served popcorn and kool-aid. Dreamy, YR

Tuesday, April 12

Dear Diary,

Mom, Mary Ann and I went to town with Fritz (our mailman) today and stayed at Aunt Ginny's. Dad went in early as he had a dental appointment. We went out to Aunt Lou's for supper. Uncle Albin showed me his pictures. From Shimota's we went to the Mount. Everyone was in my cell. I didn't really want to come back too much. I hope I want to later on.

[Every time I went home for vacations, part of me kept asking why I didn't just stay home and go to public school in Mahnomen with all my friends. I kept flip-flopping on the idea of becoming a nun or not.]

Wednesday, April 20

Dear Diary,

Not much done today. We got a big bawling out from Sister Victorine today. She said we didn't know what it meant to be a nun! I cried a real lot tonight. She didn't even come and comfort me!

168

Wednesday, April 27

Dear Diary,

We had a Sodality meeting, and Father Roger gave a talk. It was interesting. I asked Ruth what happened today, and she's still blabbing away on the routine just like a phonograph, only I can't shut her off! Golly, she's sickening. Ha. Hopefully yours, YR.

Tuesday, May 3

Dear Diary,

Judy, Alice, and Donna got bawled out but I wasn't as I was studying like a good girl! Ha. Ha. Well, I guess that's the way it goes. Innocently yours, Yvonne

Saturday, May 7

Dear Diary,

I went uptown and got Mom's birthday present. I got her a cake decorator and a dish. Mom said they couldn't make it for Mother's Day, and I cried! Sorrowfully, YR

Sunday, May 8

Dear Diary,

Here it is Mother's Day and I couldn't make it home. I sent Mom a booklet of prayers etc. It was real nice. Didn't do too much today. Lazily, Yvonne

Sunday, May 15

Dad, Mom, Sharon, Floreen and Mary Ann came to see me. We celebrated Mom's birthday that was yesterday. She is 46. They said I could go to Mahnomen High School or the Mount next year. I'm very undecided. I don't know what to do! I cried myself to sleep tonight. Questionably, YR.

The Junior and Senior girls attended a prom in the boarders' recreation room with live music every year. Boys were not allowed unless they were members of the band, and girls danced with girls. According to tradition, the Juniors picked a prom theme for the Senior class and decorated the recreation room.

I will never forget when we underclass students were given a preview of the room the day before the prom. In giant bold letters covering one wall was the banner displaying that year's theme: "RENDEZVOUS OF THE STARS."

I had never seen that word before. I blurted out: "What on earth is ren-dez-vus, anyway?" All the junior girls started to laugh hysterically. When they recovered from their hysteria, they told me how to pronounce the word. I vividly remember that scene. Today whenever I see that word, I enjoy a good laugh at my freshman naïveté.

> Sunday, May 29
>
> Dear Diary,
>
> It was Baccalaureate Sunday today. The Seniors wore their caps and gowns and will wear them every day to Mass until they graduate. They also installed new officers into the Sodality, and we had our May procession. It was beautiful. Yvonne

> Tuesday, May 31
>
> Dear Diary,
>
> Today I had my Algebra exam, and boy, was it hard! I'm really getting anxious for Thursday morning. I'll be cruising along in our dear old Ford to Naytahwaush.
>
> We put on our Freshman operetta for Mother Blandina and the Seniors. I was Madame Y, and I had to be uppity up! My hair was white!
>
> Madame Y

> Wednesday, June 1
>
> Dear Diary,
>
> Wednesday at last! Tonight they had graduation and most of the girls went home but about 30 of us are staying until tomorrow. We sang songs after the graduation and we had ice cream cones after.
>
> Anxiously, Madame Y

That summer at Home after Freshman Year, I decided to keep writing in my journal even after coming home for the summer, and that only lasted the first two weeks of June.

> Saturday, June 4
>
> Dear Diary,
>
> Floreen got stranded in Mahnomen, so I had to do all the Saturday work. Poor me! Sob Sob.
>
> We went down swimming as Don took us and Kenny had his car so he drove us back. I sat in the back seat. We drove around a while, then we went up to Belle-feuille's house and stayed till ten. I read magazines while

Sharon and Orvie danced. What a dull night. Orvie and Beans walked us home. Tellingly yours, Yvonne

Tuesday, June 7

Dear Diary,

Guess what! I'm 15 years old today. Banners Aflare. Ha.

I had a party and I invited about 14 kids. All in all there were 12 of us. I got a lot of presents such as - photo album, $3.50 in cash, two hankies, earrings, a headscarf, two pairs of shoes, a blouse, and candy. Boy, I really got some nice presents. Well, guess I'd better close. Happily, YR

Monday, June 13

Dear Diary,

My first day on my job! I was really pooped today as I wasn't used to working in the store. Sharon and I wanted to go swimming but the boys [Sharon's brothers] forgot to leave us the pick-up keys. Sadly, YR

[We could officially get our drivers' license at the age of 16, but our folks let us drive around the village before then. There were no Driver's Education classes back then.]

That summer Sharon and I often biked down to BAB on North Twin Lake to swim after work, since it was much closer than South Twin. On weekends we loved to go to Pinehurst Lodge at South Twin Lake. The beach was sandy and great for swimming—so different from weedy North Twin Lake.

Kenny worked on road construction with his Dad but came home some weekends and had a car to drive us around whenever we wanted. That gave us wheels to go to Pinehurst on our own, so we didn't have to wait for our parents to drive us there. I had mixed feelings about Kenny, but he kept trying to be around me and did not seem attracted to any other girl besides me. Mom and Dad looked with questioning eyes at their daughter, who proclaimed she still wanted to be a nun, yet was still very interested in going out with boys.

We teenage kids loved playing the jukebox in Pinehurst lodge and dancing to our favorite tunes. Girls danced together since the boys just weren't that keen on dancing. The jitterbug was our favorite dance. We inserted our nickels into the jukebox to play rock and roll tunes of the 50's such as:

"Johnny B. Goode," by Chuck Berry.

"Jailhouse Rock and Hound Dog," by Elvis.

"Rock Around The Clock," by Bill Haley & His Comets.

"Tutti-Frutti," by Little Richard.

"Whole Lot of Shakin' Going On," by Jerry Lee Lewis.

We girls danced around the lodge's circular floor and returned to the booth where the boys were sitting. We sat, talked, and sipped our pop when we weren't dancing.

Besides work and play, I practiced the organ most afternoons and had choir practice every Friday evening with the choir members. Father Gus came to help select hymns to fit the scriptures or holy days. Sharon and I attended Mass every morning to be the "altar-girls" since boys didn't seem to participate in daily Mass. We felt special to do this during the week, as only boys were allowed this privilege on Sundays. We took turns ringing the bells during the Offertory and enjoyed reciting the Latin responses. (At this time, the Mass was recited only in Latin.)

Another incentive to attend daily Mass was that Father gave Sharon and me a quarter every day after Mass for our services. (We never told our parents that this was another reason we attended daily Mass.) Those quarters became our monetary bank for feeding the jukebox at the lodge.

My parents didn't discuss my school plans for my sophomore year until the middle of the summer, when Dad was home for the Fourth of July.

"Vonnie, we think it's time to talk about your sophomore year. We know the nuns gave you a four-year scholarship, but why not take this next year and go to Mahnomen public high school? Boys seem to be important in your social life, and you could compare the differences between boarding school and being at home going to public school."

"Well, I still get homesick when I'm at the Mount and miss you and my friends, but I'm learning so much in my classes there. The nuns are strict, and there are lots of rules. It's hard to explain, but it's like I have an inside magnet pulling me there," I replied.

Mom and Dad told me to give this decision a lot of thought and prayers. We decided to give it another month to figure out my choice. I realized I had to spend time and give this lots of considera-

Me in the summer, visiting Paul Bunyan
Land in Brainerd

tion. It was another big decision to mull around in my head. I knew what my parents preferred. I should be so thankful that they gave me a choice in this crucial decision. I certainly knew what Fr. Gus wanted. Why didn't I go along with their thoughts? I needed to think of others, not just myself. I needed lots of time to talk about this with Sharon.

Having lots of sleep-overs together, Sharon and I wrestled with choosing schools. Being together was the most significant pull to going to Mahnomen. The previous year of being separated was heart-wrenching, and could we do that again? This summer made us even more aware of how we needed to be together. We were almost like Siamese twins who had been separated and suffered the consequences.

On August 1, after gut-wrenching talks trying to make up my mind, the Mount won out. I would return as an aspirant. My parents gave in, and I ran over to Sharon's house to tell her my decision. What I was about to hear was a total shock.

"Vonnie, I don't want another year not having you with me at school, so I am going to go to the Mount next year as an aspirant! Mom and Dad agreed and are willing to pay for everything, and they think I'll get a good education." She added, "And, of course, they know how much I have missed you this past year."

What??? I couldn't believe my ears. The world became a rainbow of sparkling colors as we hugged and danced around the room, shouting for joy and happiness.

"But, Sharon, do you truly want to become a nun?" I asked as we sank onto her bed, giddy with excitement.

"Well, this will be an excellent way to find out, and besides, we can be together. If I were just a boarder, we'd be apart most of the time."

I was thrilled with her decision to come with me to the Mount. I didn't care if she became a nun or not. We would be together! That was the most important thing.

With that fantastic news dancing in our heads, we immediately put our heads together and began making plans for our sophomore year—reunited!

Chapter Nine

My Sophomore and Junior years: 1955-57

Education is the passport to the future,
for tomorrow belongs to those
who prepare for it today.
Malcolm X

Sophomore Year: 1955-56

T he world became a whirlwind of joy-filled activity as I helped Sharon prepare for boarding school. After all, I had spent one whole year as an aspirant and could give first-hand advice. Aunt Ruby was over the rainbow with happiness that her daughter, too, wanted to be a nun just like me. Uncle Howard took another view of the matter.

Uncle Howard took Sharon aside. "Sharon, I know the real reason why you want to be an aspirant. Just know that if you go ahead with this plan, you will stay the entire year no matter what happens," he told her. "I will miss you terribly. You're my right-hand girl, and I've never been away from you. It's going to be a whole different world for me with you gone."

He knew his daughter too well. Sharon was not going with the intention of being a nun, but she was going so she could be close to her best friend. He knew how lonely it had been for Sharon the past year without the companionship and closeness of her closest cousin, Vonnie.

I caught myself smiling all the time, just thinking how great it would be to have Sharon with me at the Mount. And to think she would be an aspirant sleeping in the same dormitory and being with me day and night.

Oh, I kept pinching myself to ensure this wasn't all a dream. My very best friend would be there to share all our thoughts and secrets. Could anything be better than this?

As we were together sewing name tags on her clothes, choosing her Sunday dress, making lists of all the things she needed to bring, we talked nonstop about what the Mount would be like as an aspirant. She had visited me a few times, so it wasn't like it would be a total unknown. As we worked together, Sharon shared her reasons for making this decision.

"You know, Vonnie, I've been so lonely this past year not having you with me at school. It was hard not having you here to study with me and do things together after school and on the weekends," she went on to say. "I didn't have any close friends to be with as Maxine wasn't here either. She went to Mahnomen to work and live at a doctor's house."

"Oh, Sharon, I keep thinking I'll wake up and find all of this a dream," I said as I gave her a big hug. "This will be the best year yet!"

August slipped into September with only a week before school started. Sharon and I worked in the store up until that time. Our folks said we should take a break so we would have a week to get packed and spend more time with them and our friends in the village. Of course, there might be last-minute school supplies to get. Mom and Dad were thrilled to have Sharon go with me as they knew how much I had missed her in my freshman year.

Labor Day, September 5, arrived. Mom and Aunt Ruby decided to be the ones to drive us to the Mount. It was a whole new feeling leaving home this time. Sharon was going with me! After hugging everyone in our family, we giggled and waved goodbye as the car drove away. This time we didn't have to say goodbye to each other. It seemed too good to be true. I felt like I was the luckiest girl alive to have my best friend and cousin by my side. I could hardly wait to see the aspirants from the previous year and introduce them to Sharon.

On the way to Crookston, Mom and Aunt Ruby took turns reminding us of last-minute things such as needing to put our studies first and obeying the rules. Aunt Ruby reminded Sharon that she would have to complete the school year even if she wanted to quit halfway.

This year, when we arrived, I knew exactly where to go. Taking our suitcases down to the dormitory, we saw that other aspirants had come before us. I looked around the dorm and was thrilled to find two unoccupied beds side by side. Sharon and I quickly put our suitcases there to make sure we had beds next to each other.

After claiming our beds, I grabbed Sharon's hand and ran to introduce her to my closest friends, Bonnie, Ruth, Donna, Marguerite, and Corrine. I shared the good news that Sharon would be an aspirant with us for her sophomore year. Bonnie turned to the girl next to her and said, "I'm happy too, as my sister, Dolores, decided to become an aspirant. She'll be a freshman."

Mom and Aunt Ruby patiently waited for us. They called us to say they had to leave, and we rushed back. Aunt Ruby shook her head, saying she couldn't believe the small closet space and dresser, much less the sheets hanging around our beds. Even though she wanted to stay and help Sharon unpack, we assured her we could do that later.

Sharon and I walked them out to the car. Aunt Ruby tearfully said to Sharon, "Oh, my girl, I hope you know what you have signed up for. Remember you can call anytime and be sure to write every week. We are going to miss you." With that, she hugged Sharon and got behind the steering wheel.

Mom hugged me tightly and told me how she hoped I had made the right decision. "I will miss you so much, but I'm happy Sharon will be here with you. I put lots of stamps with the stationery and envelopes in your suitcase." After making me promise to write home every week, she wiped away her tears, got in the car, and waved as they slowly drove away.

Sharon and I headed for the dormitory to unpack before going to the recreation room. The laughter and talk of the other aspirants settling in were reassuring. I couldn't wait to hear what they had done over the summer, as well as to have Sharon and I share the summer we had.

I suddenly realized how much the friendships of my fellow aspirants in the previous year meant to me. I hoped Sharon would feel the same after a while. Because we aspirants were such a small separate group from the boarders, we automatically bonded with the common goal of becoming a nun.

The next day, we received our class schedule: Latin 1, Biology, American History, Religion, English, Music, and Piano/Organ. We had no electives. Sharon and I chose to sit next to one another for every class, and it seemed too good to be true. How could I ever thank Sharon enough for deciding to join me at the Mount?

The first two weeks were tough for Sharon as she tried to get used to the strict routine, rules, and being away from her family. Even though she had me by her side, she was still homesick. I tried to console her by saying that I had experienced the same thing last year. For me, daily life now felt comforting in ways I found hard to explain, like wearing comfortable broken-in shoes.

One afternoon after classes, Sharon broke down in uncontrollable tears. Sobbing, she asked Sr. Therese, our new aspirant mistress, for permission to call her dad to say she wanted to go home. Uncle Howard tried to comfort her, but he reminded her that it was her decision to leave home, and she would have to stay the year. Returning to her cell, Sharon flung herself on her bed and wailed. Why had she come? I reminded her that she and I could go home for MEA vacation to help with the choir, and that was only a month and a half away. Then we'd go home again for Thanksgiving vacation, even though that seemed eons away for her. As for me, I felt so much more at home here at the Mount, and I hoped Sharon would too.

As more weeks went by, Sharon became more used to the routines and rules, but she confided in me that she realized this was certainly not the life for her. Who would ever want to live a life with such strict rules and boundaries? I tried to cheer her up and talk about all the positives. We were together. We were getting a good education. We were the only girls from our village daring to be different. Laughingly I said, "And just think Sharon, we don't have to spend time each day wondering what to wear!"

Sharon missed her Mom's baked goodies, but having Sr. Christine's freshly baked treats every day after school was a good substitute. We looked forward to them every afternoon, wondering what Sister had baked for us. The gooey caramel rolls became our absolute favorite. Every day after our snack, we returned to our cells to take off our uniform clothes and put on jeans for outdoor recreation.

Sr. Cyprian, our biology teacher, was stern and all business. Being fifteen years old, we girls could hardly wait to get to the chapters on the human body, sexual reproduction, and other bodily functions. Much to our disappointment, Sister skipped those chapters.

With a clearing of her throat, those chapters became anathema. Being obedient students, no one dared ask why. After all, she was the teacher and knew best. But at night, gathering in designated cells, we sophomores tried to figure out the textbook's meaning as we diligently studied the illustrations. Why didn't we examine the chapters on the sexual parts of our bodies? Did she think we were too young to learn about that? Not teaching us made us even more curious.

Our English teacher, Sr. Basil, chose safe books for us to read, but warned us that there were individual book titles that we were not ready for at our young age. Those books were locked up in a cupboard, and that was all we needed to tempt us to search for the closet to sneak a look at the forbidden titles. Where was this cupboard? Who would be the first to find it? The game was on to see who the winner would be.

Luckily for us, one of the boarders found the forbidden closet in a small alcove off the library. She couldn't believe her luck to discover the door unlocked. Sr. Leocadia, the librarian, unexpectedly walked into the room, but the student already had three titles written down: *Catcher in the Rye*, *Lord of the Flies*, and *The Scarlett Letter*. News spread quickly among the students about the titles. Even though we didn't have a library in Naytahwaush, I knew we could find the books in the Mahnomen public library. Sharon and I would have some summer reading to do.

At the Mount, the nuns required every student to join the Sodality of Mary. The Sodality had monthly meetings and chose officers at the beginning of each school year. The Sodality prefect (a senior girl chosen by the nuns as an exemplary student) led these meetings. As a member, we dedicated ourselves to saying the daily rosary. At each meeting, we learned more about Mary's apparitions and miracles.

(The Sodality is not a mere pious organization. The first of its rules states that the Sodality, "is a religious body which aims at fostering in its members an ardent devotion, reverence, and filial love towards the Blessed Virgin Mary. Through this devotion, and with the protection of so good a Mother, it seeks to make the faithful gathered together under her name good Catholics, sincerely bent on sanctifying themselves, each in his state of life, and zealous, as far as their condition in life permits, to save and sanctify their neighbor and to defend the Church of Jesus Christ against the attacks of the wicked.")

I know we girls did not realize the original intent of the Sodality. It was a religious organization imposed on us to become pure and loyal followers of Our Lady. In October, we students said the daily rosary outside by the grotto dedicated to the Blessed Virgin.

Like my freshman year, I had the privilege of going home during MEA vacation to work with the choir. Father Gus asked that Sharon come with me as she had an excellent voice to help the others. The nuns decided to give no objection. When Father Gus arrived at the Mount on that Tuesday afternoon, we were anxiously waiting outside with our suitcases and smiles on our faces. The ride home flew by as we talked nonstop, sharing stories of how Sharon was trying to adjust to convent life and, despite all, how great it was to be together. Father hoped this idea of ours to attend the Mount was worth it. He was still not happy to have lost his organist.

Sharon and I went to daily Mass to appease him, and we worked extra hard teaching new hymns to the choir. Our families were thrilled to have us home for this short time, spoiled us with all our favorite foods, and asked us constantly what we wanted to do. Those five days disappeared so quickly and, before we knew it, we were back at the Mount.

Thanksgiving vacation arrived a month later. Sharon was over the moon to be going home again. When Mom and Aunt Ruby came to get us, we were surprised to see Flo in the car. Mom asked us to wait with Aunt Ruby in the recreation room. She and Flo needed to talk with Sr. Austin. Why were they doing that? Mom said she would explain everything when they returned. Sharon and I begged Aunt Ruby to explain what was happening. Why were they talking to Sr. Austin? Had something happened with Flo? "Please tell us, Aunt Ruby, please!" I begged.

Aunt Ruby smugly smiled and told us to wait and see. "Are you two all packed?" she inquired as we tried to question her more about what was happening. "We're so glad you'll be home with all of us for Thanksgiving."

Sharon and I looked at each other, bursting with curiosity and questions. "Come on, Aunty Ruby." I pleaded. "Please tell us why Flo came with you. We'll act surprised when Mom and Flo come down to explain. Please, pretty please?" I couldn't stand the wait any longer.

At that moment, Mom and Flo walked into the rec room. Sharon and I burst out in one voice: "What's happening, Flo? We can't stand another minute of suspense."

Flo smiled, looked at us, and said, "I'm going to finish my senior year of high school here at the Mount as a boarder."

What??? Sharon and I looked at her as if a meteor had just fallen at our feet. Firing off question after question, Mom interrupted to say that Flo would tell us all about her decision on the way home. We picked up our suitcases and flew out of the building as if we were rocket-propelled. Mom and Aunt Ruby laughed as they tried to keep up with us as we rushed to the car.

"Okay, Flo, tell us, tell us!" we panted as we scrambled into the back seat. "You sit between us so we can both hear you better. How come you didn't let us in on this plan in your letters? When did you decide? What made you do this?"

We peppered her with so many questions that she didn't even have time to answer one before we asked the following question. Mom turned around and said, "Girls, give Flo a chance to talk and then ask more questions."

Flo looked at us and said, "Well, first of all, the classes offered at Mahnomen High School aren't preparing me very well for nurse's training. I've heard you two talk about the challenging classes here and the study halls you have to attend. If I learn how to study well and get good grades, nurse's training will be easier."

She continued, "Besides, I've been lonely. It'll be fun to be with both of you." We looked at each other but didn't want to pop her bubble of hope. She didn't know how little time aspirants and boarders spent together. But at least we'd be in the same school. Maybe, because she was my sister, the nuns might make exceptions. This ride home proved to be the fastest trip ever. We talked nonstop, making plans and telling Flo what to expect when she returned with us after vacation.

I thought Flo was courageous and daring to make this change in the middle of her senior year. I sure hoped she would be happy at the Mount. Getting good grades must be vital for her. Or was Flo keeping something from us? What was the real reason she made this life-changing decision? If Flo wouldn't tell me, I'd have to try to wriggle the truth out of Mom.

Thanksgiving vacation flew by as we sewed name tags on Flo's clothes, bought nylons and a Sunday uniform dress and personal toiletries. She had a going-away party with some of her closest friends. Sharon and I were thrilled that they invited us. I think her friends wanted us there to answer all their questions about attending a boarding school. They wanted to know what Flo would experience, since none of them had ever gone away to school.

Flo told us she wanted to get a good education, but I wanted to ask Mom if this was the real story, and I realized I had never given it any thought that she might be very lonely without Sharon and me. Mom assured me both reasons were the truth. Then she added that the nuns gave them a significant tuition discount because Flo was the second in our family to attend the Mount. Mom reiterated her belief that a good education was the best gift she could give her girls, and she was ready to sacrifice everything for that.

Flo and Mary Ann.

In turn, Mom asked me to tell her the truth about my choice to be an aspirant. Did I regret my decision? I shared that I missed being at home, but I felt a real inner calling to be a nun. Living with the nuns brought an inner peace that I had never experienced before. It wasn't easy to explain. I admitted that my first year had been challenging—as I learned to live in such a different regulated environment—but the commitment of being an aspirant kept burrowing deeper into my mind and heart despite the rigid rules and hardships.

This second year was much more comfortable. I loved having Sharon there and now I'd have my older sister too! I hugged Mom and thanked her again for letting me follow my dreams. Of course, I missed her terribly, but I knew that was one of the sacrifices nuns made when they chose their vocation. A nun had to put God before family. I tried not to think about that, because I loved my family so much. Why would God demand giving them up? I pushed those thoughts away, and decided to enjoy every minute with my family.

The Saturday after Thanksgiving, Sharon, Flo, and I gathered in our kitchen to bake cookies and bars to take back to school. Of course, Rice Krispie bars were at the top of our list. Uncle Howard had not been to the Mount, so he and Aunt Ruby said they would drive the three of us back. Sharon promised him she would be the best tour guide ever to show him the school.

As Uncle Howard placed the three suitcases into the trunk, Flo and I hugged Mom and Dad for our farewell. I saw the pained look on Mom's face as she waved goodbye. Dad stood with tears in his eyes as he placed a comforting hand around Mom's neck. They were losing two of their girls. Mary Ann jumped up and down as she waved and shouted her goodbyes. Now she had Mom and Dad all to herself.

When we got to the Mount, Flo and I hugged Sharon's parents and thanked them for the ride. As Sharon left to give her Dad and Mom a quick tour, I took Flo to the office. She needed to find her room number and the name of her roommate. Seniors were assigned the best rooms and had more privileges than their younger classmates. They got to sit in the back of the study hall, were first in line for everything, and were highly respected by all.

I proudly told everyone we met in the hallway that Flo was my sister and had just joined us. We walked up the flight of stairs to the bedrooms and met her roommate, Joyce. Since I needed to get back to the dormitory, Joyce promised to help my sister with everything. I quickly hugged Flo and raced back down to the dormitory to unpack and visit the other aspirants. I wanted to share the good news of having my sister here at the Mount. When Sharon came back, it was time for supper.

That first week proved to be difficult for Flo. All the classes were new, and she studied extra hours to review the material presented in the first few months of the school year. Some of the seniors took on the role of study buddy to speed up the process. We looked forward to the weekends so we could spend time together. Friday night movies were great because Sharon, Flo, and I sat together, laughed, and shared popcorn. Boarders could walk downtown every weekend, but aspirants could only do that once a month. Sharon and I looked forward to being with Flo on the Saturdays we could go. We laughed as we shared our spending money to get the biggest ice cream cones we could afford. Just being off the school grounds felt so liberating.

On December 8, Feast of the Immaculate Conception, new students were enrolled in Our Blessed Lady's Sodality organization. Flo and Sharon became enrolled members that day and received their certificates as I had received in my freshman year. My certificate read:

> "Sodality of Our Blessed Lady: This certifies that Yvonne Rumreich was received as a member of the Sodality duly erected in the Mount St. Benedict Academy under the title of Immaculate Conception and St. Gertrude the Great and is therefore entitled to all the indulgences, favors, graces and privileges which other Sodalists enjoy, and upon death will receive from our Sodality all the suffrages which are of custom offered for Sodalists departed. In Witness whereof our signatures hereunto affixed. Crookston, Minnesota, December 8, 1954. Rev. Roger Schoenbeckler OSB (Director) and Lois Spors (Prefect)."

On feast days such as this, every student received a holy card at their place in the dining room. Another treat was grape juice that we all pretended was natural wine. With all our giggling and laughter, a passer-by might think it was wine. On the serious side, the nuns ensured that we knew what the feast was all about and why we were celebrating it.

Because the Nativity play had been such a success the year before, Father Gus requested that his three parishioners be allowed to return home early for Christmas vacation to prepare for Christmas Eve. The nuns hesitated, but granted his wish if we completed the homework for the days missed. Sharon, Flo, and I were ecstatic, and Flo was anxious to see her school friends. We all looked forward to the tasty cookies and candies our moms always made for the Christmas season. Of course, we were happy to see our families too!

Father Gus drove up to the Mount to fetch three excited girls who couldn't wait to get home for Christmas. We excitedly talked about ways we could make the Nativity play even better this year. He laughed and said, "I wish I could bottle up all your enthusiasm and uncork the bottle during the long winter months when you girls aren't at home!" He continued, "It'll be great to have our organist back as well as our two good choir members. We have missed you."

The Nativity play went off without a hitch. Our church members and choir shared how much they enjoyed it and also how much they missed us. At times like this, I felt guilty for abandoning them during the school year. Was I meant to be a nun, if it meant depriving them of their organist? Was I being selfish?

With these thoughts rummaging through my head, I tried to justify leaving home during my high school years. Maybe Mom was right. If I had a vocation to be a nun, it would still be there after I graduated. Or would it? I enjoyed the challenges of trying new things and showing my strengths even when times were tough. As the nuns said, "Pray for your vocation. Be strong. Sacrifices are a part of becoming a nun, and do it for the honor and glory of God."

January 2 came too soon for all of us. Saying goodby to family and friends was difficult after a fun-filled two weeks of Christmas vacation. Easter seemed so far away for our next home visit. At least, I had Sharon and Flo return to the Mount with me.

In February, Sr. Austin announced that there would be a posture contest for three months, since posture was such an essential element of good health. All girls must participate. We were to stand tall, sit straight at our desks, and walk properly. The faculty nuns would be the judges watching and checking us at various times. Every student must work diligently to improve her posture. I had never heard of such a contest. Why not try to be the best? Sister did not mention any prizes. Maybe this was their idea of not looking for material rewards in this world?

It became a game with us aspirants as we kidded each other. "Hey, Sharon, watch that walk. Is that as straight as you can sit?" "Yvonne, did I see you slouching again?" "Donna, there is a posture contest going on. Did you forget?" At least, during the cold winter months, we had something to talk about other than schoolwork.

On the last day of April, Sr. Austin called the students together for a "Posture Celebration Party." With a twinkle in her eye, she told us to stand tall, sit straight, and then we could celebrate. Sr. Austin brought out a silver crown and solemnly proclaimed that the faculty had chosen the posture queen for the year.

"We are proud to announce that Yvonne Rumreich is officially the new Posture Queen of Mount St. Benedict Academy." I gasped and walked up as straight and tall as I could to receive my crown. As

Me as Posture Queen.

she placed the crown on my head, Sr. Austin whispered to me. "Keep working at it. You seemed to be the most improved student." I didn't know if that was a compliment or not, but I smiled and accepted my crown! At least I was a queen of something.

Sharon learned the Gregorian chants and liturgical music with me because she was an aspirant and attended daily chant practice as I did. Sr. Kathleen had Sharon and I work together to prepare for Holy Week. One of the few pluses of being an aspirant was going home early with me on vacations to help with the choir. Even though Flo was not an aspirant, the nuns decided to let her come with us when Fr. Gus requested it. The nuns started to realize how difficult it was for our choir not to have an organist.

As we practiced for Holy Week, I suddenly realized how much I loved Gregorian chant. It had a peaceful, mystical quality. Singing in Latin, the music reminded me of a meandering brook winding its way through a quiet forest. The notes were medieval shapes with fascinating names: quilisma, podatus, pressus, tristropha. Since there were no definite rhythmic patterns, we had to carefully heed Sr. Victorine's baton strokes as she directed. Sr. Kathleen played the organ for all the services. As I watched her feet dance on the foot pedals, I hoped to do the same when I became a nun.

Sr. Kathleen continued to be my piano and organ teacher. She was the one I could always go to whenever I needed advice or doubted if becoming a nun was the path I should continue. Sister felt like my guardian angel, always ready to protect me and encourage me along the way.

In May, we always had an impressive procession from the chapel to Mary's shrine located behind the school building near the nuns' gardens. All the nuns joined the students.

As we walked to the shrine, we sang: "O Mary, we crown thee with blossoms today! Queen of the Angels and Queen of the May." The Sodality Prefect placed a beautiful crown of flowers on the head of the statue. After the crowning, we all said the rosary by the shrine and sang more hymns to honor Mary.

In early June, our parents came to the Mount for Flo's senior graduation. Afterward, we all left for home to begin our long-awaited summer vacation. Flo had been accepted at St. Cloud Nursing School and would start in the fall for her training. She was excited to be home for a few weeks before leaving for her summer job waitressing at a restaurant in Beaver Bay on Lake Superior's north shore. The tips for waiting on tables would come in handy for spending money in the fall. Another plus was being there with her best friend, Babe.

Returning home, I thought Sharon and I would take a little break and then return to our summer jobs in Uncle Howard's store. The day after I came home, Fr. Gus came down to talk with me. He needed someone to drive a school bus each day to pick up kids that lived in the country for the two weeks of catechism classes. Since I would turn sixteen in a few days, I should practice driving more and get a driver's license. Mom and Dad thought I was a bit young to drive a bus. Father Gus told them that there wasn't much traffic on those country roads. He wanted someone responsible and would have one of the nuns ride with me.

With that, my folks agreed I could take on this task. Dad spent hours giving me driving tips and even tried to teach me how to parallel park as he knew that would be part of the test. We had no reason ever to parallel park in our village, or Mahnomen, for that matter. People used angled parking on the streets in Mahnomen. In our town, there were no streets, just dirt roads.

The day after I turned sixteen, Dad drove me to the big town of Detroit Lakes, twenty-five miles away, to take the test. In those days, there were no classes to take to learn how to drive, and you simply learned from your parents or older friends. Dad was an excellent driver, so I was fortunate to have him as my teacher. There was no way Mom could teach me as she was the worst and most nervous driver ever. On the way to take my test, Dad tried to calm me down. "You can do whatever you set your mind to do, my girl. Just smile and act like you know what you are doing."

Trying to follow his advice, I felt good about everything the driving examiner told me to do until we got to the orange cones he had placed on the street for parallel parking. Getting nervous, I managed to knock over some of the cones but not all. On my second chance, I again knocked over cones. The instructor tallied up my points and told me I passed, but barely. Oh, well, I was only concerned that I had passed the road test! Now I could drive the school bus to pick up kids for catechism.

Little did I know that the school bus was one of the older yellow buses from our school. Maybe they thought it wouldn't be too much of a loss if something happened to the old bus. Fr. Gus knew how to persuade people when he needed anything, so getting the bus was another example of his persuasive power.

Dad came to my rescue again. He showed me that shifting gears in the bus was the same as a car, and the big difference was the size and length. If I needed to back up, I just had to make sure there was plenty of room to do that. I was more than nervous about backing up this monster, but Dad again assured me that I could do it. Driving the bus was another way for me to help the church. Father Gus gave me a list of all the homes I needed to go to for my job. Dad and I did a practice drive, so I knew the routes and time it would take to drive to the different places.

That Sunday, the nuns arrived. Father told me to come to the rectory to meet them. There were two older nuns, but no Sr. Kathleen! How I wished she had been sent back to our village that summer. Father explained to the nuns that I would be the bus driver for picking up kids to attend catechism classes. He felt one of them should ride with me to greet the children and help with an emergency if there was one. The nun named Sr. Charlotte said she would be the nun to come with me.

On Monday morning, I drove the bus to pick up Sr. Charlotte. Mom suggested that I wear a dress for the occasion out of respect for the nuns. Imagine my surprise when Sister took one look at me and told me that my sleeveless dress was immodest and not to wear it again. I bit my tongue and couldn't wait to share this with Mom. How prudish this older nun was, I thought. Here I had worn a dress and not jeans for this job. I was unhappy to hear this, and hoped I would never be like that nun when I entered the convent.

When I told Mom about Sr. Charlotte's reprimand about wearing sleeveless dresses, Mom shook her head and smiled. "Well, Vonnie, I don't agree," she said, "but for two weeks, I think you can find clothes with sleeves on them."

I decided the school bus should have some music for the kids to enjoy while they rode. Ernie, my first-grade boyfriend, was very mechanical-minded, and I asked him to help me get the radio working on the bus. He got some tinfoil, tinkered around with the sound system, and made it work. The kids loved the music, but I'm sure Sr. Charlotte would have preferred hymns.

The music helped soothe my nerves when I backed the bus up on the narrow driveways. With the kids telling me to go a little more to the left or right, I managed to avoid going in the ditches. The two weeks went by quickly, without any accidents. I was a little richer when Fr. Gus generously paid me for my efforts. When I tried to refuse the money, he insisted.

When I shared the story of how Sr. Charlotte disapproved of my sleeveless dress, he laughed heartily. I didn't think it was amusing! With a twinkle in his eye, he asked me if that were the kind of nun I would become.

"Maybe you should reconsider what you want to be," he said thoughtfully. "It's not too late to change your mind."

I shared that the more time I was at the Mount, the more confident I became about becoming a nun. "I don't ever want to be a crabby old nun, and I want to make people laugh and happily learn about God," I retorted.

After driving the bus those two weeks, I resumed working in the store. Sharon and I were glad that we didn't have to leave home to work as Flo did. Happy to be employed as Uncle Howard's two favorite store clerks, we continued to invent ways to entice customers with new products. The vendors knew we were gullible and always had samples of new products they gave us to try, and then we figured out ways to sell them.

Mom (right) and her friend Dorothy at a picnic that summer.

Our summer flew by as we worked every day except Sundays. Every week we had choir practice. I enjoyed being the director and organist at the same time. In my spare time, after working in the store, I biked to the church and practiced on the pump organ to prepare for the weekly choir practice. Having had two years of organ lessons with Sr. Kathleen, my skills were much more advanced. Thinking back to my first attempt to play the organ with one hand while pumping the pedals in and out made me laugh out loud. I have come a long way since then. Father Gus asked me to play the organ for Masses at another mission church in Island Lake. It was about fifteen miles from Naytahwaush. The choir promised to practice the hymns a half hour before Mass each Sunday. I agreed.

Enjoying my time with Mary Ann that summer.

Sharon and I took up the usual summer activities of swimming, dancing, going out with the boys, and having fun with our cadre of friends. I decided that I would be a teenager just like my friends during my summers, and I could think about being a nun when I returned to school. It was my summer break so going out with boys was part of my vacation.

We learned about the new outdoor theatre built near Mahnomen. Since the theatre charged each person, we kids figured how to save money. Before we got to the drive-in entry, some kids got in the car trunk to avoid paying. The driver drove to the elevated mound near the speakers and parked, opened the car's trunk, and the kids got out quickly. They jumped in the car, we paired up, and waited for the movie to start.

The person on the passenger side rolled down the window, placed the speaker's box on it, and rolled the window up as far as it could go. Mosquitoes were a nuisance, as well as the windows getting steamed up. Such were the trials and tribulations of outdoor movies!

Life was great that summer until one day in July. Father Gus appeared at our doorstep when I came home from work at the store. The Post Office was empty, and Mom and I were the only ones home at the time. "Phil, I need to talk with you," he said with such a severe face. "I'm glad Vonnie is also here." I wondered what on earth was on his mind. What had happened?

Fr. Gus sighed deeply and said, "I'm being transferred to Detroit Lakes at the end of this month to replace Father Andrew. He will become your pastor." He continued, "Phil, as you know, we Benedictine monks have no choice in the decisions of where we go or how long we stay, and the Abbot determines our fate."

I jumped out of my chair sobbing and ran to give him a big hug. How could they do this to us? Father Gus was the best priest ever and had been so good to me. How could they take him away?

Mom told me to sit and listen to more of what Fr. Gus wanted to share. "I've loved being in Naytahwaush and being your pastor. This new assignment is so hard to accept, but I wanted to share it with you before I tell the rest of the parishioners on Sunday," he continued. "Phil, you have always been such a good listener whenever I needed a person to turn to, and I just needed to have you advise me on the best way to tell the parish."

Then he turned to me. "Vonnie, I want you to think seriously about becoming a nun," he said as he looked at me. "Both your Mom and I feel you are too young for such a serious decision in your life."

I was sobbing too much to try to listen to that. I was only thinking about what life would be like without him and his praise and encouragement as his organist at St. Anne's. Why did that Abbot have to go and upset our apple cart and take away the priest we all loved and admired?

Father continued to share that Fr. Andrew had had a stroke and couldn't continue being the pastor of such a large parish as Detroit Lakes. Mom told him that he would leave a deep hole in everyone's heart and that it would be difficult to heal when he left us.

She turned to me and said, "Vonnie, this is another example of what can happen if you decide to become a nun. The Rev. Mother decides where you go and for how long. See how difficult this can be? Are you ready to make sacrifices like Father Gus now has to do?" I didn't even want to think about myself. This talk was about Fr. Gus, not me.

At the end of July, Fr. Andrew arrived. I didn't like him immediately, and he was not happy to be assigned to such a small parish in the middle of nowhere. He showed it in his talk and manners.

We had a huge farewell party for Fr. Gus. I'm sure Fr. Andrew could see how much we loved Fr. Gus and didn't want him to leave us. That didn't help matters any, and we all knew that this would be a difficult transition. We didn't want a new pastor, and our new pastor didn't want us.

Fr. Andrew (left) and Fr. Augustine (right)

A few weeks later, Fr. Andrew appeared in the store to get some groceries. George Norris had just given Sharon and me our summer haircuts, in George Norris style—short! Fr. Andrew took one look at us while we were stocking the shelves with new products. He started laughing and sarcastically said, "What lawnmower ran over the top of your heads?"

We were so angry and upset, but we didn't dare utter the words bubbling up in our heads. How could a priest be so crude and rude? From that day on, I knew that I would never like him. Where was Fr. Gus when we needed him?

One night in the middle of the summer, at a sleepover, Sharon said, "Vonnie, I realized this past year that I don't want to become a nun. The rules are too strict, and it's not the life for me."

"Oh, Sharon, this past year was the best because you were with me." I cried. "Why not try it for another year?"

"No, but I've thought that I might go back as a boarder," she replied. "I want to be a nurse like Flo, and I know that the Mount gives us a good education. But, for sure, I don't want another year as an aspirant. The boarders have more freedom."

I was thrilled that she wanted to go back. At least, we would see each other every day. As a boarder, Sharon would have a bedroom with two or three students rooming together, instead of the big dormitory. And being a boarder meant she could go home any weekend she wanted. She promised to go downtown with me on the Saturdays I was allowed to go. We would try to sit together in as many classes as we could.

"Sharon, I don't want to become a boarder because I still want to try becoming a nun. I feel that God wants me to be one, even though it is challenging to follow all the rules." I responded. "I feel like it's the right choice for me."

"If you're so set on being a nun, why are you going out with boys?" retorted Sharon. "What if the nuns find out?"

"I need to find out both worlds. How else will I know which vocation to choose?" I retorted.

Sharon agreed and said it was more fun when we both did the same things. It would be terrible if I insisted on staying home while she went out and had a good time without me during the summer, and I heartily agreed.

The next day I shared with Mom what Sharon and I had talked about at our sleepover. "Mom, I'm so happy that Sharon will be a Junior with me at the Mount. I'll miss having her as an aspirant, but she doesn't want to be a nun like I do."

I continued, "Each year I'm at the Mount, our aspirant mistress explains more about the Rule of St. Benedict and what that means to become a nun following his rules." I knew I wanted to be a teacher so I could do that following his practice of "Ora et Labora" (Pray and Work), all for the honor and glory of God.

Taking on the life of a nun, dedicating oneself to God, was very appealing to me. To spend my whole life helping others was what I wanted. Each year at the Mount made this more clear to me.

"But, Vonnie, you're saying this, but yet you don't act like someone wanting to be a nun when you are home in the summer," Mom responded.

"Mom," I said, "I just told Sharon that I feel I need to experience a regular teenage life when I'm home, so I can compare and make the right decision." I added, "Isn't it alright to see both sides?"

Mom hugged me and shook her head. "Oh, Vonnie, you are quite the unique, stubborn girl," she laughed. "I'm happy that Sharon will be with you another year at the Mount. As far as your vocation, remember that it is a huge decision. Pray for the right decision, my girl. Just don't ever lose your zest for life, no matter what you choose."

Junior Year: 1956-57

Flo left for nurse's training, and after Labor Day in September, Sharon and I set off for the Mount. We parted ways when we got there, and she headed for the boarder's area, and I returned to the aspirant's dormitory. It would be strange not to have Sharon with me all the time, but we promised to stay as close as we could during our classes together.

On the first day of classes, Sr. Austin gave her usual introductory speech laying out the year's rules and regulations. No new surprises.

Each class received a roster of classes for the year. As a Junior, my classes were: Religion, Latin II, English 11, World History, Plane Geometry, Music, Piano, Organ, Physical Education. Why Physical Education? It was a new class. Our first two years were informal sessions after school. Did they hire a new teacher for the class?

We soon learned that a college graduate became a postulant in the fall. Her name was Miss Janet. (Adding "Miss" to a postulant's first name was a sign of respect, as well as a tradition at the convent.) She became our new Physical Education teacher. From then on, Phys Ed was considered an academic subject to be graded on our report cards. We didn't know what to expect.

Learning the art of archery became our first challenge with Miss Janet. Sharon and I were excited. Even though men and boys used bows and arrows for hunting deer on our reservation, we never did. Miss Janet explained the archery rules and demonstrated how to hold the bow and arrow. We were to try and hit the bull's eye target standing down range.

Sharon shot her first arrow and hit the mark. I was next in line. Eager to do the same, I snatched the bow and arrow, didn't listen for directions, and accidentally released an arrow. Whoosh, the arrow landed within inches of Sharon. Our teacher was upset with my rash behavior; she told me that I was banned from the sport until I could learn how to listen and follow directions.

That evening at study hall, Sharon pulled me aside and said, "I thought you were happy I was here with you, Vonnie. Why did you try to kill me today?" We giggled and giggled, trying to muffle our sounds. After that disastrous beginning, I tried to avoid archery the rest of that year whenever we had a chance to choose an after-school activity. My Native American genes weren't working!

I didn't get to be with Sharon as much as I wanted. We saw each other in classes and some Saturdays we went downtown together.

Sr. Josepha was our class advisor. She was quite the character— tall, skinny, wrinkled as a prune, with the habit of constantly tugging back the coif on her face when she got excited about something. Sister got excited about anything that pertained to the news or any historical fact that caught her fancy. She lived, ate, and breathed history and, of course, taught all the history and social studies courses.

Her broad smile always showed off the spaces between her front teeth. We knew how to make her smile: Just bring up the latest news fact or article you had read or had heard on the radio. Incidentally, this constantly improved one's grade for the report card. We girls vied with one another to be the first to share the latest tidbit of news to impress her.

The Junior class traditionally presented a play each spring to entertain the rest of the student body. After finding a mystery-comedy for an all-girl cast, Sr. Josepha took on the role of becoming our directress. We had more laughs trying out for the different parts she had already pre-determined. I ended up being a hick country girl that spoke in a dialect. The rest is history!

Costumes were simple, with several of the characters wearing their bathrobes. I had a simple blouse and skirt, and my hair needed fake braids with pieces of straw sticking out at intervals. A bale of straw was my chair as a reminder of my primitive farm upbringing. At this point, I can't remember the plot. Still, visions of Sr. Josepha—constantly tugging at her coif and adjusting her rimless glasses as she reprimanded us for not remembering our lines—remain vividly in my mind.

My junior play. I'm second from left (with braids).
Sharon is second from right. Marguerite far right.

Another tradition was that the Juniors planned the Prom for the Senior class. Sr. Josepha collected us to decide on the theme for that year. She strongly suggested an Asian theme to relate to our World History classes. We needed to include some historical trivia and Asian skits with music. Peering at us with her darting brown eyes, pulling on her coif, she coyly remarked that she knew we could create the best prom ever. How could we say no to her? Asian theme, it was.

Immediately after sharing that bit of news, she had another announcement. She shared that the class advisor always received a gift at the end of the year. She declared that she did NOT want such silly gifts as towels and washcloths because she would have to give those to the motherhouse. Instead, she wanted us to consider a black suitcase with a red lining. Sister said she needed a nice piece of luggage when she visited her mother.

We all looked at each other in disbelief. Sr. Josepha seemed too old to have a mother still on this earth. Standing there with mouths open in disbelief, she whispered not to say anything about this to anyone else. When Sister left the room, we all giggled, wondering how old her mother must be. Next, how would we find money to get her a suitcase? Much less, find a black one with a red lining.

Since Sharon was our class president, she felt responsible for finding the much-coveted suitcase. Not really knowing where to find one, Sharon wrote to her Dad to ask for his help. After many attempts to check out different luggage places, Uncle Howard found the suitcase of Sr. Josepha's dreams. He told Sharon not to worry about collecting money from her classmates. It would be his gift to our class. If Sharon weren't the class favorite before this, she now was. What a fantastic leader we had chosen to be our class president.

As for preparing the Asian theme, we divided into groups to work on the music, decorations, historical trivia, and a skit. I was in the music group. With Sr. Kathleen's help, we decided that three of us would perform Gilbert and Sullivan's "Three Little Maids from School" from *The Mikado*. We found records of Asian music to play in the background to enhance the theme. All of us worked together to create decorations to transform the room into an Asian paradise. The countless hours we spent after school to work on this meant that I had much more time with Sharon, an unexpected blessing as well as a fun, creative, productive venture.

We had the week before the Prom to decorate the rec room. No students could enter except us Juniors as the theme needed to be a total surprise for the Seniors.

Since we girls were supposed to be learning etiquette during our time at the Mount, the nuns decided that every girl had to wear a formal to attend the Prom. They imposed regulations about the formals. No girl could wear a strapless gown or have a plunging neckline. If you wore a strapless formal, you had to wear a bolero with it. No boys were allowed. Girls must dance with girls, but not too close!

The night of the Prom, the rec room looked like an Asian fairy-tale with Asian tunes reverberating in the background. We Juniors beamed as we looked around and admired our efforts. Even Sr. Josepha proudly presented it to all the nuns and declared it was her idea. Before the dance began, we Juniors put on a skit that included Asian trivia, and we performed our musical. After that, a small band of male musicians entered the room and set up their dance instruments. (The only boys allowed in the room.)

When the band began to play, we girls checked our dance cards to see which girls we would dance with next. Several nuns chaperoned to ensure that girls were not dancing too close together, mainly when the band played a slow dance. Non-alcoholic punch and cookies were available during the evening. By 11:00 p.m., the Prom ended. Unlike regular proms, we had no date to drive us home, and we simply had to retire to our rooms or dorm.

After Prom, things settled down for us Juniors. The Seniors had final recitals, Baccalaureate services, a week of wearing their white caps and gowns to Mass, and the special privilege that last week of no study halls because they had finished all their exams.

After graduation, Sharon and I packed our suitcases and waited anxiously for our parents to come and get us. To think that the following year we would be Seniors!

It felt good to be back working at the store, bantering with the weekly salesmen, and trying new products. One afternoon that summer, Uncle Howard took Sharon and me aside to share his shocking news. He told us that he had decided to sell the store, and the new owners would take over in a few weeks. He asked us to stock the shelves, help with inventory, and be ready to do whatever he needed us to do in the next two weeks. Sharon and I couldn't believe the news. "Uncle Howard, why are you selling?" I asked in total disbelief.

Uncle Howard explained that it was the right time, and he needed a change. When he shared that they would be selling their house to the new owners, Sharon blurted out, "Where are we going to live, Dad?"

"Well, my girl, we are looking for a home in Mahnomen. Until then, we can rent the teacherage across the street," he answered. "It will be quite a change for all of us." I stood there in total shock. How could this be happening? Moving to Mahnomen? New neighbors?

I did not like what I was hearing. I started to cry and hugged Sharon. "Please don't do this, Uncle Howard!" I cried. My world seemed to be crumbling apart with all these recent changes. How long before they moved to Mahnomen? Sharon would be so far away. How could I not have her next door? My stomach turned like Aunt Gerda's butter churn. Life was not fair! Wait until I shared this with Mom and Dad, or did they already know?

The next few weeks were a blur of frantic activity as we worked long hours to prepare the store for the new owners. The day arrived: Another new chapter as the village store now no longer belonged to a family member. Aunt Clara sold it to Uncle Howard in 1938. Now, in 1957, it came to be owned by a family called Olsens.

Mom tried to soften the blow. She hired me as her assistant in the Post Office. Since the Post Office was inside our house, it made this job a very convenient one. When no one needed stamps or money orders, we could do other activities in our home. When customers needed something, they simply rang the bell attached to the post office counter. The noon hour, of course, was the busiest time when the mailman brought the day's mail. Other times we baked, cleaned the house, read books, did the laundry, or did other chores.

Knowing that this was my last summer at home, I was happy to have more time with Mom and Mary Ann. Dad was, once again, doing road construction work in South Dakota, and Flo was at nurse's training in St. Cloud.

Mary Ann was eight years old and spent a lot of time with our cousin, Roy Allen, who was the same age. That left many hours for me to enjoy Mom's company. She taught me to crochet and knit. I even learned how to make bread and shape the dough into buns, caramel rolls, rohlickes, and loaves. I loved the aroma of fresh-baked bread. To spread butter on the warm slices, watch it melt, and add a spoonful of homemade jam or jelly was always a slice of heaven.

Before they moved to Mahnomen, Sharon and I spent every available minute together. One night at a sleepover, Sharon started crying. "Vonnie, I know you aren't going to be happy with my news." she sobbed. "I've decided to go to Mahnomen High School for my Senior year. I don't want such a structured, strict way of living as I experienced at the Mount." She went on to say that she wanted to have more fun in her last year of high school. Living in Mahnomen, she wouldn't have the long, dreaded bus ride to and from school every day.

"I gave it a try for two years," she continued. "It was not a good fit for me, and I did it to be closer to you."

We talked long into the night, and I shared that I wanted to continue at the Mount as an aspirant. In the second half of my Senior year, I would take the next step of becoming a nun by becoming a postulant. It was the path I felt God was calling me to follow.

I knew Sharon had not been happy at the Mount, yet, I was disappointed that we would not have our senior year together. I couldn't be selfish and upset that she made this decision. I realized that as a postulant, I would not have any contact with her that second part of our Senior year, anyway. So, that was another reason not to object.

Suddenly, it dawned on me how different our lives would soon be. Sharon would graduate from Mahnomen and go on to nurse's training. I would graduate from the Mount and become a novice in the convent.

"Sharon, I still want to keep going out with our friends," I shared. "I think that if I go out with boys now, I won't be tempted later on in life."

We giggled and promised to spend every living moment we could together before I left in the fall for the Mount.

That summer, every Sunday morning after Mass at St. Anne's, I drove to the Island Lake church as they still needed an organist. I became friends with Doris, one of the girls in the choir who was my age. Doris' brother, Con, had dated Flo the year before. One Sunday morning that summer, while I talked with Doris, he came over and asked if he could take me out. Doris laughed and said, "Only if you bring me along." That started my summer romance with Con. Mom and Dad shook their heads and wondered why I was still interested in boys, if the convent was my destination.

During the remaining weeks before Sharon moved to Mahnomen, we spent many hours swimming and hanging out together after my Post Office work. After supper, we joined other kids at Pinehurst lodge and spent our money on the nickelodeon playing our favorite dance tunes, especially ones that called for the jitterbug moves. The circular dance floor was perfect for dancing the bunny hop. Even though the boys seldom danced with us, we girls did not let that prevent us from dancing to almost every song played. Elvis Presley tunes were our favorites.

The summer slipped by. Sharon left for Mahnomen, and I packed my suitcase and set off for the Mount. How strange it was not to have Sharon join me. Here I was, a seventeen-year-old, soon to give up the worldly enticements.

Or was I?

Chapter Ten

My Senior Year: 1957-58

Graduation is an exciting time.
It's both an ending and a beginning;
it's warm memories of the past
and big dreams for the future.
Anonymous

I n the fall of my senior year, I returned to the Mount alone as I had done in my freshman year. Sharon and I promised to write every week to share the happenings of our senior year. I knew many challenges and changes lay ahead of me. The most significant change was preparing to become a postulant. In my first three years as an aspirant, we had little time interacting with the postulants except at evening recreation and choir practice. There was an aura of mystery about them, and their black garb set them apart. I couldn't wait to don that outfit, but I didn't know much about what it meant to become a postulant. When I first saw the postulant garb, I remember how ugly I thought it was. Now that I would be wearing it after Christmas, I felt differently. It would mean that I was seriously taking a further step of dedicating my life to God.

If postulants had already completed their senior year of high school when they came to the Mount, they attended Junior College upstairs in the convent area. Postulants ate their meals with the nuns and went to more prayers than we did. The postulants' dorm was across the hall from the aspirants, but we weren't allowed to enter it. I was sure that I would learn the ins and outs of being a postulant during my fall semester.

That fall, it was a big surprise to discover that Marguerite and I were the only ones in our senior class who chose to return as aspirants. The rest of our aspirant group, Ruth, Donna, Corrine, and Anne, decided to return as boarders and not take the next step of becoming a postulant. How different it would be to have only the two of us continue. Marguerite had not been my closest friend the past three years, but that was about to change.

"Hey, Marguerite," I laughed, "Can you believe that only we Indian girls decided to take on the challenge of becoming a postulant?"

"Yeah, and to think we come from warring tribes! You Chippewas drove us, Sioux, out of Minnesota and into the Dakotas!" she retorted. "We better make sure to leave our war bonnets back on the rez." We both giggled and promised to forget that part of our history.

With new freshman aspirants joining our group, they took our the empty beds of our friends who now lived as boarders in another part of the school. As the oldest of the aspirants, Marguerite and I needed to be leaders and help the newbies. It felt strange to have only the two of us as aspirants out of our senior class, instead of six of us. We definitely would get to know each other now!

Sr. Victorine was not only the aspirant mistress, but also the postulant mistress. She arranged special times with Marguerite and me to share the expectations and rules of being a postulant and learn more about the Benedictine way of life.

My senior academic classes were religion, English XII, Social science, chemistry, music, economic geography, typewriting, GAA (Girls' Athletic Association), and piano and organ. One of my least favorite classes was economic geography. There were only three students: Marguerite, Michaela, and myself. Sr. Leocadia was our teacher, and we met in the library every day. Marguerite and I decided that the nuns didn't know what other class to offer Michaela as she had some learning disabilities. Since we were aspirants, they decided we should start learning about making sacrifices for others' good. Need I mention that we were not pleased with this sacrifice?

None of us girls had heard of GAA and wondered how that would differ from last year's Physical Education classes, and I soon learned it was just a different name to put on the report card. Nothing else had changed.

GAA originated in 1920 to allow girls to participate in volleyball, dance, tennis, bowling, archery, and softball. (I learned that in 1907, people considered girls' basketball harmful for girls as it could cause overexercise and heart lesions. Besides that, they felt it was being too rough and tumble. There was concern that unfettered girls' athletic competition would harm female participants physically and psychologically, and detract from—or even diminish—their femininity. Competitive sports were too masculine, unhealthy, and inappropriate. Many men felt that women belonged in the kitchen, not on the playing fields.)

Because the Mount did not have the facilities to offer many sports, we continued to play softball and have archery classes when weather permitted. In the winter months, we had skating. Of course, walking around the school grounds was always encouraged as a good form of exercise. Without a gym, our athletic opportunities were minimal.

That fall, during a softball game, I was pitching a ball. The batter connected, and the ball came straight towards me. As I swerved to catch it, the ball landed on my nose instead of in my hands. Blood gushed from my nostrils and wouldn't stop. Two of the girls came to my rescue and rushed me inside to get help. Since the bleeding wouldn't stop, one of the nuns drove me quickly to the hospital next to the Mount to have my nose cauterized. That blow to my nose only exacerbated the earlier injuries done to my nose: falling off the couch three times as a baby—breaking it each time—and having my nose punched several times when I was trying to learn the art of boxing.)

The nuns decided to have my nose examined by a specialist since I had trouble breathing through both nostrils. The doctor determined that it was necessary to re-break the broken bones blocking the nasal passages.

After getting my parent's permission, the doctor scheduled the surgery. Mom arrived to be with me. The doctor explained to Mom that he could also straighten the bump on my nose while breaking the bones. That part of the surgery was considered plastic surgery and was not covered by insurance. Because the cost was prohibitive, I didn't beg to have it. My parents had done enough for me. Another argument I used was that I should not be vain about my looks since I would be a nun.

To this day, I can remember the shocked look on Mom's face when she visited me after the surgery. Bandages covered my nose, the area around my eyes was black and blue, and the rest of my face was all swollen and purple.

Mom gasped, "Oh, Vonnie, how much does it hurt?" She held my hand and tried to soothe me as I sobbed with pain.

"Oh, Mom, I sure hope that this surgery was worth it. What if my nose is more crooked than before?" I cried.

Mom assured me that the doctor said the surgery was success-ful and that the most important thing was that my breathing ability would improve. "You'll have to be careful not to injure it again." she continued. "No more tomboy moves for a while!" We both laughed, and I promised to try to follow her advice. Visions of a tomboy nun danced in my head.

Mom stayed with me until I returned to the Mount the follow-ing week. My nose was very tender and sore—no more softball for me that fall!

I continued my organ and piano lessons with Sr. Kathleen. Since it was customary for seniors to perform a piano recital in the spring of their senior year, Sr. Kathleen suggested that Marguerite and I start preparing for it in late fall. After choosing the recital pieces to memorize, we spent hours practicing in the music conser-vatory. I knew Marguerite was much more talented than I was in pi-ano, so I decided I'd have an organ concert instead, but spending hours practicing in the chapel proved to be extremely difficult.

I had to find hours that the nuns were not singing their Divine Office. Since they prayed five times a day, I tried to juggle practice times between my classes and the nuns' chanting hours, so few hours were available. After a few months, I realized how futile this was. By the time I gave up the idea of having an organ recital, it was too late to memorize enough piano pieces for a piano recital. My stubbornness in insisting on switching to an organ recital backfired. I realized even more clearly that stubbornness was a character trait that proved both a weakness and strength in my actions. I should have presented a piano recital.

When Thanksgiving vacation rolled around, I was anxious to return home. Mom wrote to tell me that Father Andrew found an organist to replace me, so I did not have to spend time practicing with the choir. After Fr. Gus left us, it just never was the same. I rel-

My senior photo.

ished not having to spend time with Fr. Andrew preparing for liturgies. Since this holiday and Christmas would be the last time I spent with my family, I was thankful to have uninterrupted time with them. Thanksgiving vacation seemed strange without Sharon next door to us. I traveled miles to Mahnomen instead of walking a few steps to visit her. We tried to squeeze in as much time together as possible before I returned to the Mount.

At the Mount, Sr. Victorine gave Marguerite and me a list of supplies we needed to buy before becoming postulants. We needed to create new name tags. Sr. Victorine explained that the nun died who had the R5 number, so it was available to become my number. It was a blessing to sew only a single-digit behind my initial instead of a double-digit! Sister suggested that we use red embroidery thread on our clothing, a color easily seen by the nuns who sorted the laundry.

During one of our sessions to learn more about becoming a nun, we discovered that our convent had 335 nuns. Most nuns were out in the missions teaching or nursing, and some nuns did housekeeping work. I quickly said I wanted to be a teaching nun, and Marguerite said she wanted the same. Sr. Victorine reminded us that you didn't always get what you wanted in the convent, and it was up to the Reverend Mother to determine that.

"Well, Sister," I interjected, "I always wanted to be a teacher, so I'm sure that's what she will choose for me." Sr. Victorine tried to hide a smile. "Yvonne, you will have to learn how to accept the will of God and learn the vow of obedience."

About a month before Christmas vacation, the seamstress nun measured Marguerite and me for our postulant garb, another exciting step closer to becoming a real nun. Whoever designed the drab postulant's attire was not the most creative designer. Maybe the dress was intended to make one feel less worldly. The dress was one piece, with a plain bodice, a pocket, long sleeves, and large pleats in the skirt. The black, removable cape—with a white detachable collar—covered the bodice while a shoulder-length, black net, see-through veil covered our forehead and hair.

It was customary for a Senior to become a postulant when she returned from Christmas vacation. When I went home for Christmas, I shared my supply list with Mom. She wondered why I had to buy two dozen cloth diapers. Blushing, I told her that nuns did not use Kotex because it was too expensive. We had to use folded diapers for that time of the month. The diapers were laundered in a separate sanitized machine and returned to us to use for the next menstrual period.

Mom said she would gladly furnish me with my monthly needs. I told Mom I had already suggested that to Sr. Victorine. Sister's response had been, "No, Yvonne, that is not acceptable. We lead a simplistic life as nuns." Shaking her head, Mom wondered what she would learn next about convent regulations, and said this rule was like returning to the medieval days. I certainly agreed.

"But, Mom, I better begin my life as a postulant by following their rules," I added. "I'm sure there might be a lot of other rules that will be harder to follow."

Next on the list was that I had to buy at least six men's t-shirts. When I had inquired why we needed t-shirts, Sister explained it was a form of modesty. I decided to ask Dad to go to the men's store and buy a size small for me. Dad looked at me, shook his head from side to side, and followed that with a definitive, "NO!" He reminded me that everyone knew him at the men's clothing store in Mahnomen, and they also knew he had only girls. The store owner would question him and want to know why he was buying such a small size since he always bought a large. Dad did not want to have to explain why.

"Vonnie, you will have to go in and buy those t-shirts yourself. If you have decided this is the life for you, then you'll have to take the bull by the horns and do what you have to do."

I pleaded, but Dad insisted I had to do it myself. He gave me the money, but would not go with me. While in the store, I also had to buy twelve white men's hankies. When I asked Sister about buying cloth handkerchiefs, she said Kleenex was too expensive, and laundering cloth handkerchiefs was much cheaper.

Mom bought some red embroidery thread so that we could start embroidering R5 on the t-shirts and hankies, as well as each diaper. There was nothing feminine about t-shirts, and at least I could still wear my bras under the t-shirt. No one except my family would know all the layers of modesty under the postulant's garb. I swore them to secrecy on all the embarrassing purchases I had to make for my postulant's required list.

As if all of that wasn't bad enough, I had to buy a half dozen long, black, cotton stockings and a pair of black shoes that looked like old Grandma shoes. The closest town with an extensive selection of shoes was in Fosston, about twenty-five miles from home. At least no one there would know me when I had to go in and try on shoes like that. I also had to get a pair of flat black shoes for working outside or casual wear after school and on Saturdays.

I savored every moment of my time at home that Christmas because I knew it would be the last time with my family. Nuns did not spend holidays with their families, and Sr. Victorine shared that nuns only return home for a two-week family visit every three years. Yikes, was I ready for such a cutting of family ties?

Days flew by. Suddenly it was New Year's Eve. Sharon and I talked about what we should do to celebrate my last night of freedom. Why not double-date with Manny and his best friend, Duckhead? We could go to the Flowing Well Tavern for the New Year's Eve dance. I told Mom and Dad our plans.

Once again, my folks shook their heads and wondered about this daughter of theirs that seemed to have two different personalities—the party girl and the convent girl. Oh, well, why not let their middle daughter enjoy herself before heading for the convent?

The boys had the unmarked bottle with a colorless liquid called vodka tucked in their jacket pockets. I pledged my freshmen year not to imbibe until I was eighteen, and I had been faithful to that promise. The temptation to celebrate my last night before entering the convent took precedence, so I decided to break my pledge for this one evening. We set off for the dance, dressed in our poodle skirts and sweater tops, and proceeded to have fun drinking, dancing, talking, laughing, and making fools of ourselves.

Who knows where I got the bubblegum I was chewing when we walked, a bit unsteadily, to the car after the dance? I got in the back seat with Duckhead and did not need the gum when he kissed me. How did the gum end up in Duckhead's hair? Giggling, we tried to remove it, but we couldn't get it out of his curly black hair.

When we drove up to my place, Mom and Dad were up waiting for us. Mom came out to the car. She said we should come in for something to eat and drink. There was no way Duckhead wanted my parents to see what their daughter had done to his hair. The guys quickly said they had to leave. Sharon and I giggled. We got out of the car with a quick goodby and thanks for the night of dancing.

Trying to be as sober as possible, we told my folks we weren't hungry and needed to sleep. After all, I needed to return to the convent the next day to become a postulant!

After packing up my supplies the following day, I ran around to say goodby to my extended family and friends. I explained that the next time I'd come home would be in June after my senior graduation. Hugging and crying, I said goodby with a pounding headache from the night before.

After arriving in Crookston, it was even more difficult to say goodby to Mom and Dad. Watching them get into the car to return home without me brought tears to my eyes. I knew I wanted to become a nun, but leaving family was devastating. Yet, when I prayed, I just knew that God was calling me for a different life—one that meant putting God before family. It was a sacrifice I needed to make in entering the convent. There was an inner calling within me that never seemed to go away. I wanted to dedicate my life to God, no matter how difficult it might prove to be.

Trying to explain why I wanted to become a nun was a challenge. What was drawing me into this monastic way of life? There was still that desire to do something that no other girl from Naytahwaush had done, but it was much deeper than that. The chance for me to dedicate myself as "God's chosen one" was a special gift I felt I had received. Today was that next step after my three and a half years as an aspirant: Becoming a postulant!

After Marguerite and I arrived, Sr. Victorine directed us to the postulant dorm, where we unpacked our suitcases. Our new postulant uniforms lay on our beds. The dorm was smaller than the aspirants' dorm across the hall but looked just the same. We would share the bathroom with the aspirants, and their rec room.

When we finished unpacking, we went to the rec room. There Sr. Victorine explained the procedures to become a postulant. As postulants, we could now enter the convent areas. As far as praying with the nuns, we now were expected to attend the Divine Office's evening prayer called Compline.

She explained that the ritual for becoming a postulant involved making a formal request before all the nuns in their refectory at the evening meal. Sister handed us a typewritten note containing the words we needed to say. Wishing us the best, she told us to return to the dorm and put on our postulant garb. We were to return to the rec room when we were ready to put on the veil so she could help us with that.

Marguerite and I giggled when we pulled up the long black stockings and put on our black heeled shoes. It felt like going back to my childhood wearing long, brown-ribbed socks. We were abandoning the modern nylons of our high school years and replacing them with leggings of yore. Changing from my worldly clothes into the garb of a postulant created an overwhelming feeling of excitement within me, and a realization of my serious commitment to follow my desire to become a nun.

We followed Sr. Victorine to the nun's refectory when the bell rang for the evening meal. A chill of awe and excitement overcame me as I crossed the threshold into the silent refectory. Many people make new resolutions on January first, and here I was, making a total life change.

The refectory was stark and felt like a tomb with all the nuns seated silently at their assigned places with bowed heads. There were a few holy pictures and a giant crucifix on the wall behind the Reverend Mother's front table. The sub-prioress and the oldest nuns sat nearest her. We postulants were the lowest in rank and were to sit at the ends of the tables that created a U-shape on either side of the front table.

As instructed, Marguerite and I walked toward the head table and knelt in front of the Rev. Mother seated in the middle. Kneeling on the cold, brown-tiled floor with my arms extended in a crucifix position, I heard the echoes of my trembling voice, "I humbly beg, for Jesus' sake, to be admitted as a postulant and to learn the ways of St. Benedict."

The Reverend Mother, who was about to approve or disapprove of my entrance into the postulancy, had no idea what I had done the night before. This very girl asking for her approval had decided to live it up in the worldly sense by having her last fling before officially entering the convent as a postulant.

My poodle skirt with a sequined sweater and high heels worn at last night's New Year's Eve dance party was in stark contrast to this postulant's garb that I was now wearing twenty-four hours later. Doing the jitterbug on the dance floor at the stroke of midnight was not entirely fitting into this scene of austerity and silence.

Hearing the Reverend Mother's voice brought me back to reality. "Yes, Miss Yvonne, you are now accepted as a postulant in our Benedictine community." (Our postulant name involved adding a "Miss" before our baptismal name, and I now officially became Miss Yvonne.) Was I ready for this?

After hearing my acceptance, I stood up, bowed, and took my place at the end of one of the tables. There was total silence except for the nun chosen to do spiritual reading while we ate. We kept our eyes cast down during the meal except when the nun seated next to us passed food dishes.

After the meal, we emptied any scraps into a container passed from nun to nun. The serving nuns brought dishpans with hot soapy water and a small mop on a wooden handle to wash our dishes. Well, let's say the water was soapy and hot when the first nuns used it.

Two nuns at a time took on the task of washing and drying each other's dishes. One washed, and one wiped. The cleaned plates were placed upside down on the table for the next meal. Silverware needed to be in the correct place beside the dishes. When we finished, Rev. Mother led us in a prayer of thanks before solemnly leaving the refectory in silence. To think that a few weeks ago, I was part of the students' refectory filled with laughter and constant chatter!

As a postulant, I had many new rules to learn. One was always to hold your hands under the postulant cape when walking as a form of modesty. Getting used to being called "Miss Yvonne" seemed so strange and formal, but it was another step into the world of becoming a nun.

As postulants, we attended classes with the rest of the seniors but did not have after-school contact. We had our postulant dorm for sleeping and attended special classes to learn more about living the Benedictine rule. We joined spiritual reading with the aspirants each day and shared rec time with them. Since there were only two postulants, I appreciated having recreation with the aspirants.

After Compline, we observed the strict night silence that involved no talking in the evenings. Nuns could talk during recreation times after lunch and the evening meal. Since we were still going to school, Miss Marguerite and I were allowed to speak during the day, and only kept silent during meals and after Compline in the evening.

One day in the spring of the year, Sister told me I had a visitor. I walked to the visiting area. Sr. Sophia, the office nun, told me I had a visitor in the guest room. There stood Con, grinning like a Cheshire cat. I couldn't believe my eyes and rushed up to hug him. It was a total surprise and shock to see him. I heard some "Ahem, ahems" coming from the office. Giggling, I suggested we go outside to talk since it was a lovely spring day.

"What on earth brought you here? How did you even know where I was? I haven't seen you for so long!" I asked as the words spilled out of my mouth.

Becoming a postulant. Me (left) and Marguerite.

"Well, I got a job brick-laying in Crookston. I have been thinking of you and wanted to see you," he replied. "I asked your folks if they thought it would be okay to visit you. So they told me where to find you."

At that moment, Sr. Sofia decided it was time to shake some rugs and see what was happening with us. Con and I laughed and moved down the steps and found a bench to sit on to continue our conversation. Con wanted to know if I was serious about becoming a nun. What an interesting question as I had not been writing to him or hadn't seen him for a long time. When we had gone out together during one summer, he seemed somewhat shy and never expressed his deep feelings. I had a big crush on him at the time, but didn't think it was mutual. Now, all of a sudden, he appeared at the convent.

"Well, Vonnie, I came to see if I could make you change your mind," he said as he took my hand.

"Wow, Con, I thought you had never gotten over your crush on Flo," I replied. "I thought I was just someone you took on the rebound."

I suddenly realized that he had liked me in a way that I had not known until now. I was flattered.

"Con, I never knew you felt so attracted to me!" I responded. "I appreciate your concern and feelings for me." We talked for quite a while, and then I hugged Con and thanked him for his visit. After assuring him that I would become a nun, he walked away. I once again had a tugging in my heart, but I knew that this new life required certain sacrifices. I needed to dedicate my life totally to God and no human.

My senior graduation ceremony.

In June, we graduated from high school and had two weeks to go home to vacation with our families. My family attended my graduation ceremonies and then brought me home. I arrived just in time to go to my cousins', Sharon and John, graduation from Mahnomen

Graduation party. Sharon, John, me (left to right).

High School. After graduating with eighteen students at the Mount, seeing over a hundred graduates from their class was very different. After the graduation ceremony, we all went to Sharon's home for a celebration meal. It was the first time many of my relatives saw me in my postulant's garb.

"How long will you have to wear that outfit?" was their first question.

I explained that I received the postulant garb in January and would take the next step in becoming a nun in July. I'd then be called a novice and wear the regular nun's habit. "I can't wait for that day,"

I said with an excited voice. "The only difference will be that my veil will be white and not black like the professed nuns."

"What is it like being a postulant?" my cousin Linda asked. I tried to share that being a postulant was the second phase in becoming a nun. My three and a half years of being an aspirant were like the introductory phase, and gradually I was learning the life of what it meant to be a nun. As a postulant, I was with the nuns during meals and prayers but did not participate in their daily rituals. As far as being a student, I was with the other students during the school day, but was like an outsider who couldn't join in their social activities.

"Why do you want to be a nun?" asked another cousin. "It doesn't sound like much fun!"

I laughed and said, "You don't go into the convent to have fun. It's a way to give up lots of things for the honor and glory of God."

At that moment, Aunt Ruby called us over to enjoy some of her baked goodies. As we started to walk over to the table overflowing with cookies, cake, and bars of every kind, my cousin grabbed my arm and asked, "How long can you be home?" I shared that I had two weeks to be with them.

Knowing it would be a long while before I would have another vacation with my family, I stayed close to home and enjoyed family time together. Spending lots of time with Sharon was high on my list ,since we had so much to talk about and share.

Sharon and I decided to drive to Detroit Lakes to visit Father Gus at his new parish. It would also give us more time to be alone and test Sharon's driving skills, as driving was not one of her favorite activities.

"Let's hope there are not many cars on the road," I said to her. "I have come this far in becoming a nun and want to discover what being a novice is all about. Keep your eyes on the road, Sharon!"

Our folks made sure we had called Father Gus to find out what time was best to visit. It had been two years since we had seen him. The surroundings in this large parish seemed so formal compared to Naytahwaush. Wow, he even had a parish secretary who informed him that his guests had arrived.

Feeling a bit awkward in this unknown territory, Sharon and I looked at each other, wondering what would happen next. Father

Gus came out of his office with a big smile on his face. He made us feel right at home and took us into his office.

"Well, my favorite girls from Naytahwaush, sit down and tell me what I owe the pleasure of this visit to?" he started saying as he motioned for us to sit in two comfortable chairs.

I giggled and said, "Well, we're not here to confess our sins!" That broke the ice. We settled in like old times and told him about graduation and our decisions for the future. Sharon shared that she had decided to attend nursing school in Grand Forks, ND.

"As for me, I guess you can tell what I am still planning to do with my life," I said, "I know you didn't think I should make that decision at such an early age."

He replied, "Vonnie, I still don't think this is the life for you. You are too filled with a zest for life. Please remember you can leave at any time before you make final vows."

I looked at him and wondered why he had never approved my decision to become a nun. At that point, he changed the subject. He wanted to know all about our families and what was happening in Naytahwaush.

His secretary knocked on the door and said an emergency had come up and needed him. With that, we said a quick farewell as Father gave us each a big hug and said how he missed us and being a pastor in Naytahwaush. Sharon and I reluctantly walked with him out of his office and waved a sad goodbye. I wondered if I would ever see him again.

On the way back home, Sharon and I spent the time remembering all the good times we had when Father Gus had been our priest. "Remember when..." we'd each say and then have a good laugh, especially remembering being his altar girls during weekdays.

"Of course, our parents didn't realize he paid us a quarter each day we went to Mass," I said, "They thought we were such religious little girls!"

Sharon said, "And how about when we competed on who could save the most souls from Purgatory?" One story led to another. Before we knew it, we were back at Sharon's, all in one piece. No accidents!

The night before I returned to the Mount, Sharon came for a sleepover. John, my cousin, who also had graduated with us, came over to visit and say his goodby. We started talking about our future, and John shared that he was going to Bemidji State College to become a teacher.

When asked what I would be, I said I had always wanted to be a teacher, but the Reverend Mother would decide. That was part of being a nun. My family once again just shook their heads and wondered how their independent daughter would fare in that type of setting.

Everyone decided we should end my last evening by playing a game of canasta, a game that had become the family's favorite game next to whist. Sharon and I talked until late into the night after the card game.

The following day we drove Sharon back to Mahnomen.

After another tearful goodbye, she promised to come to the Mount for my novitiate ceremony in July. Mom, Dad, Mary Ann, and I drove off to Crookston. My two-week vacation had gone by too quickly.

When we arrived at the Mount, the folks again asked me if becoming a nun was the life I wanted, and I said it was. Tearfully, we hugged and said goodbye. I loved my family, but I knew I wanted to find out the real meaning of living the life of a nun. Tomorrow was the beginning of a week-long SILENT retreat.

How could I survive a week without talking?

Chapter Eleven

My Novitiate 1958-59

To pray, to hope, to love ...
to see things in new lights ...
what better curriculum for a canonical year?
Anonymous

W hen we returned from our home visit, Miss Marguerite and I looked at each other, realizing what a serious commitment we were about to make. Here we were, eighteen-year-old girls, just out of high school and making our life decisions. Our inner fears became somewhat tamed as we talked and realized that we had the year of Novitiate and three years of the Juniorate before we made our FINAL commitment of vows. We would be the ripe old age of twenty-two before we crossed that bridge. In the meantime, we promised to help one another in the process. After all, since there were only two of us in our group, we had only each other to share and work out any further challenges along the way to the final profession of vows.

Since we were the first-ever from our Indian reservations to become nuns, we were determined to be the best nuns ever. We would make our people proud, even though the convent instructed us in the rules of humility.

In the history of our tribes, we Ojibway chased the Sioux from Minnesota into the Dakotas. Was the fighting spirit going to be tamed in our convent setting? Miss Marguerite and I had constantly competed in our high school studies and piano to see who could be the best. Could this critical component of each of our personalities be tamed in the Novitiate? How would that play out in our striving to become more humble than the other? How would the convent life teach us about the dichotomy of pride vs. humility?

Before becoming a novice, one of the preparations was to have an eye exam and get rimless glasses. My black cat-eye-rimmed ones were not allowed: They were too worldly and brought attention to one's face.

Nuns needed to be concerned about their inner beauty, not physical beauty. We also had to have a physical exam to ensure we were healthy specimens.

The next step was to spend time with the seamstress who would sew our nun habits, including even our underslips. After Sister finished our measurements, we met with Sr. Victorine, who gave us a lecture on the meaning of wearing a religious habit.

Sister explained that religious habits were the most recognized sacred symbols for centuries to proclaim that the wearer consecrated herself to God. Since the early Church, men and women who wanted to give their lives to God have donned modest, austere clothing to reflect their spiritual commitment.

A Benedictine nun's habit consists of a tunic, belt, scapular, and veil, all black. Under the veil is a white pleated headdress called a coif, which frames the nun's face. Over the coif, Novices wear a white veil but fully professed nuns wear a black one.

"Every piece of garment you have is blessed," said Sr. Victorine. "The beautiful blessings explain each item's meaning and help a nun to live her vocation as a bride of Christ."

"The belt reminds us that Christ wore chains," she said, referring to his obedience. "The scapular represents our commitment to conversion—to take on the yoke of the Lord, which is sweet. A yoke is usually carried by two: We carry half, and Christ carries the other half."

The veil is the sign of the nun's consecration. "You put the veil on, and you know you belong to God," she continued. "You are not your own. The veil and coif cover the nun's hair, which the Scriptures call a woman's 'adornment,' to protect her from vanity and to remind her that she is given entirely to God."

"You act as you wear," she said. "If people wear jeans and T-shirts, they act differently than if dressed in a suit. A certain dignity goes with wearing the habit; one is expected to carry a certain nobility. Clothing does express your heart."

Benedictines wear black tunics, she explained, both as a sign of repentance and because it was the cheapest fabric in the fifth century when the Italian, St. Benedict, founded the order. "Wearing the habit is also a sign of poverty," she said.

After sharing the symbolism of the clothing, Sr. Victorine reviewed what the year of Novitiate would require of us. She reminded us that it was a time of intense spiritual growth both as individuals and community members. A novice immerses herself in the Benedictine identity, and seeks God with the support of the Benedictine community.

"You will intensely study the Rule of St. Benedict and the meaning of monastic profession through the guidance of your Novice Mistress," she continued. "As a novice, you will engage in many hours of prayer and some work within the monastery. Remember the motto of St. Benedict: 'Ora et Labora.' Pray and Work."

"It is a time when you may not speak to the professed nuns in our convent, and you may talk to the Novice Mistress and each other during evening recreation. Silence is the essential key to becoming closer to your God during this year." She added, "You already know that this is a year of decisions that requires a year in which you can not see your family members."

I thought how difficult that would be for me. It was part of the testing ground to determine our dedication and sincerity as novices. We could only communicate with our family by writing a letter at Christmas and Easter.

To prepare us spiritually for our Novitiate, we needed to participate in a week-long retreat of total silence. I had participated in three-day retreats during my high school years, but this retreat felt like a "go-for-the-gold" one with much higher stakes. I needed to prove I had the mental and spiritual stamina to become a nun.

Retreats included hours and hours of meditation, but no one explained or showed us how to meditate. Sr. Victorine told us to choose a spiritual reading book and then meditate on what we had read. I don't know why I didn't just ask how to do that! Maybe I thought meditation would act like osmosis and simply seep into my soul.

Our first meditation of the day was early in the morning, and I must admit that many of my meditative moments included an early morning nap. All the people who knew me could understand what a massive challenge it would be to be silent for a week. Being silent required lots of energy!

During our retreat, I had my first introduction to the daily routine of a nuns' prayer life:

6:00: Divine Office of Prime and Lauds

6:30: Morning Meditation

7:00 Daily Mass

7:30 Breakfast

8:00 Gregorian chant practice

8:30 Work of the day/Classes learning about Benedictine Rule

11:30 Divine Office: Terce, Sext, None

12:00 Lunch

12:30 Recreation

1:00 Divine Office: Vespers

1:30 Work of the day/ Spiritual Reading

5:30 Divine Office: Matins

6:00 Evening meal

6:30 Recreation

7:30 Divine Office: Compline/ Stations of the Cross

8:00 Evening silence

(During our retreat week, we did not have classes or recreation because we could not talk.)

A few times during that week, I slipped a written note to Miss Marguerite. I wanted to know if the silence was as hard for her as it was for me. Another time I wanted to know if meditating was getting any easier. I guess I just needed to know how she was faring during all this silence. I couldn't talk to her verbally, but no one told us we couldn't write messages. Somehow, those seven long days and nights ended with my meditative skills still at the primitive level. I told God I was positive it was a sure sign for me to become a nun since I had survived that week of silence. Praise the Lord!

Right after our retreat, Sr. Victorine shared the procedure for choosing our nun's name. "When you become a nun, you must renounce the world and all of its possessions," she said. One way to do this was by taking a new saint's name to replace our baptismal name. She gave us the form to fill out with our three requests saying we had a few days to think about it before submitting our choices to the Rev. Mother.

That night Miss Marguerite and I talked about names to choose. Since Father Augustine had done so much to help me in our parish, I decided on his name. Then I told Miss Marguerite that I'd write it three times instead of choosing three different names to make sure I got my choice. She looked at me, giggled, and said that her priest also had been very good to her and her family. Why not do the same as I did? So the next day, we handed our forms, sealed in an envelope, to Sr. Victorine. She gave them to Mother Mary John. I secretly felt proud of my creative ability to get the name I wanted.

I was excited about the next step in my journey: Becoming a novice with a wedding ceremony. I would enter the chapel as a bride of Christ dressed in a white bridal gown and veil. The nuns kept a wardrobe of used wedding gowns that people had donated in previous years for this occasion. Miss Marguerite and I went to see which dress was the closest fit for each of us. We had no choice but to take the wedding dress that fit. The nun in charge handed us a veil to go with the dress. Having had no experience in this area, I had nothing to compare with other wedding gown choices. It simply was exciting to think we would be dressed in a wedding gown to marry our Saviour, Jesus Christ.

July 2, 1958, arrived—my wedding day! We were two excited eighteen-year-old girls getting a new name and donning the Benedictine nun's garb. Our parents and family members had been invited to the Mount to celebrate with us for our bridal day. We shivered with excitement having them here to join all the nuns in our new commitment. I was sad that Fr. Gus could not be with me (even though I knew he still did not approve of my choice), but he had previous commitments that he could not change on this day. It did not bother me that Father Andrew couldn't make it!

The first shock of the morning started when I put away my cat-eyed rimmed glasses and donned my rimless ones. (A sign of giving up worldly possessions.) I looked in the mirror and quickly bade goodby to my vanity. I looked like I aged twenty years with such plainness.

Two nuns came to our postulant's dorm to help us with our bridal gowns and veils before entering the chapel. Butterflies danced in my stomach. Today was the day I had looked forward to since that September four years earlier when I left home to be an aspirant. As the organ began to play, it was our signal. We began solemnly walking down the aisle to the front pew.

Dressed in my bridal gown.

As I got near the front, I spotted my family on one side of the aisle and Miss Marguerite's family on the other. I smiled at my family with tears of happiness and excitement, and took my place in the front pew. The Mass began.

After the sermon, Mother Mary John walked up to the altar, turned around, and faced the congregation. She welcomed everyone and then called me to come forth to receive my habit and a new name.

"Yvonne Marie Rumreich, from this day forward, as a new member of our Benedictine community, you will be known as Sister Mona."

What? Had I heard her wrong? I was supposed to be Sr. Augustine, as those were the three names I had given for my choices.

"Excuse me," I whispered to the Rev. Mother as I looked at her in utter disbelief, "I didn't ask for that name."

It was the Rev. Mother's turn now to look at me in disbelief. Who was this young woman already questioning decisions made by her? Bending down, she whispered back, "You don't look like an Augustine. We already have a Sr. Monica, the name of Augustine's mother, and Mona was the closest name I could think of that had a connection to St. Augustine." With that short explanation, the next thing I heard was, "Go and get dressed, Sr. Mona!"

With a heavy heart and a new name that I had NOT chosen, I obediently walked from the altar, out of the chapel, and downstairs, where two nuns were waiting to help me dress in my new nun's garb. As I tried to wrap my new name around my head, I heard Marguerite's footsteps right behind me. I tearfully turned around to ask her what name she got. She started to cry and said the Rev. Mother gave her the name of Sr. Isabel, in honor of Rev. Mother's favorite niece. Then she blurted out, "I bet Mona wasn't the village prostitute like Isabel was in our Indian village."

Feeling so sorry for her, I suddenly didn't mind my new name at all. In fact, it had rather a nice ring to it.

The next thing I knew, two nuns in the downstairs room helped us shed our bridal attire to replace it with our new nun's habit. We replaced our silky nylons with black cotton stockings, and our feet slipped into black stodgy-heeled shoes. Over our bra, we added a t-shirt, followed by a floor-length brown/white seersucker slip with two huge pockets.

Next came the black-flowing habit secured at our waist with a three-inch, black, woven cincture acting as a belt. The waistband had hooks and eyes to fasten the ends together. Then came the scapular, which covered the front and back of the habit.

On our arms, we put on black nylon sleevelets with elastic around the top end to keep in it place above the elbow and grosgrain ribbon with snaps to secure it at the wrists. The nuns pulled our hair back to fit underneath a white cotton skull cap.

They placed the pleated white coif under our chin, pulled the ends tightly around our face, and secured them on the top of our head with a big safety pin. The coif ends were "braided" to shape the back of our heads. A stiff white piece of plastic shaped into a rectangular frontal piece covering our forehead had ties in the back to fit our head. Onto this frame, they pinned a long cotton white veil that came down three-quarters of the length of our habit. We were now fully dressed as a novice.

As we returned to the altar, Rev. Mother bowed and asked us to face the congregation. In solemn tones, she proclaimed the two new members of their Benedictine community: Sr. Mona and Sr. Isabel. Everyone clapped. We slowly walked back to our front row seats, and the rest of the Mass resumed.

After Mass, all the nuns went back to their refectory. Sr. Isabel and I celebrated with our family and friends in the students' refectory to eat a special feast, including a bridal cake.

After eating, everyone gathered outside to talk and enjoy the special occasion. Before I walked out to join my visitors, Flo and Sharon grabbed me and took me into the girls' bathroom so they could see the multiple layers that were part of a nun's habit. They shook their heads.

Sharon quickly said, "I'm sure glad I don't have to put on all those layers every day. Think how hot it must be in the summertime. Vonnie, oops, I mean, Sr. Mona, you even sweat when you wear shorts. What on earth are you going to do now?" We giggled and returned to spend the afternoon taking photos and visiting with the rest of the family.

The celebration came to an end later that afternoon. I hugged everyone and tried not to let my pleated coif get in the way as we kissed and said our goodbyes. Tears were in everyone's eyes as they walked to their cars. I, too, cried as I waved goodbye and walked

The day I became Sr. Mona.

back through the convent doors. I realized that I now had a new family, the Benedictine community of Mount St. Benedict. I must say goodby to the family that had been a part of my life since I was born.

Because we were now officially nuns, Sr. Isabel and I moved up to the monastery's nuns' quarters, a dorm that we shared with junior professed nuns. (Junior professed nuns had three years after the Novitiate to determine if convent life was their true vocation, and if so, they took the next step called final vows to remain forever in the convent as the bride of Christ.) The dorm was similar to our postulant dorm, as we still had the white sheets pulled around our beds to act as a privacy barrier. Having only two habits and two pairs of shoes, we didn't need much closet space. The small dresser held our underwear, hankies, and a few personal articles such as a comb, brush, and toothbrush.

As novices, we could not speak with any of the professed nuns because it was our year of silence and meditation. We met our novice mistress, Sr. Aquina, the nun we could talk to during the year at the given recreation times and classes when she taught us about the Rule of St. Benedict.

She was a tall, thin nun who had a lovely chuckle when she laughed. She shared with me that she had grown up in Fosston, a town somewhat near Naytahwaush, and I felt an immediate bond with her. Sister must have realized the difficulty of young women trying to adjust to the trials and sacrifices of the Novitiate. She shared that she would try to make the transition from a world of chatter to a world of silence as easy as possible.

I looked forward to recreation time after the noon and evening meal to break the silence of the day. During the summer and early fall, the nuns spent much of their recreation time gathered together outside under the trees helping with garden produce such as shelling peas, snapping beans, or husking corn. We novices sat separately from the other nuns and could talk among ourselves with our novice mistress. Our small trio was in stark contrast to the large groups of chattering nuns.

The professed nuns had their vast recreation room, but we had a separate small room where we played board games or enjoyed simple daily conversations.

During inside recreation, Sr. Aquina demonstrated how to darn the holes in our black stockings whenever that might be needed. I hoped my stockings would last a long, long time without getting holes!

She also taught us to walk in the corridors with downcast eyes and hands folded under our front scapular in silent prayer. She explained how important it was not to speak unless we confessed a fault. When this happened, we were to quietly knock at her door, say, "Praise be to Jesus Christ, I have a fault to confess," get down on our knees, and tell what we had done wrong. Depending on the severity of the fault, she sometimes gave us extra prayers to say. If we had offended another nun, she had us confess publicly in the refectory as we knelt and told the nuns our misdeed. Then the Rev.

Mother would give us a penance to do and for all to hear. I wondered then and there how often I might experience that.

Since we needed to keep busy this Novitiate year, Rev. Mother decided to have Sr. Isabel and me refinish all the floors of the older nuns' private bedrooms. When we worked in a nun's bedroom, she had to move elsewhere. After helping each nun move her personal belongings, we removed all the furniture from the bedroom into the hallway to refurbish the floor. We did all this in silence.

Since the bedrooms were small, we each were assigned a different room. They gave us paintbrushes, putty knives, rags, and a gallon container of varnish remover. We poured the smelly liquid on the floor, spread it on the narrow boards with the paintbrush, and waited to have the varnish remover on the floor start to bubble. When that happened, we tackled that area with the putty knife to scrape off the layers of old varnish.

Even though the directions stated that the room should be well ventilated, that was impossible as most bedrooms did not have windows. It was a slow and laborious process, but it kept us busy and productive most of that year. We often wondered if the fumes might affect our brains and that we might be brain dead by the end of our Novitiate.

Because we were doing such an excellent job on the bedroom floors, Rev. Mother decided to refinish the recreation room floor. Because that floor space was so huge, they brought us an electric scrubber to remove the varnish after we had hand-brushed it on the floor.

Of course, we also had other chores to do. One was to help in the laundry the day that sheets were washed and mangled. I can still remember my first disastrous day in the laundry.

Sr. Bertha, the head nun in the laundry, told me to get on one side of the gigantic mangle and had another nun stand on the opposite end. Sr. Bertha and another nun fed the sheets into the mangle wide enough for an entire sheet's width. As the sheet came through the mangle, I grabbed the end. It was scorching hot and burned my fingers, and I dropped it immediately. The sheet proceeded to get tangled as it rolled back toward Sr. Bertha.

She yelled at me, stopped the mangle, and tried to get the tangled sheet out. How was I to know how hot the sheets were when they had gone through the mangle? Of course, I could not speak to a professed nun and had to hang my head in shame. I wished there was a saint of laundry to pray to, so I wouldn't fail again. As the next sheet came through, I knew I had to grab the end no matter how hot it was.

My next lesson was to quickly fold the sheet with the other nun on my side before the next sheet came through the mangle. My fingers were tingling and blistered by the end of my laundry work. Finishing the sheets, I rushed back to the convent to confess to Sr. Aquina my fault for tangling the sheet. I wanted to get there before Sr. Bertha reported my misdeed.

That night, I knelt in the refectory to admit my weakness for causing distress and problems in the laundry room. After that incident, I never was a favorite of Sr. Bertha. She cringed every time I had laundry duty. My fingers became a bit more callused over time as they grabbed the hot sheets. I dreaded laundry duty every week.

If I was not great at folding sheets in the laundry, I soon learned that I was even worse at pleating coifs with Sr. Inez. Our coifs were rectangular pieces of linen that looked like dishtowels when washed, and to transform them into coifs was an art form. Sr. Inez told me to observe her as she went through the laborious steps.

The coif machine had a hand crank like the old wash machines, and each turn of the crank would pull the wet material backward to make a creased pleat. When the rectangular piece was all pleated, Sister placed heavy flat irons on top and, like magic, shaped the pleats into the hourglass shape of a coif.

When it was my turn to try, I started cranking the material into pleats. Somehow the pleats didn't magically stay together like when Sr. Inez did it. After many attempts, I successfully pleated the whole piece, but when I tried to shape the pleats with the heavy irons, they all bubbled up out of control. After an afternoon of messed up coifs, Sr. Inez lost her patience and told me to stand and watch.

Sad to say, I never successfully pleated a coif. Sr. Inez asked Sr. Aquina to give me other duties. She asked to have Sr. Isabel return each week, since she had learned so quickly. Secretly, I was thrilled to be relieved of that duty. Folding scalding hot sheets didn't seem so bad after all.

Another job was to help in the kitchen when the farmer brought the milk disks to be washed and dried. Cleaning the milking equipment was a tedious job taking about an hour, and I don't think that the farmer realized that we nuns in white veils were not supposed to talk with him. He must have thought I was retarded: I was only able to smile and nod my head as he shared stories from the farm.

We could write to our family during our Novitiate year at Christmas and Easter, so I decided to write a little each day to share my life in the Novitiate. When our novice mistress announced a few weeks before Christmas that we should begin to write our Christmas letter, I was so proud of myself because I had pages and pages and pages already written. When I brought my epistle to be mailed to my parents, Sr. Aquina gasped.

"Sister, you are not to be writing every day, just a short letter to wish your family a Blessed Christmas." Because I was so upset and had tears in my eyes, she told me that since I had not understood the rules for writing at Christmas, she would make an exception and mail my pages. But, I was to follow the rules for the Easter letter!

In my parent's Christmas letter, they shared that Aunt Clara was at St. Francis Hospital, located on the adjoining property to our Motherhouse. Mom said they drove slowly around the Mount whenever they visited her in the hospital, hoping to see me walking outside, and that never happened. It made me sad and lonesome to think that they had been so close but yet so far.

Sister Isabel and I wondered what the next big job might be when we finally finished applying new varnish to the rec floor. The lingering varnish remover odor still clung to our nostrils, as well as the smell of the varnish itself. Doing all this work on our knees in our nun's garb was no easy feat.

By the time we completed refinishing all the floors, it was springtime and time to do spring cleaning. Our next job was to wash all the windows inside and out in the monastery. The ground-level windows were not difficult to clean, and we used vinegar water and newspapers to accomplish this job. It was just like I had done at home when Mom and I cleaned windows.

The challenge came with the windows on the second and third floors of the convent. Sr. Isabel and I learned to be creative when we tried to clean the outside of the upper story windows. After opening the window, one of us perched on the window sill while the other pressed down on the other's legs to prevent her from falling out the window. Of course, all this had to be in silence.

One day the Rev. Mother walked by and saw us. She chuckled and told us to be careful, but soon returned with a candy bar for each of us as a bit of gratitude for our hard work. We were giddy with excitement like little kids in a candy store who received an unexpected treat. We silently bowed our heads in gratitude before enjoying the sweet morsel. Life was good! We were thrilled.

In June, the diocesan priests always came to our Motherhouse for a week-long retreat. Sr. Aquina instructed Sr. Isabel and me that we should never let the priests see us if we were outside. Priests strolled around the premises for their meditative times. The nuns worked hard to make the areas spick and span for the priests. One day, my job was to sweep the sidewalks. Somehow, the timing of my sweeping occurred when the priests were coming for their daily walks.

Remembering the warning not to let the priests see me, I looked up and saw some priests approaching. It so happened that the bakery window was nearby on the ground level and open. It was the closest exit I could find. I panicked and crawled through it, broom and all. Sr. Christina, our dear baker nun, was busy kneading bread. She looked up just at that moment to watch this unexpected visitor come tumbling through her window. To this day, I can still see her open mouth and startled expression staring at me in disbelief. Since I could not talk to a professed nun, I just got off the floor, bowed, took my broom, and ran out into the hallway.

Luckily for me, Sister was a very quiet nun who seldom spoke. She grew up in a Bohemian village with Czech as her primary language, which limited her English. I'm sure she wouldn't have found words to explain to the other nuns what had just happened. The incident became her secret and mine. Therefore, I did not end up confessing that misdeed in the refectory.

Despite the year of silence and the limited number of people we could speak with, Sr. Isabel and I had a competitive year of togetherness in everything we did. We raced to see who could get to the chapel first, say the most novenas and Stations of the Cross, and work the hardest. We even competed in Lenten fasting, which resulted in losing weight and moving the cincture fasteners to a different notch. Of course, she won on being the best coif maker and rule-follower.

In July, we finished our Novitiate year, our year of silence. Never in my life would I have believed that this would have been possible for me to accomplish. It was a gift of time and quiet to search into my inner being and become spiritually aware of inner peace. Silence and separateness from others made this possible. It was now time to learn the ropes of becoming a Junior Nun.

Chapter Twelve

My Juniorate: 1959-61

Education is the sum total of one's experience,
and the purpose of higher education is
to widen our experiences beyond the
circumscribed existence or our own daily lives.
Mortimer Adler

A fter the year-long Novitiate, Reverend Mother arranged a meeting with Sr. Isabel and me and asked if we wished to continue on our journey of becoming professed Benedictine nuns. We both answered that we chose to follow our vocation of dedicating our lives to God. After the year of concentrated prayer, I felt an inner peace and connection to my God. Spending the rest of my life dedicated to His service felt like the right path for me. I felt honored to be called a bride of Christ.

Sr. Isabel and I joined the annual summer retreat for all the nuns. On July 11, 1959, we took our next step on the road to becoming a full-fledged nun. We had a special ceremony and Mass for this event and invited our families to join in this special celebration.

It began with a Mass. After the sermon, Mother Mary John walked up to the altar and addressed the congregation. She called the two of us to the altar and had us openly profess before all that we wished to take our Benedictine vows of stability, fidelity to the monastic way of life, and obedience. (Implied are the promises of poverty and chastity in the Benedictine vows, but stability, fidelity, and obedience receive primary attention in the Rule of St. Benedict, perhaps because of their close relationship with community life.)

The ceremony was called Simple Profession of Vows, in which we pledged our vows for three years. At the end of these three years, I would have the opportunity to make my Final Vows if the monastery and myself felt I was ready to make a life's commitment to be a Benedictine nun. After reciting our vows, Sr. Isabel and I exchanged our white veil for a black one. We could now have the privilege of speaking with all the members of our community of nuns. Our year of Silence was over.

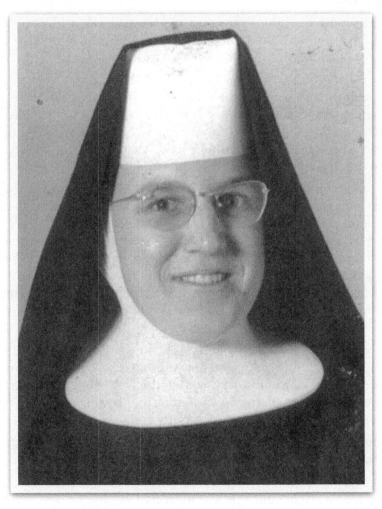

I received the black veil for Juniorate.

After Mass, we celebrated a special meal with our families. The joy of seeing my family after a whole year was overwhelming, and it seemed like we could not stop hugging, laughing, crying with everyone trying to talk at once. Since it was a lovely day, we went outside after our celebratory meal and sat in a circle on the convent grounds to catch up on the past year's events. I explained to my family that I would spend my first two years of Juniorate at our Motherhouse, where Sr. Isabel and I would go to Junior College with the other Junior nuns.

Becoming a Junior nun gave me the privilege of having a two-week vacation with my family. My parents were overjoyed to return to Naytahwaush with their daughter, the nun.

During those two weeks, it was so strange to have so many people gawk and want to come up to see if it was really me dressed as a nun. There were more stares as I walked into the Pinehurst Lodge one day with my family—a nun in a place where they sold liquor! Dad wanted to show his friends that I was still his daughter, so he ordered a beer for me from the bar. How could I refuse?

We had many family gatherings with Mom's family in Naytahwaush and Dad's in Mahnomen. Aunts, uncles, and cousins joined us for picnics and meals where I feasted on favorite family recipes. It also was a time of much laughter as we shared childhood stories. Every night my family and I played cards, including poker. I won a few dollars, so the family wondered what I would do with that since I had taken the vow of poverty. I assured them I would share my vast winnings with the nuns when I returned to the convent.

The nuns had instructed me to be very modest and not let my family see me without my habit. How on earth could that be in our tiny house with one bathroom and sharing a bedroom with my little sister? I threw caution to the wind and let my family see me in my nightclothes. After all, they were family, not strangers.

The two weeks whirled by, but I felt so lucky to have the opportunity to be with my family and strengthen family ties. After all, it would be another three years before I could do this again.

I felt special in my role as a nun, but I also sensed a feeling of separateness. Choosing this vocation had set me up on a pedestal, and I realized that I was different. It was hard to explain, but I had built an invisible wall with my vows and dedication to God above family. When the time came to return to the Mount, I realized that separation more deeply. And yet, I was anxious to discover more about the life of a Junior nun.

During the summer, most of the teaching nuns returned to the Motherhouse before leaving to attend colleges and universities in various places to complete their educational degrees. For the nuns remaining at the Motherhouse, the Rev. Mother allocated different summer jobs for them to do.

She assigned me to work at our nursing home for the elderly, a few miles from the Motherhouse. Since this was a brand new experience, I wondered what my duties would be. That first morning, Sr. Imelda, the head nurse at St. Vincent's Rest Home, introduced herself and said she would be my supervisor for the summer. She had a twinkle in her eye and a lovely smile. I liked her immediately and had a feeling we would become great friends.

For the first few days, I shadowed Sr. Imelda. Since I did not have the training to be a nurse, I was to keep the patients happy by spending time with them. My job involved:

- Talking with the patients (which was no problem for me).
- Encouraging them to share stories of their lives.
- Making them comfortable.

Many of the elderly could walk and get around by themselves, but some were bedridden.

As the weeks went by, I became a hairdresser for the women who wanted their hair washed, curled, and coifed. They shared their life stories as I worked with them, which kept me entertained. Because I had grown up with a card-playing family, I played cards with those who asked me to join them. I fed the patients that were not capable of doing it themselves. Some wanted me to sit and pray with them, while others wanted to sit and talk or listen to their story. I grew to love being with the senior citizens and looked forward to being with them every day.

Toward the end of the summer, Sr. Imelda came to me and explained that some night nurses had taken ill. Would I be willing to do night duty with her?

I quickly said, "Sure, Sister, but I have no idea what night duty involves."

"You will do just fine, Sr. Mona," she replied. "I will be on duty also. We continually make the rounds to make sure all the patients are sleeping and helping those who might be awake." She then reassured me that I could come and get her if I needed help.

The first hours of that long night went smoothly. Then Sr. Imelda had an emergency with one of the patients, and I was on my own. I checked on several patients and then heard moans coming out of the room on my right. I rushed into the room, and this gigantic gent was moaning and struggling to get out of bed. He said he needed to go to the bathroom. Before I got to his side of the bed, he was on the floor and peeing without control.

I knew Sr. Imelda couldn't come right at that moment. What on earth was I to do? I had to clean him up and then attempt to lift him back to bed, but he was like a helpless giant of dead weight. To this day, I will never know what forces from above gave me the strength to get him back in bed. After cleaning him, I cleaned up the mess on the floor. I quickly added a few extra prayers that he would be alright despite the fall. By the time I had everything back in order, the gent was loudly snoring as if nothing had happened. This night duty life was not the quiet, peaceful shift I thought it would be!

When I reported to Sr. Imelda, I told her of my disastrous experience. She immediately went to check on the old gentleman. He was fast asleep, and Sister assured me that he would not be sleeping so peacefully if he were injured. When we checked on him in the morning, he was all smiles and acted as if nothing had happened the night before. I was one happy nun—with a bit of a sore back—who hoped that was the end of my night duties.

All the nuns returned to participate in a three-day retreat at the end of the summer. Sometimes this was when Rev. Mother handed out the assignments for the coming year, if she had not done it earlier in the summer. After our retreat, the teaching nuns left for their year's duties. The Motherhouse seemed quiet without several hundred nuns running around.

A few years before I entered the convent, Mother Mary John created Corbett College at the Mount. Having a junior college meant that the young professed nuns could remain at our Motherhouse to get their first years of a college education. Staying at the Mount saved money on tuition, room, board, and supplies, and it was staffed by teaching nuns from our convent.

In September, we began our first days of college and had most of our classes in the recreation room set aside for Junior nuns. There was a long wooden table that took up most of the room. The second-year Junior nuns joined us, so Sr. Isabel and I were not alone in our small classes.

I will never forget Sr. Patricia, our English, Literature, and Latin professor. She was a nervous perfectionist, constantly pulling her white handkerchief from her pocket to wipe the sweat from her face and neck. We soon learned that she appreciated having the windows open for fresh cool air. As soon as she entered the room, we vied with each other to get "brownie points" by being the first to open the window. Her nervous twitches and redness of her face were a daily part of each class.

As we studied Chaucer and *The Canterbury Tales*, she expected us to read the different passages using the Old English pronunciation. Sr. Patricia had us keep meticulous notebooks in all the classes she taught us. We had to hand them in periodically so she could read and edit our notes. If you only got an A, it was a disappointment because she gave an A++++ for exceptional work.

All of us immediately checked to see who got the most +'s and strove to get more than that the next time. Heaven forbid if you ended up with a B as a grade. It was like getting an F in other classes. Sr. Patricia had raised the bar so high, so our job was to study and get the best grades possible. We all stayed up beyond curfew each night to get the most +'s possible.

In contrast, Sr. Lamberta, our biology teacher, was the exact opposite in temperament with her easy manner and calm demeanor. Even her gait as she entered the room made you relax and yet aspire to do your best. Biology became a favorite subject because of her teaching style and her attempts to make learning meaningful and fun. We had frog dissections in the lab to learn their anatomy and trips to the pond to discover their natural habitat.

Sr. Lamberta had us getting up before dawn to go bird watching. Sr. Isabel was a naturalist for learning bird calls and recognizing the various birds. I wondered what had happened to my Indian heritage, as I seemed to lack the ability to learn from Mother Nature.

In Naytahwaush, we lived among the lakes and trees, but I had never taken the time to listen intently and learn the sounds and gifts of Mother Earth. Now, at age nineteen, I attempted to cultivate a closeness, awareness, and appreciation of Nature and its contributions to humankind.

Father Roger, our chaplain and teacher, taught theology and Bible classes at Corbett College. Since he could not enter the convent area, we went downstairs to his high school classroom when he was not teaching the Mount students.

Studying the Bible was a new class for me. Learning about the Old and New Testaments required hours of reading, and it wasn't easy to understand the meaning of the different passages. I remembered the gold-edged, red leather Bible at home that was more of a decoration on the bookshelf than a book to be read. Father assured us that the Bible was a book to read and studied throughout our lives. We should not have to worry about reading and digesting every page during our two years of college study.

Sr. Mary Magdalene taught us Speech Arts. She detected my lisp and prepared tongue placement exercises to overcome it. I became very conscious of this imperfection and nervous when I had the duty of reading during meals in the refectory. She critiqued me every time, and that made me even more nervous.

I have no idea why Sister decided we needed to take lessons in ballet for that class. Our habits covered our ankles, and the clunky nun shoes didn't lend themselves to graceful ballet moves. I can still picture us singing and moving to the music of the five movements:

Here's position number one

Arms are out/Just like the sun

Toes are out/Heels are in

That is how we begin

Here's position number two

Arms are out/You know that's true

Legs apart/Nice straight knees

Toes are out if you please, etc.

Needless to say, no ballet company rushed to sign us up as the ballerina nuns in action!

Sr. Isabel and I continued our piano and organ lessons, so daily practice became a part of our routine. Of course, we also had our daily Gregorian chant class after breakfast with Sr. Victorine. Junior nuns had lessons to learn more about chanting the Divine Office. Each nun had to lead the chants, which included solo singing. When it was your turn, you spent many hours of practice to do it perfectly.

Our Junior mistress, Sr. Mary Ann, taught us the Rule of St. Benedict in a weekly class. We needed to be well versed in what it meant to be a Benedictine nun and learn about the life he designed for his followers.

During those two years at Corbett College, we also had work duties in the laundry, kitchen, coif room, candle house, or bakery, and we had our daily prayers to attend. After supper, we had recreation time followed by Compline and nocturnal silence.

Looking at the transcript of grades during Junior College, I realize how busy I must have been studying to try to get all A's and going to classes: Liturgical Worship, World Cultures, Latin of the Breviary, Masterpieces of Literature, Speech Arts, Theology, Medieval Latin, Dogmatic Theology, Sacred Scripture, Intro to Philosophy, American Masterpieces, American History, and General Biology.

In the Juniorate, we could have visitors on designated Sundays. I will never forget one Sunday when my parents brought a picnic lunch to share with me on the convent grounds. Dad decided it would be fun to take me downtown Crookston to get some ice cream. I quickly said I would love to, but I had to obtain permission to leave the convent grounds. He looked at me in disbelief.

"What do you mean?" Dad asked. "You are a young woman. Are you telling me that you have to ask permission for simply going with your family to get ice cream?"

He shook his head and wondered what else his daughter had to do in this life she had chosen. At that moment, the bell rang for Vespers. I told my parents that I needed to go for prayers but would ask if I could go and get some ice cream with them afterward. Would they mind waiting while I went for afternoon prayers?

Once again, Dad shook his head. He and Mom said they would wait, yet questioned why I couldn't skip one set of prayers to be with my family. After all, they had limited Sundays to visit me. I promised to be back in less than half an hour. I rushed off to prayers, hoping my Juniorate mistress would give me a positive answer to get some ice cream.

My mind was not in my prayers that afternoon, as I kept wondering if I would get permission to go. I rarely left the convent grounds, so the thought of a delicious ice cream cone with my family overrode any spiritual thoughts. It seemed like Vespers would never end. As soon as we said the last Amen, I rushed up to Sr. Mary Ann, who was still praying in her assigned chapel space.

I whispered, "Sister, can I please have permission to go downtown to get ice cream with my folks? They are waiting for me at the picnic table."

She raised her head from her prayer, looked at my pleading face, and nodded yes. My face lit up like a Christmas tree bulb. Smiling, I quickly added, "Thank you!" genuflected, and hurried out of the chapel. Giddy with excitement, I rushed to the picnic table to announce my good news. My parents later shared that I acted like a young child who had received a special treat.

Even being in the car with my family was a treat. Dad said I should get a double scoop, and I quickly agreed. It wasn't easy choosing which flavor, but peppermint bonbon and maple nut won out. Now the challenge was to prevent ice cream from dripping on my newly pleated coif. If it did, I would have constant reminders that week of my ice cream excursion and the pleasures that it had brought. We sat outside the ice cream shop and savored our treats. Relaxing and talking about more news from home was a perfect ending to our Sunday visit.

Before they left, Dad asked if Sr. Christina might be in the bakery. He had met her the day I made my first vows and spoke Bohemian to her, making her feel special and happy. (I had shared with him the story of flying into her bakery on my broomstick during the Novitiate.) She was from Pisek, North Dakota, where many Bohemians had settled, including my Dad's family. Sister spoke broken English and had no one in the convent who knew the Czech language. During that conversation, she told Dad how great it would be if he stopped to see her whenever he visited me.

Since Dad spoke the Bohemian language very well, he always tried to take some time to visit and talk a little Bohemian with her. Her family rarely saw her, so she always loved to spend time with Dad. As a little gift of appreciation, she made sure he walked away with some of her special bread and sweets. Of course, Dad left smiling as he clutched his prized homemade goodies.

While Dad chatted with her, the rest of us stayed outside and shared some final stories. The bell for Matins rang, and I had to bid farewell once again to my family. A few tell-tale ice cream drips on my coif would be a special reminder of our fun visit.

When all the teaching nuns returned to the Motherhouse in June, it was a beehive of activity. Nuns went as pairs to teach catechism for two weeks in parishes that did not have Catholic schools.

It was exciting to think back to when the nuns came to teach us in Naytahwaush for two weeks in the summer, and now I was the nun and not the student! The first summer after a year of college, my assignment was to teach with Sr. Alexine in Grygla, a small parish in northern Minnesota. We stayed with Mr. and Mrs. Gonnering, a childless couple who loved the nuns. They met us with open arms, showed us our bedroom, and then brought us back to their living room to enjoy the best homemade rhubarb cake I had ever eaten.

They shared the history of the small parish and brought out a photo album. Mrs. Gonnering proudly showed pictures of the before and after of their church. The highlight of their history was telling about a certain priest named Father Aarden. He had been their assistant priest for a few years and had helped the parishioners rebuild their church. The couple said he was like a son they had never had ,and hoped that I would have a chance to meet him one day!

I just knew it would be a fun two weeks staying with such warm and welcoming hosts. I also liked Sr. Alexine as she was very patient with me and helped me prepare my catechism lessons every night.

We ate all our meals at the Gonnering home and taught our classes in the church. Sister gave the younger children to me to train and prepare them for their first confession and communion. Even though I was nervous thinking about this task, I knew that she was a master teacher and would help me anytime I ran into a problem.

The two weeks went by so quickly, and Sunday morning arrived. All went smoothly and without problem as the children were eager to learn. After Mass, when people wanted to take my picture with the children, Sister explained that I could not have my photo taken since I had not taken final vows.

Once again, I inwardly questioned the strict rules of the convent. When I asked Sister about the ruling, she explained that it wouldn't be proper for people to have photos of nuns if that nun chose not to make her final vows. Somehow that didn't sound too sensible. However, my job was not to question the rules, but to obey them.

In my second year of Juniorate, Flo told me she was getting married and wanted me to come home for the wedding to play the organ in our St. Anne's Church. I felt so honored and could hardly wait to tell the nuns.

Sr. Mary Ann responded, "Sr. Mona, nuns don't go home for weddings. It was lovely that your sister wanted you to attend and play the organ, but that is not possible."

"But, Sister, it would mean the world to her to have me there. Can't you ask the Rev. Mother for this special favor? Or can I?"

I met with the Rev. Mother and when she told me my request was not permissible, I cried. How could she be so cruel and not think of my family and their needs? Could this not be an exception to the Rule? She assured me that there would be many sacrifices that I would have to make as a nun. This sacrifice was one of them. My sister could come to visit, and bring her bridal dress to show me, but that was it. No more discussions on the subject of going home for the wedding would be allowed.

I spent many nights crying in my pillow and trying to make sense of such strict rulings. I knew I had to give up my family, but this seemed cruel and insensitive. If my God was so loving, why weren't the convent rules? Did they not see that I had given up so much to become a nun? Why this restriction? I realized that I must search for the answer through prayer and meditation.

Mom and Flo found it hard to believe that the convent's rules could be so strict and unyielding. They tried to make me feel better and made the sacrifice of driving the seventy-five miles to visit and console me. They even brought Flo's wedding dress for me to see. As they shared the wedding plans, I cried and realized once again that I could not attend or play the organ for Flo's wedding Mass. Why? Why? Why?

Mother Mary John came down to the visiting room to assure Mom that this was a convent rule. If she allowed me to go home for a wedding, other nuns would expect the same. Being a nun involved sacrifices, and this was one of them. Mom tried to explain how difficult it was to find an organist and how much this would mean to the family. Mother Mary John left the room after saying she was sorry, but she could not make exceptions.

We all sat there crying, but we realized we could not change anything. The bell rang for prayers, and I had to leave. Crying and hugging them as they left, I felt a heaviness and wrenching in my heart. How many times would I miss being with my family on different occasions? This convent life was not the easiest to live. I told myself that my folks did not raise a quitter when things got tough and felt I needed to pray harder. I so wanted to be a good nun. That meant sacrifices, but right now, I wasn't doing such a great job accepting them. Yet, I still had this inside yearning to conquer all and follow my dreams and ambitions to be the best nun ever.

Sharon found a letter I had written to her on March 15 of 1960:

"Joy is the echo of GOD'S LIFE in us."

Dear Sharon,

Happy Birthday! I surely hope you didn't think that I had forgotten your Birthday and I'm sorry to be a wee bit late in sending you greetings. I was going to make you a birthday card, but we went on a trip this weekend, so please forgive me. I hope you had a lovely day today, and I remembered you special in my prayers. What did you do to celebrate since you are now no longer a teenager?

You'd never guess, but I was actually in the Cities this past weekend. Our English class went down to see the play "As You Like It" presented by St. Catherine's College. The play was just superb. We left Friday afternoon, stayed overnight at Little Falls nursing Home, went to the play Saturday afternoon, and left for home Sunday morning. I've not enjoyed myself like that in a long time.

I got permission to call Flo, so she and Romie came over to see me Saturday evening. It was so good to see them again, and we had such a good visit. Flo showed me her invitations, napkins, and wedding book. I'm getting so anxious. No, I can't go to the wedding even though I want to so badly. This is a good sacrifice for me, and I shall offer it up for Flo and Romie. I'm sure that everything will be gorgeous and you'll look dazzling in orchid. Don't get a big head now!

I got the flu the weekend before this, and so I wasn't able to make it to Moorhead that weekend. The flu is really making its rounds and Sister Isabel is in the hospital with it now but is feeling much better.

How is everything coming along with you? Mom said you're working in O.B. now. How do you like it? You ought to see the new nursing home in Little Falls. Is it ever nice and the rooms are just lovely. Sister Mary Kevin and I slept in one of the infirmaries and we had more fun. Sr. Ricarda goes to school there so she came to the Cities with us. I thought I might run into some of our good Twin Lake friends but didn't.

You didn't tell me who Linda went to the Prom with. Please greet her and all the rest of the family for me. Tell Linda I shall write to her at Easter. I'm glad your Birthday is in Lent so that I could write you a few lines. If you ever come near Crookston, be sure to come and see me.

May God Bless You on this your 20th Birthday, and may Our Lady protect you!

Happy Birthday, again! Bye. Love, Sister Mona

After finishing my second year of college at the Mount, that summer I taught catechism for two weeks in Moorhead, MN. Since Moorhead was a large city, I stayed with several nuns in our convent there. Compared to my first summer's experience in Grygla, this was not nearly as exciting and fun. I realized I loved being in small parishes in the wilderness, which was more like the area I had grown up in.

After teaching summer catechism, we returned to the Mount for summer classes and our annual retreat.

It was the custom of the Motherhouse to send nuns to begin their teaching careers after completing two years of Junior College. Sr. Isabel and I were excited to think we would soon be in a classroom, despite our lack of classes teaching us how to teach. Even though I had two years of college, I had not received any classes explaining teaching methods.

After our annual retreat, each nun received her yearly Obedience assignment. On this slip of paper, Reverend Mother wrote the place we'd be assigned for the coming school year. My mouth fell open in total surprise when I read: "Sr. Mona, you will be teaching in Asherton, Texas."

What?? I couldn't believe my eyes. Texas was such a long way away. I rushed over to Sr. Isabel, "Where are you going to be?" I breathlessly asked.

"My obedience says, East Grand Forks, MN." Sr. Isabel calmly stated. "I will have to find out who the principal is and what grade I'll be teaching. What does yours say?"

Trembling, I blurted out, "Can you believe I'm going to Texas, to our Mexican migrant mission? Oh, wow, I wonder what grade I will have and what it will be like in Texas. I hope Mother Mary John didn't make a mistake."

Just then, before I had a chance to find out more about my assignment to teach in Texas, the bell rang for prayers. Later that day, I met Mother Mary John in the hall. Still trying to believe my obedience slip, I thanked her and shared I had never been to Texas. I told her it was the biggest surprise in my life.

"What will it be like at this Mission? How can I prepare?" I said, as questions tumbled out one right after another.

She smiled and then chuckled as she told me that she was sure I would do well in Texas. "Go and find Sr. Caroline, the principal of the Asherton School," she said. "Ask her what you need to do to get ready for your mission work in Texas."

When I found Sister Caroline, I told her that I was so excited to teach at our Texas mission, and what did I need to do? What did I need to bring? What was it like in Texas?

"You will find out when you get to the mission, Sr. Mona," was her reply. "We will decide your duties at that time. Now enjoy the rest of the weeks before we leave. The other Sisters, Sr. Mary Ellen, Sr. Marian, and Sr. Margaret, have all been teaching there before, and they will help you when we arrive."

Since I was the first Junior nun ever assigned to the Texas mission, she told me I should check with my Junior Mistress to find out what restrictions I might have during the year. She would also talk with Reverend Mother about having a Junior nun on her Mission.

She added that since we had a five-day journey driving, we would depart for Texas a week before the other nuns went to their missions in Minnesota.

"By the way, do you have a driver's license?" she asked. I assured her I did. "Well, we must make sure it is up to date, as you will drive some of the time. Sr. Marian also has a driver's license, so you two will be the main drivers."

With a renewed license and a mind overflowing with questions, I saw Sr. Marian walking outside one afternoon. I rushed over to talk with her. "Hi, Sister, I'm Sr. Mona, and I'm going to Texas with you!" I said excitedly, "Sr. Caroline didn't tell me which grade I'll be teaching, so I thought I'd ask you."

Sr. Marian looked at me with a peculiar expression and said, "I don't know, but I'm sure Sr. Caroline will let you know when the right time comes."

Realizing I wouldn't get an answer, I thanked her and said I was excited about coming to Texas and hoped we would become close friends in the coming year. As I walked away, I wondered why no one would tell me what I would teach or any details about my new Texas life.

Once again, I must practice patience and wait. What would my life in Texas be like?

Chapter Thirteen

My Texas Years: 1961-63

The magic in new beginnings
is truly the most powerful of them all.
Josiya Martin

The day arrived in August of 1961 for Sr. Caroline, Sr. Margaret, Sr. Marian, Sr. Mary Ellen, and me to pack the car with our meager belongings and set forth on the five-day trip to Texas. The trunk was crammed, loaded down with our suitcases and and school supplies for the coming year.

The challenges began before we even started the journey! Sr. Marian got in the driver's seat with Sr. Caroline next to her. When the rest of us nuns climbed into the back seat and closed the doors, the back end sagged dangerously close to the ground. They now had one extra person in the car, which made a big difference. Realizing that we had only a few inches to spare, Sr. Caroline told Sr. Marian and me that we needed to be extra careful and avoid big bumps and sharp inclines on the road as we drove.

Waving goodbye to the cadre of nuns that gathered for our Texas send-off, I had a strange lump in my throat and a churning in my stomach. My career as a teaching nun was about to begin. I had a big responsibility to prove that a Junior nun could do anything a final professed nun could do. I wondered what adventures lay ahead in teaching Mexican migrants at our farthest mission. At the same time, I felt special trying to figure out why Mother Mary John had chosen to send me so far from home that first year.

On the way, Sister Caroline shared a bit of the history of our Texas mission. The parish, called Our Lady of the Immaculate Conception, began in 1939. In 1943 Mother Monica sent four sisters from our convent to Asherton, Texas, to establish St. Thomas Elementary School for the Mexican children. Our Motherhouse chose Asherton as its first distant mission outside of Minnesota because of its poverty and Hispanic population. I tried to visualize what the school looked like and its surroundings.

Then the discussion led to what everyone had done that summer. After that, Sr. Caroline said, "Sr. Mona, our tradition is to stop for lunch at Sr. Mary Ellen's home in Rosen, MN. Her family loves to have us visit them, and it is right on our way."

Once we got to Sr. Mary Ellen's home, the warmth and laughter of all her brothers and their wives and kids, as well as her parents, made it so easy to fit right in. Delicious aromas filled the room. The tables were ladened with several meat dishes, an abundant array of home-grown vegetables, and several salads. It was enough food to feed an army. No one could resist the homemade pies and desserts even after filling our stomachs with the main courses. By the end of the meal, we hated to leave the comfort of Sr. Mary Ellen's fun family, but we needed to move on.

The other tradition on the way to Texas was to spend that first night on the road at the Benedictine Motherhouse in Yankton, SD. It was quite a contrast after being in the cheerful, noisy family atmosphere at noontime and then entering into the convent monastic silence. Yet, the hospitality of the nuns was appreciated. We had an early bedtime because we would leave right after Morning Prayers and breakfast.

As we drove off, Sr. Caroline informed me that Sr. Marian was an excellent driver, but I needed to help out since we had long days of driving the 1500 miles to Asherton. She thought we should exchange drivers every time we needed to stop for gas. I hoped I could impress Sr. Caroline with my driving skills.

When the gas dial hovered near empty, Sr. Marian spotted a gas station. The steep incline to the gas pumps proved too much. The car's back end objected with a loud, painful scraping sound as we pulled up to get gas. Lesson learned: no more gas stations with that type of incline.

After filling the gas tank, it was my turn to get behind the wheel. To leave without further damage to the car, Sr. Caroline decided the best strategy was to have some of the nuns get out of the car while I slowly maneuvered the vehicle from the gas station.

Sr. Caroline always followed the same route every year to and from Texas. That meant that we stayed at the same motels and ate at the same restaurants familiar to her. Staying in a motel was a new experience for me, and it was fun sharing a room with only one other person. What a change from dormitory living! One bathroom for two people was a luxury I had never had in my life.

Instead of reciting the Divine Office while traveling, we prayed the rosary together in the car. We prayed all three mysteries: the Glorious (The Resurrection, The Ascension, The Descent of the Holy Spirit, The Assumption, and The Coronation); Joyful (The Annunciation, The Visitation, The Nativity, The Presentation at the Temple, and The Finding of Jesus in the Temple); and Sorrowful (The Agony in the Garden, The Scourging at the Pillar, The Crowning with Thorns, The Carrying of the Cross and the Crucifixion.) As we recited the prayers of a rosary three different times, we tried to visualize each of the mysteries as we prayed. It was our way to practice meditation on the life of Christ.

After many hours on the road, I finally found the courage to ask Sr. Caroline questions that had been circling in my brain. "Sister, what grade will I be teaching?" I innocently asked.

There was a long pause. Then, finally, Sr. Caroline informed me that I would not have a classroom. Instead of teaching a specific grade, I would be responsible for various tasks around the convent and helping the other nuns in their classrooms. She explained that I was replacing Sr. Marian, who had done these duties for two years.

The local parish had just built a new classroom during the summer so that Sr. Marian could teach the fourth, fifth, and sixth graders. Having this new classroom would ease the teaching load of everyone.

She went on to say, "It has been challenging to carry out my responsibilities as Principal while also teaching fifth through eighth graders." She explained that Sr. Margaret taught second through fourth graders while Sr. Mary Ellen taught kindergarten and first graders.

"Now that we have an extra nun and an extra classroom, it will be much easier for all of us. Sr. Mona, you will be helping each of us teachers as we need you. On Mondays, you will do the laundry, and on Fridays, you will clean the house. Every day, you will make lunch for all of us." As I listened, I fought back my tears and tried to look like I accepted all that she was saying.

Then she said, "You'll help all of us in between those tasks, and after school, you will drive some of the nuns to Carrizo Springs to teach catechism. There is no Catholic school there, so we give weekly catechism classes to those children."

My head was spinning with all of this new information. Now I knew why Sr. Marian had been so secretive when I asked her what grade I would be teaching. I thought right then and there that I should change my name to Sr. Cinderella. Oh, my, this would be a year of learning and non-stop work. I prayed to whatever saint might help neophytes like me head for unknown territory. The other nuns had been strangely silent as Sr. Caroline shared all of this. I decided not to ask any more questions. Instead, I'd wait to let things unfold when I got to our mission.

Despite the bombshell news of my coming year's tasks, all was going smoothly until the following day when we stopped for gas. In those years, the gas station person always filled the gas tank, washed the windows, and even checked the oil under the hood as a courtesy.

Stopping at a gas station meant that it was also a bathroom break for us. Seeing five penguin-like-looking women in a line waiting to go to the outside toilet was a spectacle just in itself. This time there was an added treat for the bystanders staring at us. Sr. Mary Ellen had to go so badly that she bolted out of the car and headed for the toilet. Before we knew it, she disappeared. The rest of us nuns looked around and discovered that the door to the women's restroom was still open. Where on earth was Sr. Mary Ellen?

Sr. Caroline went into the women's toilet, and just after she closed the door, Sr. Mary Ellen emerged from the men's toilet saying, "Honestly, a man could suffocate in there!"

The rest of us laughed hysterically and almost peed in our pants when she said that. We pointed to the sign that said MEN above the door from which she had just emerged. Unfortunately, she had been in such a hurry, she hadn't read the signs. The man at the gas pump tried not to laugh as he finished filling the gas tank. I am sure he had a good laugh later, telling others his story about the nun who used the Men's toilet. After that experience, you can be sure we all carefully checked out the signs whenever we stopped for gas.

Immaculate Conception Church in Asherton, Texas

As we traveled further south, I was amazed as I listened to the different speech patterns of the people we encountered in restaurants and at the gas stations. I had never been this far South, and had not realized how Southerners talked. The way they spoke felt like molasses was slowing swirling around, with no time frame to meet. I loved to listen as the waitresses smiled at us and said in a drawl, "Honey chile, what are you all wantin' to order today?"

The patterns of the countryside also acquired a different look and feel. The forests and lakes of the Midwest were nowhere around. As we arrived in southern Texas, I saw the desert scene of cacti and rolling tumbleweeds for the first time in my life. I didn't even remember seeing cactus in our geography books.

Then came acres of flat fields, irrigation systems, and oil rigs scattered along the roadsides pumping oil. The searing sun's rays seeped into the car, and my first experience of extreme heat made me begin to question why we had to wear all the layers of clothes here in the hot South.

Was this heat going to be the starting story of my life in Texas? I sweated even thinking of it. None of the other nuns complained, so

I thought it better to keep my thoughts to myself. After all, I was the neophyte baby nun among them. Each of them had spent several years in Texas, so I must take my lessons from them.

Suddenly, we left the tarred roads and drove on dirt roads with dust flying all over. As plumes of dry dust escaped into the car, we quickly shut the car windows. The little wooden sign on the side of the road had the word Asherton written on it. The nuns became excited, cheered, and said, "Home at last!"

Looking ahead, I saw a beautiful stone church looming before us as Sr. Marian pulled up to the building near it. Sr. Caroline turned to me and said, "Well, Sr. Mona, here is your new home for this year. We hope you will come to love this place just as we have. The Mexican people are so loving and appreciative of all that we do for them."

With that said, we got out of the car into the most oppressive heat I had ever felt. Sweat trickled down my face, and I hadn't even done any work yet!

Next to the church was a building that I assumed to be the priest's home. Next to that was another stone building: The new school. As we each grabbed our suitcase from the trunk and followed Sr. Caroline into the stone building, the nuns told me this was both our school and our convent. Opening the creaky screen door leading into the school, I saw unfinished wooden floors in the small hallway that led to three rooms with no doors, just door frames. I stared around me in wonderment. I had known poverty on the reservation, but the old school buildings I had attended seemed rich in comparison to this.

As soon as we got inside the tiny school hallway, we put down our suitcases. Sr. Mary Ellen ran into the first room on the left and said, "Well, this room will soon be teeming with my little darlings." With that, Sr. Margaret walked into the middle doorway and commented that it would be great to see her students again.

Then we all entered the third classroom that Sr. Caroline said was hers. She immediately said, "It will be so wonderful to have another classroom so I won't have so many students this year." She turned to Sr. Marian and said, "Let's see how the new classroom is coming along before we go into the convent."

I followed the nuns as they walked out of Sr. Caroline's classroom and outdoors into the oppressive heat. About a hundred feet away was an old building that looked like a garage with a three-sided concrete block addition.

Sr. Marian squealed with delight and immediately raced over to inspect the building that didn't yet have windows. She opened the door and crowed with joy. Unfinished as it was, she was ecstatic and thrilled to have her very own classroom. All the other nuns entered the room and oohed and ahhed. The spacious, well-furnished class-rooms at the Mount were luxurious compared to the Asherton class-rooms.

Memories flooded my mind. Except for the soaring heat, this village reminded me so much of Naytahwaush, where I grew up with its dirt roads and tar paper houses. The cacti and sagebrush in Texas replaced Minnesota's pine and oak trees. It was like going back in time. What would the convent be like inside?

Walking back to the school, I discovered that the small hallway in the school entrance had a door leading into our convent area. Opening the door, I saw a long hallway. On the left side of the hall-way was the wall that separated the convent from Sr. Caroline's classroom. Sr. Caroline entered the first room on the right, her com-bined bedroom and office. I followed the other nuns to the next room on the right, a small bedroom that the four of us were to share.

As I stood in our bedroom doorway, I saw four beds with a tiny dresser next to each bed. There was no privacy. There wasn't even enough room to have poles with sheets pulled around each bed as we had at the Motherhouse.

Immediately on the right of the doorway was a door that opened to a small closet. Opening that door, I saw two huge nails protruding on each sidewall with two hangars dangling from each nail. Sr. Marian chimed in, "Look, Sr. Mona, we each have a nail to hang our habits." I didn't know whether to laugh or cry. The wall in the back of the closet had floor-to-ceiling shelves that held the bed and bathroom linens encased in plastic bags.

Walking into the bedroom, I realized that the door on the op-posite wall opened into the bathroom containing a toilet, bathtub, and an old-fashioned washing machine tucked into one corner.

Smiling, I said to myself, "Well, at least there is an indoor toilet with a door to the bathroom for a little privacy!" Then, looking at the washing machine, I realized it was like the old one with wringers that Mom used to have when I was growing up. At least this one was electric.

Since I was the baby nun, I took the bed that remained after the other nuns chose theirs. Before we unpacked our suitcases, the nuns were anxious to show me the rest of the convent. The hallway that separated the classrooms from our convent led into the combined living and dining room. The spartan living room had a couch and a few chairs to sit on. The dining room table and chairs butted up to the living room space. An open doorway led to the kitchen, with another door leading to the outdoors.

The kitchen was small, with a refrigerator and stove on the left as you entered. Some cupboards and a sink with a window overlooking the fenced-in area outside were on the opposite wall. Outside, there were orange trees and a clothesline sagging from its poles.

More memories leaped into my mind as I compared the small four rooms in this convent to our four-roomed home where I grew up. Here, though, we had five grown women, not two adults and two kids.

We were a long way from the Motherhouse, and we would be here for a whole year. But, looking at the bright side, I decided it was good to have such a small living space as it wouldn't take as long to clean. I just hoped that all the nuns proved to be compatible, with a keen sense of humor.

Sr. Caroline announced that she and Sr. Marian would drive to the nearby town of Carrizo Springs to the grocery store to buy food for our supper and the days ahead. The Mexican women usually cleaned the convent before we arrived and placed some food in the refrigerator. Somehow the communication to the parish priest didn't reach him in the mail before we did. That meant we needed to clean the convent.

While Sr. Caroline and Marian went shopping, the rest of us got to work to make the beds, sweep and dust, and prepare the convent for living. Since it had been vacant all summer, there was dust everywhere. With no air conditioning, we turned on a few fans. Looking at all the cracks in the walls, I soon realized how difficult it was to keep the dust from blowing into the convent. My Cinderella days would be busy ones.

By the time Sr. Caroline and Sr. Marian returned, we had the place looking clean enough. We were ready for some food. Exhausted, we all decided to go to bed early.

The next day I learned more about living in Texas. Winds blew fine sand and dust through the windowsills, doors, and all the cracks in the walls covering everything with a veil of dust. Preventing this dust from coming into the house proved futile, so dust became a part of our daily lives.

We began working in the classrooms to get them ready for students. The nuns explained that we were not only teachers, but also janitors. Keeping our school clean included the two outhouses on the playground. Sr. Caroline said we would take weekly turns on that task. I looked outside at the outhouses, and memories of my elementary school days flooded my mind. The only difference was that I hadn't been required to clean the outhouses of my childhood!

The desks in the classrooms took me back to my early elementary school years when I sat in desks connected in long lines with wooden runners. The sizes of the desks increased as I went from the second/third-grade classroom to the desks of the upper-grade kids, but the classroom size did not.

Sr. Marian was giddy with excitement because her new classroom had moveable desks to arrange in various formations. The concrete floor and concrete block walls looked bleak, but nothing could dampen her spirit of having her very own classroom.

There was a stage on one side of the room in Sr. Margaret's classroom. Windows on one wall looked out onto the playground. The other walls separated her classroom from Sr. Caroline's and Sr. Mary Ellen's.

Each classroom had one of the walls lined with an antique slate blackboard. There was little room to walk around because the desks on the wooden runners filled the entire room. However, if an adult walked sideways, you could try to squeeze between the rows.

In the front right corner in Sr. Caroline's classroom was an upright piano. Sr. Caroline told me that she played the piano and organ, but I would take over her musical duties, since I also played both of these instruments. I was sure I would soon learn more details of what that meant. My work schedule included being a part-time assistant teacher, cook, housekeeper, janitor, and musician.

As I went into each classroom, I asked how I might help during the coming school year. First, I went into Sr. Mary Ellen's room. She taught the youngest students and shared that she could have as many as sixty on her attendance list at the height of the school year. Thank heavens, she went on to say, not all of them showed up each day for school; there were not enough desks if they did.

When her classroom became overcrowded with little cherubs, she couldn't possibly stop each time a child needed to go to the toilet. Since the youngest students knew very little English and were naturally shy, they often peed in their pants or on the floor before asking to go to the outside toilet. At that point, the unfinished floor-boards of the classrooms were a godsend as the wood absorbed the wetting, and classes went on.

After that explanation, Sr. Mary Ellen asked me to take some of her students into the hallway each day to teach them basic English. So I now discovered one of my future teaching duties—teaching English to children who knew no English from a teacher who knew no Spanish. That should prove challenging and most likely very frustrating for the students and myself. I hoped Sr. Marian might share some teaching strategies she'd learned when she was the flunky Cinderella nun.

When I went into Sr, Margaret's classroom, she explained that working with her students would vary from day to day, depending on the needs of the students. Flexibility was the key. She would appreciate an extra pair of hands, and was sure we would get along very well.

Sr. Caroline called me into her classroom to explain how she planned on using my time for her students. "Sr. Mona," she said, "Many of my students need extra help in reading." Then she told me I would take a small group outside each day, find the shadiest area, and teach reading from the few basal readers available. I hoped that Sr. Marian would come to my assistance and tell me how she had handled that.

Before walking over to Sr. Marion's classroom, Sr. Caroline called me back. "Sr. Marion is from Boston, you know. She still has the Bostonian accent of dropping her "r's" in words and says many words differently than we do in the Midwest." But, she continued, "I want her students to hear the correct pronunciation, so I've decided you will teach them spelling."

I wondered where I would do that. Sister quickly added that I would teach spelling in the church, since the students could use the church pews for desks and have the kneelers as their seats.

"I'll go with you to explain all this to her," Sr. Caroline said to me. Sister Marian was busy removing stickers from the newly placed windows that the parishioners had installed that morning. "I love my new classroom!" she exclaimed. "It all seems like a dream, and I can't wait to see my new students."

Sr. Caroline laughed and again shared how happy she was to have fewer students. She then told Sr. Marian that I would become the spelling teacher. Each day I would take one grade to the church to teach spelling, and Sr. Marian could work with other students teaching another subject.

On Fridays, I would give the spelling tests for all the students in her classroom. During that time, Sr. Marian would go to Sr. Caroline's room to teach art. That gave Sr. Caroline extra time to do administrative work. Since our rule was not to question authority, we did as told.

Those first days in Texas taught me how loving and affectionate the Mexican kids were. During our first days of cleaning the school, we had a constant supply of children running in and out to hug the nuns and welcome them back. When the limited amount of English words failed to convey the message, the smiles and hugs of each child did.

Sr. Caroline gathered us for a meeting on the Friday of that first week after having the classrooms ready for the students' arrival the following Monday. She explained that life would be easier this year, with an extra nun to help. Since Sr. Caroline was both our principal and Superior, she said the nuns needed to have their lesson plans completed and approved by her every Sunday evening for the following week. This ritual was part of their teaching schedule.

Because I did not have a classroom, I was exempt from creating lesson plans. As for my schedule, Sr. Caroline reviewed my duties, reminding me that Mondays were laundry days, and that would take most of the day. Tuesdays through Thursdays would be regular school days for me. During those days, I must help each nun in her classroom, doing whatever they needed help with for that day. On Fridays, I had to clean the house and prepare the evening's meal.

During the week, Sr. Caroline told me that each nun would take a turn to cook the evening meal.

Sunday mornings were busy as we attended Mass in Asherton and Carrizo Springs. In addition to attending Mass, it was customary to visit some elderly couples before returning home. After lunch, we had the afternoon to complete lesson plans, create worksheets for the week, and personal time to write letters to our family. How could I possibly write all that had happened my first week in Texas in a letter?

The following week, school started. Since it was Monday, I knew that meant laundry day for me. Before school started, Sr. Marian had shared the basics of doing laundry in Texas. First, I filled the washing machine with pails of hot water from the bathtub, added the detergent, and then placed the soiled laundry for washing. Next, I filled a bucket with cold water into a container for the rinse water.

The bathroom was not that big, so there was very little room to perform the routine of washing and rinsing clothes. When the machine finished washing a load, I put each piece of laundry through the wringer and into the rinse tub. Because all water was scarce, I used the same wash water for the second load. While that second load was washing, I took each piece of laundry in the rinse tub and put it through the wringer again.

After placing the clean, rinsed items in a laundry basket, I walked outside to our sagging clotheslines. Using wooden clothespins, I attached each item to the clothesline. We had long-forked wood poles to prop up each line, so the clean clothes would not touch the dusty ground underneath. As I hung our laundry, visions of helping my Mom hang clothes ran through my head. I wished she were here now to help me fix the sagging lines!

At recess time, the big boys from Sr. Caroline's classroom came into the convent to empty the rinse tub of water. When they returned, I drained the washing machine water for them to carry out for me. At noon, we repeated this process.

The boys poured the water under our orange and lime trees in the backyard since we had so little rain to keep the orange trees watered. Once a week, ready or not, the trees got watered! (It must have been enough moisture because we managed to pick oranges and limes whenever we wished during their bearing season. The trick was to enjoy their juiciness without having any of the juices drip onto our coifs to create yellow stains.)

By the time I finished with the two loads of laundry, it was time for me to prepare lunch. The students lived close by, so they went home to eat their tortillas and beans while the nuns came in for their light lunch with a sandwich or soup, and fruit.

After lunch, I washed the dishes and the kitchen floor. Because of the vast cracks under the screened door, it was a constant struggle to clean the kitchen floor. When finished with lunch duties, I drove daily to pick up our mail at the post office down the road.

Sr. Marian had earlier explained the ritual for picking up the mail. She told me that I was not to look at the mail when the Postmistress gave it to me. The easiest way to do this was to shut my eyes when she did and quickly put it in a bag. I asked what was so important about not seeing who got mail. Sr. Marian said this was the protocol and not to question it. Having grown up with the Postoffice in our home, I wondered how Mom might have handled this situation. For me, I was stunned.

To this day, I wonder what Mrs. Hearn, the Postmistress, thought when every day, after greeting her, I shut my eyes to receive our mail? Was there a lack of trust that we might go through the mail and know who was getting mail, or was it a sign of control by the Superior? As the new nun on the block, I decided not to question but do as told.

I returned to the convent and placed the mail in Sr. Caroline's office-bedroom. Next, I went to help in Sr. Mary Ellen's room.

The room was alive with talk and laughter, all in a language foreign to me. Sr. Mary Ellen knew Spanish and was busy explaining to the little ones what to do. Some students were in their second or third year in First Grade because they needed to learn sufficient English to pass onto Second Grade. (Because their parents migrated up North for many months of the year, the children's time in a school classroom was limited. So, it took them longer to acquire enough English to pass on to another grade.)

When I asked Sister what I should do to help, she just laughed and said to go around the room and see that every child had at least one color crayon to make a picture. The smiling faces and multitudes of hugs as I moved from one child to another were rewards enough for me after my first laundry day. Before I knew it, the cowbell rang in Sr. Caroline's room. All the kids cheered and raced out of the classrooms marking the end of their first day back in school.

After supper that evening, Sr. Mary Ellen brought a strange-looking contraption into the living area. She placed it on a dresser standing next to the hallway doorframe. I immediately asked, "What is that?"

Sister laughed and explained that it was an antique hectograph machine for creating worksheets. The machine was a metal frame with four legs and a handle on the side attached to a gelatin pad bound tightly to rollers. It could replicate five different sets of worksheets, if one used every inch of the roller space.

Sister showed me the process. First, she made sure that she rolled the gelatin pad to its beginning spot. Then, Sister moistened the pad with a wet sponge. After carefully placing the ink side of the master worksheet copy onto the moist gelatin pad, she smoothed and rubbed it carefully to avoid any wrinkles.

After removing the master copy, she took a sheet of blank newsprint—white printing paper was too expensive—to make twenty-five to thirty copies, depending on how well the ink template transferred onto the paper. Because there were spaces on the roller for just five different worksheets, the nuns had to take turns deciding who needed worksheets for the following day.

Memories of my first-grade experience came rushing back. I recalled how I helped Mrs. Tviet create worksheets on her gelatin cookie sheet pads. This antique copier was a step-up in the world, but I never thought I would be copying worksheets with gelatin fifteen years later. It was another example of the poverty of this mission school.

That first week the nuns discussed plans for teaching catechism classes in Carrizo Springs, the neighboring town. The church was called Our Lady Of Guadalupe. Its pastor, Father Schweider, wanted the nuns to teach catechism classes to the children in his parish, since he did not have a Catholic school. So, of course, the nuns agreed; they didn't want to miss out on opportunities to bring God's message to the people, especially the children.

Carrizo Springs, a relatively wealthy town with many Anglo residents, was about ten miles from Asherton. It had the only big grocery store within miles, a weekly newspaper, shoe repair shop, clothing stores, several gas stations, hospital and clinic, public school for grades K-12, several churches, and tarred streets. Asherton had one small service station, a small general store, a post office, and the Catholic church. I now understood why our Motherhouse chose Asherton to serve the poorest of the poor.

Because all the children in Carrizo went to public school, we needed to teach classes after the students finished school for the day. Sr. Caroline explained that we would attend Sunday Masses in Carrizo Springs the following Sunday to set up registration for the catechism instruction. Then, depending on the number of children and the grade levels, she would decide how many classes were needed. It was good to know that we would not start catechism classes in Carrizo for the first two weeks of school.

Not used to the heat, I felt like an overheated oven. My white handkerchief was in constant use as I tried to wipe the sweat rolling down my face. As for my coif, it wilted like a flower left without water. Each day it drooped lower and lower. There was no escape and no air conditioning. Why didn't we send a plea to the Reverend Mother to allow us Texas nuns to have a different wardrobe for this desert climate? I sweat just thinking of how hot it was without air conditioning. Somehow, I made it through that first week in the sweltering heat and was thankful for Saturday, the day we nuns took our weekly bath.

Saturday evening, we took turns bathing while the others sat in the living room to prepare their newly pleated coifs for the upcoming week. With each day's heat, the coifs began to sag more and more so that by each Saturday, they were almost limp across our bosoms.

I can't imagine how we managed to wear one coif for a whole week. If we accidentally spilled something on our coif during the week, the only alternative was to turn it over and wear it that way. Our prayer then was not to spill again. To keep the coif pleats together in the excessive heat, we threaded a needle with white thread to sew between the pleats to keep them tight and close together.

(We had packed a metal-like, sturdy box with our extra coifs when we left Crookston. We mailed this container—packed with our dirty coifs—back to the Mother House each month. They were laundered and given to Sr. Inez to work her magic of pleating them, before they were returned to us.)

Even though we had to wear our coifs for a week, I could not exist wearing my habit for more than one day because I sweat so much. Since I always had tell-tale salt rings covering the back of my garb, I developed a new nightly routine.

The habit we wore each weekday was polyester material. I discovered that if I washed my habit in the tub every night and then hung it on the outside clothesline, it was magically dry in the morning, and the ugly salt rings had vanished. So, every morning, I rushed out to pull my habit off the clothesline, hoping nobody would see me in my white nightgown and night veil.

After a few weeks of listening and learning the Spanish hymns, I became the organist, and Sr. Caroline became the choir director. Of course, everything was in Spanish, and I did not know any of the hymns, or Spanish. I soon learned that the rhythms they sang did not match the notation on the music page. My task was not only to play the notes, but also to learn the rhythm patterns they were used to. Thank heavens the choir was very patient with me. I had to keep one eye on the notes and one eye on Sr. Caroline's directing to keep the music and their singing synchronized as well as I could. I wondered whether I would ever succeed at this challenge.

Father Francisco was the pastor who lived in the rectory between the convent/school and church. His mother was his housekeeper. I learned that he had a stuttering problem during the first Sunday Mass I attended. In the 1960s, Mass was in Latin. That helped Father a bit with his stuttering because it had a rhythmic stance, just as the Spanish language did. But, when it came to the sermon, that was a different matter. He decided to share it in Spanish and English so that the nuns would understand him. With his stuttering, the sermons went on forever. In the oppressive heat, this was not a blessing.

The first time we had a High Mass, which included lots of singing on the priest's part, I realized that he did not stutter while singing. I so wanted to ask him to sing his sermons, but that would not have been the best idea in the book.

One day Father came over to the convent to bring us a cold beverage (would you believe a six-pack of beer?) and it was the most welcoming cold drink, compared to the warm water we drank from the tap. Dad would have laughed and enjoyed watching his nun daughter savoring a refreshing, cold beer! Father stayed to share the extra beer and, in his stuttering voice, told us how his older brothers used to lock him in their home basement to scare him. His stuttering was the result of that prank.

Continuing with his story, he explained how his speech impediment almost kept him from the priesthood. Finally, his superiors at the monastery decided to send him to a particular speech school to rid him of his stuttering. He stayed there for a year. When he returned, he proudly went up to his superior and glibly said the following line: "She sells seashells down by the seashore."

The superior smiled at his great accomplishment but then was aghast when Fr. Francisco then added: "b-b-b-but wh-wh-who w-w-wants t-t-to s-ss-pend the r-r-est of the-their l-l-ife s-sa-saying only th-tha-that?" Despite everything, Father was able to laugh at himself. As for his parishioners and us, we continued to sit through two sermons every Sunday, one in Spanish and one in English.

On my "teaching" days, I began with some first graders gathered around me on the wood-splintered floor in the school hallway. Since the hallway was the entrance for anyone coming into the school, it was a busy place filled with constant distractions as I attempted to teach. It was also the major pathway for students who needed to use the outside toilets.

Another distraction was having an old refrigerator in the hallway. The milkman tried to walk around us every few days to deposit the milk cartons into the fridge. His coming and going became an excellent teaching tool for my students, as I taught them English words to match the interruption. For example, milk (leche) and Man (hombre) became two words they learned well. I needed to develop other words and gestures to fit our multiple distractions in the hallway and increase their English vocabulary.

If that teaching situation wasn't tricky enough, I faced the challenge of teaching reading to ten upper-grade students outside, under the palm trees. Students had to share a basal reader as they leaned up against the school wall. Students became distracted whenever a car drove by, birds sang in a tree, or if a person walked nearby. They decided it was more fun to check these moving objects rather than read what was on the page or answer discussion questions.

The desert winds often became extremely strong, making the dirt around us mini dust tornados. We spent more time choking and coughing than reading aloud when the dust swirls started. I'm not sure how much the students improved in reading with all those outside distractions.

Because students needed to write in their spelling books when I taught Sr. Marian's fourth-through-sixth graders, the wooden pews gave them seats to sit on while I explained the lesson. When they needed to write in their spelling books, the kneelers became a place to sit while the pews became their desks. I kept praying that teaching in the church within sight of the statues of Jesus, Mary, and the saints would promote their spelling ability.

When time allowed, I went into Sr. Margaret's classroom to see who needed any help. Sometimes, I again ended up in the hallway to give her students a bit of English tutoring. This space, as always, led to using the surrounding environment to teach some English words as people came and went during our tutoring sessions. Teaching students in this non-classroom environment led me to develop a teachable-moment type of teaching. I learned to go with the flow and not get uptight.

When we finished teaching the kids in our school, three of us nuns hopped in the car and drove the ten miles to Carrizo Springs to teach catechism to the public school kids there on Monday through Thursday afternoons. One nun taught in the parish hall, and two in the church—one in the front and the other in the back. Being low on the totem pole of seniority, I never got the hall. It wasn't the ideal teaching situation, but there was no other place to teach. After being in school all day, the kids were tired, but they tried hard to listen and learn, since they loved the nuns.

The nun remaining at the convent was the cook for that evening, and Sr. Caroline then had time to take care of some of her administrative duties. After supper, we spent the time correcting papers or making worksheets on the infamous gelatin machine.

Fridays were cleaning days for me, which meant getting on my hands and knees to scrub the unfinished floorboards of our convent. Each Friday, I set out to clean the rooms, which meant getting rid of as much of the accumulated dust as possible. No matter how hard I tried, I never seemed to win that battle. The last thing on the cleaning list was the floors. Dust seeped through the cracks as quickly as I wiped it away.

One particular Friday, when I washed Sr. Caroline's office-bedroom floor, I reached under her bed with the rag, instead of pulling the bed away from the wall. All of a sudden, a scorpion scuttled out from underneath the bed. I grabbed the broom and tried to kill it as it headed down the hallway. Sad to say, the scorpion escaped out the kitchen door under the big, open crack. Happy that I was not stung, I learned a lesson that day of never washing any part of the floor that was not visible. That meant moving beds or making sure I could see where I was cleaning. Nun versus scorpions!

Imagine my surprise when I awoke one night and heard strange rustling noises and scurrying sounds in the hallway. I didn't dare get up to find out the cause of the sounds. The following day I asked the other nuns. They all laughed and said, "Welcome to Texas and the land of cockroaches." The cockroaches ruled no matter how clean we tried to keep our convent. With a building filled with so many cracks and crevices, it was impossible to get rid of them.

Sr. Marian was so frightened of the bugs that she refused to retrieve potatoes from under the cupboard with her bare hands. Finally, she solved the problem by taking a big cooking fork and stabbing each potato she needed. There was no way she wanted to have a cockroach crawl on her hand. Often the potatoes already had holes to mark where the cockroaches had chewed. I began to sense how Texas grew everything bigger than life-size. Cockroaches and scorpions were no exception and part of our daily life.

Did I forget to mention tarantula spiders? One day, the nuns pointed out a tarantula spider on the ground when we walked to the church. Somehow, I naively never expected to see one in the convent.

As I mentioned before, we had one small closet with a nail for each of our habits. This closet also had a single light bulb dangling from the ceiling. One evening, I opened the door, turned on the light, and saw a colossal tarantula spider crawling on one of the shelves. I screamed and yelled, "Tarantula!"

Sr. Marian screamed without even seeing it, and she immediately jumped into the bathtub. Sr. Margaret ran to get a broom. I stood frozen to the spot. She brought two brooms, handed one to me, saying I should hold the dangling light bulb with the broom handle while she would try to kill the spider with the other broom. I panicked. Just as she struck, I jumped back. As I jumped, I dropped the broom. With that, the dangling light bulb hit Sister in the back of her head.

268

Surprised, she leaped back before she was able to kill the spider. She quickly closed the closet door. Sr. Mary Ellen rushed to find old towels to place under the gaping space between the floor and the door frame. We certainly did not want that spider to crawl into our bedroom that night. In the midst of all of this, Sr. Marion was still screaming from the bathtub to find out if we killed it.

After an almost sleepless night of worrying about the tarantula, morning finally dawned. It was then that I realized that my shoes were in the closet. With daylight to help her, Sr. Margaret cautiously opened the closet door to find the spider, but it remained hidden.

Just as I grabbed my shoes, Sr. yelled, "Drop them. The spider is in your shoe!" I screamed as my shoes clattered to the floor. As the spider tried to scurry away, Sister Margaret came to the rescue and deftly killed it with the broom. After that scare, we decided to have someone nearby whenever we opened the closet door!

Our school grounds became the outdoor movie theatre for the village on Friday nights. Parishioners helped set up the screen and projector as well as benches. Admission was ten cents. We nuns got in free, and were even treated to flavored shaved ice served in conical paper cups. People loved the movies, even though they were vintage. It reminded me of my Friday movie nights in Naytahwaush, but there we had the shelter of a building. Here in Asherton, since rain was a scarce commodity, movies took place almost every Friday.

Washing our dusty car. Sr. Mary Ellen, Sr. Marian, Sr. Margaret (left) and me (right).

Two nuns drove to Catarina, Texas, on most Saturdays to teach catechism. Caterina was even smaller than Asherton, with a population of about 200. However, no group was too small to share the Lord's gospel, so Catarina became a Saturday mission.

One Saturday that fall, the nuns encouraged me to try my hand at making bread. We had all grown accustomed to Sr. Christina's homemade bread at the Motherhouse, and we found bought bread unsatisfactory. My first bread baking attempt failed miserably, but the nuns encouraged me to try again. Eventually, some Saturdays became bread-making days for me. The outside temperature and the kitchen temperature vied with one another as the oven heated up for the bread. Dripping with sweat and thankful that I could don a new coif the next day, I gladly baked to make the nuns happy.

One Saturday that I wasn't making bread, Sr. Caroline asked me to find a good recipe for making caramel candy. I paged through an old cookbook and tried one that I thought would be good. She and Sr. Marian went to Carrizo Springs to buy the ingredients.

The first batch of caramels turned out so well that Sr. Caroline decided that I should make another batch. She wanted a sweet treat to bring to Fr. Schweider, the pastor in Carrizo Springs, so making caramels became another task for me on Saturdays that I didn't bake bread.

After cooking the caramels, I cut and wrapped each piece in wax paper. Everything went well until one time when I overcooked the candy, which became challenging to cut. Not prone to swearing, I used words that qualified for my list of sins for my next confession. As I attempted to cut the candy, every piece became more complicated than the last one. Breathing a sigh of relief when I finished the arduous task, I gave Sister Caroline the box of cut caramels that she and Sr. Marion set off to give to Father Schwieder.

After they left, as I was cleaning up, I discovered the tip of the butcher knife was missing. Had it broken off when I was cutting the caramels? Had it been broken before that?

Visions of newspaper headlines such as, "Nun kills priest by planting tip of a butcher knife in caramels," or "Priest dies from unknown causes after eating caramels delivered by nuns," sprang from my imagination.

What was I to do? I didn't have any way to warn the priest. Should I assume that the knife was broken before I cut the caramels?

I was shaken and nervous, and I couldn't live with myself if I didn't say something.

As soon as the nuns returned, I nervously shared my dilemma. Sr. Caroline went straight to her office to call and warn Father of the possibility of a piece of steel hidden in one of the caramels.

I am happy to report that the priest lived. Father said he would be cautious with each chew of the caramel, but he didn't want to waste any piece of the delicious candy! Over the years, Sister trusted me to make the caramels, but she always warned me to check the knife blade before cutting!

December rolled around. Sr. Caroline gave me new hymns to practice for the Christmas liturgies. She explained that we would be practicing the "Las Posadas" song with the choir. This song did not need organ accompaniment because we would be singing it in procession outside. I learned that the words "Las Posadas" (Spanish: "The Inns") depicted a religious festival celebrated in Mexico and some parts of the United States between December 16 and 24.

Las Posadas commemorated Joseph and Mary's journey from Nazareth to Bethlehem, searching for a safe refuge where Mary could give birth to the baby Jesus. The nine-day novena represented the nine months of pregnancy, and a small child dressed as an angel led the procession through the town streets.

There are two parts to the traditional posada song. First, those outside the house sing the role of Joseph asking for shelter. Then, those inside respond, singing the innkeeper's part, saying there is no room. The song switches back and forth a few times until finally, the innkeeper agrees to let them in.

Sr. Caroline explained that everyone would process around the church. Some choir members would then go inside the church and sing the innkeeper's part. The rest would stay outside and sing the part of the pilgrims. Afterward, all would go inside the church for prayers and more singing.

Experiencing this emotional procession and heartfelt singing, I realized how unique this tradition was and loved every minute of it. The sincerity of the Mexican people and their love of Our Lady of Guadalupe continued to amaze me. My love of them and the privilege of working and praying with them brought me to my knees with gratitude. How fortunate I was to have this as my first teaching mission.

In the spring of the year, I began feeling pain in my right knee, especially when I had to kneel for daily prayers and Mass. Not wanting to complain, I endured this for several weeks. Then one Friday, while scrubbing the floors, the pain became intolerable.

After school, I went to tell Sr. Caroline about it. "Let me see your knee right now," she said. I sat on her bed, lifted the multiple layers of my garments, unhooked the garter holding up my black stocking, and bared my knee. She gasped. My knee was bulging and red.

"You need to see a doctor before this gets worse!" she quickly exclaimed.

She immediately called our visiting school nurse, Mary Ellen Blackard, who had often told Sr. Caroline to call her if we ever required medical attention. After all, we nuns rarely got sick or needed any medical treatment. Sr. Caroline asked Mary Ellen which doctor to call.

Within the hour, I was in the doctor's office. Once again, I bared my leg, but I felt embarrassed to do this in front of the male doctor. He shook his head and asked lots of questions: "How long had this been painful? Why didn't I come in sooner? Did I know what could happen if this didn't get treated?"

He softened his tone, seeing the pained expression on my face. I was like a little girl, feeling admonished for something I should have known not to do. I explained that I got on my knees each week to scrub all the wooden floors and also washed the kitchen linoleum floor each day on my knees.

"Well, Sister, you will not be doing that for a while. I need to drain the fluid build-up and give you medication to prevent more infection. I'm also ordering some crutches for you. For the next week, I want you to elevate your leg until this swelling goes down." Then with a twinkle in his eye, he said, "Since you're a nun, I think you know about obeying orders, right?"

I nodded my head and smiled. After all, that meant a vacation from scrubbing the floors for some time!

During that week, I reflected on my year in Asherton. Coming to this Texas mission had helped me realize how much I wanted to teach and work with the poor. It had been a challenging year, with the oppressive heat and poverty, but living with and learning to love the Mexican people had far surpassed any physical hardships. The migrant families had won my heart and soul, and I hoped to return the following year.

Returning to Minnesota in June, I engaged in our annual summer retreat. I spent time praying and seeking guidance for my decision to make final vows. Did I want to become a full-fledged member of the Mount St. Benedict community? Being a nun, I felt I could dedicate my entire life to God. With His love and protection, I just knew I could overcome any obstacles that might arise in the future.

Yet, what if I didn't get assigned to Asherton again? Would I be happy to be a nun serving people in Minnesota? Was it the Mexican people that made me want to take final vows? Could I be as excited about being a nun in a different situation and place?

What about my family? I had not seen them for a year. We wrote weekly letters to each other, but I didn't have the pleasure of being with them physically. Would I spend years in Texas and only see them infrequently, in the summertime? Was I willing to place them on the back-burner of my life? Taking final vows meant severing myself from them and having a home visit only every three years. Was I willing to sacrifice that after everything they had done for me during my life?

Obedience was not an easy vow for me. I realized what an independent thinker I was. Giving up my will and accepting the will of my superiors would be necessary, if I chose to make these final vows. Would this continue to be a stumbling block for me?

Poverty was not a challenge. The convent took care of all my physical needs: food, clothing, shelter. I never handled money, but went to my superior, got down on my knees, and asked for whatever I needed.

Being celibate was more problematic, since I still felt attracted to the opposite sex, at times. Yet, being with other women who had chosen this vow of celibacy made it much more manageable. I realized we all had chosen a Higher Love as our one-and-only. I lived with all younger nuns in Asherton (except for our principal), which fulfilled my need for close friendships. I decided that giving up the idea of marrying and having my own family was a sacrifice I would make. After all, I now could spend my time embracing all the families I worked with within my mission, wherever that might be.

Yes, I wanted to make my final vows. After a week of intense prayer and meditation, I wrote to my parents to share my final decision and invited them to celebrate with me on July 11. In our exchange of letters during the past year, my parents realized that I was happy and excited to be a missionary nun in Texas, so they were prepared for my decision to take my final vows.

The morning of July 11, 1962, Sr. Isabel and I dressed in long, flowing, pleated black robes over our regular habit. We processed into the chapel for this profound moment, dedicating the rest of our life as a nun.

After the sermon, the Reverend Mother called Sr. Isabel and me to the altar to profess our Benedictine vows:

STABILITY: This vow binds one to a specific community. (Benedictines are not an Order, in the generally accepted sense of the term. Each monastery is autonomous but belongs to a Federation.)

CONVERSATIO MORUM: Usually translated as "conversion," which means to live monastic life as it should be lived. (Benedictines do not make vows of chastity or poverty, but to live a monastic life properly, one must be chaste. The Benedictine understanding of religious poverty is quite radical: it means more than living frugally. There can be absolutely no private ownership

Mary Ann, Me, and Floreen on the day of
my final vows.

of anything, although, of course, the community as a whole must own things.)

OBEDIENCE: This vow meant we were to imitate the obedience of Christ "who came not to do his own will, but the will of his Father."

After reciting my vows, I received the official Benedictine wedding ring. It symbolized my marriage to Christ, and was placed on the same finger that brides wear their ring. When we both had said our vows, Sr. Isabel and I returned to our pew, and Mass resumed. Again, a deep surge of love filled my inner being. I felt like I now really belonged. Making my final vows cemented my commitment to serve God with my whole heart and soul. I was His bride forever.

After Mass, we had a big celebration meal with our family, friends, and the other nuns. I was now officially a member of the community.

The day of my final vows, with Mom and Dad.

Family photo taken at my final vows. Me, Mom, and Dad (front).
Mary and Flo (back).

Since nuns could have a family visit every three years, I returned home with my family for a two-week stay. My parents were thrilled, and so was I! Mom and Dad now accepted the fact that their middle daughter meant what she said about becoming a nun. They were proud and ready to show her off to family and friends.

My sister Flo now lived in the Twin Cities and had two children, so we drove there and visited them. It was great to be back with family and see people I had not seen in years. My younger sister, Mary, was twelve, almost a teenager. That made it possible for the two of us to be together for the whole two weeks at my parent's home.

We spent time visiting family members and old friends and, of course, playing cards every evening. Dad kept reminding me to pay attention to the cards played and remember them. Each time I played the wrong card, I usually caused us to lose. He tried to be patient with me as I explained I had not played these card games for a long while. His ability to remember cards played was phenomenal, while mine was not. He forgave me. How could he get mad at a nun? Especially his nun daughter?

After my home visit, I returned to the Motherhouse to take two college classes: Benedictine History and Readings and Composition. There was newfound freedom being a final professed nun at the Motherhouse. I was officially finished with special training, and I could mingle with all of the nuns, not just a small group of those preparing to become full-fledged nuns.

While we were taking summer classes, the day arrived for receiving our coming year's obedience. My hands shook as I opened the envelope. YES!! I jumped up and down with excitement. My assignment was once again to teach in Texas. I rushed to find Sr. Marian. She was also running to find me. Yeah! We were both returning to Asherton and learned that the other nuns were also going back.

This time I knew what lay ahead and was not disappointed that I would not have my own classroom. It would have been great to have that, but I was ecstatic to return to the Mexican people. They had won my heart. How wonderful to return, no matter what type of work I did.

In the latter part of August, we drove the same route to Texas that we had driven the previous year. Catching sight of the beautiful stone church, my heart sang. I was still Sr. Cinderella, the flunky nun, but I knew a bit more of what to expect this time around. But then, on second thought, one never knew what to expect in Texas.

As you know, Sr. Mona is a derivative of St. Monica's name, and I learned to like it very much. It was short, easy for the kids to pronounce and spell, and I always had the picture of the smiling Mona Lisa to think of in my mind. But, unfortunately, these positive aspects came to a grinding halt when Sr. Marian's brother-in-law, Greg, wrote to chide me about the Spanish meaning of my name. He wanted to know if any Mexican children laughed when I told them my name. He said it meant a feminine monkey. That's all the other nuns needed to add to their teasing.

Sr. Marian found a box of letters containing those she had written to her sister, Susan, and Greg during this time. She sent me the following letter I had sent in my response to Greg:

Dear Greg,

This is just a note to thank you for your latest discovery concerning the Spanish meaning of Mona! Sister Marian is gloating in this latest meaning of my name. But, the woe of woes, "mona," also implies ape! I made the matter worse by saying that "chunga" probably meant an ape.

Since all this has come out, I've become quite tamed and have had no opportunities to display my natural climbing talents. I can only thank the dear Lord that He made a St. Monica to validly claim that my name is an English derivative of her name. My latest motto: "Down with Spanish language; up with the English." Of course, this is all in fun, and we've had more laughs over this new tidbit of knowledge. Signed, Sister M.M.(Mona-Monkey!)

Greg sent me his apologies. (Sad to say, I looked for his letter but have lost boxes of correspondence I once had over the years, so I cannot share Greg's letter with you. Greg McDonald became a famous author of the Fletch series of comedic mystery books and later movies starring Chevy Chase.) Not to be outdone, I wrote the following "poetic" response to him:

IN GRATITUDE
Your humblest apologies were joyful received
And I'm sending this note to make sure you'll be relieved
Of your sleepless nights due to an academic interpretation.

Your profound supernal view was so artistically displayed
Concerning the name "Mona" which you so vividly portrayed
And will always be treasured as a source of great consolation.

St. Francis of Assisi has become to me a special friend
And someday in heaven when we meet, I'll gladly lend
My smile (for a while) in exchange for his hee-haw (under supernal law.)

Somehow I don't picture heaven as so aristocratic
And maybe Brother Ass and Sister Donkey can make it more democratic.
If they could get more fans of your appeal to abolish "stuffiness."

Sister Virgin or Sister Debutante is quite an honor to bestow
And with that feather in my veil, I can really start to crow.
About the greatness of a certain name known as Mona.

Your ideas against ordinary conventions are true signs of your cre-
ative mind
And have proved to be a lifesaver and answer I've tried to find
As a rebuttal to those "taunting, jeering, demeanors of my dignity."

Seriously I never lost any sleep over this entire ordeal
And to be thoroughly honest, it hasn't affected my eating at any
meal.
But how else would I have rated a letter from Sr. Marian's famous
brother-in-law?

A final hearty Texas thanks to you for your letter
And it couldn't have explained the name "Mona" any better,
Now I'll have to think of another name to see if I'll rate another
letter.

As I analyze my poetic attempt to respond to Greg, it follows
no rules of rhyming poetry. I must have decided to be creative myself and make up my own AB rhyme pattern followed by a non-
rhyme line!

A month or so after we returned to Texas, Sr. Marian took Sr.
Caroline grocery shopping as usual. The unusual aspect of this shopping trip was that they met people from Vermont. In their conversation, the topic of piano lessons came up.

Sr. Caroline told them that she had a nun among our small
group who could teach piano lessons to her two girls. You can imagine my surprise when I learned that I now had become a piano
teacher. My immediate response was that I had never taught piano.
Sr. Caroline assured me that I would do just fine. The girls and their
mother would be coming on Saturday morning for their first lesson.

Saturday morning arrived. Connie and Ginny Tidd—and their
mother, Betty—appeared at the convent door. Sr. Caroline happily
introduced me. Nervously, I explained that I had no idea how advanced they might be, nor did I have any piano books. In addition to
that, the piano in the classroom needed tuning.

Sr. Caroline simply smiled, asked which girl wanted to be first.
She then told me to give them each a half-hour lesson. Thankfully,
the girls arrived with their piano books. Unfortunately, I did not
have any of my own to improve my playing. Sr. Caroline decided to
stay in the back of her classroom to talk with Mrs. Tidd during the

lessons. The girl I was not teaching sat at one of the desks to do her homework.

Connie and Ginny were quite advanced pianists. I listened to them play from their books. I tried to remember some of the helpful hints that Sr. Kathleen had shared with me during my high school years. I couldn't believe that Sr. Caroline had done this to me. It had been some time since I had played the piano. How on earth could I teach these girls anything?

The girls told me they wanted to learn some new sheet music to play for their grandmother at Christmas. I told them that they were my only pupils and I did not have any sheet music, so they would have to buy the pieces they wished to learn.

I will never forget the following Saturday when Connie came with Grieg's "Hall of the Mountain King" and Ginny with Beethoven's "Moonlight Sonata." I felt I needed to practice the same pieces, to give them some helpful teaching hints. No such luck! Sister told me that she was sure I could do it without buying the music. How I managed to act as if I could teach them anything is still a mystery. They had the determination to learn those pieces, and I could only play the act of an encourager.

The grandmother flew in from Rhode Island for Christmas. The Tidds invited us nuns over to their home to meet her. After a lovely meal, the first thing on the agenda was for the girls to give a mini-recital. Nervous as a wet hen, I quickly and quietly sent several prayers to every saint above that all would go well and that the girls would impress their grandmother.

You can imagine my shock when Betty asked her mother to reciprocate by playing some of her favorite music selections. It was then that I found out that she was a concert pianist. That's why the girls wanted to impress her so much. My following prayers were prayers of utter thankfulness that Connie and Ginny were so talented and ambitious. Their ability to play their chosen pieces had nothing to do with my teaching—only their talent!

Later that year, Sr. Caroline mentioned to the local Postmaster, Mrs. Hearn, that I was giving piano lessons. The next thing I knew, I had two more pupils to teach. This teaching situation proved to be pure drudgery. The kids did not want to take lessons, but their mother insisted. They chose to practice little, if at all. It was like pulling teeth to get any musical sound out of those piano keys. They were true beginners and stayed in that category for that year. Finally, I begged Sr. Caroline to let me talk to their mother to stop their lessons at the end of the year. What a contrast from the Tidd girls!

As for my other duties that year, I followed the path of my first year, but everything was a bit easier now that I knew the expectations of the housework and classrooms. The heat was still atrocious, but the joy of working with the Mexican migrants made up for any discomfort. I also enjoyed working with the nuns at our mission.

Toward the end of my second year in Asherton, Sr. Caroline surprised all of us at supper one night. She had just talked with Fr. Schweider in Carrizo Springs, who told her that he contacted Mother Mary John at our Motherhouse. He wanted to know if she could send another nun, the following school year, to start his new school. Father planned to build four classrooms and an office on the land opposite the church. Sr. Caroline was all excited. She said she was sure to be chosen as the new principal. After all, she had been in Texas for so many years, had administrative experience, and knew many people in Carrizo Springs.

We all agreed that she would be the person chosen because of her experience and expertise in running a school. Sr. Caroline agreed. For laughs, she then said, "Well, we all know the nun that it will NOT be. That is our baby nun, Sr. Mona."

With that, we all laughed hysterically and agreed. As the talk continued, Sr. Caroline said she would be helping Father with his plans for the new school. If she were to become the new school principal, we wondered who would become the principal in Asherton?

We finished our school year and returned to the Motherhouse for our annual retreat and summer obedience. Sr. Marian and I were assigned to attend St. Catherine's College in St. Paul, Minnesota. We both decided to register for Spanish classes. Unfortunately, much to our disappointment, they were only offering Intermediate Spanish and would not allow anyone in the class that had not taken Beginning Spanish. Learning Spanish would have helped us tremendously if we returned to Texas.

Since my sister Flo lived near the college, I visited her family several times that summer. Mom, Dad, and Mary Ann drove to the Twin Cities, so we were together as a family, which I loved. I shared Texas stories and explained how much I missed them, and how much I loved teaching the Mexican children. Telling them how much I loved their weekly letters, I shared that it wasn't the same as visiting in person, so I loved having these visits with them. I told them I didn't know my assignment for the next school year, but I would let them know as soon as I received it.

That summer, I took an Applied Music class to help me with my piano teaching, a course in Logic, and a class called "Principles of Learning and Teaching in the Elementary Schools." It would be my first class in learning HOW to teach! I managed to get an A in the last two courses, but only a B in my music class. I decided not to share that tidbit of info with anyone, except Sr. Marian. She knew I did not feel competent to give piano lessons; I only did it because I had no choice.

We received an envelope with our assignment for the coming school year in the last weeks of summer school. I so hoped I would return to Texas. With shaking hands, I opened the envelope and screamed out in total disbelief. It said: "Sr. Mona, you will return to teach in Texas, but this year you will be the principal and first-grade teacher at the new school in Carrizo Springs, Texas." WHAT???? Was Mother Mary John out of her mind?

Sr. Marian read hers and came running over to see why I was screaming. For once, I was speechless. Then, still shaking, I handed her my obedience slip. Her mouth fell open in shock. "Oh, no, wait until Sr. Caroline hears about this!" was her immediate response.

It so happened that Sr. Caroline was attending the same college that summer. Because she was a senior nun, she lived on campus. We younger nuns lived off-campus, at a house owned by our Motherhouse.

I certainly was not looking forward to meeting up with her the next day. I knew she must have been in total shock, realizing that she was not the new school principal in Carrizo Springs. I was sure she had already questioned everyone to find out who it was.

My mind was in complete turmoil. Did Mother Mary John know that I had never taught in a classroom? That I was only twenty-three? That I knew nothing about being a principal, much less starting a new school? What had caused her to make this kind of decision? All I knew was that one did not question one's obedience slip. What would tomorrow bring?

Sr. Caroline was there to meet us as we all piled out of the station wagon in the parking lot the next day. She rushed up to Sr. Marian, asking what her obedience assignment was. Relieved that Sr. Marian was not the new principal, she asked me if I was returning to Texas. Of course, I nodded in the affirmative. Then, Sr. Marian blurted out, "And can you believe Sr. Mona is going to be the new principal in Carrizo?"

Sr. Caroline stopped as if a semi had hit her, turned around, and yelled at me, "That was to be my job! What on earth was the Rev. Mother thinking when she gave it to you! It's not fair!"

I started to cry and said I had no idea and didn't know why. That was a wasted day of study and classes. I was an emotional wreck, trying to imagine how I would carry out my assignment for next year.

I was thrilled that Sr. Caroline wasn't in any of my college classes that summer, and that she was living on campus. How could I live with the jealousy and anger of Sr. Caroline? I avoided her as much as possible. What would it be like when we were back at the Motherhouse, planning for our Texas return?

Chapter Fourteen

My Texas Years 1963-67

The best education is not given to students; it is drawn out of them. It is the supreme art of the teacher to awaken joy in creative expression and knowledge. Good teaching is more a giving of right questions than a giving of right answers.

Anonymous

The rest of that summer of 1963—after receiving my new Obedience to be a principal and first-grade teacher—I spent every free minute trying to learn a principal's responsibilities. My biggest challenge was the role of becoming a principal and starting a new school with zero experience. The best resources for me were the nuns that had been, or were currently, principals of other schools.

But, of course, I also wanted to acquire as many tips or strategies for teaching first graders as I could. With all her years of teaching first-grade Mexican migrant children in Asherton, I knew Sr. Mary Ellen would be a great source of helping me teach first graders when we were in Texas.

I didn't go to the Reverend Mother for guidance, because she was so distant from teaching and principal duties. I was also so excited about my new assignment that I didn't want Mother Mary John to know how insecure I was. Otherwise, she might have questioned her decision to assign me as the new principal in Carrizo Springs. Plus, if I did go to her, I knew she would tell me to ask Sr. Caroline for advice. At this point, I was afraid to tell the Rev. Mother the vehement adverse reactions that Sr. Caroline was feeling and displaying toward me. It would be like being a tattle-tale, and I didn't want to fuel the fire.

A few days before we left for Texas, Mother Mary John blessed us and wished us the best of success in our upcoming school year, especially with the Our Lady of Guadalupe School in Carrizo Springs. Looking at Sr. Caroline, she said, "Please be there to support Sr. Mona in every way you can. She is young and inexperienced, but I am confident that she will bring her enthusiasm and zest for life to the work needed to start a new school."

Then Reverend Mother explained that I would live in Asherton, rather than alone in Carrizo Springs. Father Schweider had purchased a car for my travels back and forth.

As she talked, I tried to look brave, but, inside, my stomach was in knots. I wondered if I should try to meet with her alone at this last minute to change her mind and have Sr. Caroline be the new principal. Yet, she just said she was confident I could do the job. Obedience was one of the vows I had just taken, so I decided that I needed to accept her decision and not question it.

I felt so inadequate. Even if I did my utmost, I needed all the blessings and prayers that the entire convent could give me. Was there a saint to pray to for one's feelings of inadequacy?

Our trip to Texas followed the same travel stops as the previous two years, but my mind was unsettled. I tried to figure out all the complexities of being a principal and starting a new school. Having a disgruntled superior did not make it any easier.

Nuns in Texas. Sr. Mary Ellen, Me, Sr. Marian,
Sr. Caroline, Sr. Margaret, Sr. Noreen. (L to R)

I needed to learn how to walk that tightrope of independence and yet still be dependent on the other nuns. I knew Sr. Caroline would be challenging to live with. Her dreams of being the new principal had been crushed. Somehow, I must learn to ask for assistance but still be assertive in my final decisions.

Since we did not have a new Cinderella flunky nun to replace me, that meant that life in Asherton would take on another change. Sr. Caroline told us that every nun would have to take on more cooking, cleaning, and laundry duties. She designated Saturdays as our cleaning and laundry days.

The day after we returned, Sr. Caroline told me that the two of us should drive to Our Lady of Guadalupe Church in Carrizo Springs to pay a visit to the parish priest. First, she wanted to introduce me to Father Schweider, as the school's new principal. Then, the three of us could discuss plans for the coming school year. Driving up to the rectory, I looked over at the construction area to see if they had completed the new school. It didn't look finished.

Our Lady of Guadalupe Church in Carrizo Springs, Texas

After Sr. Caroline introduced me as the new principal, Father shared that I would start teaching in the parish hall because the new school was not ready. The new school's name was Our Lady of Guadalupe School, taking the same name as the parish, unlike the

Asherton school, whose name was different from the parish church. He then added that his parishioners had decided they wanted a first grade *and* a kindergarten class. Well, that was news to me as well as to Sr. Caroline. She quickly assured him that she knew of a likable candidate in Asherton for the additional teaching position.

Father turned to look at me for approval. I said I would find a person as soon as I could. He then went on to say that the kindergarten class would begin classes in the garage near the hall. He assured me that all of this was very temporary.

Since Carrizo Springs would have its own school and teacher-principal, Father requested that I become the organist for one of the Masses on Sunday. Unfortunately, their organist had recently moved away. He would try to hire another, but until that time, he needed someone. Sr. Caroline assured him that I could do that, and that she would come with me every Sunday to direct the choir. Now I would have two Sunday Masses to prepare for—one in Asherton and one in Carrizo Springs. Oh, well. What was yet another challenge to add to my list?

It began to feel like Sr. Caroline was the principal instead of me. Here she was making all the decisions as I stood by, not knowing what to do. I felt very uncomfortable. What was Father thinking? Time would tell.

I couldn't wait to see the new school buildings, so Father proudly walked across the open area between them and his rectory to show us the current status of the new school. Butterflies flitted in my stomach as I stared at the buildings. My first authentic teaching assignment!

In front of us stood an elongated, blue concrete building divided into four classrooms, each having a door leading to the outside. A cement walkway connected them to the office building. Father explained that he planned to build another four classrooms parallel to these with a playground in-between. He designed the school to be u-shaped, with the office space and bathrooms joining the classrooms on one end. Since the school was just across the road from the church and community hall, it would be easy to take the students to visit and attend Mass.

Walking into the unfinished classrooms, I first noticed how light-filled they were because the outside wall was all windows. The windows had divided-glass sections to open or close. Built-in shelves were underneath the windows for storing supplies and books. The new smell was refreshing, and I was overcome with excitement to think I would be teaching in this brand new school that I loved already. It was so different from the Asherton school that I didn't want to look at Sr. Caroline's face to see how she reacted.

After looking at the classrooms, Father took out a key to open the office building. Inside were materials and textbooks from the Archdiocese. Father said the office furniture and desks for the classroom were to arrive the following week. He shared that the school would hopefully be ready for occupancy in a month.

Sr. Mona (me) in front of new school office.

"Sister Mona, I hope you can put up with the inconvenience of waiting to start in the new school," he said.

What could I say? "I'm sure we can," I responded with as much confidence as I could muster. He smiled at that. Secretly, I was glad that he addressed me and not Sr. Caroline.

"I'm going tomorrow to pick up your new car in Dallas. Then I'll bring it to Asherton for you," Father added. "I'm sure you will want to have your own transportation and not depend on the Asherton nuns' car."

My heart skipped a beat to think of the upcoming responsibilities. Hopefully, Father would not discover that I had never taught in a classroom before this, much less that I had no experience of what it was to be a principal. I thanked him for showing us the new school and that it would be great to have the car for traveling back and forth from Asherton.

On the way back to Asherton, I told Sr. Caroline how shocked I was to find out that we would also start a kindergarten class. But, unfortunately, there would be little time to find a teacher at this late date.

"Don't worry, Sr. Mona, remember that I have been teaching here for over ten years. I know all the people in the village and will find someone," she assured me. What else could I say?

She also reminded me that she was my Superior. I needed to report to her every day when I returned from Carrizo Springs. She wanted to know what happened during the day, and share whatever Fr. Schweider said whenever I talked with him. Oh, dear, she could not accept that she was not the new school's principal.

I decided I would not let this bother me and that I would do everything in my power to make this new school the best that ever existed. My energies were better spent learning the ropes of becoming a teaching principal, rather than being upset with Sr. Caroline's demands as my superior

The next day Sr. Caroline invited Aurora Villaneuva to visit with us at the Asherton school. Sr. Caroline explained the available kindergarten teaching position to her, and wondered if she would be interested in it.

At this point, I interrupted Sr. Caroline to tell Aurora that I was the new principal. Then, I explained that our new school wouldn't be ready for about a month. Would she be willing to teach in a garage until our school classrooms were completed?

Aurora was a soft-spoken, gentle young woman, but she was still self-assured. She shared that she had worked with young children, and was currently taking classes to become a teacher. She looked at us with excitement in her eyes. "I don't have a degree. but I love children," she added. "I will do whatever you need me to do as your kindergarten teacher."

"Great!" I responded. "Since you speak both English and Spanish, you'll be a great asset when we work with the parents during school registration and the school year."

Once again, I so wished that I was able to speak Spanish. Having Aurora as the kindergarten teacher to translate for me was a blessing. Sr. Caroline interrupted to say that she would assist us because both of us were new to teaching and running a school.

I explained to Aurora that I would be living with the nuns here in Asherton, but would be getting a car from the Carrizo parish so we could ride together each day. Driving to and from school would allow us to discuss ideas and work.

I shared that the pastor was willing to get us whatever we needed regarding teaching materials. At this point, Sr. Caroline again interrupted to assure Aurora that she could also help us in every way. An hour later, we had a kindergarten teacher. I thanked Sr. Caroline for her help.

Father Schweider arrived with the brand new, flaming red car the following Monday. Sr. Caroline immediately went out to share the good news that she had found a kindergarten teacher for him. Did he want to meet her now?

Father looked at me and asked if I could bring Aurora over the next day. I realized that he detected Sr. Caroline's need to be in control and how subtly he was deflecting this control towards me, his neophyte, young principal. For this, I was grateful. I quickly thanked him, and asked what time would be best for our visit. He handed me the keys and said he would be at the rectory any time after Mass.

Aurora and I drove over the following day to visit with Father. He was very impressed with her, and happy to have a Hispanic kindergarten teacher. He wanted to share the new school buildings with her and proudly showed her the school office with its supplies.

I was surprised to see that a new mimeograph machine and all new office furniture had arrived. Seeing everything so fresh and up-to-date caused me to think again how different this was from teaching in Asherton. I had to keep pinching myself to believe that Aurora and I had the privilege of starting a brand new school! Oh, my, when the Asherton teachers at St. Thomas School would see the mimeograph machine, they would think it was a bit of heaven compared to their old gel copier.

Everything in the new buildings smelled pristine and untouched. When Aurora saw the spacious classroom that would soon house her students, she clapped her hands in glee. We decided that her kindergarten classroom should be the first one and that my first-grade class would be next to hers to create a chronological order.

Father explained that he had waited for so many years to have a parish school and that, finally, his dream had come true. The other two classrooms would be used for grades two through eight catechism classes after school. He asked Aurora if she would be willing to teach catechism classes as part of her contract. She readily agreed.

He asked Aurora to return to the rectory to discuss her contract while I stayed in the office to check out the school supplies. I hoped that her salary would be much more than the meager pittance we nuns received. Maybe his parish could pay higher wages than the $1.00 a day that Asherton could afford.

When they returned, Father took us across the road to check out our temporary school quarters. He suggested that I teach my students in the parish hall and Aurora in the parish garage. The big drawback of teaching in the parish hall was removing everything each Friday afternoon because they used the parish hall as their hospitality room after the two Sunday masses. Not wanting to complain, I smiled and assured Father that we could make sacrifices until our new classrooms were ready. How could I object to anything when his dreams of having a parish school were about to come true?

After seeing the hall and garage, Aurora and I realized we had lots of work ahead to make the temporary "classrooms" workable and inviting. So every day, we drove in our bright red car to Carrizo Springs and worked like mad women trying to make the hall and garage look like classrooms. Despite the long hours and hard work, we had many laughs as we created our transitional teaching spaces. I realized what a great choice Sr. Caroline had made in asking Aurora to become the kindergarten teacher.

Aurora was a hard worker and willing to consider all kinds of ideas as we worked together. With portable blackboards, benches and tables instead of desks, and storage boxes holding our materials, we tried to decorate the walls to bring color to the drab surroundings. Knowing this was for just a short time, we were willing to endure the inconvenience.

Each day we walked across the road to encourage the workers at the new school and praised them for what they were doing. We hoped they knew how badly we wanted them to finish the buildings.

After Sunday Masses, we set up a registration table for our K-1 classes. We discovered that our classes would begin with ten students each, knowing more students would attend as migrant families returned from the North.

Father told me that I would not have to be concerned with the tuition or finances; his secretary was willing to do those jobs for the new school. I just had to teach and run the school as efficiently as possible.

The first day of school arrived, and I was as nervous as the new students. Parents drove up to the church parking lot and proudly presented their children as Aurora and I stood outside the parish hall with welcoming arms. Aurora's calm, yet inviting, personality made everyone comfortable.

I hugged each child and parent, telling them we were so thrilled to start our new school with their precious darlings. Then, we invited everyone into the hall to explain our agenda and school plans. Part of the welcome speech included sharing our hopes of moving to the new buildings in October. We would do our best teaching in the hall and garage until then. Everyone was accepting of that and thanked us for coming to their parish. At last, they had their Catholic school! All of our students were Hispanic.

Aurora and I discovered how grateful the parents were to have their children in a Catholic School. They made a point to thank us again and again when they picked up their children after each school day. They did not seem to care that our teaching environment was in the garage and hall.

Every Friday after school, Aurora helped me cart my supplies to the garage, and every Monday, she helped me return them to the parish hall. Oh, how wonderful it would be to teach in our new classrooms! The two of us appreciated the drive to and from school as it gave us time to discuss and plan for the next day's adventures of teaching the little darlings entrusted in our care.

Every Sunday, we nuns attended the 8:00 Mass at our Immaculate Conception Church in Asherton and then got in the car and drove to Our Lady of Guadalupe Church in Carrizo for their 10:00 Mass. Sr. Caroline directed the choirs, and I played the organ for those Masses. Almost every Sunday after Mass in Carrizo Springs, we visited Mom and Pop Willems, who had been special friends of the nuns ever since the nuns had arrived in Asherton years earlier.

Mom and Pop Willems were a Belgian couple who were staunch, loyal parish members. They lived right across the road from the church. Mom Willems was outgoing and filled with energy, while Pop Willems was the quiet, reserved person whose shy smile won everyone's heart.

They were ecstatic to have their own nun for their parish, and they became my sentinels of love and support—My new Mom and Dad away from home! Because they lived so close to the school and church, I learned to rely on them for sage advice and constant encouragement. They loved Aurora and adopted her as one of their own, as well.

Some Sundays, we nuns stopped to visit Mrs. Powers, an elderly widow who also was a staunch supporter of Our Lady of Guadalupe Church. Her son, Dick, owned huge agricultural fields and always brought us nuns fresh vegetables during the year.

Then, one day he appeared at our Asherton convent, carrying a television. We couldn't believe our good fortune. Because we were not allowed to have a TV in our convent, Dick found a place for it in Sr. Caroline's classroom. Then, of course, he sent an electrician the next day to have it properly connected.

How could we ever thank him? Dick was rich and had everything he needed. Sr. Caroline immediately thought of making caramels for him and creating a thank you card, pledging lots of prayers on his behalf. In addition to his frequent donations of fresh veggies, Dick made sure we always had all the food and trimmings for every holiday. Dick and his mother had such a soft spot in their hearts for us nuns, and they often expressed their appreciation for everything we did for both parishes.

Sometimes we also visited Mr. and Mrs. Jung on Sundays as we drove back to Asherton. They lived between the two towns on a small ranch. Mr. Jung used a wheelchair and enjoyed having the nuns stop by for a short visit. Their son, Kenny, who owned the local gas station in Carrizo Springs, was an excellent mechanic and took care of any car problems we ever had.

Every Sunday, the Asherton nuns needed to share their lesson plans with Sr. Caroline. I did not, since I was my own principal! Sunday afternoons were ours to prepare our weekly lesson plans, create worksheets for the students, and write letters to our families. I secretly said a special prayer of thanks as I saw the nuns struggle with their ancient gel copies while, in stark contrast, I could create my worksheets on the mimeograph machine in my office at school.

On September 14, 1963, during our letter-writing time, Sr. Marian wrote this in a letter to her sister, Susan:

> I'll now proceed to Carrizo. Sister Mona has the privilege of teaching over there, and she loves every minute of it. As yet, she is teaching in the parish hall since the school is not yet completed. She has everything she wants over there, and we are, in fact, her poor country cousins. Just yesterday, Father Schweider went to Dallas to get a car for her use in driving back and forth each day. It is a new Falcon and quite the thing—a bright, bright, red color. So all she all she needs now is a siren.
>
> Sister really has the stories to tell every day on her return home. On the first day of school, the tiny tots were to make introductions under Sister's supervision. She had them repeat after her, "My name is...." Everything went according to her outline until she came to one little boy. Sister instructed, "My name is Henry Vargas." No response — She tried a few more times. I guess without success. Finally, after much coaxing, he whispered in hardly an audible voice, "My name is Henry Vargas." The next day when Sister looked at the class list, she howled, and the light dawned — His name was JUAN Vargas!! (I guess he gets an A for Obedience, huh?)

The Tidd family became an integral part of our lives socially, and I continued to give piano lessons to the girls on Saturday mornings. It was puzzling how Sr. Caroline allowed us to be with the Tidds and the older people we visited in Carrizo, but was so strict in other areas of our lives.

The Tidds invited us to their home for meals, and we reciprocated, but most of the time, we went to their home in Carrizo. They would even plan outings for us. The whole family—Russ, Betty, Connie, Ginny, and Steven—would have us all pile in their big van, and off we would go to explore places in the area. We didn't need seat belts, and we were packed together like a can of sardines.

We often went on short trips to Eagle Pass, Cotulla, Dilley, Crystal City, or Laredo to see some historical sites and learn about their history. We took picnics to enjoy along the way at a roadside park or artificial water hole. Each outing was an exciting adventure filled with laughter. Just being together was the best entertainment. Some of the time, Sr. Caroline stayed back at the convent.

Russ always teased us about not belonging to the right church. The Tidds were staunch Episcopalians, so we spent lots of time arguing about who belonged to the right church. All in fun, as we loved our new friends and the joy that they brought into our lives. Russ worked for the Border Patrol and knew Spanish, so he always gave me a rough time asking why I was teaching in Texas and not learning the people's language. My comeback was that there just were not enough hours in the day to try and squeeze in time to study Spanish.

For me, teaching in Carrizo Springs felt so much different than teaching in Asherton. Even though Aurora and I were teaching in makeshift classrooms, the flavor and feel of a big town compared to Asherton were prevalent. Mexican people lived in Asherton, no Anglos. In Carrizo Springs, it was different, as there were many Anglos. The prevalent prejudice kept the Anglos and Mexicans segregated. There was even a Mexican Baptist church and an Anglo Baptist church. Even though our Lady of Guadalupe Church opened its arms to all, we had only Mexican children in our school. I wondered when that would change.

Carrizo Springs had a shoe repair shop, and the owner, Jack Springs, was the town's bachelor. He was a big supporter of Our Lady of Guadalupe, loved the nuns, and offered to repair our shoes. Jack never let us pay for the shoe repairs. Instead, he laughed and said he hoped we would help save his soul as he repaired our soles.

In October, we pushed toward the grand opening of our new school. Aurora and I spent hours and hours getting everything organized in our new classrooms the weekend before the first day. We designed bulletin boards and wanted our rooms to be inviting, yet educational. It was exciting to smell the fresh paint and see brand new furniture, actual blackboards, and spacious shelves lining the walls under the ample windows. We even had teachers' desks and comfortable chairs. Aurora and I felt like royalty!

Father ordered desks for all four classrooms. We would use the new school for the catechism classes for the public school children every afternoon, after regular school days. Aurora and I, as well as two of the Asherton nuns, would be teaching these classes so that we could have four sessions each day.

Our new office had the mimeograph machine, desk, and chairs. It looked dignified and official. I only wished that I felt more qualified. I did everything I could to act like I knew what I was doing.

When the Asherton nuns came to our grand opening, I felt uneasy as our school differed drastically from their impoverished school. It seemed like they were the developing country cousins in contrast to the richness of our new school.

The first week in the new school was like having your favorite ice cream whenever you wanted. The students were so excited to each have a desk and be in a real classroom with blackboards, bookshelves, individual cubbies for their belongings, and their very own playground.

Robert Tito, the church custodian, was more than happy to be the school custodian as well. His smiling face and concern for all the little ones were a special blessing for us. He spoke very little English, so I was happy to have Aurora translate. She was a Godsend also in working with the parents who did not speak English.

Having Aurora's expertise gave me an excuse not to study Spanish. The current philosophy on language acquisition was that the students would learn English more quickly if we didn't speak their language! To this day, I regret not knowing Spanish. Unfortunately, I was so busy trying to wear so many hats that there were never enough hours in the day for language study. I didn't even have a Spanish-to-English dictionary. I picked up a few common phrases, but could not carry on a conversation.

In October, the public school superintendent, Mr. Taylor, called to meet with me at our new school. He wanted to talk with me about Title One funding. I remember how nervous I was to meet him. But, as we spoke in my office, I decided to be very honest with him. I shared that I had never been a principal before, did not know anything about Titles or funding, and that I would be so appreciative if he could help me learn.

He smiled and, with a twinkle in his eye, said, "Sister, I appreciate your honesty and willingness to learn. You can rest assured that I will help you get all the funding we can get for your students, and will be here for you at any time."

We became friends, and he made sure that I learned more about the different Title programs over the following months. As a result, our school became even richer in resources.

1963 was the New Math implementation year, so the Archdiocese sent us all the manuals and workbooks for the new program. Besides everything else that was so new, I now had to learn how to teach this New Math, so I had to learn right along with the students. There were workshops in San Antonio, but the distance, and our busy schedules, made those impossible to attend.

Our schools were also required to implement new physical education programs and work on wellness and nutrition. I researched different ways to help the students become more physically fit. I came up with balance beams as one method. Since the commercial beams were so expensive, I showed a picture of them to one of our talented woodworking parishioners. Within two weeks, we had the balance beams that only cost the price of the materials. Because of the generosity of the woodworker, we then had money to buy playground equipment to encourage our students to become more fit. I was able to find funding for milk and healthy snacks for the students.

In addition to everything else, Aurora and I spent many hours developing ways to make learning fun for our students. I enjoyed this new freedom, new responsibilities, and the chance to create this new school. Because the parishioners were thrilled to have a Catholic school for the first time in their history, I wanted them to be proud of our school and students.

Father Schweider was living his dream to have a Catholic parish school. He was a quiet man, but he assured me that I should feel free to ask for help at any time, and that he would be there to assist me. He must have sent our Motherhouse money for my salary, but he never discussed that with me. (I learned later that Father Francisco was paying $1.00 a day for each nun in Asherton. I only found that out when he came over one evening to tell Sr. Caroline that he was sorry that he did not have money that month for the wages, which amounted to $120.00 for four nuns.)

Hearing this made me wonder what Fr. Schweider was paying for my wages since his parish was better off financially than Asherton. But, because Father told me that his secretary handled the finances, I decided it was none of my business. I had enough to do without getting into that.

Every day when I returned from teaching in Carrizo Springs, I had to report to Sr. Caroline if Father Schweider had visited the school. Knowing she was highly interested in the happenings at my school, I still resented having her question me.

A few months after moving into our new buildings, Betty Tidd came over to our school one day. By this time, Betty and I had become great friends. She shared that she'd dreamt about learning to play the organ for years. Would it be possible for me to give her organ lessons? In addition, she wanted to learn how to play the hymns for their small church.

Betty had also become our school nurse in Carrizo. I called on her whenever I needed help with any medical needs at our school. She kept us well stocked with bandaids and gave us an overflowing First Aid kit to place in the office. She was always only a call away for any emergency. Because she was a nurse and was always there to help us nuns in any medical need, I felt teaching her the basics of playing the organ would be a small way to thank her for all she did for us.

Friday afternoons became our time for organ lessons, so I drove to her Episcopalian Church to teach her using their organ. These lessons became our bonding time, and a time for teaching Betty the hymns she wanted to learn. I told Betty that these lessons would be our secret and there was no charge. I didn't think Sr. Caroline needed to know, as this was a decision I made that involved my school. When I gave lessons to Betty, Aurora used this time to prepare her lesson plans for the following week. She appreciated having that time at school and didn't have to take materials home.

A few months into the school year, the Archbishop of San Antonio sent a letter to all the nuns in his Archdiocese inviting us to a FREE movie in San Antonio, a city about 115 miles away. The film, *Lilies of the Field*, was at 10:00 a.m. We had to forgo a Saturday morning sleep-in if we wanted to go.

Excited about the chance to see a big-screen movie, we got up at 6:30 in the morning. Sr. Caroline opted not to go, so the four of us jumped in the car and headed north to see the movie. On the way, we talked and laughed, wondering if they awarded prizes for nuns traveling the farthest to attend this free movie. We all fell in love with Sydney Potier and loved the movie.

In the movie, Homer Smith (Sidney Poitier) is an itinerant jack-of-all-trades who stops at a farm in the Arizona desert to obtain water for his overheated car. There he sees several women working—very ineptly—on a fence. The women, who speak very little English, introduce themselves as German, Austrian and Hungarian nuns. Before he knows it, Mother Superior persuades him to do a minor roofing repair. He stays overnight, assuming that he will be paid in the morning.

The next day, Smith tries to persuade Mother Superior to pay him by quoting Luke 10:7, "The laborer is worthy of his hire." Mother Maria Marthe responds by asking him to read another Bible verse from the Sermon on the Mount: "Consider the lilies of the field, how they grow; they toil not, neither do they spin. And yet I say unto you that even Solomon in all his glory was not arrayed like one of these."

Mother Maria likes things done her way. The nuns have essentially no money and subsist by living off the land, eating whatever vegetables the arid climate provides, and some milk and eggs. Even after being stonewalled when asking for payment, the nuns persuade Smith to stay for another meal. He agrees, against his better judgment, to remain an extra day to help them with other small jobs, always with the faint hope that Mother Maria will pay him for his work.

As Smith's skills and strengths become apparent to the nuns, they come to believe that God has sent him to fulfill their dream of building a chapel for the townsfolk (who are Mexican and impoverished) as the nearest church is miles away.

Sidney Potier teaches the nuns English using songs and the Bible. One of the songs was the famous "Amen" song that we nuns sang all the way home. It was an unforgettable movie about nuns struggling to build a chapel, and later a school, for Mexican immigrants. We drew many similarities between the film and our Texas work.

School life progressed well with no problems until the day that Robert Tito came rushing to my classroom in real distress. It was Friday, November 22, 1963. He was sobbing and trying to tell me something. Then I heard the words, President Kennedy. The first graders came running up and asked him in Spanish what was wrong.

He told them that our President had been shot and killed in Dallas a few minutes earlier. My students began to sob. I rushed to Aurora's room to share the news and asked her to talk with Robert Tito to learn more.

Totally in shock, we gathered our little ones together and immediately walked over to the church to pray the rosary for him, his family, and our country. So many people came in and joined us as we prayed in disbelief of the tragedy that had just happened.

That weekend, we nuns sat glued to the TV in Sr. Caroline's classroom from Friday through Monday. We were in a state of shock over Kennedy's assassination, and immobilized while the horrific scenes unfolded in front of us. Sr. Marian, being from Boston, had met some of the Kennedy clan, and she shared her Kennedy stories with us. We kept asking ourselves, "How can our country ever recover from such an act of violence?"

We were trying to teach those last days before Thanksgiving, but it was difficult for everyone. We were all still in shock over the death of our beloved, young President. The children kept asking, "Sister, why did the President die? Why would someone want to kill him?" When we dismissed our students for Thanksgiving vacation, we asked them to pray for the Kennedy family and our country. As I hugged each student good-by, I told them how thankful I was to be their teacher and how grateful we must be for our new school.

Sr. Caroline seemed to become more accepting that she was not the principal of Our Lady of Guadalupe School, and her demands of having my report to her each day lessened.

At Christmas time, Sr. Marian and Sr. Margaret went out to try to find an evergreen tree. They came back with a small tabletop tree that looked similar to the Charlie Brown version. In Sr. Marian's letter to her sister, she wrote the following:

December 1963

So many times I've mentioned our sole closet in this home, haven't I? Well, on one of its uppermost shelves neatly tucked away rested our Christmas decorations. To get them down either requires a tall ladder from the garage — or Sr. Mona. (We sometimes refer to her as the missing link or a very close semblance to our ancestors — only because of her talent to climb, of course.)

Being my lazy self, I asked her to do her climbing stunts last Saturday to reach the packages for me. She obliged, of course, while I did the heavy looking on and supposedly held her back or braced her someway. My helpful hand was no earthly good when the shelves tumbled down and Sr. Mona with them. By some freak accident, she landed on her feet and in one piece. The only broken thing happened to be a splintered mop handle.

Any normal person would have gone for the ladder to fix the shelf but not Monique (another nickname), for she hurried right up again to repair the damage. Don't ask us how that happened because we don't know. The whole thing was funny afterward, but Sr. Mona claims she prefers to get laughs in another manner.

As long as I'm telling stories about Sr. Mona, I might as well tell you about learning the song "Jingle Bells" with her class of first graders. After they'd practiced the song a few times, Sister said anyone having little bells could bring them to school for the sake of accompaniment. The next day one of her pupils greeted her with a clanging cowbell on a wire. He was thrilled to death, and Sister tried to be thrilled also while the class attempted to sing above the sound of the bell.

Once again, Sr. Marian's family outdid themselves with the multitude of Christmas gifts for her, but also for the rest of us nuns. Smoked turkey, ham, jams and jellies, nuts, and candy were some of the bountiful treats hidden in the most beautifully decorated packages I had ever seen. The convent living room looked like a decorated department store with all her boxes overshadowing the Charlie Brown tree! Mom sent my favorite treat of popped wild rice, which was shared and enjoyed by my fellow nuns.

In my letters to my family, I shared many stories of trying to be the best principal and teacher I could be. I knew that my parents had hoped I would have received a Minnesota assignment so that they could visit me more often. Despite that, they were happy to learn how much I loved teaching the Mexican migrant children, and that I had fallen in love with the people.

At this time, Mary, my younger sister, was fourteen, and my older sister, Flo, was twenty-six, married, and had two children. My parents were in their mid-fifties and did not travel much outside Minnesota. I knew better than to ask them to drive the long distance to Texas to visit me. Communicating every week through letters was a comfort and kept us informed of what was happening in each others lives. My Texas letters often became Texas-sized in length as I tried to explain my new assignment and adventures as a teaching principal in our new school.

In the middle of March 1964, we were preparing for Holy Week, and I wrote to my family telling them about all the liturgies we needed to prepare. I shared how challenging it was to fit in extra choir practices at both churches and carry on our regular duties. I always got a weekly letter from home, and this week it did not arrive, so I decided to grumble a bit to the other nuns that Saturday evening.

"I hope nothing has happened. Mom is so good about writing every week, " I told the other nuns. None of them were very sympathetic and told me I should be thankful for the weekly letters I had received. Just at that moment, there was a knocking at the door leading into our convent.

Sr. Caroline walked down the hallway to see who was at the door. We heard Sr. Caroline say, "Good evening, won't you please come in?"

I wondered who this impatient person was, and what could they want this time of the evening? There were lots of footsteps following Sister down the hall. Looking up from my lesson plans, I screamed, dropping my lesson plan book. Who should be standing before me but Dad, Mom, and Mary Ann! How could this be? I had just complained about not getting a letter, and here they were in person, standing in our living room.

Jumping up and down in total excitement, I continued to scream and cry simultaneously as I frantically hugged each one in disbelief. Scrambling to find more chairs, the other nuns joined in the laughing and crying as I introduced them to my family. After much commotion of talk and laughter, Mom and Dad shared the story of how this trip happened.

Unbeknownst to me, they had been writing to Sr. Caroline and the others to plan this surprise trip to Texas. The nuns had helped them get a motel in Carrizo Springs since we did not have room in our convent, and there was no motel in Asherton. Sr. Marian writes about their surprise visit in the following letters to her family:

March 8, 1964:

...Did we get news here the other day!! Sr. Mona's family wrote to Sr. Caroline telling her that they were planning a surprise visit on March 21 through that week until Holy Thursday. Everyone knows but Sr. Mona. I tell you — you'll hear the uproar in Massachusetts — and there is no doubt about that. Sr. Caroline is just great and is making arrangements for me to take Sr. Mona's first-grade class in Carrizo — so she can be completely free to tour the country and show off Texas to her family. What a break! It will be a "once in a lifetime" for sure. How lucky Sister is to have Sr. Caroline — in some circumstances, we wouldn't even be allowed to miss a prayer, much less be free as a bird. Anyway, I could hoot every time I look at Monique and think of her great surprise.

March 21, 1964:

..Man, what a shock! If Sr. Mona is never quite the same again, we'll know why. Last night after we were all preparing for bed, Sister's family came. Monique was making her lesson plans for the coming week, complete with night veil when Sister Caroline brought her family into the house. She looked up and just stood there — with her mouth open (for a full minute, it seemed.) I think she then proceeded to a scream followed by a flood of tears. Of course, the rest of us didn't help matters much, but I honestly wondered if Sr. Mona would ever be able to stop. Although we are thrilled for Sr. Mona, today we are a little green with envy. After dinner, she took off — and I mean jet propulsion style too. (Personally, I don't think she'll ever again land.) She won't be back until Tuesday sometime. They plan on going to Laredo today. Then, if at all possible, they will go into Monterrey. (That is if Sr. Mona can get in that far to Mexico since she is a religious.) From there, they will hopscotch to Corpus Christi to view the Gulf. What a life, huh?

My family joined us for Mass in Carrizo Springs on Sunday morning. I couldn't believe that Sr. Caroline had arranged for Sr. Marian to take my first-grade class for three days and let me travel with my family. It all seemed like a unique, wonderful dream unfolding that would suddenly disappear.

My family had never been to Texas. They wanted to visit my area and had the idea to cross into Mexico, since Nuevo Laredo was only forty-five miles away. I remember my Dad asking me if I knew enough Spanish to be their interpreter if we drove into Mexico. I assured him I knew enough to help us get by. (This would be sufficient fodder for my next confession).

Crossing the border, I became the person the police scrutinized and questioned, not my family. When they heard my name was Mona, the entire group of security men started to laugh. I tried to repeat my name, emphasizing the "a" at the end, but they continued to laugh. I was Sr. "Monkey" to them, and after a few more questions, we were finally allowed to go across the border into Mexico. My family wanted to hear the entire story of my name and its connotations in Spanish. That led to more laughs.

Arriving in Monterrey, the traffic was heavy, and Dad was nervous. He kept asking me to translate the Spanish road signs for him. The tension grew as I only knew "Alto." Stopping for a red traffic light, Dad had his window rolled down. A young Mexican man poked his head in and started asking questions. Of course, I had no idea what he was saying. That made Dad even more nervous. He quickly rolled up his window and turned to me to say, "Vonnie, I thought you said you knew Spanish!"

I wish I could tell you that my Spanish improved during that trip, but when I couldn't even tell him the word for the men's bathroom, it got even worse! How we made it through that trip with my meager Spanish vocabulary is beyond me.

Dad wanted to get some good tequila while in Mexico and bring some home for his buddies. We found a tavern and walked in. All talk ceased as I, a nun in her full garb, entered the room. Obviously, this was not the place where nuns hung out! The tavern keeper just stood there staring, unable to look away from the nun bellying up to the bar.

Thank heavens, the only necessary Spanish word was "tequila." After asking for tequila, Dad motioned that he wanted to sample some. Shaking his head, the bar keeper bowed to me, then poured tequila for everyone. Dad was delighted with the taste and bought four bottles. I chose not to walk out of the tavern carrying a bottle of tequila. My walking *into* the bar caused enough of a shock.

(The sad part about this story is that they served Dad the best quality, but sold him poor quality bottles. Dad discovered this when he arrived home to share the tequila with friends and family.)

Mom loved eating beans, and we certainly had plenty of chances to have beans for breakfast, lunch, and dinner. I can still see Mom savoring every meal as she ate her fill of beans. Mom began moaning from her overindulgence of this favorite food on our way back to Texas. We had to make many stops along the way for Mom to relieve her "bean illness."

It still seemed like a beautiful dream that my family had traveled all the way to visit me in Texas. I was delighted that they spent a few days after our Mexico trip visiting with the nuns and our friends, the Tidds and the Willems. Betty Tidd helped Mom recover from her bean overindulgence, for which Mom was highly grateful.

When we returned to Carrizo Springs, it was with pride that I showed off our new school. Since it was Easter vacation, my family did not get a chance to see my wonderful little first graders, but they were very impressed with our school.

Saying goodby after a week with them was a difficult and tearful farewell. Even my fellow nuns cried. How special I felt to have had such a wonderful visit with my family. Sr. Caroline pulled out all the stops to make them feel welcome. It just so happened that Sr.

Caroline was originally from Mahnomen, MN, so my folks knew her family, and they had great stories to share.

(The tequila, beans, and my name episode became the highlights of conversation whenever my family would recall our Mexico trip. Of course, for every story that Dad shared of their Texas trip, he had to preface it with my inability to speak Spanish. Dad never let me forget it. It was the most fantastic trip for all of us to be together, and something I will treasure forever in my heart despite my limited Spanish vocabulary.)

Our trip to Mexico. Dad, Mom, me, and Mary Ann.

The following are two letters that Sr. Marian wrote after my folks left.

April 5, 1964

...Let's go back to Sr. Mona! She is gradually getting into the swing of things again, although we hear another fragment of a conversation she had during her glorious visit with her family each day. It's incredible how it can string out over such a lengthy period of time. I'm beginning to believe that none of them slept at night in those motels where they stayed. Otherwise, how could they possibly have said so many things or seen so many sights? The last two nights, we sisters enjoyed her family too, at which time we sat up until all hours just gabbing and laughing.

April 10, 1964

"....Sr. Mona has a chronic latecomer each morning in her first-grade class. The girl usually tries to appease things by offering some tidbits to her teacher. The little cherub hasn't tired of her ailment, but Sr. Mona has long since quit asking for excuses. So last week, when the tardy tot pulled in about fifteen minutes late for school and placed a lovely bouquet of flowers on Sister's desk, "Monique" hardly looked up from her reading class. It was only later at recess that the reason for the girl's tardiness leaked out. Her aunt had been picking the flowers for Sr. Mona, and in the process of gathering the blossoms, she was bit by a rattlesnake. A good excuse for her tardiness this time, wouldn't you say?

The spring of the year was time for First Communion celebrations. No matter how little money the families had, the boys and girls looked like they had just stepped out of a fashion shop with their new clothes. Boys wore black pants, white shirts, and even ties. The girls wore white dresses decked out in veils and white shoes.

To prepare them for this special occasion, we spent months teaching catechism classes about the Sacraments of Penance and Communion. To help the children practice going to confession, we nuns pretended to be the priests and sat in the priest's chair. We wanted to make sure that each child knew the formula of words for their First Confession: "Bless me, Father, for I have sinned. This is my first confession. These are my sins."

Telling them to make up some sins, we heard everything from "I killed my brother twice, I hit my sister fifty times, I said bad words to my father seventy times." Having no sense of numbers or what sins were about, we nuns kept asking WHY our little innocent children needed to go to confession!

One little boy got so nervous when we practiced for the first time, I heard sobs coming from his side of the confessional. I tried to reassure him that everything was alright and not to worry, but his sobs got louder and louder. I got up from the priest's chair in the enclosed area of the confessional and went out to see what was the matter with this little darling. A puddle of water trickled from behind the curtained door of the penitent. He had been so nervous, he peed in his pants and didn't know what to do. One more reason why innocent children should not have to go through this.

At that time, the Catholic Church was very strict about not touching the Communion host with your fingers and not letting it touch your teeth before swallowing it. How does one explain this to little ones? Now the fear of the confessional was replaced by the fear of doing the wrong thing when receiving communion. I will never forget little Luis on his First Communion Day. He was so nervous that he gagged on the host. His father rushed up to take him out of the church. What happened to the JOY of receiving sacraments for the first time? I often wondered if the boy ever got over the fear of receiving the host.

The bishop came every other year to our area to administer the sacrament of Confirmation. On the years that the bishop came, I hoped one of the other nuns would teach the Confirmation class, because the students needed to memorize many answers from the catechism. One never knew which child the bishop would quiz during the ceremony. During the questioning, we nuns almost peed in our pants in nervousness. We so hoped the kids would respond well and correctly.

I remember that spring when the bishop came over to our convent after Confirmation. The protocol was to kneel and kiss the bishop's ring whenever he appeared. After doing that, he told us that he had decided we all could sleep in the following day and not have to say our Divine Office.

I felt that we nuns deserved more than one day's late sleep after our many hours of teaching to prepare the students! I don't think he realized how difficult it was for these children to learn the catechism in their second language. Instead of sleeping in late, I thought canonization would have been more appropriate for both the students and us.

Since it was the rule that a nun could be a Superior at one place for no more than six years, Sr. Caroline knew she would not be returning the following school year to Asherton. It was a total surprise to get our next year's Obedience in May instead of summertime.

We nuns hurriedly opened our envelopes to find out where we would be the following year. Sr. Caroline learned that she would be a principal at Thief River Falls in northern Minnesota. Sr. Margaret also would be leaving us for another teaching assignment in Minnesota. The other news was that Sr. Mary Ellen would be our new Superior. That came as a big shock. Sister had been teaching first grade all the past years, but now she would be promoted to teaching the seventh and eighth graders, and taking on the additional role of Superior and Principal in Asherton. Sr. Marian and I were thrilled that we would be returning to Texas. We now wondered which nuns would join us to replace Sr. Caroline and Sr. Margaret for the next school year.

The Mexican village loved Sr. Caroline. She had been with them for over ten years and had won their hearts. They, in turn, had won hers. The farewell that the parishioners gave her was fit for a queen. The singing, banquet, and embraces were part of the festivities. The local women prepared the delicious tamales, tacos, and beans of all kinds, as well as the sweets she so loved.

Sr. Caroline had mellowed despite our challenges since I became the principal at Our Lady Of Guadalupe School. That drive back to Minnesota was bittersweet as she shared beloved stories and experiences over her past years in Texas. I could only imagine the sadness she must have felt, knowing she wasn't coming back. I was so thankful that my Obedience stated that I would return to my precious people in Texas.

Our summer of 1964 was spent in our annual retreat and then off to St. Catherine's College for summer school. Still unable to take a beginner's Spanish class, I took Teaching of Math at the Elementary level, Social Dynamics of Behavior in the School-Age Child, and Applied Music. (I knew I had to get better in piano and learn new techniques for my piano teaching.)

Father Schweider requested another nun for our school to add a second grade. So we now had three new nuns joining our Texas family. Sr. Colette became the first-grade teacher to replace Sr. Mary Ellen, Sr. Rosalia took Sr. Margaret's second- and third-grade classroom, and Sr. Noreen joined me in Carrizo Springs to teach second grade. Lots of changes.

Sr. Marian used her new math skills and figured out that the common denominator for all our ages was twenty-five for the coming school year. Our Texas mission life required young blood and the willingness to take on any challenge that presented itself. We learned quickly to say, "Yes, I can do that!" without batting an eyelash.

After squeezing our six bodies into the car, we began our trek to Texas in late August. Sr. Mary Ellen continued the tradition of stopping at her family's home on the way down, but we persuaded her to find some new routes to Asherton. She readily agreed, and we found ourselves exploring Oklahoma City and Dallas for two of our stops on the way.

We were awestruck as we drove several times around the area where Lee Harvey Oswald had shot President Kennedy. Each time we got another look at the warehouse area, we continuously missed our exit. We thought we would never leave Dallas with all the traffic and one-way streets.

As we chatted during our five-day trip to Texas, we tried to figure out plans for adding a sixth nun to our small convent. With Sr. Noreen joining us, we now were up to five nuns sleeping in the same space as four of us had in the past years. Adding another bed to our dormitory made our close quarters even closer. Figuring out which side of the bed to get out of without bumping into the other nun took cooperation, plus coordination. Finding the hammer, we added another nail in the closet for another set of habits. Having such a limited wardrobe was essential.

Space-wise, it made me wonder why Rev. Mother decided not to have Sr. Noreen and I live in Carrizo Springs. It would have been so much easier, not only for living space but also for travel. Once again, one did NOT question the Mother Superior! It was good that we were all young, flexible, and pliable, and with an open mind willing to sacrifice anything to teach our beloved Mexican people.

Sr. Marian wrote this letter to her family:

August 1964 letter:
Our new nuns are loving their first hours in Texas...
-the lines of people that welcomed us home with the usual embraces,
-the $70.00 worth of food that filled our shelves donated by the Carrizo Springs people
-the priceless smiles on the sparkling faces of the children,
-the spotless house we stepped into,
-best of all: the six inches of rain Texas received last night after a completely rainless summer...
All these things are new to them, and although older experiences for us nuns returning, we shall always remember these moments with joy even after Texas is only a memory.
This year we are planning on having a hot lunch program in school. We are eligible for special dispensations by the government offered only to one other school in the nation. The children have to pay only 10 cents for lunch, so we are hoping many will take

advantage of the program. In order to have lunches, we needed a place to eat.

So Father Francisco had to build a $14,000 hall this summer and put us in debt for a while. It is very nice though and really a necessity. Now there will be a place to hold parish doings. I'm doubly glad since most of the extracurricular activities last year were held in my classroom.

We ate dinner and walked to show the new nuns the town. They saw their first tarantulas — one dead and one very much alive. We also saw a centipede a good three inches in length. I guess the heavy rain last night brought all the wildlife out of their homes. I don't know whether to be glad or sad that we could not point out a rattler, but it wasn't bad for the beginning, was it? Greg, your book "Running Scared" is still on top here. Sr. Mona enjoyed it on the trip.

Adding another grade to Our Lady of Guadalupe School in Carrizo was exciting. We could now offer Grades K to 2 for the parish. Instead of transferring to the public school, my first graders could advance to the next room, and a new teacher. Because we still had small classes, we could give so much more attention to each child. The parents were thrilled about that. Aurora was such a valuable asset, and she continued to take care of the Spanish translating whenever I needed help. Superintendent Taylor continued to offer assistance with the Title programs.

I will never forget the morning that fall when I was teaching my little first graders. We had left the door open since a lovely breeze was coming from that direction. Suddenly, an older woman clutching her rosary beads entered our classroom on her knees. She crawled to me, grabbed the bottom of my habit, and began crying and talking in Spanish. I didn't know what to do, so I immediately asked my students what she was saying.

One little girl rushed up to the woman and asked her what was wrong. Her son had just been in a horrible car accident and was not expected to live. She immediately implored Our Lady of Guadalupe to save her son and promised to make a "promesa" on her knees from her house to the church.

She not only went to the church but then came on her knees to ask me to pray for her son, since I was a nun and close to the Virgin Mary (in her way of thinking). Feeling so humbled, I told the little girl to tell the dear lady that I would definitely pray for her son and then helped her up from her bruised knees. I decided to gather the students and walk to the church to recite the rosary for her son. The grief-stricken woman was so grateful. I, once again, admired the deep faith of the Mexican people and their devotion to Our Lady of Guadalupe.

Another letter Sr. Marian sent to her family:

November 27, 1964

...Yesterday, Thanksgiving, was a perfect day, weather-wise (otherwise too). The people of Carrizo donated everything for our dinner, and we had everything, believe me. We sent over food for six priests at Father's home, so we had quite a bit to prepare. We had the bird stuffed and ready for the oven by ten o'clock the night before Thanksgiving. Sr. Mona was going to put the bird into the oven just before she popped into bed. Of course, she jumped in last, as usual. The rest of us nuns were already under the covers when Sister came bellowing into the dormitory. She announced that the broiler went on instead when she turned the oven to 200 degrees.

We all drudgingly fell out of bed and met in the kitchen. The funny part of the story is that our broiler hasn't worked for years, but tonight it seemed to be — according to the concerned turkey roaster, namely Sr. Mona. After a few moments of examination, we came to the conclusion that the reddened coil was the standard procedure for a warming oven. We also decided that Sr. Mona had never before taken time to look in the oven when it was first heating. I think it was at that time that the dear one knelt for our individual blessing before going back to bed. Only kidding, but it is one more thing to razz Sister Mona about.

With all the things we had yesterday to make our day so wonderful, it made me ashamed to see poverty at its peak. Someone sent us a box of clothes for small girls, and we thought of a family in school here. We have three girls from this family in school already — one in first and two in the primary. The other day, while driving by their house, I noticed a little sister in their yard playing with black diapers (made from rags). Yesterday we went to the house with some clothes.

Sr. Mary Ellen first asked in her best Spanish if they wanted the clothes. She then motioned for me to bring the box into the house. What a sight! The house consisted of 1 1/2 rooms, with two large double beds — no chairs — junk on the beds used for everything, I guess. The father was sitting on the bed holding a sick baby, crying in a pitiful little voice. The infant had the mother's apron wrapped around it for warmth. It seemed like there were a dozen little diapered children playing on the floor, but I guess there are only eight in all. One of the little girls' diapers was made out of an old curtain. The house reeked of kerosene burning somewhere. To see the children, you'd think they had everything, as they looked so happy. They shouted to us from blocks away as we left. They are so beautiful, and what a shame that they hardly have a chance in life.

After sharing this story with the rest of us nuns, we decided to do everything we could to help the neediest families in the village. Food and clothing were first on the list.

Fr. Schweider was so happy to have his school growing. He often came over to talk with the children and visit them in their classrooms. His dream was coming true, and he supported us in anything we needed. Robert Tito kept the school immaculate and always had a beaming smile on his face. Aurora told him in Spanish how much we appreciated his efforts.

One afternoon after school, I moved a bookshelf to get something that had fallen behind it. I screamed. Robert Tito came running. I pointed at the black spider with the red hourglass on its body. I had been warned about spiders, and I knew this one was venomous. Robert, my hero, killed it and smiled, all the while bowing to me as he was leaving the room. My scant Spanish vocabulary knew the word "Gracias," I repeated as he smiled and bowed to me!

The spring of 1965 brought unwanted changes. Fr. Schweider was transferred to another parish. We now had Father Green as our pastor of Our Lady of Guadalupe. He came over to check out the school and asked for a meeting with me.

His first words were: "I don't believe in Catholic schools, so we will not be adding another grade next year. I want this to be a catechetical center instead. We will not need to add more classrooms. Four rooms will be enough, and maybe we will continue with a K-2 school for a while."

I was dumbfounded. No matter what I said, the new pastor refused to listen. I pleaded and shared the plans for a K-8 school that Father Schweider had discussed with me. Father Green stubbornly stated that instead of adding to the school, he planned on building a new rectory for himself. One of his excuses was that the expenses of running a school were too overpowering for the budget.

In addition to everything else, he also wanted a kindergarten teacher from his parish, not someone from Asherton. Listening to him go on and on about his plans was too much news to swallow all at once. I realized we now had a priest with a completely different mindset than Fr. Schwieder. I did not like this man at all. Yet, I was the principal and first-grade teacher and needed to obey. I would not go down without a fight and needed time to formulate powerful arguments.

Like Father Schweider, I, too, had dreams of adding on a grade each year, as well as having our own convent in Carrizo Springs. The Asherton convent could not house another nun. We were bursting at the seams with six of us.

Now all these dreams came tumbling down as I listened to this new priest's plans and ideas. We were not on the same wavelength. I needed to talk with Reverend Mother in Crookston to see what recourse I had, or what rebuttals I could make in retaliation. Or maybe I had none, since he was the pastor.

Driving back to Asherton that afternoon was a challenging ride. I shared with Aurora what Fr. Green had said about hiring a kindergarten teacher from Carrizo. Then I also told her and Sr. Noreen that he didn't want to add additional grades to our school. Before discussing this with Rev. Mother, I would ask the other nuns for ideas on the best way to stop Father Green's plans.

With heavy hearts, we drove back to Asherton and hoped for the best. Aurora—the gentle soul she was—told me that she knew I had to do what the pastor wanted. She said that she would like to further her education. These two years of teaching experience would help her finish her degree more successfully. I couldn't believe how she could accept the termination of her teaching career at our school in such a gentle manner.

I would have been ranting and raving.

The following week, Father Green met with me and said he knew one of his parishioners that he thought would be a good fit for our next year's kindergarten. Her name was Bessie Herzog, and he wanted me to interview her for the position. He felt that the parish trusted her, and since she spoke Spanish, she could communicate with the parents. Aurora had done this so well in the past two years, and he knew I needed someone on our staff who could speak Spanish. I had already talked to Rev. Mother, who told me that each parish priest had the right to decide the future of their parochial school. She would speak with him, but urged me to accept his decisions at this point.

I met with Bessie to learn more about her and her teaching experiences. It was challenging to find a teacher ready to work for the pay given at our school. She would practically be donating her time as a parish member, but she was so excited to be a part of our school.

Bessie took on the teaching position to become our next year's kindergarten teacher. Even though it was a "done deal" before I even interviewed her, I was glad to discover her enthusiasm and love of teaching young children. She assured me that she would diligently encourage Anglos to send their children to our school. Our school numbers were small, and as a long-standing parish member, she felt she could change that. I hoped more Mexican children would also attend the following year. We needed numbers to prove the importance of having a Catholic School in Carrizo Springs.

That spring, there was a diocesan teacher's meeting we nuns had to attend in San Antonio. The six of us nuns piled in the car and set off for the 115-mile trip. When we got to the building, we noticed a nearby movie theatre advertising *The Sound of Music*. We had heard about this film, and couldn't believe there was an early afternoon showing. We decided to go to the morning meetings and then take the afternoon to see the movie. Of course, it would be educational, besides being entertaining.

After the movie, we happened to pass a music store on the way to our car. It just so happened that my parents had sent me $25.00 for Christmas, and I had been keeping it safe for something I really wanted. Fortunately, I had put the money in one of my slip pockets that morning just in case I found something to buy in San Antonio. I saw a guitar in the storefront, just like Maria had in the movie.

I told the other nuns I needed to run into the store for a minute and then I'd meet them at the car. I rushed in and told the shopkeeper that I was in a hurry, had just seen *The Sound of Music* movie, and wanted to buy the guitar in the window. I said it looked just like the one Maria had in the film. The shop owner looked at me, got the guitar, and I dug in my pocket to get the money to pay him.

When he saw the $25.00, he laughed heartily and said that my money would not even buy the baritone ukulele displayed in the window. I couldn't believe my ears. $25.00 was a lot of money to me. When he returned the guitar to the window display, I started to cry and told him about the poor Mexican children I was teaching, and how I wanted to play the guitar for them as Maria did for the Von Trapp children. He stared at the crying, blubbering nun in front of him. Then after a brief hesitation, he reluctantly reached for the ukelele.

"Sister, I am a Jewish man and have never dealt with a crying nun before. I can't believe what I am about to do. Take the ukulele, which costs a whole lot more than your $25.00."

I was taken aback and started to cry tears of joy this time. He kept shaking his head and stroking his beard. When he handed me the ukelele, I looked up at him and said, "But sir, Maria's guitar was in a case."

Placing his hands on his head in utter bewilderment, he stared at me again and walked to the back room of his shop. He came back with a case. I screamed in joy, saying that was it almost like Maria's and how happy he had made not only me, but also the children.

"Dear Sir, I will never forget you and will pray for you every day!" I was ready to kiss his ring as I did for the bishop, but instead ran and gave him a big hug. Realizing the nuns were waiting for me, I rushed out of the store. As I was leaving, I heard him mutter, "What a story I have to share with the Rabbi. Who will ever believe it?"

The nuns were about ready to come and see what on earth was keeping me. When I raced to the car like Maria did when she arrived at the Von Trapp home, they were dumbfounded. Where and how did I get the guitar? I said I would share the story on the way home after carefully placing the ukelele in the car trunk since we had no room inside.

As I shared my story of trying to get a guitar like Maria's, the nuns hysterically laughed when I told them that he was a Jewish man who never saw a nun cry. When we got to the convent, Johnny Joe, one of the eighth-grade students, happened to be at the playground. He was so curious when I took the ukulele case out of the trunk.

"Is that a guitar, Sister? The case looks smaller than a guitar case."

I opened the case for all to admire my new possession. Johnny Joe asked if he could try playing it because he could play the guitar. I told him to be extremely careful, and within moments, he tuned the strings and played beautiful melodies. His innate talent came so naturally as he plucked the strings. Suddenly, I knew who my ukulele teacher would be, and hoped I would soon play a few tunes for my students.

With his help, I learned how to play a few chords of simple tunes such as "Kumbaya" and "Frere Jacques." (My ukulele playing never was great, but to this day, sixty-six years later, I still have my ukulele in the same case.)

The school year came to an end. We returned to the Motherhouse, and when I spoke to Rev. Mother about the plight of Our Lady of Guadalupe School, she told me I must accept Fr. Green's decisions. Crying, I told her how difficult that was. She reminded me of my vow of Obedience, no matter how difficult it was to accept a decision, even this one.

I spent the summer at St. Catherine's, but I had no time for another session of Applied Music. Once again, the college did not offer Beginning Spanish. My classes were "Literary Criticism" and "Human Growth and Development."

I remember I decided to be creative for my critique of *Anna Karenina*. I chose to write it in rhyming couplets. Proud of my hours of using this poetic format, I was dismayed by the professor's remarks: "Sister, I spent so much time wondering which rhyming words you might choose to complete the next line, I lost any sense of what you were trying to say. Next time, do a normal critique."

We had a five-question open book exam for my Human Growth and Development class. Undaunted by my *Anna Karenina* failure, I decided to try my creative juices again. This time, I answered each question in a different literary format, including a short play with characters, a dialogue between two people, and a poem.

Mr. Burns, our professor, was ecstatic that one of his pupils had thought outside of the box and commended me in front of everyone. I realized then that you win some and lose some, but the winning indeed felt good!

Our summer obedience came out late, but I learned I would be returning to Texas. I requested another session with Rev. Mother to ask for advice on how to handle my dealings with Fr. Green. Mother Mary John explained that each pastor has his ideas. We nuns served the parish and did what they asked us to do. She, too, had hoped we would have been able to have a K-8 grade school. Telling me to do my best and make our K-2 an excellent example of teaching and learning, she gave me her blessing.

Returning to Texas, Sr. Noreen and I set off for Carrizo to meet with Bessie, plan our school year, and check out the attendance list. She said parents were disappointed not adding the third grade, but they still supported a K-2 Catholic school. They felt it an honor to have nuns teaching their children.

Bessie was able to help me learn more about the parish and created ways we could become more involved with the teenage kids of the parish. We started a Youth Group together, which made the pastor extremely happy.

Another letter that Sr. Marian wrote:

April 1965:

Friday being Good Friday, we "good" nuns were quite quiet and subdued. I got some letters written, and my clothes cleaned. Saturday, things really began to pop. Sr. Mona dove into a few cookbooks and almost didn't resurrect. At least she didn't until she had our Easter menu ready. I think she decided to go the way of the church and change traditions, or else she just found a foreign cookbook.

Anyway, we spent almost all Saturday making Sunday dinner. The manager, Mona, had me rolling her bread into bunnies and twisting strips of dough into long ears and short tails. She found a frozen salad recipe that took six nuns and two days to prepare. We did stick to mundane things in regard to ham, mashed potatoes, and carrots, but we left for outer space in the dessert line. Some kind of parfaits in two tones was on the agenda, and for a sidekick, there was a jelly roll filled with ice cream.

That Easter meal was a never-to-be-forgotten story that the nuns often shared. It brought many laughs in the years to come whenever we nuns got together to share our Texas tales and adventures.

It was always fun to share stories each evening when we gathered for supper and recreational time together. Here is one of the stories that Sr. Marian wrote to her sister Susan:

May 1, 1966 letter

Sr. Rosalia picked up a note the other day written by one of her third-grade "loving" Christians:

"Dear Betty, I will fight with you. Will you fight with me?" Love Ida

Then one of Sr. Mona's thoughtful first-grade philosophers decided she would be a nun when she got big. Why? Because she could love God more, wear a long dress but most of all because she could write on the blackboard. That's called a correct hierarchy of things, right?

And just this minute, Sr. Mary Ellen read a section of an original paragraph in which one of her eighth-graders (a future genius) wrote that "Robert E. Lee said after he died, "Make your sons

Americans." We might add that we are TRYING, but we wonder how effective we are.

I sound like a broken record, but we are leaving right now for supper at Tidds. Not much time left to squeeze in before we pack them off. You asked about Mr. Tidd. He is in the Border Patrol, not the service, and they are being transferred to Vermont.

We nuns realized how much we would miss our special friends, the Tidd family. They had become family to us, and we were always invited over for any special occasion, such as seeing the girls go to their Prom dances, birthdays, and holidays when possible. Spending time with them always led to lots of laughs and tons of stories. How difficult it would be without them. My piano and organ teaching would now become a thing of the past, and I would undoubtedly miss those special times together.

Our last supper with the Tidds was a tearful one. How would we survive without our dearest friends who had brought such joy and fun into our Texas lives? We promised never to lose touch and be forever friends.

The rest of the 1965-66 school year flew by. Sr. Noreen and I got more involved with the Carrizo Parish as Bessie found more ways for us to work with the teenagers. We began visiting more homes and working with families. Of course, this pleased Fr. Green.

I was genuinely enjoying this independence outside of the convent. Going on bike rides with the kids and keeping the long skirts from getting tangled in the spokes and chains was a constant feat, but worth the fun of the rides. Meeting and planning ways for the youth to help the community meant spending evenings and some Saturdays away from the convent. I thought how much easier it would be if we had our own convent in Carrizo, but that was not to be. I needed to make the best of the situation.

When we returned to the Motherhouse that summer of 1966, we all had to take a "Diocesan Workshop in New Catechetics" before heading off to other universities for our regular summer courses. The records showed that I got my first C in college. What a disappointment! I learned this was the common grade given at workshop sessions, but still, I was not happy. That summer at St. Catherine's, I took three classes: Elementary School Music, Children's Literature, and Documents of Vatican II and managed to get an A in all of them. I had to keep up my pattern!

My course in Vatican II documents was exciting as we learned about all the new changes. These dogmatic changes opened the doors and windows of the church to further reforms in other areas. To create changes, John Paul XXIII had called forth the Vatican II Council, which convened from 1962 to 1965.

More than 90,000 nuns left the church after the rulings of Vatican II. It became a time of significant change and freedom. Nuns were no longer required to wear habits or cover their hair. I wondered how long it would take for our convent to make some liberating changes.

The summer obedience for the 1966-67 school year came out while I was at St. Catherine's. I was thrilled to return to Texas and happy when I found out that the same six nuns would be returning. Once again, the six of us started our Texas trek and looked forward to another new route and new sights to see along the way. Sr. Mary Ellen, our superior, was open to new ideas. It was different from all those times that Sr. Caroline followed the same route to Texas.

The most fun experience was finding an outdoor theatre near our motel stop in Oklahoma. The billboard advertising the movie had the title: *Who's Afraid of Virginia Wolf.*

"Oh!" I glibly said, "That must be a new fairy tale movie playing on the words about the Big Bad Wolf in the *Little Red Riding Hood* fairy tale. Shall we go?"

Because we had not been to an outdoor movie since our high school days, everyone thought that would be a fun adventure. No one knew us in Oklahoma! It would be a new experience to add to our Texas trek.

When we got to our motel room, we ate supper. Since the film started at twilight, we decided to put our nightgowns on to be ready for bed after the movie. We covered them with our black habit and replaced our black shoes and stockings with our Texas slip-ons. Laughing, we ran out to the car and rode to the drive-in theatre.

Forgetting that the back end of the car was almost touching the ground with all the suitcases, Sr. Marian tried to park the car in the sloped area by the speaker—not possible—so she told us we would all have to get out of the car while she parked. As we dismounted the vehicle, we suddenly heard car horns. People around us rolled down their windows and yelled, "Way to go, Sisters! Hope you like the movie!"

Watching a movie about two dysfunctional couples airing their grievances was not quite what we had expected. As the movie progressed, we giggled at our innocence of thinking this would be a fairy tale. We had decided it would look too conspicuous if we all got out of the car in the middle of the movie and went back to the motel. Instead, we watched it until the end, and decided to wait a bit before all piling out so Sister could back the car up without damaging the back end.

People around us also decided to wait for the comic ending of watching five nuns bail out of a car. Once again, horns tooted, and people yelled, "So whatcha think of the movie, Sisters?" That was the first and last outdoor movie we ever experienced on the way to or from Texas! We blushed and raced to get back in the car as soon as Sr. Marian backed down the slope.

Our school year progressed without too many changes until December when Sr. Marian received a letter from Mother Mary John. Sister was to leave Texas and return to St. Catherine's College to finish her degree. Sister Judith would replace her in January.

The letter was a total shock for Sr. Marian and the rest of us nuns. How could we lose our fun, gregarious, loving Sr. Marian? What plans did the Rev. Mother have for her? Saying goodbye to Sr. Marian was the most challenging school year experience. She had arrived in Texas in 1959 and taught for seven years in Asherton. During our Texas years together, she had become my best friend and confidante. I would miss her exuberant personality and friendship. Life would not be the same. Her students cried when they heard she was leaving. She was their favorite teacher.

Sr. Judith, her replacement, was a year younger than I, and a good friend. I immediately sent her a letter about teaching in Texas. I shared about the poverty, her classroom-to-be, and the joy of working with the Mexican people. Because of the intense heat, I suggested that she shave her head to get the "Yul Bruner shaved head look" like the rest of us when she arrived.

Just before Sr. Marian left, we received a letter from Reverend Mother stating that our Motherhouse was designing different ideas for modifying our habits. Since we were so far from Minnesota, we could create our modified version with certain restrictions. The color must remain black. Our habit's length must be no more than thirteen inches from the floor, but we must retain our black shoes and stockings. Our headgear must include a veil that extended to below our waist, but we could show a bit of hair.

None of us nuns knew anything about sewing or creating a modified habit. Oh, it would be so wonderful not to have multiple layers of cloth in this heat of Texas. Finally, we could simplify our garb, but how? What could we do?

The next day at school, I told Bessie Herzog about our dilemma. She got so excited and said that she was a seamstress and would be happy to help us design a new habit. She knew parish ladies would help sew them. What a godsend for us! I couldn't believe my ears. Wait until the nuns in Asherton heard the good news!

All the nuns were excited and had Bessie come to our convent to discuss creating our new look. We had a fun but exasperating time trying to develop a suitable pattern that met the requirements from the Motherhouse. My question was: "Why can't we wear regular clothes with a short veil?" No, we had not been given any special privileges for teaching in the Texas heat.

Since we no longer needed to wear the coif or front headpiece, we needed to design a new head covering to connect to our veil. We discovered that if we cut white Hilex containers into rectangular shapes, they could support the weight of the waist-length veil. Why did the veil have to be waist length? To this day, I wonder why we didn't ask for a special exemption for clothing in the Texas heat. It would have been the perfect timing for such a question. I guess we were just thrilled to have even a minor change.

In the meantime, we nuns were trying to figure out how to fix the little bit of hair that would show in our new head covering. Some of us had entered the convent in the pin curl era, others in the wave era. Those that had natural curls didn't have any problems. After buying combs, brushes, and bobby pins, we experimented with the bit of hair we had on our heads.

It so happened that the five of us living in Texas had not recently cut our hair, but Sr. Judith decided to shave her head right before she came, instead of waiting until she arrived in Texas. Her head was just stubble. Oops, what was she going to do?

I have no idea who bought the new black material for our new habits, but they were sewn and ready to wear within a month. Bessie said all this was a gift from the parishioners, and we shouldn't ask about the cost.

We were ready to don our new look and asked Fr. Francisco to come for a sneak preview on Saturday night. We were "coming out" the following Sunday morning at Mass. Who could ever forget the look on his face as we six nuns sat in a semi-circle when he came into our living room?

As I said before, he had a stuttering problem, and our look added to that problem. He looked at us one by one, and when he saw Sr. Judith, he could not help laughing. We had told her that no one would notice that her hair was a bit more than stubble, and she had believed us.

Each of us had our hair fixed in the same style as when we entered the convent. Sr. Judith's stubble was too much for Father. He pointed to her and said, "M-M-M-m-my G—g-g-God Y-y -y ou l- look j-j-j-ust l-l-l-like J-j-j-ulius C-c-ceasar!!" With that, Sr. Judith jumped up crying, and ran to the bedroom and never returned. Father apologized and left. Our fashion show did not go quite as planned.

Here was my new look as a nun!

The following day, we wore our new modified habits. Sr. Judith did not. When we went to Carrizo Springs for Mass, I was anxious to show off the new look. Fr. Green took one look, shook his head, and said, "If you nuns are changing, then go all the way. Why keep those ugly black stockings and shoes, and the long veil?" Our excitement over having a modified habit lessened as we realized how true that statement was. Once again, the bubble burst.

Having a shorter habit and fewer layers of clothing did help a bit in the heat. My little first graders were amazed when they walked into my classroom after we changed to our new look. "Oh, Sister, look, you have legs! And hair!" How I laughed and hugged them. The innocence of children was always such a delight to experience.

I so loved teaching the little ones and enjoying the warmth and love of the Mexican people. I hoped I would have many more years to be with them. The fourth year of having our school in Carrizo Springs included more involvement in parish activities. Even though we were not expanding the school, we used the extra two classrooms for meetings with the upper-grade kids and high schoolers. Bessie proved to be an excellent catalyst for creating more opportunities to work with the people outside of the school itself.

Life was good. Teaching in Texas those past six years made me realize why I had become a nun: To serve the poor, and teach those hungering to hear God's message from women who had dedicated their entire lives to Him.

The new look and the ukulele. Sr. Mona and students.

Chapter Fifteen

My Minnesota Years: 1967-69

We don't grow when things are easy.
We grow when we face challenges.
Anonymous

W hen we returned to the Motherhouse that summer of 1967, it was interesting to see the different modified habits that the Minnesota nuns were wearing. None of them were designs a person could get excited about, and many nuns chose to keep the old garb.

I returned for classes at St. Catherines as I had done the previous summers. The summer obedience of 1967 arrived before we finished the summer session.

WHAT?? It did not say I was returning to Texas. Instead, I was assigned to St. Jude's School in Mahtomedi, Minnesota, to teach eighth grade. WHAT?? My world turned upside down as I read and re-read my obedience slip. Not returning to Texas broke my heart. I had never taught older kids. Why did I have to leave my beloved people in Texas? I never had a chance to say goodby. Six years of living and teaching in Texas, being so independent, so close to the Mexican people, was now no longer to be a part of me.

I didn't know how to handle this news. My best friend, Sr. Marian, was not there to console me, since she had finished her degree during the past school year. What lay ahead for me? My vow of Obedience tested me to the greatest extreme. I took the vow and now must follow, as I had promised.

Returning to the Motherhouse, I went to Rev. Mother and shared my distress. "Sr. Mona, our life of dedication involves many changes. You did fantastic work in Texas, but a young nun needs to experience many different teaching environments," she told me. "Now it is time for you to move on. You must not get too attached to any one place."

Crying, I told her that I just never wanted to leave Texas. She tried to console me by saying that she was sure I would learn to love Mahtomedi, and I must take up the challenge with my zest for life and teaching at a Minnesota mission. Leaving her office, I knew I must face my new assignment with courage and determination to become the best eighth-grade teacher ever.

When I met Sr. Agatha, my new principal, I felt her kindness and empathy as I shared my trepidations about teaching older students. "Sister, I only taught first grade when I was the teaching principal in Texas," I said. "I don't know a thing about eighth-graders."

She chuckled and said she'd be there to guide me; she was not only the principal, but also the seventh-grade teacher. She assured me that it would take time, but knew I could do it.

Mom and Dad were ecstatic that I would be teaching in Minnesota even though it was about a five-hour drive from them. Flo and family lived in Richfield, MN, about a half-hour from Mahtomedi. My younger sister, MaryAnn, was in nurses' training in Minneapolis, only about a half-hour away. With family nearby, I now could visit them more often. That was a privilege I did not have in Texas. I must look for all the positives in my new teaching assignment in Minnesota.

Arriving at the school and convent in Mahtomedi, I immediately noticed the lovely stucco house next to the school. A beige stone church stood nearby. Sr. Agatha welcomed me and said my bedroom was upstairs, facing the school. Walking up the steps, I wondered how different it would be having my very own bedroom, for the first time in my entire life. Having privacy during this challenging transition was a blessing in and of itself. Sister explained that there were several bathrooms in the convent for the ten nuns to share. *What a luxury!* was the first thought that came to my mind.

That evening, I met all the nuns I would share the convent with during the coming year. As Sr. Agatha introduced them to me, I suddenly realized the only young nun among them was Sr. Shawn, who

Mom and Dad were glad I would be closer.

had been a year behind me in high school. When Sister introduced Sr. Macrina as our housekeeper, I took a double-take. Our very own housekeeper? That meant I didn't have to spend time preparing meals, doing laundry, or cleaning the house. That was yet another gift! I must remember to make sure I took time to tell Sister how much I appreciated her and her work for all of us nuns.

Having a housekeeper would give me more time to prepare my teaching lessons. I knew I would need every spare minute I could get trying to learn how to teach eighth-graders. I wondered what it would be like living with older nuns. Time would tell.

The next day Sr. Agatha took me over to the school and showed me all the materials and textbooks in my classroom. We had a week before school started. I opened each text with terror in my heart and realized that the midnight oil would be burning as I tried to learn math, history, science, and literature concepts that eighth-graders needed to study.

After decorating the classroom for my students, I spent hours and hours poring over the textbooks and asking Sr. Agatha a million questions about the best ways to handle big kids. Eighth-graders all knew how to hold their pencils and how to write their names.

The first day of school arrived. As I watched the students come in the door one by one, I realized many of them were taller than I was. Well, at least I had thirteen years more experience and six years of teaching under my cincture.

Maybe the best way to start was to share a bit about myself, my growing up on an Indian reservation, and the wonders of teaching Mexican migrants in Texas. I would try to weave these stories into each subject we were to study throughout the year. Then, hopefully, the students would feel more comfortable sharing a bit about themselves. Storytelling was vital in finding out who we were and what we brought to the class. I needed to get to know them personally to meet their individual needs in the coming school year.

When we opened the US history text, I asked the students what they already knew about the subject. As they shared, I wrote their ideas on the blackboard and was amazed at how quickly their responses covered the board. After having everyone write all the words on the blackboard in their notebooks, I shared that my ancestors were the original people in this great land. Pulling down the US map, I told the story of my Indian village in northern Minnesota. Their first assignment was to find out how their family had arrived in America, and be ready to share the next day.

So far, so good. The rest of the day flew by as I attempted to learn what they knew about each subject area. Why teach something that they already knew?

That first week became one of learning the workings of the convent, school, and church. Unlike Texas, I did not have the duties of a principal, the role of organist, or household duties. This left time to dedicate solely to my teaching, which I needed desperately.

Living with older nuns and being in a convent that did not visit the students' homes became stumbling blocks for me. How did they get to know the people? In the evenings after our meal, the nuns were satisfied to knit, play a few board games, correct papers, or read the newspaper. Each evening became like the one before, with little of the laughter I had known in Texas. The camaraderie was definitely not here. I felt stifled and wondered how I would ever fit into this type of life on a Minnesota mission.

By Christmas, I knew things had to change. I could not keep up with burning the midnight oil, trying to keep a few pages ahead of my eighth-graders. They were smart kids and eager to learn, but it required me to be knowledgeable in too many subjects.

Sr. Agatha had been so helpful, so I went to her with my new master plan for changing the way we taught the upper grades. She excelled in math, and Sr. Hyacinth loved history, so why couldn't we departmentalize and each teach to our strengths? Sister was open to change and called Sr. Hyacinth for a meeting to discuss my idea. We would divide the sixth through eighth graders among us. Science and language arts were to be my subjects. Sr. Florentine taught music for all the grades. (I never thought I would be teaching with the amazing Sr. Florentine who taught me piano and organ in grade school!) Each of us would be responsible for the physical education of our current grade.

I was thrilled that these two nuns were willing to give it a try for the rest of the school year. If it didn't work out for the best, we would revert to grade-level teaching the following year. We spent the rest of our Christmas vacation preparing for the new change, which meant creating new class lists and a teaching schedule since the students would change classrooms for each subject.

My students had told me that the public high school was buying new science lab equipment and tables. I called the principal and asked what they were doing with the old ones. The next day the tables arrived at our school. The custodian and some fellow parishioners helped me create a science lab (without any actual lab equipment) in my classroom. Chairs and tables replaced desks. I was excited beyond measure for the possibilities for teaching science. We could start with biology and use specimens from Nature around us with a hands-on approach. Who knew what that could lead to in the upcoming months?

Teaching literature and grammar was my strength. I knew I wanted to teach how to diagram sentences, just like Mr. Searls had taught me in seventh and eighth grade. Poetry, short stories, and novels were already in our textbooks. I would find a great read-aloud to begin each class session. I hoped the students would love having multiple teachers and moving to different classrooms. We nuns would keep our grade levels for homerooms, where students would begin and end their school day.

All was going well at the school, but I still struggled at the convent. Living with older nuns was not easy, and some were not very happy with the changes I persuaded Sr. Agatha to attempt in the school. They acted out their hostilities in subtle ways during recreation, meal times, and weekends.

I shared my frustrations in a letter to Mom. I explained that living with some of the older nuns was extremely difficult. I never wanted to become like them and would leave the convent before that happened. She immediately wrote back and said she had a meeting in the Twin Cities the following weekend and would come to visit me.

Mom was distraught. She told me that she and Dad did not raise their girls to quit when things got tough. She asked me to remember how I had gone against their advice to join the convent. Now, just because it was a situation I didn't like, I would give up?

Crying, I told her that I loved my teaching, especially since we had departmentalized the upper grades. It was the convent living that was not what I had expected. I no longer had the independence I had in Texas, and I missed the Mexican people.

"Vonnie, is it just the older nuns' behavior, or could it be your inability to do all the things that you want to do that are making you want to leave?" Mom wisely asked. "Promise me that you will take time to think and pray about this before you do decide."

Mom always knew best. She possessed that fantastic quality of helping people step back and look at the entire picture before deciding.

I kept thinking and praying about my vocation. If I had a real vocation, why would I keep questioning it? It was true that I missed my Texas challenges and freedom, but I had taken a vow of Obedience. That meant I was to accept my yearly assignments, make the best of them without constantly questioning and comparing. Yes, I would stay and be the best nun I could be.

During the rest of the school year, I became acquainted with many of the students' families, especially the McCarthy family. The McCarthys had seven children and they lived right across the street. Ruth McCarthy became the replacement for Betty Tidd in my life. She would even come with me—with last minute notice, late at night —to pick up a nun at the Minneapolis airport. I had her daughter, Diane, in my eighth-grade class and her son, Danny, in my seventh-grade class. Both were enthusiastic students and eager to learn new ideas and create projects outside of school hours.

Trying to overcome my fear of horses in Mahtomedi.

Danny was one of the reasons that gave me the impetus to set up a hands-on science lab. Creating a lab would take brainstorming and research. Since there were many engineers and scientists in our parish community, I would begin with them. One of the parents discovered that Macalester College in St. Paul, MN, offered an eight-week science lab class for elementary teachers the upcoming summer. Maybe I could apply for that.

Applying and being accepted that spring meant I had to ask Rev. Mother for permission to attend, and forgo teaching the two weeks of Catechism that all teaching nuns did every summer. It was possible to stay at our Mahtomedi convent and drive daily to school. I explained how important this class was for my teaching, and how the parents were willing to help with the cost. When the answer came back in the affirmative, I was on cloud nine and sent a lengthy letter of gratitude to her.

The workshop was mind-boggling, and as they presented each new concept, my mind whirred with ideas of how to modify it for my classroom.

Being in Mahtomedi as I attended classes, I shared some ideas for hands-on learning in science with interested parents. Parents of the upper-grade students were excited and wanted to know what kind of equipment I might need.

Before I knew it, science equipment began appearing in my classroom, including a special microscope for the overhead projector. The microscope gave us the ability to study and watch specimens in pond water! Due to the parent's generosity, the science lab became a reality.

After the workshop, I returned to the Motherhouse for our annual retreat and annual obedience slip. What would happen if I didn't return to Mahtomedi after all I had prepared for the coming fall? I tried not to think of that and prayed that I would be ready to accept whatever I was assigned. That retreat revolved around the constant prayers of my acceptance of decisions made by Rev. Mother. I needed to learn Obedience with no questions.

A few days after our retreat, we received our next year's assignment. With trembling fingers, I opened the envelope. "Sr. Mona, you will return to Mahtomedi for the 1968-69 school year." My heart swelled in happiness. I would be able to teach in my new science lab using the latest equipment and my newfound knowledge of teaching hands-on science classes!

Returning to Mahtomedi to start my second year of teaching upper-grades, I felt so much more confident. And, I was thrilled that the nuns wanted to continue with departmentalized instruction.

With all the excitement of the science lab, students in my language arts classes then wanted to know if we could start a drama club. The public school kids had one. Why couldn't we? I realized not every student was a biology enthusiast, so why not offer something for the wanna-be thespians? There was no crash course in creating theatrical productions, but the students' enthusiasm was all we needed at that point.

We decided on a Grimm's fairy tale play. The hysterical beginning was the role reversal for the King and Queen. Lynn became the tall King with her bubbly personality, and short, demure Danny became the Queen. Amidst many laughs and bantering—and my many flubs learning stage directions—we pulled it off. Even some of the old nuns had a good laugh the night we presented it for the school.

Life on the convent front remained, for me, an uphill battle. The older nuns still shook their heads at Sr. Mona's "escapades." When the assistant priest and I planned a weekend retreat with the eighth-graders, the older sisters rolled their eyes even more and wondered what the world was coming to.

Fr. Mielke came with his guitar, and I, with my ukelele. I hoped we were starting a new tradition for the eighth-graders: camping out and experiencing the wonders of God's Nature in the wild. We sat around the campfire, singing songs and telling stories to create bonds that the inside of classroom walls could never accommodate.

For me, these after-school activities kept me believing that I had made the right choice to remain in the convent. I wrote to Mom to say that I had given it much prayer and thought and would remain a nun.

Late in May, a letter arrived for each nun from our Rev. Mother. It was our summer catechism assignment, as well as our summer college assignment. I had not taught summer Catechism all those years when I was in Texas—we always arrived back in Minnesota after the weeks of Catechism were finished—and the prior summer, I had the science workshop. But that was about to change: I would be teaching summer catechism classes.

The tradition of the Motherhouse was to always send an older, experienced nun with a younger nun for those two weeks of teaching in parishes that did not have a Catholic School. My assignment said I would teach with Sr. Judith, a year younger than I. In other words, I was to be the "older" nun!

The assignment stated that we would teach in Kelliher at the parish in northern Minnesota run by Father Aarden.

Little did I know that meeting Father Aarden that summer would change my life forever...

Epilogue

My Native Naked Voice

Two years ago I took a class called , "The Naked Voice" which asked us to write a portrait of our own voice. I think it is fitting to end a book in which I hope I have found my written voice. We need both the written and oral power of our voices to make a change in the world in which we live. May each of my readers find their strength in the voice they received at birth.

MY VOCAL PORTRAIT

With a traumatic entry into this world, my voice started very weak from the almost-death experience caused by the excessive ether given to my mother during the birthing process. My helpless whimpers turned into loud squalls as I became stronger. Bonding with my mother made my voice one with hers, and I became a "Mommy's baby" afraid to become detached from my source of life.

Mom's nurturing and belief in my potential led me to find my voice. At age six, I became a more independent, vocalized first-grader who loved to read aloud and one who imitated her mother's slightly off-key Catholic hymns that she sang while doing housekeeping chores.

My Dad danced in and out of my life because of his adventurous travels to work in Alaska, serving the Navy in Papua, New Guinea, and road construction jobs during summers. I did not realize how musical his voice was until later in grade school. I then learned that music was a vital element in his family as every family member played a musical instrument. His family sang both Bohemian and contemporary songs together.

I loved being in plays and using my voice to imitate characters, such as memorizing the poem "Lil Orphan Annie" for a talent show and making her come alive for the audience. My singing voice was not exceptional, so I chose to play the piano and organ and let my cousin and sister do the singing.

I thought I had a decent singing voice until I joined the Benedictine Academy for girls as an aspirant. There we aspirants learned Gregorian chant, which we practiced daily. I can still see Sr. Victorine, the choir mistress, coming over to me that first week of chanting as I sat in the pew singing loudly off-tune and not realizing that I was not in sync with the other chanters. "Yvonne, listen to the person next to you and see if you can match her voice," was the request whispered in my ear. That was my first experience in voice recognition and needing to listen to pitches.

Spending fifteen years chanting the Divine Office daily and leading the Gregorian chants a cappella strengthened my voice, yet I knew my voice was more robust in the drama department. I loved dramatically reading stories, telling stories, and putting genuine expression into my voice to become the characters within the pages. It brought me special attention and compliments, which I thrived on throughout my schooling from grade school through high school and college.

In high school, every girl needed to be a chorus member. I learned I was a medium soprano with a minimal range at our vocal tryouts. My singing voice became more melodic when I learned how to play the ukulele and sang folk tunes with my fellow nuns as a form of recreation. Lacking the ability to harmonize, I sang the basic melody line.

As a teacher, I realized the power and persuasion of my voice, and the world became my stage. My first graders were mesmerized when I became the character's voice in stories and dramatically spoke while reading. Playing and singing simple tunes on my ukulele made me feel like Maria in the "Sound of Music."

Piet, who had a voice like melodious thunder, sang with extreme gusto at every church service. Rather than singing, I took on the role of organist and piano player since I was definitely out of my league with his voice. His love of music in singing and listening to classical music infiltrated our two children, who became beautiful vocalists and musicians. I was the catalyst who taught them music from the Treble Tot course with rhythms to KinderKeys and onto later keyboard lessons. Their voices became exceedingly well trained with private voice lessons. My voice was that of an encouraging mother and teacher.

Over the years of teaching and being an educational consultant, my musical and speaking voice did improve. I remember being at a teacher's conference and singing with all my heart. The person next to me turned and said what a beautiful, melodious voice I had. At that point, I felt that the weak, whimpering voice of my birth had blossomed into an agent of strength and beauty.

I still can not harmonize, but I love my speaking voice and my ability to use it to express who I am and what I think. My voice has created changes for me as I have vocalized through different chapters of my life.

I desire to make my voice heard to create positive changes within our world of confusion and difficulties. I want to speak up for the minorities and those in need, whether in spoken word or singing. I want my voice re-membered as one who stood up for what I believed in — a voice as a vocal gate to those in need.

May my voice sing Alleluias until my last day singing praises of others.

May my voice be a solace for those who seek justice and peace in this turbulent world.

May my voice cause us to remember our ancestors and all the gifts they have given us.

May my final words be: Alleluia, I was born the daughter of Phil and Bo!

Acknowledgments

How does one acknowledge all the people who have intersected my life and made this book possible? I give thanks to:

My ancestors...

My family...

My village...

My teachers...

My students...

My friends...

My community of nuns...

A special thanks to Judy Aiken Greeley (Sr. Marian) who let me share letters she wrote during our Texas years, and our years of friendship.

And, of course, my editor: Eric Wyatt, who believed in me and challenged me to put into writing the story of my life. Because of his great teaching and classes on writing, my two books became a reality:

Intersecting Traditions (My story from birth to age 29)

Intersecting Heartbeats (My story from age 29 to the present).

Thank you, Eric, for all your expert guidance and hours of work to bring my words into book form.

Thank you to everyone who has intersected my life and helped me in creating my memories and traditions. You will always remain close to my heart.

Appendix A

A Sketch of the Early Life of the Hon. Peter Roy, My Great-Grandfather

(Written by himself, and discovered after his death)

I was born in the year 1828, on the twenty-third of February, below Fort Francis, on the banks of Rainy Lake River, on the American side, at the junction of Rainy Lake and Little Forks Rivers. My grandfather came to that area about 1810 and opened a farm. He must have had about fifty acres of land under cultivation. About the time I left the place, he used to raise quite a lot of wheat, barley, potatoes, rutabagas and tobacco, and different kinds of vegetables. He had quite a lot of stock, such as horses, cattle, hogs, and chickens.

One winter, he lost about twenty horses; they strayed away and started to go back to Cass Lake, where my grandfather first commenced to farm. The horses came across a band of Indians and were all killed for food.

When I got to be old enough to see what was going on, my father was trading with the Bois Fort bands of the Chippewa Indians. He used to go to Mackinaw annually, make his returns and buy goods for a year's supply.

About the year 1838 or 1839, my father took me down to La-Pointe, it then being the headquarters of the American Fur Company. He left me with my uncle Charles LaRose. At that time, my uncle was United States interpreter for Daniel P. Bushnell, U.S. Indian Agent. I went to the missionary school (Presbyterian), which was under the charge of Rev. Sherman Hall. Grenville T. Sprout was the teacher. Charles W. Horup was the Great Mogul, having then lately been appointed by the American Fur Co. to take charge of all the Chippewa trade. Lyman W. Warren was in that capacity before. He was the father of Truman A. Warren, now at White Earth.

In the year 1845, I went in a store as a salesman for Leopold and Austrian and remained in that capacity until 1849. I was appointed United States interpreter for J.S. Livermore, United States Indian agent. I remained interpreter during his term of office, also through J.S. Watson's term as Indian agent and a part of David B. Herriman's term.

In the fall of 1853, I was elected as representative in the territorial legislature, and I was afterwards elected twice to the state legislature in 1860 and 1862.

I claim to be the first native-born representative in the territorial legislature. I also claim the same thing in the state legislature: that is to say those born within the boundaries of the state of Minnesota. There had been some natives who went to the legislature before I did: such as W.W. Warren, Finley, and Gingrass, but they were born in Wisconsin and Michigan, except, I am not very certain about it. Alex Faribault, I understand, though, he was born at Prarie Dwchine.

[On the occasion of Peter Roy's death, the following telegram was transmitted to the largest newspaper in Minnesota.]

Daily Globe, St. Paul

Wednesday, June 22, 1881

Death of one of Minnesota's Old Settlers

(Special Telegram to the Globe)

Little Falls, Minn., June 21 - Hon. Peter Roy dropped dead at 10:30 this morning while sitting in his chair in front of Hoffman and the sheriff's.

Peter Roy was one of the best known characters in Minnesota. He was born about fifty years ago at LaPointe Indian agency, Lake Superior, his father being a Frenchman and his mother a Chippewa Indian woman. In 1851 or 1852 he removed to Minnesota, settling in the vicinity of Crow Wing agency where he engaged in trade with the Indians, whose confidence he gained and ever afterwards retained. In 1853 he removed to Little Falls, where he opened a hotel, and kept it with signal success for many years.

In 1853 he was chosen a member of the territorial legislature, and served with ability and satisfaction to his constituents. He was returned to the State legislature in 1862, and severed the term with honor to himself and credit to the community.

During his residence at Little Falls he served several terms as city marshal, and on several occasions he served as escort and interpreter to bands of Sioux and Chippewa Indians on their periodical visits to Washington, and assisted greatly in obtaining a recognition of their rights of property. For nearly two years he has been troubled with consumption, and his friends have for months past been painfully cognizant of the fact that his end was near.

A week ago last Thursday, he came to St. Paul and placed himself under the care of Dr. Hand. He was troubled with a distressing cough and pains and swelling of the limbs. After a week's treatment, he started for home on Friday morning last, feeling greatly improved in health and hopeful of complete recovery. He arrived safely, but died as indicated above without a moment's warning, within a square of his residence. He leaves a wife and eleven children in poor circumstances, though at one time he was one of the most prosperous men of the northern part of the State.

Mr. Roy is universally spoken as a man of warm, generous nature who had few enemies and many warm friends. His death will be universally regretted.

Top: Frank Roy, Vincent Roy, E. Roussin, Old Frank D.o.,
Bottom: Peter Roy, Jos. Gourneau (Gurnoe), D. Geo.
Morrison."

**The photo is labelled Chippewa Treaty in Washington 1845 by the St. Louis
Historical Library and Douglas County Museum, but if it is in fact in Washington, it was probably the Bois Forte Treaty of 1866, where these men acted
as conductors and interpreters.**
(Digitized by Mary E. Carlson for The Sawmill Community at Roy's Point)

Appendix B

Handwritten Notes I Found From Mom

I found several pages of handwritten notes from Mom on which she had written her thoughts on the Ojibway people, I want to share exactly what was on those ten pages as I feel it is part of my history. There was no date on these notes and I am presuming she wrote these when we were writing our Naytahwaush history when I was in sixth grade:

Ancestry: Peter Roy's life

Early Life on Reservation:

Reasons for moving

Life of Early Indian

Seasonal work:

  Spring - fishing, sugar making,

  Summer - gardening, gathering herbs, cherry picking

  Fall - Ricing, hunting

  Winter - Trapping

Religion: Great Medicine, Episcopalian, Catholic

Education: Government Day and Boarding Schools, Catholic School

Artifacts: Beading, Diamond willow, Buckskin

Ojibway or Chippewa; peaceful tribes (Algonquin stock)

Settled in land of Upper Great Lakes in Minnesota, Michigan, and Canadian

Ontario and Manitoba. Now live on reservations in these states.

Indian name means Tail Skins as their dress had points hanging down before and behind.

Tribesman well built, tall and agile.

Expert hunters and fisherman.

Good gardeners: Raised corn, beans, squash, sweet potatoes. Fertilized ground with uneaten bits of fish.

Transportation by foot, drag and canoe.

My grandfather, Peter Roy a Chippewa Indian(both Mother and Father half-breeds) was born on banks of Rainy Lake on the American side. He was appointed U.S. Interpreter. In 1853, he was elected a representative in the territorial legislature and elected twice to the Sate Legislature. He was engaged in hotel business in Little Falls at the time of death. He accompanied many Indians to Washington, D.C. to intercede in making their treaties. In 1853 married to Philomene Chaunard, also of Indian descent.

Grandma Roy moved to White Earth Reservation in order to acquire land claims for her children. My mother's land was about five miles from Mahnomen, county seat of Mahnomen country. After her marriage to Alphonse LaVoy, farmed this land until her health broke, then moved to Naytahwaush, an Indian village on North Twin Lakes. There my father engaged in livery business. Had a large barn where he kept white and Indian people's horses. Also ran a livery to other towns such as Mahnomen and White Earth.

I was five years old when we moved to Naytahwaush. The older Indians still wore their Indian costumes with feather headdresses. These Indians were a very saving and hard working group. Each year they had seasonal work which both the men and women partook.

In Spring the Maple Sugar Harvest was a big event. Each family had their area known as their sugar bush. They erected their teepees and lived at this spot while the trees were tapped for sap. They used birch bark for the containers to catch the sap. Also used birch bark in teepee construction. They used large iron kettles over an open fire to cook the sap. They made syrup, sugar and sugar cakes. They always saved enough for their own use before selling any. They stored the sugar in birch bark baskets and (wigum) bark ones to preserve the sugar.

Fishing, especially netting, was also a spring industry. Some of the fish was smoked to preserve it. Fish was a daily food of the Indians. In the summer, berry picking, such as strawberries, raspberries, pin and choke cherries, blueberries. Some of the berries were dried for future use. There was an abundance of snake root (a medicinal root) and Indians dug the root and sold it to buy groceries.

In the fall, the Wild Rice Festival was the main event. A large lake named Rice Lake supplied most of the rice. Here again the Indian families moved to the Lake, built their camps and remained until it grew too cold for harvesting. There was no waste as they had a committee who governed and no ricing was allowed until the rice was ripe enough. Then only certain days were ricing days giving the proper time to get the most of the crop. Again, the Indians kept enough of the rice for themselves before selling any. The Indian women helped finish the rice. First, they would parch the rice. This was done by placing rice in a barrel which was set over a fire in a hole in the ground. The rice was stirred so it wouldn't burn. The men then tramped the rice by putting on moccasins and tramped off the chaff. The women would then fan the rice by using birch bark to toss rice in the air. This would remove the hulls. Finished rice sold for ten cents a pound at this time.

The men also hunted in the fall and much of their food consisted of wild game and rice.

In the winter, the men trapped and much of their income was from the sale of hides. Many animals were used for eating also such as muskrats, rabbits and deer. The deer hides were used in making moccasin bags and, of course, drums. The women did beautiful jackets decorating with bead work.

The first religion of the area was Grand Medicine. I remember spending afternoon with my parents watching the ceremonies held every Spring. They built a long meeting house where the Medicine Men conducted the services. Again there were many teepees erected and the Indians lived in them at the location near the Meeting House. They used large kettles and prepared food for the entire group during the sessions. Dog meat was their main meat. One year our pet dog disappeared and we were sure it ended up in one of their kettles.

The first Religious group to come to Naytahwaush was the Episcopalian church headed by Bishop Whipple. The church was built in 1894. The first minister was Rev. Geo MannyPenny, a full blooded Indian. The services were all in the Chippewa Language.

The Catholic missionaries from St. John's started to come to the area in the early 1900's. After my parents moved to Naytahwaush, Fr. Felix Nellis, who was located at Ponsford, came to Naytahwaush and remained about a month each time he came. He roomed and boarded at our house, saying Daily Mass in our dining room. Indians came for miles to attend daily Mass. The Sunday Mass was held in the school house. Soon after, plans were made to build a church.. Some revenue was obtained from the Indian Department. My parents donated much of the lumber. Fr. Felix was also a good carpenter and with help of Indian men, began construction. The church was completed before my Mother's death in 1918. Although the priest could hold Mass only at intervals, the Indian people gathered each Sunday at the church for Rosary and other prayers. They had two societies, St. Joseph for men and St. Mary's for women.

The first Day School was a government school. Philip Starr from Oklahoma was the teacher. He taught all grades and was a very intellectual man and very interested in teaching Indian children. Later in life, he wrote a book of poems. I have here an excerpt where my name is mentioned as he was being transferred.

Some of our best friends of the Twin Lakes School
Were Fairbanks, Douglas, Pellands, Browns and LaVois,
Who were always the best of friends to us
And sympathized with us in our sorrows and joys
And they did things, too, once staging a program
Which altered the Superintendent's determination
To move us away from the Twin Lakes School
To put us in charge at another location.

An amusing incident ended that special program
When Philomine LaVoi in a cute little recitation,
Requested Mr. Hinton to alter his plan
And leave unchanged the current situation,
To which he arose, eulogized the fine program
And, virtually, admitted he had made a mistake.
Then, addressing Philomine, in a quite pleasing manner,
Said, "And Mr. Starr will remain at Twin Lakes.

The Indian Department also established boarding schools on the reservation, one at Beaulieu and one at White Earth. At both Day School and Boarding Schools clothing was issued, such as corduroy clothes, shirts, stocking and shoes. Noon meals were given at Day Schools. Many Indian children also went away to government schools at Tomah, Iowa; Flandreau, South Dakota and Wahpeton, North Dakota. The school at White Earth was run by Benedictine Sisters of St. Joseph, Minnesota. I attended this school from second grade. It was closed in 1969 and is now a museum.

The excerpt Mom mentioned was from a poem book called *The Starr Gang and Other Poems*, by Philip A. Starr, Sr.

On the first page Mom wrote: "This book was written by my First Grade Teacher at Naytahwaush, MN. To be given to Yvonne when I pass."

This bark wigwam, built about 1870, on the White Earth reservation.

The photos on these pages represent some of the artifacts and details of my native ancestry. The photos of the wigwam and the couple ricing were taken from a booklet, *On the Reservation*, published in 1986 by the Minnesota Historical Society. The beadwork is from a postcard, representing the artistry of Marcie McIntire, from the Grand Portage reservation. The baskets and birchbark items were all created by people from White Earth Indian Reservation. The prayer comes from a prayer card I was once given.

Gathering wild rice.

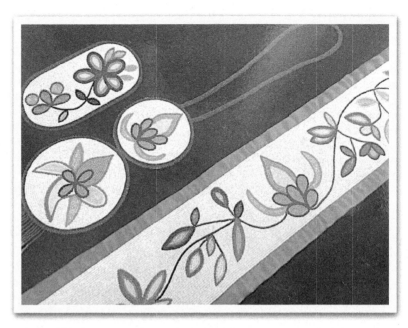

Intricate Ojibwe bead embroidery is frequently created using floral designs.

Ojibwe artifacts made in Naytahwaush that I have in my home: Woven Ash wood basket and birchbark pieces.

Grandfather,
Great Spirit, look
at our brokenness.
We know that
in all creation only
the human family has strayed
from the Sacred Way.
We know that we are the
ones who are divided and we
are the ones who must come
back together to walk in the
Sacred Way.
Grandfather, Sacred One,
teach us love, compassion, and
honor, so we may heal the
earth and heal each other.

From the Ojibwe

Appendix C

History of Naytahwaush

On the following pages, I have provided scans of the History of Naytahwaush compiled by my sixth-grade schoolmates and I during the 1951-1952 school year, under the guidance of our teacher Vivian Bisek.

Pages 351 to 377 are the original history our class wrote. Pages 378 to 387 are the pages added in 2011 by the fifth-grade class at Naytahwaush Community Charter School.

GRATITUDE

We are very grateful to Mr. Harold Emerson (May-zhuc-e-be-nais) and the late Adele Northrop for all of the information they so generously gave. We appreciate a great deal the time they spent in our class room working with us.

We are no less thankful to the following for their help;

Howard La Voy
Mrs. John Terway
John Terway
Mrs. Alois Rumreich
Mrs. Josephine Robinson
Mrs. Anna Goodwin
Late Mrs. Kate Douglas
Miss Elverum
Miss Shields
Father Casmir
Father Augustine

HISTORY OF NAY-TAH-WAUSH

by

The Sixth Grade Social Studies Class

School Year 1951-1952

Bellefeuille Ernest   **LaFriniere** LeRoy
Benson Vernon   McDougall Maxine
Boswell Russell   Murray Fred
Foxx Isabelle   Murray Frieda
Goodwin Gloria   Olson Myles
LaVoy John   Rumreich Yvonne
LaVoy Sharon   Turner Edward
LaFriniere Cecelia   Turner Orville
LaFriniere Gary   Villebrun Josephine
                    Wadena Charles

Teacher: Vivian Bisek

Nay-tah-waush

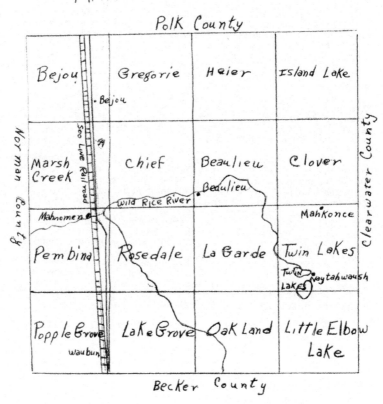

356

HISTORY OF NAY-TAH-WAUSH

Nay-tah-waush, located in the south central part of
Twin Lakes Township, in Mahnomen County, is snuggled along
the shore of North Twin Lake. It is on the White Earth
Indian Reservation. Nay-tah-waush is not incorporated into
a village; therefore, it is uncertain just what the population is. However, it is estimated that approximately
sixty families make it their home; almost a hundred
families are listed on the school census. Nay-tah-waush
is a Chippewa word which means "smooth sailing". The lakes,
streams, forest, etc. help to make the surroundings very
beautiful. The highest altitude in the county is Strawberry Mountain, a wee bit to the east. In the Chippewa
language, it is called Gah-o-dae-mi-de-nogal which means
strawberry shaped hill. It was named by Ah-bid-way-we-
dung (Mr. Emerson's grandfather) because it is shaped
exactly like a strawberry.

The village was first called Twin Lakes (Gah-nee-shoo-
oum-mon) because of the two lakes located here. Ah-bid-
way-we-dung also named it. While it is occasionally
referred to as Twin Lakes, the name was changed to Nay-
tah-waush about 1906 because the mail was being missent to
another place in Southern Minnesota also called Twin Lakes.
Our village was named after Nay-tah-waush, an Indian Chief,
who moved here from Fish Lake in 1888. He wintered with
the De-daus-e-gay family on Ah-bid-way-we-dung's camp site.
This was on the north shore of the north lake. Later the
chief built his home by all the pine trees planted past the
Elmer Olson's home. This is now known as The Norway Tree
Plantation. There is still a plain landmark where the
chief had his home. It is an elm tree, still in good shape,
standing a few feet away--next to the C.C.C. Trail.

Some of the natural resources are fish, wild rice,
lumber, and furs. Most of the fish caught is eaten, but
nearly all of the wild rice and furs are sold. Fuel is
made from the forests. Much of the soil is sandy and some
of the gravel is used for road construction. However, in
places the soil is favorable to agriculture so some farming
is carried on. Sap from maple trees is gathered and made
into syrup or maple sugar. Much of this is sold commercially.
The Chippewa handicraft is of excellent quality. Skins of
animals are used to make belts, purses, and moccasins.
Various grasses are used to weave baskets of different kinds.
Many of these things are sold to tourists during the summer.
An abundance of wild fruit is found and used for food by
the natives; some, such as blueberries, are sold.

"From time immemorial the Indians told their sons
and daughters the historic events, sites, names, and
heritage of their ancestors, which method has followed
repeatedly down through to generations. My ancestors
are as follows:
1--Gah-sha-sha-gis, died some 400 years ago of old age
at Camp ground of his hunting grounds northeast of Elk
Lake now known as Itasca Lake, Clearwater County, the
source of Mississippi River and the Indian Mounds are the
historic sites.
His son:
2--Bah-be-quew-o-ski-sig, born at east end of Cass Lake on
north side of the outlet of Mississippi River. Ne-e-ish
was his nickname, his leadership and understanding was
respected by his tribe and it is possible that he was the
first Indian ever to blaze trees in line which signified
this is his birthplace, timber, and land. Died of old
age and buried at west end of Rice Lake, now known as
Lower Rice Lake, Clearwater County, on south side of the
outlet of Lower Rice River.
His son:
3--Way-zah-wag-e-quo-ung, born at Elm Ridge west side of
the river between the lakes now known as Bemidji, Beltrami
County, and was killed in the battle between the Sioux
Indians and Chippewas on east side of Stillwater. Many
battles were fought for the right hunting grounds and
ownership of land.
His son:
4--Ah-bid-way-we-dung was enrolled; born at Camp ground
east side of Rice Lake now known as Lower Rice Lake, Clearwater County. He took part in 1889 Treaty. Died April,
1890, at Big Bend-now in Mahnomen County. He was 98 years
old.
His son:
5--Be-daus-e-goy was enrolled; born at Star Island, Cass
Lake. Took part in 1889 Treaty. Died at Nay-tah-waush,
Mahnomen, County, November 27, 1937. Helped to build Red
Lake and Beaulieu Trails when county was a wilderness. He
was 90 years old.
His son:
6--May-zhuc-e-be-nais (Harold Emerson) is enrolled. Born
October 12, 1877 at north shore of North Twin Lake; now
living at Nay-tah-waush, Mahnomen County." .....Former
Game Warden, Former Wild Rice Director, First Notary
Public in Nay-tah-waush; now a member of the School Board,
Draft Board, and Indian Council.

When May-zhuc-e-be-nais started school, the teacher
was unable to correctly pronounce his name so gave him the
name of Harold Emerson. Mr. Emerson did not start school
at Nay-tah-waush but at Beaulieu where his family lived

before moving here. The school was one room and all the
pupils sat on a long bench. The only other furniture was
the teacher's desk and a stove with a big pile of wood in
the corner behind it.

Besides Ah-bid-way-we-dung and Be-daus-e-gay (ancestors
of Mr. Emerson's), Mane-do-ge-shig and May-nay-way-bineis
were early settlers with homes also on the north end of
North Twin Lake. Another settler was Ah-ke-way-zance who
had his home between the lakes (now known as Pinehurst).
His wife's name was Shawnun-ge-shig-oquay; she died in Mr.
Emerson's home in 1916. Ah-ke-way-zance died in 1894, and
is buried in the Indian Cemetery near the south lake. They
lived in this area long before the White Earth Reservation
was set aside in 1868. Virgin forests surrounded the lakes
and abundant wildlife furnished food.

In 1869, a Civil War Veteran, Henry H. Beaulieu and
his family moved in and built a home near Ah-ke-way-zance's.
The Pinehurst Garage and Boathouse stand there now. Mr.
Beaulieu acted as foreman for the government's Indian
Office. He cut pine timber on the east and west shores of
North Twin Lake. Some of the old stumps can still be seen
between Pinehurst and Kohler's Store. He floated the logs
in Twin Lakes Creek to Wild Rice River Saw Mill (now near
the village of Beaulieu--just above the present Beaulieu
Bridge). The east side of the river was all lumber yard.
Mr. Beaulieu built a dam at the outlet of Sargent Lake and
another dam down the creek to supply enough water for
floating the logs. The timber operation was intended for
the Indian's benefit. At this same period, the White Earth
Lake Saw Mill was located on the west shore for the same
purpose. This later burned.

In 1886, Mr. Tyler Warren (after dissolving his part-
nership with a Wild West Show which traveled all over the
states, and with head quarters in Philadelphia) built the
first frame house in this area. It was on the east shore
of the north lake. He became a government surveyor and
timber estimator. He was also the first grain farmer doing the seeding of small grains by hand; he cut the grain
with a cradle and threshed by hand. The ground on which
the baseball diamond and school now stand was cultivated
by him with the use of oxen.

George Kitchum was the first white man to build a
home on the north shore of the north lake. This was in
1887. Kitchum and Warren cut roads open by the north side
of Sargent Lake; thence northwest to Wild Rice River
(Beaulieu).

Other early settlers were Frank Shanahan, Fred Bigwind, Anyweush, Littlewolf, Pemberton, Foxx, Morgan,
Wadena, and Douglas families. Many of their descendants
are living here today. Besides the natives, there are
few French, Norweign, German, and Dutch people living in
the community.

Under the treaty of 1889, the Indian Office moved
the Indians by bands--such as Mille Lacs, Gull Lake,
White Oak, Fond du Lacs, and Pillager--from different
parts of the state to the White Earth Reservation. Indians
from Cass Lake, Leech Lake, and Winnibigoshish Lake belong
to the Pillager Band. The Ottertail Band of Pillagers were
not removals and were permitted to come in with equal
rights as a result of a document signed by the head men of
the Mississippi Band, dated July 5, 1872, and approved by
Congress in 1875.

It was mostly the Mille Lacs that settled in the "Twin
Lake" area. They were housed in two large log houses. One
was built near the Warren's home and the other house was
built near the present Norway Tree Plantation--about two
hundred steps north of the northeast end--by the old
Beaulieu Trail. Here, too, land marks can be plainly seen.
This group of removals were in primitive society; their
recreation was squaw dancing, war dancing, LaCrosse game,
and, annually, the Grand Medicine Ceremony. This was
usually held during the spring or summer, and the Indians
would camp out for ten or fifteen days. The last Grand
Medicine Ceremony was held here in 1919. The two log
houses were gradually vacated as the occupants went to live
on their allotments. Mr. Warren used the log house near
him for a Blacksmith Shop. This is on the southwest corner
of the school ground and often some metal, iron, and horse-
shoe nails are unearthed.

In the winter of 1894, the Wild Rice Lumber Company of
Ada, Minnesota, built a logging camp on the northwest end
of Bass Lake for pine timber operations. Mr. Andy Remark
of Ada was the general manager; Tyler Warren supervised the
cutting of the pine timber, building of the logging roads,
and hauling operations with the use of horses. The cutting
was mostly on the south and northwest side of Bass Lake.
Most of the logs were hauled across the ice of the lake--by
the north and south side of Tower Hill. Some hills were
cut down and make wider so that the logging sleds could get
through to the east shore of North Twin Lake. This logging
road crossed the Henry Pemberton grain field--just a little
ways north of Kohler's Store. In the spring of 1895, Mr.

Charles Gardner of Beaulieu was overseer for taking the
logs across the North Twin Lake Inlet. Special cut trees--
from fifty to sixty feet long-- were chained together to
form a ring large enough to hold approximately a thousand
logs. These logs were moved across the lake by means of
cable and crank operated by eight or more men from a flat
boat heavily anchored. This was repeated until all logs
were across the lake and into the inlet, thence into the
creek to Little Rice Lake, and on to Sargent Lake Inlet,
then down the creek. This drive of logs was hung up by
reasons of low water west of the present "Ranch" so the
company built a dam about a half mile south from the highway 31 bridge on Twin Lakes Creek. The drive resumed in
the spring of 1896. This was the last drive of pine logs
in the Twin Lakes Creek, and also the last drive for the
Wild Rice Lumber Company.

In 1894, the government built a saw mill six miles
southeast of Twin Lakes and another one five miles southwest. The E. E. Miller Farm is now located on the latter.
Both mills sawed pine and furnished lumber for the Removals'
homes, most of which were built on allotments. In 1913,
Mr. Andrew Rogalski cut hard wood timber northwest of Nay-
tah-waush, and hauled the logs to his mill located at the
west end of Sargent Lake. During the year 1915, he cut
pine timber on the northwest end of Bass Lake and hauled
the logs, on ice, across the South Twin Lake, thence to
Lego Lake, and landed on Rogalski Lake-his new mill site.
This was the last pine timber operation in this area. The
large scale cutting and transporting of logs and lumber
has changed to portable mills and trucking.

About 1889, a one arm man by the name of Minito-
mah-koa carried mail on the Red Lake-White Earth Trail.
He was mail carrier for a long time. He would use either
a horse or a pony. A long rope was tied to the pony's
neck and Minito-mah-koa, holding onto the rope, would walk
beside the animal. Once in a while he would ride. During
the winter, Minito-mah-koa would travel in the day time
only; on hot summer days, he'd stop at some shady place
for a nap until almost sun down. Then he would continue
his travel in the cool nights. He usually carried lunch
with him. Often he would stop at Warren's to let his pony
feed on the grass in their yard.

Star Bad Boy had the first Post Office about 1906.
Mr. Weston, postmaster at Beaulieu, helped him to start
the mail delivery office on the condition that it would
have an Indian name. Star Bad Boy asked Chief Nay-tah-

waush if he would be willing to have the community
named after him. The Chief agreed. The Post Office was
started in the old Warren home. Mail came from Beaulieu
every Monday, Wednesday, and Saturday. For two years
Star Bad Boy handled the mail at his home. Besides this,
he was a member of the Indian Police Force for twenty-
two years. He was a fine artist, and very interested in
the school. On January 12, 1952, Mr. Bad Boy, at the age
of eighty-three years, died in a fire which destroyed his
home.

Rev. Wilkins Smith, an Indian Minister, was the
second postmaster. He had the mail delivered from his
home which was the Episcopal Mission House. He secured
the office through Mr. S. B. Olson, postmaster at Mahnomen. The next to take over the post office was Mrs.
Clara Fairbanks, who had it in her store. Later she
moved it into her home. It was in 1943 that Mrs. Alois
Rumreich took over the duties as postmistress. About
three years ago, a new post office was built. Mail now
comes from Mahnomen every day except Sundays and a few
holidays.

Nay-tah-waush had a hotel at one time, too. It was
built in May, 1915, by William Bunker. A guest at the
hotel had to pay from one dollar to one dollar fifty cents
for a room. Meals were also served. This hotel was in
operation for about ten years. Now it is a private home.

Fred Bigwind, who was married to Chief Nay-tah-
waush's daughter, owned the first store. It was located
three-fourths of a mile east of Miss Northrop's Farm.
This was about 1891. One can plainly see the cellar
holes where he had his store. One of the popular items
for sale was salt pork. At that time, the head of the
family would get five dollar rations from the government
for such things as pork, flour, sugar, and tea. Mr.
Bigwind must have strongly believed in the commandment
"Remember the Sabbath and Keep It Holy" for he would not
sell an item on Sunday. Mr. Star Bad Boy had the second
store. This was about 1906. It was located near the old
home of Tyler Warren. The next store was built in 1909
on the ground that Elmer Olson lives on at present. It
was owned by Mr. W. A. Fairbanks. There was also a
temporary store in the Guild Hall in 1913. This was
owned by Mr. Salem Fairbanks from Beaulieu who later
moved back to Beaulieu. Several families rented the
Guild Hall for homes at various times also. About 1917,
a man named Charles Potter had a Meat Market located
near Mr. Emerson's home. Cellar marks of this store are

still visible.

A cousin of W. A. Fairbanks, Mr. B. L. Fairbanks and Company had a store between the John Terway's and Mrs. W. A. Fairbank's present homes. This was in 1920. He had the store here for only a year. Then it was moved to the spot where the Gospel Alliance Church now stands. Here were two buildings--a pool hall and lunch room, and the store. Joe B. Fairbanks (Curly Joe) was the manager. Fire destroyed these structures and a new building was erected. Today church services are held in it. Mr. and Mrs. W. A. Fairbanks opened the store which is now owned and operated by Howard LaVoy. Fairbanks had two warehouses which were separate buildings; one was a log cabin. Mr. LaVoy purchased the store in 1938. Since then he has done quite a bit of remodeling. The store has been made larger, and modern equipment has been added. The warehouse is now part of the store building.

In 1911, "the Clinic" was built and paid for by the government to serve as an employee's home. Mr. Starr, a teacher, was the first to live in it, and a Mrs. Powell was the second one. It is now used as the office of the Public Health Nurse who serves the needs of the people daily. A doctor from Mahnomen also comes to the clinic every Friday to care for those that are in need of his service. At the present time, Dr. Danford makes the calls.

Public Health Service began in Northern Minnesota in 1923. Dr. A. J. Chesley (Secretary of Minnesota Department of Health), Miss Ann Nyquist (now Director of Public Health Nursing), Miss Parisian, and Miss Sherer held a clinic at the Jack Pine School, in Clearwater County, that year. Miss Parisian and Miss Sherer were certified Public Health Nurses from the University's School of Nursing. It was mainly through the services of these two Indian nurses that the confidence of the Indian people was secured. Miss Mary Martin followed into the White Earth area as Public Health Nurse.

Several nurses have been on the reservation for short periods, but the names of the following have given continuous service: Miss Adelia Eggestine was in our area, which included White Earth Village, in the days when Dr. Rodwell was the physician in charge. Many home visits were made and their means of transportation was a team of horses. Miss Eggestine went to China in 1948 with the U. S. Public Health Service and is now in the West Indies. Miss Veronica Wieber worked for many years in this area and has

a wonderful record for the work she did in the field to
eliminate Tuberculosis. For the past years she has been
head nurse at Ah-gwah-ching. Later, Miss Agnes Wiener
came to the White Earth Reservation. She is now stationed
at Ponsford. Miss Adele Northrop came to Mahnomen and
Clearwater Counties in 1936 and retired in 1951. She was
referred to as "The Nurse", and was a friend of all. She
took a great interest in community affairs and in church
work. "Her work has been characterized by state officials
as being exemplary." Miss Northrop died January 17,1952.
Mrs. Mary Stolze is now the Public Health Nurse.

There are three churches in our village. The Christian
Alliance Church had its beginning in 1926. A daily vacation
Bible School was conducted by two young ladies that summer.
It was so successful, and interest was so great that this
work was followed by a young man and his bride--Rev. and
Mrs. Floyd Pollack. They had just finished their schooling
and felt there was a great need for the Gospel. Meetings were first held in the William Bunker home until a
building was purchased and remodeled as the present chapel.
Rev. Pollack continued his work for about five years. It
was Rev. Walter Rupp and his wife who replaced the Pollacks.
Miss Elverum and Miss Shields are in charge of the church
which is referred to as the Gospel Tabernacle.

While the history of the Gospel Tabernacle Church is
comparatively new, the history of the Episcopal Church
dates far back. The following dates and material were
taken from Rev. Geo. H. Goodreid's Survey in 1949, and
also from records available in the Episcopal Church:
"The Indians now living in Minnesota are from a tribe
made famous in American Literature through Longfellow's
"Hiawatha" where the tribal name "Ojibway" was used. The
Chippewas have been exposed to missionary effort for more
than a century. In 1852, the work of the Protestant E-
piscopal Church among Indians was begun by Dr. James L.
Breck at Gull Lake; but it was not until Rev. Henry B.
Whipple was consecrated the first bishop in Minnesota, in
the year 1859 that a real missionary effort was attained.
Archdeacon Joseph A. Gilfillan served on the White Earth
Reservation for twenty-five years. It was through his
vigorous efforts, and largely at his own expense, that
schools, missions, and chapels were built at Pine Point,
White Earth, Beaulieu, and Nay-tah-waush. Samuel Memorial
Mission, Nay-tah-waush, was built about 1893 by George
Warmuth. Rev. Many Penny, a Chippewa Indian, was the first
layman stationed here. The Parish House was also built then
and remodeled in 1942 by the efforts of the Women's Aux-
iliaries of the Duluth Church and of Nay-tah-waush. Twenty-

five years ago this mission was one of the twelve Episcopal Missions in Northern Minnesota.

Rev. Edward Kah-O-Sed had charge of Ney-tah-waush, Beaulieu, and out lying missions during 1906 to 1931. He was a devout and able full-blood Indian. During his last years, he served St. Columba Church at White Earth. This church is considered the Mother Church by hundreds of Chippewas, and even a larger number of non-residents revere it as their spiritual home. The graves of three native pastors, including Rev. Kah-O-Sed, are in the church yard.

During the years 1926, and until his death in 1948, Archdeacon K. W. Boyle was our valuable friend and advisor ministering to his people. His sermons always were an inspiration, and his friendship most sincere.

Archdeacon George H. Goodreid served this Mission Field from 1945-1950. He is now rector at St. Paul's Church in Winona. Archdeacon Dell Lee Harris serves the Trinity Church at Park Rapids and the Indian Field throughout the state. He came to us in 1950.

The early clergy serving Samuel Memorial Mission and its leaders in training men for Christian Service were: Louis Many Penny--1903-1920. Samuel Memorial and St. Thomas
    Chapel at Wild Rice Rapids. This was
    located north of the present Rodwell Rest
    home.
Joseph Waukago--1900-1910.

W. D. Smith------1911-1924. Also Chapel at Bend in river.
    Location known as Washington Meadows.
    This was located near the spot where the
    Antell School stands today.

James Rice------1921-1933. Also St. Phillips, Rice Lake in
    Clearwater County.
(Died December 30, 1937.)

Archdeacon Wellington K. Boyle--1926-1941.

Wm. B. Rice (student)--1925-1930. Records show much contact
    in home.
(Son of James Rice.)

J. B. Brown-------1932-1933.

F. T. Waukazo-----1931-1932.
(Son of Joseph Waukazo)

Through these years there are many mentions of the following: Bishop Whipple, Bishop Bennett, Morrison; Rev. Chas. Wright; Deacons George Morgan and Mark Hart. Star Bad Boy--a devout church man since the church was built, and who was still an active member at the time of his recent death--was also mentioned.

Rev. Kah-O-Sed established schools at White Earth and Cass Lake. In 1925, William Rice and F. J. Waukazo were enrolled in the Kah-O-Sed School at Cass Lake. These schools were ably administered by Dr. Francis L. Carrington, Oxford University, England. The last three students mentioned above were ordained at St. Columba's Church in 1940. They are now in charge of the churches at Ponsford, Cass Lake, and Oniguim.

It takes a long time to become an effective missionary, and it is a life time labor in our Lord's work. Samuel Memorial Church is now being considered by Bishop Keeler and Archdeacon Harris as the center for this seminary training.

The Women's Auxiliary was organized at the time Mr. Many Penny was minister. His wife was the first president. Names of Mrs. Ellen Warren, Mrs. Kate Douglas, Mrs. Anne Goodwin, Cecelia Pelerin, Francis Keahand, Lizzie Roy, Irene Harris, Miss Northrop, and Josephine Robinson were mentioned. Many of these women are still faithfully working for their church.

The Sunday School was organized by Mr. Many Penny. During Rev. Boyle's service to this church, there was an active Brotherhood Organization devoted to Christian Leadership and Service."

The history of the Catholic Church is also interesting. One of the first superiors of the Benedictine Order, Abbot Alexius Edelbrock made a visit to White Earth in 1869. Father Alysious was the first priest to make a call at Naytah-waush. Father Roman was one of the early priests who attended the sick and gave the last rites. He lived at Beaulieu at that time. Today Father Roman is past eighty years of age, but is faithfully serving the parishoners at Ogema, Minnesota.

It should be remembered that Indians and Whites passed through this community when going to the Red Lake Reservation. The Trail passed from White Earth to Red Lake through the narrow pass (Pinehurst) between the lakes. Father Aloysius and Father Thomas frequently passed through on this trail. They also made some of the sick calls.

In 1916, the very first Mass was most likely celebrated here. The Mass was celebrated in various places, but most often at the residence of Alphonse LaVoy. In the summers of 1916 and 1917, Masses were celebrated in the old government school--later known as the seventh and eighth grade room. At this time there were about a dozen Catholic families. One of the most prominent promoters of the religious services, and the one person who strived to get a priest, was Mrs. Clara Fairbanks who is still a resident of our community.

In the early days there was considerable amount of logging of heavy timber in this area. Efforts were made to construct some sort of a church. In 1917, the first mission church was built and it is still being used today. The parishioners furnished some of the money, but Father Felix received a donation to finish the construction. Father Felix was the first priest who tended to the religious services regularly in the missions. Joseph Bellanger was the first janitor and faithfully did his work until his death. Mrs. Harold Emerson was the first organist.

In 1919, a big Indian Congress was held. At this Congress, Bishop Corbett, Bishop of the Crookston Diocese, came to bless the church. It was then named St. Ann--the Patron Saint of the entire mission. Besides the church here, the mission consists of a church at Elbow Lake and one at Island Lake. At present, work has begun on a church at Wild Rice Lake.

From then on various priests from neighboring parishes took care of the religious services. Some of them were Fathers Benno, Leo, Florian, Francis, Stephen, Thomas, and Constantine. Fathers Benno and Felix resided at Ponsford but journeyed here to hold services about twice a month. Fathers Thomas and Florian resided at Red Lake and also came here about twice a month. Father Benno was here shortly after the church was built (when Father Felix left) and again from 1941 to 1945. Father Francis was here at two different times--the first for a few years in the 1930's and again from 1945 to 1949. Regular Sunday Masses began when Father Benno was stationed at Beaulieu and he was able to be present every Sunday. Until Father Casmir began residing in the community, the preceding priests either lived at Beaulieu, Mahnomen, or White Earth with the pastors there. During the summer of 1951, a fine, modern residence for the priests serving this mission, was completed as a result of Father Casmir's efforts. Bishop Schenk, from Crookston, blessed the home. On November 11, 1951, Father Augustine came to serve the parish.

The Community Hall was built in 1948. Through the Indian Agency Office, Cass Lake, about a thousand dollars worth of material was donated to us from government buildings which were to be disposed of at C.C.C. Camp, Nett Lake Reservation. The school board of District 29 bought the building in which Frank Long had operated a store. This was moved to the school grounds and the school district financed the building and has supervision of it. All the families in the community donated either labor or material. Mr. William Robinson supervised the carpenter work. Other skilled workmen were Leonard McDougall, Ira White, and Elmer Olson.

"The Hall" has proved very useful as a dining hall, school room, and for activities in the community--especially for the youth groups such as Boy Scouts, Girl Scouts, and 4-H Club. The Community Council have their meetings in it, and for the past three years have had very successful Harvest Festivals here. Besides these activities, a movie is shown once a week to the public for a nominal fee.

The very first school was located near Miss Northrop's Farm. It was just a log house belonging to John Morgan. It is believed that Grace Beaulieu taught at this school. Then a Day School was built behind the Episcopal Church. Rev. J. A. Gilfillan built it. Mrs. William Maddison taught this school. This was about 1909. In 1911, the first government school was built which was the seventh and eighth grade room until just recently. All grades were taught in this room by one man named Phillip Starr. He wrote poetry. Mrs. Alois Rumreich has a book of his works which includes a poem about the people of Nay-tah-waush.

At this time clothes were issued to the school children which consisted of caps, trousers, etc. The former fifth grade room was used for a dining room and storage place for the rationed clothing. A noon meal, cooked by the teacher's wife, Ada, was served to the children. The Starrs lived at the "cottage"--another name for the Clinic.

With the ever increasing school enrollment, it was necessary to find more room for the youngsters. The eight grades were in four separate buildings. The school board was keenly aware of the crowded conditions, and worked very hard for many years to get a new building. About the time when it seemed as if the new building was a reality, World War II broke out and thoughts of building had to be set aside. Finally in June, 1950, work on a new school began, and after sixteen months, it was completed.

The **new** school is located about three blocks east
of the old one. It is very interesting to note that this
fine school building is on Tribal Land and stands right
on top of the old Indian Trail which went from White Earth
to Red Lake. From Richwood the trail lead to the north
end of White Earth Lake, then to the west side of Snyder
Lake, on to Pinehurst, and north by Pemberton's and Warren's.
Tyler Warren's home was a stopping off place. The Pemberton
and Robinson homes now stand on the original trail. Oxen
were used on this trail to transport freight. **This was
the** only means by which people could get any freight from
the railroads.

When one steps out the north door of the new school,
an old land mark can be seen across the road. It is a
narrow trail running north, and then east directly in front
of the Catholic Church door. From here it goes to Roy Lake,
then to the Wild Rice River Crossing by Bagely, on to Four
Legged Lake (south of Leonard), and then to Red Lake.

On October 1, 1951, we moved into the fine, modern,
beautiful, brick building, which cost $212,000. The fed-
eral and state government taxes helped to pay for it. The
school is a two story structure plus the basement and
furnace room. It is furnished with all new equipment.
There are eight class rooms, a science room, a sewing room,
boys' and girls' showers, lavatories, a library, nurse's
quarters, a fine kitchen, and a dining room which is also
used as an auditorium.

The people of Nay-tah-waush are very thankful and
very grateful for this fine means of education for its
citizens of tomorrow.

White Earth, Minn., July 5th, 1872

This is to certify that:

    Whereas, the Otter Tail Band of Pillager Chippewas have expressed to us their desire to come and live upon the White Earth Reservation and adopt **the** habits of Christian civilization; and

    Whereas, we remember when we were poor and ignorant, and are desirous to help others of our race to enjoy the same blessings we have; and

    Whereas: the U.S. Gov't. has appropriated $25000. to be expended for the benefit for the Indians on this Reservation in teaching us civilization and helping us to self support;

    Therefore: We the Chiefs and Head men of the Mississippi Chippewas, in open council hereby, for ourselves and our bands invite the Otter Tail Band of Pillager Indians to come and settle upon the White Earth Reservation with equal rights in respect to the lands within its boundaries.

	Wa-ban-o-quod--	his mark.
	✗ Mo zha-ke-ke-shig	" "
Witness	Mem-e-do-waub	" "
	Mino-ge-shick	" "
T. A. Warren-	I-ah-bay	" "
Interpreter	Kay-zhe-osh	" "
E. P. Smith-	John Johnson	" "
U.S. Ind. Agt.	William Superior	" "
M. S. Cook-	John Brown	" "
Clerk	Kog-og-e-we-gwom	" "
----------------------	Kah-ah-gos-de-bay	" "
A true copy of the	Shing-we-bay	" "
original paper signed	Keche-be-way	" "
July 6th, 1872.	Sang-way-way	" "

Note: Act of Congress of 1875 admitting Otter Tail Pillagers in White Earth Reservation with same rights as Mississippis in line with council proceedings.

The Store and Postoffice –
         operated by Mrs. C. Fairbanks

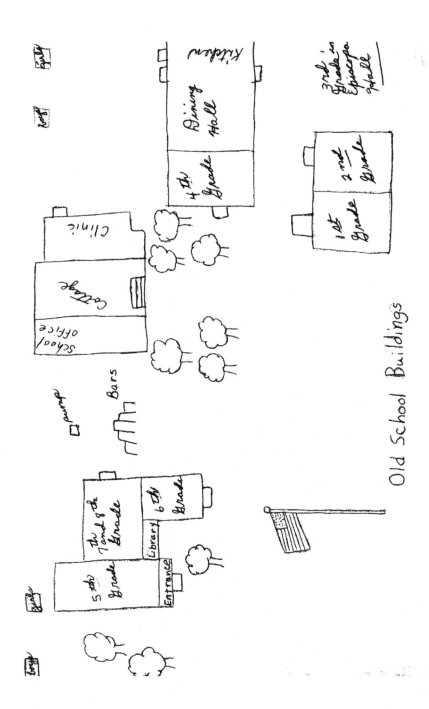

Old School Buildings

Special

Notice is hereby given that, the Northwaush Local Council will be held at Epc-Guild-Hall, Friday Oct. 27, 1939, at 7:30 pm. —

Purpose to discuss ways and help from the Pass take office pertaining to Sponsor fund for a new School building and Community Hall and to do any other business may come proper at said Council when convened —

Harold B Emerson Sec'y.
Local Council

Dated Oct 23, 1939

Roy Lake Wauk, Minn.

Roy Lake wauk Local Council held a Special
meeting at Rec. Guild Hall, Friday Oct 7, 1939, at 7³⁰ P.m.
John Coleman Local Chairman is now in
White Earth Hospital and Wm Bellanger Vis-pres.
Called the meeting to order, and stated the
business to be transact —
— Motion made, Seconded and (carried)
—that the Chairman appoint a Resolution
Committee of three (3) — carried
            Resolution Committee —
Howard La Voi, John Pemberton & Wm Hanks
     The following matters pertaining to the
Community were considered and the following
action had —
         A number of Indians present in
turn discussed, Spon share for New School
House, Chairman, Called the Resolution Com-
⊕ draft a Resolution

Resolution Com = offered a Resolution That
the Local Council go on record requesting the
WE. Res. Council approve Resolution No 1 -
$16000 from the Sale of Town Lots -
upon mater seconded That the Resolution
be adopted = Carried -

Resolution No 2 =
                    Demanding immediate Construction
of Community Hall --
     Motion made, seconded That The Resolution be
adopted Carried

Resolution No 3
                Salvaged Material of office Building
Also Known as the School Building be Transferred to
Nay Tahwahsh District - Carried

        Then was discussion of the Annuity payment
            meeting adjourned
                                HJ E

352

EXCERPTS FROM THE PERMIT FOR SCHOOL SITE

THIS INDENTURE, Made and entered into this 5th day of
October, 1949, by and between THE MINNESOTA CHIPPEWA TRIBE
of the State of Minnesota, hereinafter called the permitter,
and the INDEPENDENT SCHOOL DISTRICT NO. 29 of The COUNTY OF
MAHNOMEN in the State of Minnesota, hereinafter called the
permittee:
WITNESSTH, that pursuant to the provisions of the Act
of Congress approved October 8, 1940 (54 Stat. 1020) as
amended by the Act of Congress approved July 24, 1947 (61 Stat.
418), the permitter hereby grants to the permittee the right
to enter upon and occupy the following described land on the
White Earth Indian Reservation subject to the conditions and
covenants hereinafter contained:
That portion of Lot 2, Section 28, Township 144 North,
Range 39 West, 5th Principal Meridian, County of Mahnomen,
State of Minnesota, more particularly described as follows:
Beginning at the northeast corner of Said Lot 2, thence south
on the east line thereof a distance of 924 feet; thence west
on a line parallel to the north line of said Lot 2 a distance
of 495 feet; thence north on a line parallel to the east line
of said Lot 2 a distance of 924 feet to the north line thereof;
thence east on the north line of said Lot 2 a distance of 495
feet to the point of beginning, containing 10.52 acres, more
or less.
This permit shall terminate upon breach of any of the
conditions herein.
It is further agreed by the parties hereto that all the
stipulations and agreements contained herein shall extend to
and bind the successors and assigns of the said parties.
In witness whereof the said parties have hereunto set
their hands the day and year first above written.

Witnesses: THE MINNESOTA CHIPPEWA TRIBE
/s/ Mrs. Sara Groves   By:/s/ Lawrence Connor
                                            Its President
/s/ James Boney   /s/ Bernard Morrison
                                            Its Secretary

SCHOOL BOARD DIRECTORS   INDEPENDENT SCHOOL DISTRICT NO.29,
                                  COUNTY OF MAHNOMEN IN STATE OF
/s/ William Turpin   MINNESOTA
/s/ Mrs. Josephine Robinson By: /s/ Howard LeVoy
                                                Chairman
WITNESS: /s/ Adele Northrop
/s/ P. J. Broon   Clerk

DEPARTMENT OF THE INTERIOR Bureau of Indian Affairs Washington
Approve: May 18, 1950 /s/H.M.Critchfield Acting Assistant
                    Commissioner of Indian Affairs.

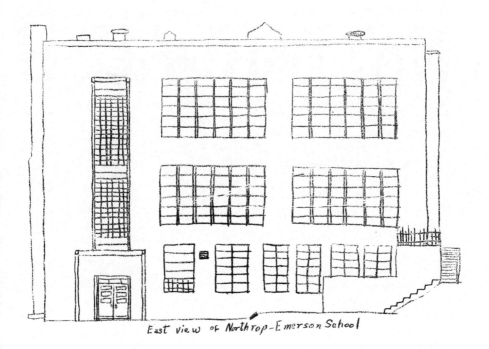

East view of Northrop-Emerson School

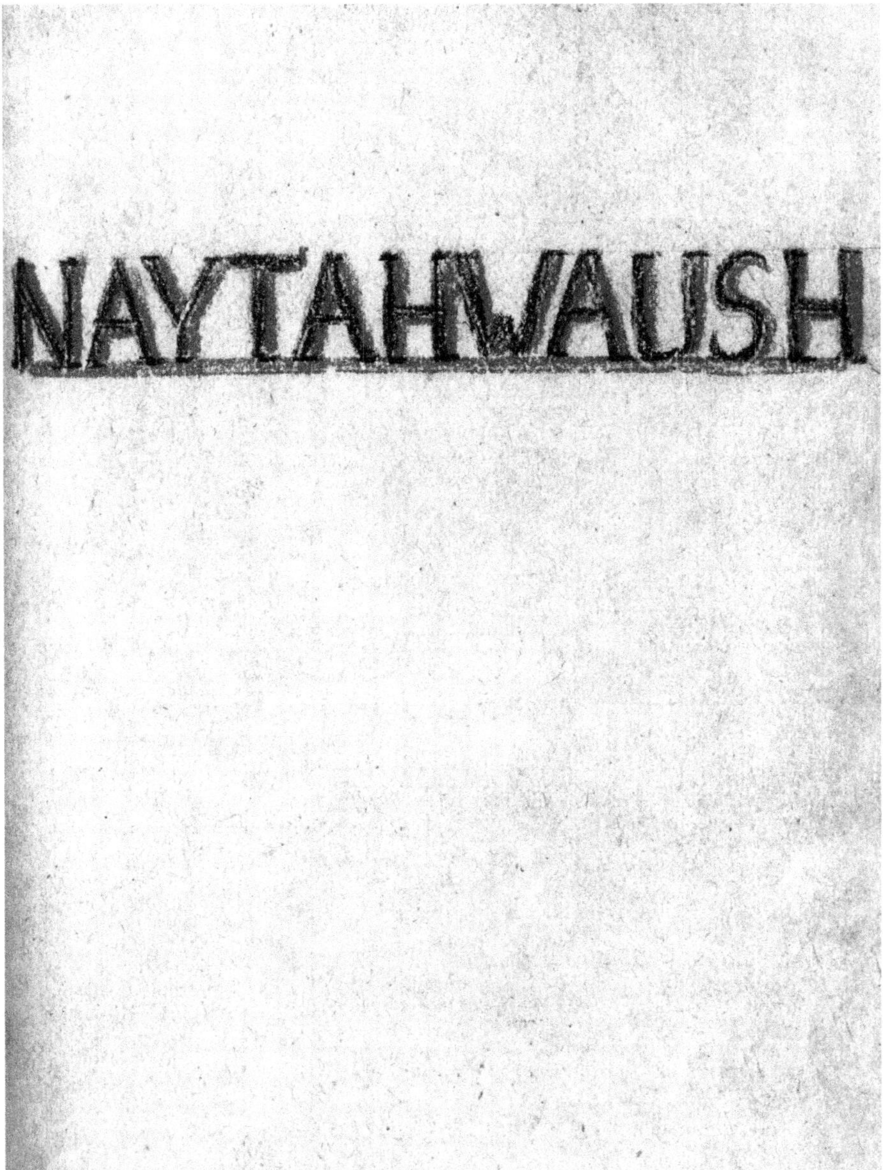
NAYTAHWAUSH

MAHNOMEN COUNTY

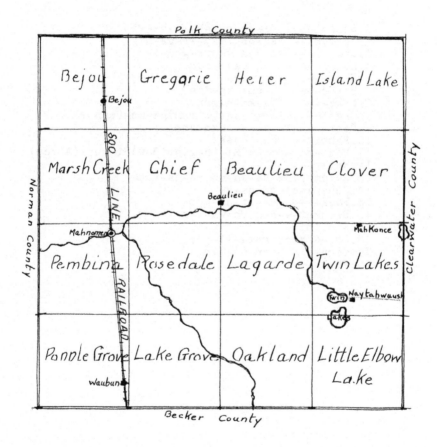

CHIPPEWA WORDS

1. School------Ge-ke-no-ah-ma-de-win
2. Church------Au-ne- may-we-ge-mig
3. Store-------A-dah-wa-we-gum-ig
4. House-------Wah-ka-e-gun
5. Bear--------Mah-qua
6. Horse-------Mish-tah-dim
7. Lake--------Sa-ka-e-gun
8. Canoe-------We-guase(birch)ge-mon(canoe)
9. Deer--------Wa-wa-shka-she
10. Rabbit----Wa-boose
11. Bow and Arrow--Mi-to-guab(Bow)Bi-quok(Arrow)
12. Water-----Ni-bi
13. Automobile-Wa-sa-mo-we-da-vaum
14. Sunshine--Wa-sa-g-
15. Book------Ma-si-na-gun
16. Blanket---Wah-bo-wa-yan
17. She-shib
18. Dried Meat-Bata-wi-yas
19. Corn------Mon-da-min
20. Fish------Gi-goo

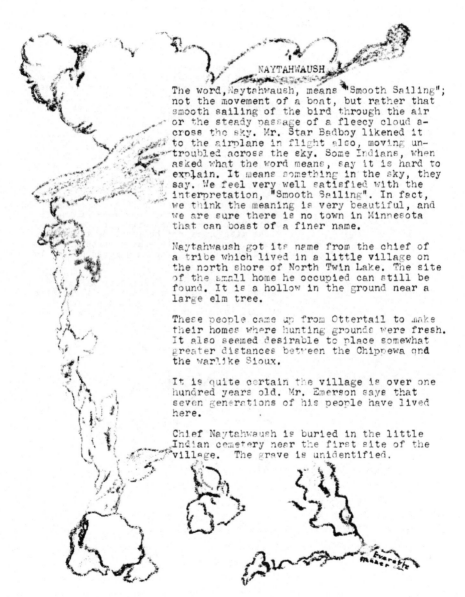

NAYTAHWAUSH

The word, Naytahwaush, means "Smooth Sailing"; not the movement of a boat, but rather that smooth sailing of the bird through the air or the steady passage of a fleecy cloud across the sky. Mr. Star Badboy likened it to the airplane in flight also, moving untroubled across the sky. Some Indians, when asked what the word means, say it is hard to explain. It means something in the sky, they say. We feel very well satisfied with the interpretation, "Smooth Sailing". In fact, we think the meaning is very beautiful, and we are sure there is no town in Minnesota that can boast of a finer name.

Naytahwaush got its name from the chief of a tribe which lived in a little village on the north shore of North Twin Lake. The site of the small home he occupied can still be found. It is a hollow in the ground near a large elm tree.

These people came up from Ottertail to make their homes where hunting grounds were fresh. It also seemed desirable to place somewhat greater distances between the Chippewa and the warlike Sioux.

It is quite certain the village is over one hundred years old. Mr. Emerson says that seven generations of his people have lived here.

Chief Naytahwaush is buried in the little Indian cemetery near the first site of the village. The grave is unidentified.

SOME "FIRSTS" IN NAYTAHWAUSH

The first post office was in the Badboy home. Mrs. Robinson's father died in 1900. Her mother later married Mr. Star Badboy. He was the first postmaster. Mr. Warren had thought of naming the post office Warrington, but Naytahwaush was decided upon.

The first school was in a little log cabin on what is now Miss Northrup's land. The first school in the present village was held in the Guild Hall, taught by Mr. Henry Warren, a cousin of Tyler Warren. This building was erected in 1892 or 1893.

The first church was the little Episcopal Church, erected in the same year as the Guild Hall. Archdeacon Gilfillan was the first missionary and builder. He traveled from village to village on horseback. He loved his work and was much loved by the Indians.

The first store was operated by Alfred Warren in a small log building. It was more of a trading post, for white man's money did not mean much to the Indians in those days.

WHAT"S IN A NAME?

When we asked Mrs. Robinson how Mr. Badboy
got his name, this is the story she told
us.

It all goes back to Star Badboy's grandfather. He had overheard some Indians
talking about an attack they were going to
make on the white people. This troubled
him. It was not easy for him to decide
what to do. After much serious thought,
he decided to go to the commander of the
fort and report what he had heard. The commander patted him and said,"You were a good
boy, but almost a bad boy!" From that time
on, he was called Badboy, and that is how
the name came into being.

Mrs. Robinson was not certain as to the
fort referred to above, but was of the o-
pinion that it might be Fort Snelling.
It could very easily be Camp Ripley, or
Fort Ripley as it was called in the early
days.

Wilbur
Norri

Mrs. Fairbanks' Story

Mr. and Mrs. Fairbanks came to Naytahwaush
from Mahnomen in 1912, January 1.They first
lived near Mr. Smith's church, using it for
a store. Six months later they moved to a new
Indian home, where Elmer Olson's home is. In
the fall of 1912, Mr. Faibanks erected a store,
a large frame building with a log warehouse behind. A three-room apartment was attached. Above
the store was a large room for the girls who
worked for Mr. and Mrs. Fairbanks. The community boomed so fast it was surprising, Mrs. Fairbanks said.

There were no good roads out here and no cars.
Mr. Fairbanks had two first class teams of horses to get freight every other day from Mahnomen. He got permission from the county commis-
sioners to build a better road so that cars
could go over it. Mr. Douglas was the foreman.
Mrs. Fairbanks fed the crew. This all took place
in their first year-1912. Mr. Fairbanks got a
new car and was the first to go over the road.
A caravan of cars came out to celebrate the
opening of the road and spent the day fishing.
They went over to where Pinehurst now stands
and admired the beauty of the spot very much.
It was then a wilderness.

At this time, school was held in the Guild
Hall, with Mrs. William Madison teaching. She
left her piano with Mrs. Fairbanks, so she had
a group of girls sing a welcome song for all the
Mahnomen guests. Among them were the Douglas
girls.

In 1915 or 16, the Fairbanks built the present
store. St. Anne's Church was built soon after.
Mrs. Fairbanks is often called the builder of
the church. There were only seven Catholic
families in the village at that time. There were
two sawmills near and the men attended all the
socials these people had to raise money for their
little church.Father Felix of Ponsford held services once a month for a short time.

The post office came to the village in the
year of 1913. Mrs. Fairbanks was the first
postmistress. Her niece, Mrs. Alois Rumreich,
is the second postmistress. Mrs. Fairbanks
retained her appointment until the date of
her retirement in the year of 1942.

People flocked to hunt and fish. They came
from far and near. Many of them were housed
in tents. Mrs. Fairbanks said she loved the
peace and quiet of this little village after
seeing some pretty wild days in Mahnomen,
which was still in its youth when she and
Mr. Fairbanks came out here to live.

The school was put up in the same year as
Mr. and Mrs. Fairbanks came to Naytahwaush.
Two Schulands with one assistant were the
carpenters.

Some of the families who lived here at the
time the Fairbanks came to the village were
Frank Pelland; the Warrens, the LaVoys, the
Douglas family,and Rev. Smiths.

The second year of the Fairbanks' residence
in the village, a Fourth of July celebration
was held. This became a tradition until in
late years. The Indians dressed up in their
finest feathers and costumes and held their
dances.

Times have changed for the village. Now Mrs.
Fairbanks occupies a modern home, fine roads
lead to the lakes, a fine new brick school
will soon be erected, and "olden days" are
just a memory.

386

Everette
Kiezer

MRS. ROBINSON'S STORY

Mrs. Robinson's father was Tyler Warren.
He came from the Mississippi tribe, settling first in White Earth, and later(1877)
moving to Naytahwaush. With his family, he
settled on the east shore of North Lake,
very near the site of Mrs. Robinson's present home. Mr. Warren was a logger and operated a saw mill also.

Mrs. Robinson said the present site of the
village had a very different appearance in
those days. It was more or less open except for the huge Norway pine trees reaching toward the heavens. These, of course,
have all been logged.

There were no roads in those days. There
were just foot trails meandering through
the woods. A few horses were used. The people loved their canoes, and traveled in
them whenever they could be used. Mrs. Robinson said they often went to visit the
three families who lived on the strip of
land between North and South Lakes. Then
they went in their canoes, except in the
winter. It was a thrilling event, she said.

Mrs. Robinson's grandmother experienced
several Sioux attacks, and could tell her
grandchildren some exciting stories of
those events. We asked her if the Indians
actually fought and attacked as history
records it. Her answer was yes--just at
dawn, preferring to attack small groups
which would be unable to defend themselves.
Favorite times were when the Chippewas
were ricing, trapping, or were in the su-
garbush. The men, they killed without mercy. The women and children they took as
captives, marrying the women into their
tribe and raising the children as their
own.

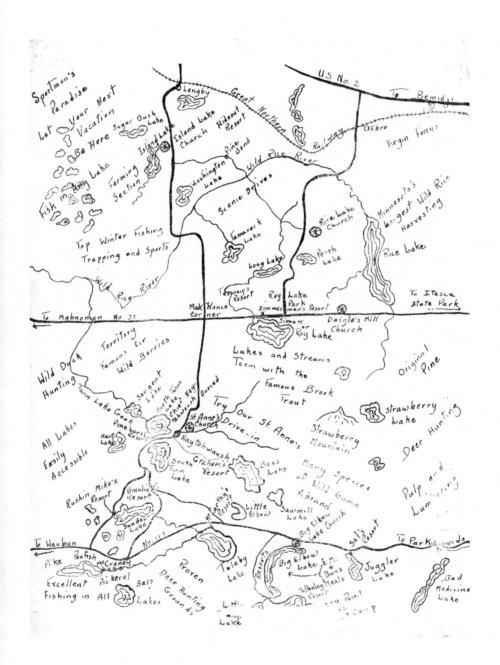

Made in the USA
Las Vegas, NV
08 February 2023

67161339R00223